*Cost Control in
the Hospitality Industry*

Cost Control in the Hospitality Industry

Agnes L. DeFranco, Ed.D., CHE
University of Houston

Pender B. M. Noriega, D.B.A, CHE
Delaware State University

PRENTICE HALL
Upper Saddle River, New Jersey 07458

Library of Congress Cataloging-in-Publication Data

DeFranco, Agnes L.
   Cost control in the hospitality industry/
  Agnes L. DeFranco, Pender B.M. Noriega.
       p.   cm.
  Includes bibliographical references.
  ISBN 0-13-575325-2
   1. Hospitality industry—Cost control.   I. Noriega, Pender B.M.
  II. Title.
  TX911.3.C65D44 2000
  647.94'068'1—dc21
                                             98-55472
                                                  CIP

Acquisitions editor: *Neil Marquardt*
Development editor: *Cheryl Adam*
Production editor: *Trish Finley*
Production liaison: *Barbara Marttine Cappuccio*
Director of manufacturing and production: *Bruce Johnson*
Managing editor: *Mary Carnis*
Manufacturing buyer: *Ed O'Dougherty*
Editorial assistant: *Jean Auman*
Creative director: *Marianne Frasco*
Cover design: *Liz Nemeth*
Cover illustration: *Leon Zernitsky*
Formatting/page make-up: *Clarinda Company*
Printer/binder: *R.R. Donnelly*

©2000 by Prentice-Hall, Inc.
Upper Saddle River, New Jersey 07458

Printed in the United States of America

10 9 8 7 6 5 4 3 2 1

ISBN 0-13-575325-2

Prentice-Hall International (UK) Limited, *London*
Prentice-Hall of Australia Pty. Limited, *Sydney*
Prentice-Hall Canada Inc., *Toronto*
Prentice-Hall Hispanoamericana, S.A., *Mexico*
Prentice-Hall of India Private Limited, *New Delhi*
Prentice-Hall of Japan, Inc., *Tokyo*
Pearson Education Asia Pte. Ltd., *Singapore*
Editora Prentice-Hall do Brasil, Ltda., *Rio de Janeiro*

To PJ, we need to talk.
To GianCarlo, take your time.

Contents

3

Setting Standards   50

4

The Menu as a Cost Control Tool   70

11

Sales and Cash Control 212

12

Sales Analysis 234

13

Labor Planning and Factors That Affect Labor Cost 256

18

*Casinos: The Wild Card
in Hospitality Cost Control* 354

Foreword

Cost Control in the Hospitality Industry is a welcome addition to the existing array of cost-control texts. Drs. Agnes DeFranco and Pender Noriega provide a fresh and realistic approach to the control and management of resources in the challenging hospitality industry, and more specifically, in food and beverage operations.

The authors initiate the discussion of controlling resources by addressing the high incidence of business failure in the hospitality industry. This creates an immediate awareness within the student that success in the hospitality industry is challenging and that resources must be controlled and used for their intended purposes if an operation is to be successful.

The text unfolds with a logical flow of information from an operational perspective and commences with a discussion of menus as the ultimate control device to assist management and integrate pricing. What follows is often called the food and beverage cycle, or the flow of food and beverage through an operation. The authors' practical experience enables them to highlight many of the unethical practices and inferior operational procedures that must be prevented in order to achieve operational success. The book addresses cash control, sales analysis, food and beverage cost controls, and the control of the cost of labor. A unique feature is the detailed section on credit and debit cards.

Also discussed are the financial areas that managers must be concerned with if a business is to become financially sound and generate a profit. Additionally, this text's value is increased by the inclusion of a chapter on gaming and gaming controls. This gives the text a competitive edge and will assist any manager involved with the gaming process.

This is not merely an academic text, for the authors' practical and varied experiences in the hospitality industry provide a strong sense of realism. Drs. Agnes DeFranco and Pender Noriega have an excellent blend of youthful and mature experience as well as a good balance of business and academic experience. Dr. DeFranco is an outstanding educator in the hospitality field and recently received the prestigious Enron Teaching Excellence Award at the University of Houston. Her sensitivity to students' needs has greatly enhanced the development of this text. Dr. Noriega complements Dr. DeFranco with a distinguished and lengthy tenure in club management in the United

States Army, in which he had overall responsibility for 31 dining facilities. In addition, Dr. Noriega has extensive experience in the operation of pari-mutuel gaming facilities. He has been committed to higher education for several years, and like Dr. DeFranco, he has a good sense of students' needs in today's educational market.

—Clinton L. Rappole
University of Houston

Preface

This text is designed to provide students, managers, and hospitality professionals with a realistic approach to controlling resources in the hospitality industry. This text differs from other cost-control books in that the authors have tried to provide insight into why many hospitality businesses fail and what methods can be used to identify and correct this. While most texts in this subject area deal with the balancing and accountability of input and output, this text provides that information and attempts to illustrate that management must also be concerned with whether products and services have actually been used for their intended purposes. If more products and services were used for their intended purposes, far more operations would be successful.

Chapters 1 through 5 describe the importance of management, control, the menu as a cost-control tool, standards, and pricing. These chapters describe why businesses fail and the importance of control as a managerial function. The menu as the driving force in the foodservice industry is emphasized because foodservice is an enormous part of the hospitality industry. Readers are provided a working knowledge of how standards must be established, monitored, and constantly controlled. Pricing is also addressed in this section because of its importance in generating profits based on the menu and standards that have been established.

Chapters 6 through 10 explain the importance of functions within the control process. The significance of purchasing, maintaining quality, and the control and evaluation of products and services are addressed, as are the vulnerability of products during receiving and the essentials of inspecting and evaluating products during receiving. Procedures for storage and issuing and the accountability of products during these processes are thoroughly explained. The exposed position of products and the array of errors that can occur during preparation, production, and service are discussed to make readers aware of the unethical practices and inferior operational procedures that must be prevented.

Chapters 11 through 14 address the issues of sales and cash control, along with procedures that should be practiced to prevent the misappropriation of funds. Credit and debit cards are discussed in detail, as they have become a common means of handling sales transactions. Analyzing sales, controlling waitstaff, and calculating food and beverage cost percentages are explained from a control standpoint. The hospitality industry is labor intensive; therefore, planning staff and labor needs in conjunction with cost control and scheduling are also discussed.

Chapters 15 through 18 highlight the types of controllable and noncontrollable items that can become an expensive part of a business operation. Because controllable costs account for such a large percentage of a manager's span of control, numerous items are addressed. The chapters that concern financial planning and budgeting may assist a manager in making a business financially sound and profitable. The chapter on gaming provides insight for managers in the casino arena. Now that gaming has become such a significant part of the hospitality industry and is growing so rapidly, many managers that have not had to concern themselves with controls in this area will have to take on this responsibility.

In short, this book provides a realistic view of daily operational procedures in the hospitality industry. Although many businesses perform these activities in a professional manner, many others constantly fail due to a lack of knowledge and willingness to accept responsibility in the area of control. Managers must understand that balanced input and output does not necessarily mean that a customer received the quantity and quality of product or service that he or she was supposed to receive. Control in the hospitality industry, or any other industry, entails much more managerial attention than just balancing the numbers.

Acknowledgments

The authors would like to thank Alan T. Stutts, Dean of the Conrad N. Hilton College, for his support and cooperation throughout the preparation of this text. Many thanks also go to Clinton L. Rappole, Douglas C. Keister, Cathleen Baird, Mary Wollin, and James Wortman for the materials and assistance in making this project a reality. Our gratitude also goes to Cheryl Adam and Neil Marquardt at Prentice Hall for their invaluable and kind comments and suggestions in all phases of the text. Lastly, our sincere appreciation to our students, who challenge us on a daily basis; and to our colleagues, who walk with us every step of the way in the education process.

We would like to acknowledge the following reviewers who gave us the most fair and critical reviews to better this book: David Barrish, J. Sergeant Reynolds Community College; William Day, Johnson & Wales University; Richard Lagiewski, State University of New York at Plattsburgh; Jay Kitterman, Lincoln Land Community College; and Terence McDonough, Erie Community College–City Campus.

1

Managing in the Hospitality Industry

Learning Objectives

After completing this chapter, you should be able to:

- describe the six elements to evaluate productivity.
- define and explain the three managerial attributes that are essential in managing the control function.
- diagram and define the four steps in the control cycle.

- outline the determining factors of ABCD classification for the security of products.
- describe the three major activities in sustaining a business operation.
- describe the major reasons for business failure.

Effective management is imperative to the success of any business operation. Management is defined as the process of getting tasks accomplished with and through people. This definition of management is exceedingly valid for the hospitality industry because it is so labor intensive. Since the overwhelming majority of tasks performed in the hospitality industry are services by employees, management leadership and interpersonal skills are essential to the success of any hospitality organization. However, because the industry is so labor intensive the managerial function of the control process must be maximized for an organization to be truly successful.

Segments of the Industry

The number of businesses that compose the hospitality industry is constantly increasing. There was always a tendency to associate the hospitality industry mainly with foodservice operations. While the majority of the industry is composed of food and beverage operations several facilities do not include foodservice as a major source of their income. Just as several hotels and motels do not include foodservice operations, several casinos do not have any lodging facilities. Therefore, although foodservice facilities and lodging facilities were accepted as the two main components of the hospitality industry, this is no longer the case. The four main components that appear to drive the hospitality industry are foodservice, lodging, travel, and gaming. From a revenue standpoint, casinos as a component of the gaming industry is now one of the fastest growing industries in the world. From a generic standpoint, this separates the major segments of the hospitality industry into those businesses that deal with food, tourism, lodging, or entertainment.

It is becoming increasingly difficult to categorize the hospitality industry. The major overview that had always been applied was foodservice and hotel/motel. These were the two broad terms that were used to encompass hospitality. An operation was considered a part of the hotel industry if it had rooms, and if it did not have rooms and served food, it was a part of the food-service industry. We now know that this does not cover the entire hospitality industry. Not only does the industry provide lodging facilities and places to eat, but it is now a big seller of tourism and entertainment. With the growth of the casino industry, selling entertainment has become a major portion of the hospitality field.

The industry previously classified casinos as hotels with facilities for gambling. Now there are several casinos that do not provide lodging and there are also agreements in some areas that casinos will not sell food. The industry had previously looked at sporting events and musical concerts as means of selling entertainment, and a substantial percentage of profit could be made from beverage and food concessions. Casinos are capable of far exceeding the amount of money made from a typical concert and they do not depend on concessions to supply a significant profit.

Therefore, rather than categorizing the hospitality industry into facilities that either provide food or lodging, we must now say that the industry is truly composed of four components—foodservice, tourism, lodging, and entertainment—and that they are all a part of the travel industry.

What does hold true is that with these four components composing the hospitality industry, we have a very labor intensive industry and therefore the demands for control are significantly higher than the demands in other industries. The hospitality industry does not deal with a product in the same manner as the manufacturing industry. Manufacturing can rapidly adjust production or place items into inventory; the hospitality industry as a whole does not have these advantages. Hospitality products cannot be placed back into inventory if they are not sold. A hotel room is one of the most perishable items in the industry. If a room is not sold, revenue is lost for that day and cannot be recovered. If guests do not play a particular slot machine for a given period, the entertainment time for that machine is lost. While you may be able to temporarily replace a worker on an assembly line, a superstar singer who cannot make a concert because of illness cannot be replaced and the revenue is lost. Contingency planning in the hospitality industry is a way of life.

While the hospitality industry may differ from the majority of industries in that it is more labor intensive and items cannot be placed back into inventory, the elements and means of accounting for resources are essentially the same. Even though the accounting methods are the same, here again the hospitality industry usually differs from other types of industry in the frequency of evaluation of financial position. Some businesses may only review annual reports, quarterly reports, or monthly reports. The hospitality industry must evaluate performance daily, weekly, or no less than each accounting period. An accounting period for the industry normally is every four weeks, yielding 13 periods annually. A manager cannot wait any longer than an accounting period to make adjustments or to address a problem. If management waits any longer than this, there will be no time for recovery. This urgency for frequent evaluations again is due to three main factors: the labor intensiveness of the industry, the fact that items cannot be placed back into inventory, and items that are in inventory are perishable.

Importance of Accountability and Control _____

The hospitality industry is growing faster than managers can be obtained. Because there are not enough qualified managers, the control and accountability of operational procedures becomes an increasing problem. The lack of accountability and control is evident in the vast amount of business failures.

As stated earlier, the elements and means used to evaluate productivity are basically the same as for other industries. However, because of the frequency in which these activities must occur, the industry has developed procedures to unify these tasks for easy comparison and evaluation. Items and activities that are essential to form an evaluation process are:

- Income statement
- Uniform systems of accounts
- National standards
- Cost-volume profit relationship
- Controllable and noncontrollable expenses
- Operating budget

Income Statement

The elements of most income statements are: sales, cost of sales, gross profit, other income, controllable expenses, noncontrollable expenses, and net income before taxes. When discussing controlling costs and profit in this industry, the income statement is our most utilized document (see Figure 1–1).

Figure 1–1   *Generic Income Statement*

Statement of Income for the Month Ended March 31, 20XX	
	$ Amount
Sales revenues	
Cost of goods sold	_____
Gross profit	
Operating expenses	
Salaries and wages	
Utilities	
Marketing	
Rent	
Repairs and maintenance	_____
Total operating costs	
Net Income	

The elements of the statement are the same as for other industries, in that managers are essentially concerned with sales and costs of these sales. However, the review of these elements most be done as frequently as possible because of the limited reaction time to make corrections. Regardless as to how effectively a manager may have scheduled employees and planned the production worksheet, a change in the weather or any unexpected major event can quickly alter the amount of resources required and can negate the most effective and extensive planning. Therefore, the essential elements of the income statement that inform us of sales and costs of sales must be continuously monitored. The frequency in which a manager must monitor the income statement in the hospitality industry cannot be overstated.

Uniform Systems of Accounts

The various uniform systems of accounts are very important in maintaining continuity within the hospitality industry. As the hospitality industry grows at such a formidable rate, experienced managers will continue to shift to new operations for career growth and upward mobility. In order for new managers to be familiar with some of the control tools, the uniform systems of accounts provide managers and accountants with a system of continuity. While there is not one accounting system that is applicable to all industries, because of the variety of sales and expense classifications, different segments of the industry do have uniform systems of accounts. The three most used uniform systems in the hospitality industry are: Uniform System of Accounts for the Lodging Industry (USALI), Uniform System of Accounts for Restaurants (USAR), and the Uniform System of Financial Reporting for Clubs (USFRC). Examples of the suggested income statement format from each system are shown in Figures 1–2, 1–3, and 1–4.

National Standards

The percentage of prime costs standards for similar types of operations are usually referred to as the national standards. Food, beverage, and labor costs are known as prime costs. In other words, they are the costs that make up the majority of the costs of a hospitality operation. The national standards for food cost, beverage cost, and labor cost for McDonald's and Burger King may be about the same. These two operations are similar in nature and therefore their food, beverage, and labor cost percentages would be very similar. However, a fine dining restaurant will provide a higher level of service and different types of products; thus, the price structure of this type of operation would be very different. Therefore, managers must be careful when using these national percentages to compare their operations as each operation may have different operating expenses. *Trends in the Hotel Industry* (published by Pannell Kerr Foster) and the *Host Report* (published by Arthur Anderson and Smith Travel) annually summarize standard performances in the hotel segment. The National Restaurant Association reports on restaurant performances. In addition, the *Business Almanac*, Dun and Bradstreet, and Robert Morris and Associates publish industry statistics and ratios.

Figure 1–2 *USALI Income Statement*

Statement of Income for the Period Ended December 31, 20XX

	Current Year	Prior Year
REVENUE		
Rooms	$	$
Food		
Beverage		
Telecommunications		
Garage and parking		
Other operated departments		
Rentals and other income	————	————
Total revenue		
COSTS AND EXPENSES		
Rooms		
Food		
Beverage		
Telecommunications		
Garage and parking		
Other operated departments		
Administrative and general		
Human resources		
Information systems		
Security		
Marketing		
Franchise fees		
Transportation		
Property operation and maintenance		
Utility costs		
Management fees		
Rent, property taxes, and insurance		
Interest expense		
Depreciation and amortization	————	————
Total costs and expenses		
GROSS INCOME		
INCOME TAXES		
Current		
Deferred	————	————
Total income taxes		
NET INCOME		

Figure 1–3   *USAR Income and Retained Earnings Statement*

Statement of Income and Retained Earnings for the Period Ended December 31, 20XX

	Amounts	Percentages
Sales		
Food	$697,000	82%
Beverage	153,000	18
Total Sales	850,000	100
Cost of Sales		
Food	245,500	35
Beverage	52,000	34
Total cost of sales	297,500	35
Gross profit		
Food	451,500	65
Beverage	101,000	66
Total gross profit	552,500	65
Operating expenses		
Salaries and wages	255,000	30
Employee benefits	34,000	4
Occupancy costs	59,000	7
Direct operating expenses	51,000	6
Music and entertainment	1,000	00.1
Marketing	17,000	2
Utility services	25,500	3
Depreciation	16,500	2
General and administrative expenses	44,200	5
Repairs and maintenance	16,500	2
Other income	(2,500)	(00.3)
Total operating expenses	517,400	61
Operating income	35,100	4
Interest	4,250	00.5
Gross income	30,850	4
Income taxes	4,500	00.5
Net income	26,350	3
Retained earnings, beginning of period	175,450	
Less dividends	(10,000)	
Retained earnings, end of period	191,800	

Figure 1–4   *USFRC Income and Expense Statement*

Statement of Income and Expense for the Year Ended December 31, 20XX	
Membership dues	$320,000
Golf and other sports—cost or (income)	
Golf Operations	100,000
Tennis	15,000
Minor Sports	10,000
Net cost of sports activities	125,000
Dues available for clubhouse operation and fixed charges	195,000
Clubhouse operating income or (loss)	
Food and beverage	55,000
Rooms	25,000
Minor departments—loss	(5,000)
Other income	20,000
Total	95,000
Deduct, undistributed operating expenses	
Clubrooms expense	20,000
Entertainment	10,000
Administrative and general	90,000
Heat, light, and power	35,000
Repairs and maintenance—clubhouse	40,000
Total	195,000
Net cost of clubhouse operation	100,000
Dues available for fixed charges	95,000
Rent, taxes, and insurance	40,000
Dues available or (loss) before interest and depreciation	55,000
Interest	50,000
Dues available or (loss) before depreciation	5,000
Depreciation and amortization	40,000
Net operating income or (loss)	(35,000)
Other additions and (deductions)—net	45,000
Net income or (loss)—to members' equity	10,000

Cost-Volume Profit Relationship

Cost-volume analysis will be explained in detail in a later chapter. The cost-volume financial profit relationship is the evaluation process that managers must use in the financial evaluation of business operations. Because of the flexibility and competitiveness of the hospitality market, this cost-volume relationship must be carefully examined so that adjustments can be made early in the accounting period.

Controllable and Noncontrollable Expenses

The reason superb management is so vital to an operation is because controllable expenses account for over 50% of the cost of running an average hospitality operation. Other managerial functions must be implemented, but none can surpass the importance of control. Over 50% of an operation is under the direct control of the manager. Controllable expenses include but are not limited to payroll, employee benefits, direct operating expenses, marketing, energy and utilities, administrative and general expenses, and repair and maintenance. Management does have strong influences over the use of these resources, thus they are deemed controllable.

Noncontrollable expenses are also expenses incurred by the operation; however, the owner or corporate office personnel most often determine them. Some examples of noncontrollable expenses include rent, depreciation, and property taxes. All of these expenses are determined at a level different from management. Thus, managers may not be able to exert direct control over these expenses to deliver more profit to the bottom line.

Operating Budget

The budget is the standard that is developed by which a business is to operate. The budget is the main tool used to compare operational actual activities against planned activities. Overall performance can be evaluated by comparing actual performance against the standards that have been established in the budget. If actual performance is thought to be significantly different from the planned performance, corrective action may have to be taken.

Managerial Attributes

Inexperienced managers often may ask how they are supposed to do all of the things that are asked of them. A manager in a hospitality operation is like a juggler at a circus. A manager has a variety of activities he or she must maintain control of at the same time. Just as a juggler may occasionally drop a ball, so will a manager. But, as we know, the show must go on. Just like a juggler, a manager must pick up the ball as quickly as possible and get it back into its normal rotation with the rest of the balls. Unlike a juggler, the show does not end, and a manager must keep juggling. Accepting the fact that all controllable tasks are a manager's responsibility is crucial in being a successful manager.

Managers must understand and accept three important attributes in managing the control function of a hospitality operation:

1. Professionalism
2. Effective time management
3. Acceptance of responsibility

From day one, in order to control operational procedures, a manager must always try to manage an operation with the highest possible degree of professionalism. A manager must be professional with his or her guests and extremely professional with his or her staff. Professionalism means having the standard and status suitable and worthy of a particular field. Some managers are always trying to get along with their employees and may have a difficult time balancing professionalism and friendships. If a manager remains extremely professional with all employees, he or she will get along with them. Several young managers become friends with employees and then experience difficulty counseling their friends as employees when they are constantly late or involved in some other infraction. As a friend, an employee should not do anything that would create a problem. For some reason numerous managers do not understand this logic. A friend is supportive, not detrimental to your success. If a manager does not understand the logic of this he or she may be looking for another job while the "friend" remains employed. The subject of professionalism and its importance to the control function will be discussed throughout the text since this is seen as a major downfall for many new managers. The inability to control employees/personnel causes many new managers to give up on the industry.

Managers must also understand the importance of managing their time. A manager's time is never listed as a controllable asset yet it is one of the most important resources to control. With the increasing cost of human resources, a manager cannot afford to waste time. This is true in any industry but especially for the hospitality industry. Time is a finite, nonrenewable asset and no manager can afford to waste any. If a manager is constantly juggling balls and stops to waste time, all of the balls will drop. So, what is wasting time? Talking with guests is not wasting time. Asking an employee if he had a good weekend is not wasting time. Wasting time is usually a result of being unorganized. Time can be wasted in fraternizing with employees during work hours. A manager should take time to plan his or her day or week and try to stay as close to the schedule as possible. If managers have to make a lot of last-minute decisions that are not the result of a change in guest count or some unexpected events, then they may have a time management problem. If employees constantly come to managers with questions concerning work procedures, managers may not have an effective training system, and the results will drain or waste their valuable time. Employees should know what is expected of them and only need to consult with the manager if there are unanticipated changes in operational procedures. If employees are well trained, they will know what to do and will not waste a great deal of the manager's time with procedural questions. Employees should be empowered and authorized to resolve day-to-day situations without always having to consult the manager.

One of the most difficult job descriptions for managers to accept is that they are to be responsible and accept responsibility. When accepting a management position an employee will normally receive some type of pay increase. In essence the employee is being paid to accept additional responsibilities. Accepting managerial responsibility means accepting the responsibility of ensuring that tasks are accomplished. Owners or stockholders do not want to hear statements such as "I told him to do it" or "Nobody told me." When an employee reaches management level he or she is placed in a position to ensure that things are accomplished. A manager must also ask questions so that he or she will be able to stay informed and keep his or her employees informed. Knowing what is going on becomes a primary responsibility.

If a manager can accept and apply these three attributes he or she will find that the ability to control will be much easier. A manager should always try to accept responsibility and do something about it, instead of avoiding problems or the situation that causes the problem. Managers are paid to control operational procedures that will determine the success or failure of a business.

Definition of Controls

Control can be defined as maintaining the necessary restrictions and accountability over the resources of a business operation. Regardless as to how one attempts to define control, one must accept the fact that it encompasses every aspect of the business. In the hospitality industry, owners and entrepreneurs are probably primarily involved in the planning stages. First-line supervisors or managers are far more involved in the day-to-day controls of the operation. Managers must plan, direct, and coordinate all operational procedures, but all is lost if the operation and the resources are not controlled.

Control is essentially a four-step cycle, as shown in Figure 1–5.

Establishing Controls or Objectives

When establishing controls or objectives, it is imperative that these objectives are measurable. Employees must be able to determine if they are performing these tasks correctly and they must know what is expected of them. Whenever possible, all control procedures should be in writing. This can be in the form of an operations manual, standard recipes, budget, and so on.

Informing Employees

Employees must receive proper training in order to comply with standards. All too often employees may be unaware of certain expectations because management did not correctly explain these expectations. Employees must be informed of standards or objectives either through training programs or through other means of standard operating procedures. They must be informed of what the measurements will be for these expectations. This step is often taken for granted, although it is one of the most important steps in the control cycle. Employees

Figure 1–5   *Control Cycle in Management*

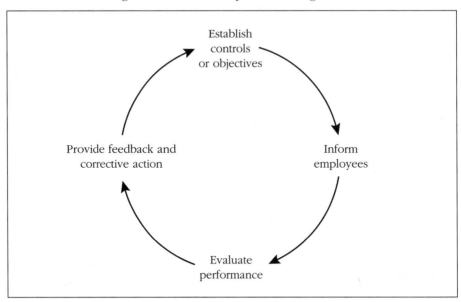

must be informed of correct control procedures or they may mimic the mistakes of other employees. If a manager says the same thing to two or more employees or corrects the same problems with two or more employees, he or she may have a communication problem. This can occur if control procedures are not correctly and clearly communicated. Once control procedures are established they must be communicated to all employees. Asking employees to demonstrate the correct procedures is one of the best ways to ensure that they understand the expectations.

Evaluating Performance

Performance must be routinely evaluated to ensure that standards are being met. If this step is omitted the operation will lose consistency, and employees will begin to think that control procedures are not important. Interest must be shown for doing things correctly. The hospitality industry is often a function of attitudes. Managers must display a positive attitude toward the importance of doing things right. If a manager does not reflect an attitude that controls are important, employees will begin to take the attitude that they are not very important. Therefore, managers must routinely and consistently evaluate employees to determine if controls are being met. Evaluation is also the step in the cycle where a manager can determine if any corrective actions have improved a previous situation.

Providing Feedback and Corrective Action

In order for the control cycle to work, employees must receive feedback on their performance. Often management only provides feedback when something is wrong. If managers want employees to continue to do things right, they must also receive positive feedback to act as reinforcements for those activities. Therefore, once performance is evaluated, positive or negative feedback must be given. Additionally, the feedback must be given as soon as possible after the evaluation. Since there are so many external influences that can have an effect on the performance of a hospitality operation, if feedback is not provided quickly and consistently, the business may not have sufficient time to make adjustments. For example, if by Tuesday it appears that an operation may not make its weekly budgeted sales, a manager has to start taking action to control all other controllable expenses or institute new plans to increase sales. It would be too late to wait until Friday or Saturday to try to take action to reduce labor and other controllable expense categories.

When providing feedback a manager has an opportunity to give instructions concerning any corrective action that must be taken. However, feedback is a two-way communication process. Effective communication allows employees to offer feedback and suggestions to enhance the business operation. The manager's willingness to facilitate open communication may result in increasing the efficiency of the organization and can develop a positive attitude among employees toward the organization. Valid suggestions and feedback can then be implemented as new controls and taken back to the beginning of the control cycle.

What to Control?

An important decision for each hospitality operation is the question of "What to control?" Obviously, because the major costs of a hospitality operation are labor, food, and beverage, these three costs must be monitored if management is to keep track and control these expenditures. Combined food and beverage costs represent one of the two highest cost categories in most foodservice operations. Not controlling the cost of sales can place any foodservice operation at a distinct competitive disadvantage. Controlling the cost of sales often determines whether an operation survives and always has a significant impact on profitability. Monitoring entails the constant surveillance and supervision of the entire control process.

When monitoring the cost of food, beverage, and labor, the entire process from purchasing, storage, preparation, and service must be scrutinized. Products must be purchased according to specifications and at the most optimal price. A minimum amount of products should be in storage to prevent waste, theft, or the tying up of funds that could be used to generate additional income. Additionally, all standards should be adhered to during preparation and service to prevent waste, ensure a consistent product, and ensure that guests are not dissatisfied. Management must remain vigilant by walking around, observing production processes, talking with customers, and evaluating results against established standards.

Management must provide feedback to employees on a consistent basis whether the feedback is good or bad. Employees need to know if standards are being met and if they are performing their tasks according to expectations. The results of monitoring should always provide some type of feedback. If constructive feedback is not given mistakes are apt to continue. If positive feedback is not given employees may feel that no one cares and mistakes may begin to occur. It is the responsibility of management to be aware that monitoring should occur and that feedback must be given in order for mistakes to be corrected or for good work habits to continue.

While resources must be controlled for an organization to operate effectively, the control measures must also be cost effective. It is imperative to point out that control as a managerial function applies to far more than just controlling costs. For managers to operate a successful operation, they must be able to control the operation itself. If managers are in control of the operation, then they stand a chance of controlling the different costs. Again, much of running an operation has a lot to do with professionalism, consistency, and attitude. Managers can tell employees to count products and to lock up products, but whether or not these activities will occur depends upon whether the employees think that the activity is important. The success of control has a lot to do with the attitude that management relates to employees concerning the importance of control. The easiest way to describe this is that a manager must be in control for controls to occur. This means action, not talk. Balancing numbers is important and essential to controls, but balanced numbers will not guarantee that the control issue is in line. Unless the culture of an organization is not to waste products, to look at products as being money, and that an operation has to be run cost effectively, there is apt to be very little cost control. This is why so many business plans look good on paper but the operations fail once these plans are applied. Controlling costs is not just about counting and locking up products in the absence of direct supervision. Controlling costs is also about the perception that employees have that will urge them to take the necessary steps to count and secure products. Therefore, managers must project an attitude that they want to run the most efficient hospitality operation possible and that controlling costs is an efficient means of aiding this operational procedure.

Providing the guests outstanding service to ensure that they will spend as much as possible, and that they will return, is just as important to the control process as locking up steaks. A facility can keep steaks locked up and accounted for, but if no one orders a steak because of poor service, an operation can end up having a high labor cost due to insufficient sales. Therefore, all operational procedures can have an effect on cost control. Before managers can control costs, they must have professionalism, consistency, and an attitude that reflects the importance of professionalism and efficiency. Once managers start from this perspective, they can ask employees to count products and secure products with the assurance that it may occur. With the understanding that all operational procedures can have an effect on control, it is then possible to discuss what should be controlled.

ABCD Classification

Some facilities use an ABCD classification for securing products. This allows them to place products into different categories for recognition of security. Items placed into category A are those that require the most control, and those in category D would require the least amount of control. For example, expensive wines over a certain dollar amount may be categorized as A and need to be locked within a precious room inside the wine cellar. Even with this method or characterization, a manager or owner must still decide which items fall into which category. Wines costing less than that dollar amount may be categorized as B and these wines may be placed inside the locked wine cellar. The decision of how to categorize items should be based upon type of operation, location, level of usage, possibility of theft or waste, and convenience to guests and employees. An example of an ABCD classification chart for a steak house is shown in Table 1–1.

Table 1–1

Category A	Category B	Category C	Category D
Wines with a selling price of over $1000 a bottle	Wines with a selling price of $1000 to over $500 a bottle	Wines with a selling price of $500 to over $ 100 a bottle	Wines with a selling price of less than $100 a bottle
Kobe beef from Japan	Prime beef steaks	All other beef and pork	Miscellaneous
	Maine lobster	All other fish	
		Poultry	
		Dry storage items	

Type of Operation

If an operation is a casino, management would place a high degree of security on tokens, cash, and means of access to any machines that dispense coins. If the operation is a steak house, management has to place a high degree of security on meats and fine wines. A quick foodservice operation may have to secure par stocks—the amount that should always be on hand between orders—of hamburger patties or other meat items. Items that represent the highest costs are usually the type of items that must have the greatest amount of control. Therefore, the type of operation will dictate which items represent the most costs.

Location of Operation

The location of an operation may also dictate which items to control and the amount of control that is necessary. A store that sells spirits and expensive wines may not have to worry about access to the products in the facility but may need to consider the threat of being robbed. Therefore, location can dictate the amount of control and in some cases the type of control. A person of ordinary prudence would have to make the decision based on the location and the demographics of that location.

Level of Usage

Level of usage is also a determining factor. The manager of a steak house may have to have a large amount of prime steaks available for easy access. As a control process, the cook may have to sign for a certain number of steaks from storage and then be accountable for those items. But remember that controls must also be cost effective. The level of usage may dictate easy accessibility to a limited amount of expensive products. While there may be less control over items that have been made available for easy access, this does not reduce accountability or preclude management from keeping the bulk of the inventory under tight security and control. One example of this is an expensive bottle of whiskey at the bar. One or two bottles may be kept at the bar for easy access by the bartender, however, the remaining stock should be under double lock. A double lock system would be accomplished by having a locked cabinet or room within the original storage area that is also locked. While storeroom personnel may have access to the lock on the storage area, only specific individuals would have access to the inner cabinet or room. However, the bartender would still be accountable for those bottles located at the bar.

Convenience

Level of usage may dictate whether products must be made available as needed. Management does not want to inconvenience guests or employees unnecessarily. If a guest orders a bottle of fine wine at an expensive restaurant, he or she does not want to wait for the employee to chase down a manager to get the key to the wine cellar. An operation could lose the guest if the wait staff is unreasonable. Additionally, steps of this nature could slow down service because it could tie up an employee for an unreasonable amount of time. Therefore, the key to what to control and how much to control must be based on what is cost effective. Accountability may often have to be substituted for locks and keys. If an employee has access to a product, management can hold the employee accountable. It is always difficult to implement changes, therefore it is important to start with control procedures rather than having to implement them later once things get out of hand.

Internal System

There will always be those unexpected extraneous activities that may cause an operation to lose products, money, and sales. The internal activities that can be implemented will at least provide a means of accountability. Internal controls and accountability should apply to the purchasing of products, to the sale and delivery of these products to the guests, and finally, to the collection of money. An internal control system should provide for accountability in each step of the operating control cycle. For example, if a case of lamb chops is purchased and there are 25 pieces in the case, there has to be a method of comparing the invoice, receiving report, production sheets, and the guest checks to reconcile that the 25 lamb chops that were purchased were indeed received, prepared, and sold and that the cash for the sales was received. For an internal control system to work, management must set the example and illustrate the importance to the employees. An internal control system depends on participation and cooperation among managers and employees.

Staying Power

The reason why most businesses have been able to stand the test of time is because they fulfill a need and operate a sound business venture. Since most businesses in the hospitality industry only generate a small margin of profit, managers must be able to make sound business decisions and not waste any resources. Staying in business in the hospitality industry is a function of three major activities that are the result of operating a sound business venture. The three major activities that can sustain a hospitality business are:

1. Fulfilling a need
2. Remaining competitive
3. Controlling cost

In order for a business to survive it must continue to fulfill a need. This may often include changing the menu over time or changing the method of delivery. Pizza Hut realized that they had to deliver pizza once Domino's came along and captured a portion of the pizza market. The delivery system established by Domino's was a means of improving guest service and seeking a competitive advantage. To remain competitive Pizza Hut had no choice but to enter the delivery business. McDonald's and Burger King resorted to serving breakfast. States bordering those that have state lotteries may consider their own lotteries. Remaining competitive is a must for staying in business.

Several businesses have actually used efficiency and control as a means of competitive advantage. McDonald's made employees out of all of us by having us clean tables. By placing trash containers at every exit, McDonald's was one of the first to cut labor costs by involving its guests in the process. By holding down costs and making products affordable, McDonald's has continuously been able to fulfill a need and remain competitive by providing a quality product and quick and efficient service. Fulfilling a need, remaining competitive, and controlling costs are essential to staying in business.

All of the essential management functions of planning, organizing, directing, and controlling are applicable to the hospitality industry but none is more essential than the control function. Controlling cost is essential to the hospitality industry since the majority of operations generate such a small margin of profit. A slight deviation in prime cost can move an operation from success to failure.

Business Failure

There are numerous reasons for business failure in the hospitality field. Individuals who started businesses that failed find it difficult to give a quick snapshot as to why their hospitality businesses did not succeed. A lot of these failures could have been prevented if sound steps had been used when developing the business plan. The proper research procedures in developing the business plan would have identified several of these problems and could have addressed alternative plans to eliminate or avoid potential problems. The importance of a well-designed business plan cannot be overstated. In interviewing several lending agencies, a list of possible causes for business failure in the hospitality industry has been established. The most predominant reasons are:

- Lack of working capital
- Inexperienced managers
- Inability to control operational procedures
- Competition
- Employee theft
- Wrong location
- Wrong concept
- Inadequate Inventory control
- Poor credit practices
- Too much personal income
- Wrong attitude
- Not knowing yourself
- Unrealistic expectations
- Lack of planning

Lack of Working Capital

Lack of working capital has been the downfall of a vast number of businesses both large and small. The unpredictability of guest count along with needed repairs and hidden costs can cause businesses not to be able to meet their financial responsibilities. Several businesses do not take into account the fact that the life cycle curve will normally have an effect in the growth of all businesses.

As illustrated in Figure 1–6, the majority of well-planned businesses will have a normal growth pattern. This normal pattern will take organizations

Figure 1–6 *Business Life Cycle*

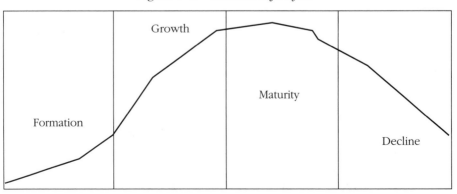

through four stages: formation, growth, maturity, and decline. Not planning early and not understanding the life cycle of business can cause failure during maturity and decline.

Most hospitality operations will do an excellent job of developing a business plan for opening an operation to get through the formation and growth stages; however, plans are not well developed to deal with maturity and decline. A major problem is that the growth stage is misinterpreted by most businesses. The growth stage, or honeymoon period, that usually occurs when an operation first opens is not long lived. If the business plan for opening an operation is researched and well developed, the operation will usually experience a good financial start. In fact, in many cases, the operation may exceed expectations for the first year or two. Owners often misunderstand this fantastic beginning. Several owners will begin to overspend during the growth stage or withdraw too much money out of the operation as they anticipate that this increase in sales will continue. Instead of planning for maturity and a possible decline in sales, some owners will begin to expand in different areas of the operation with the attitude that sales will continue or increase, and therefore bigger is better. Because of this misconception, if there is an unexpected change in business income or expenditures, many businesses are not able to meet their financial commitments.

Trying to anticipate hidden costs is a monumental problem for all business activities. Because the service industry is so labor intensive and must deal with such a large number of perishable products, anticipating hidden cost presents even more of a challenge. Unlike manufacturing, inventory cannot be held until sold. If refrigerators or other types of equipment need to be repaired or replaced, the decision to take action cannot be postponed. If an operation runs out of food items and cannot feasibly go to its main suppliers, items may have to be purchased at a local grocery store at a much higher cost, which in turn will cut into profits. Not accounting for maturity and decline will cause operations to be unprepared to deal with the unpredictable changes in the market place and other unforeseeable activities.

Inexperienced Managers

A lack of managerial training continues to have a negative effect on operations. As previously stated, management is viewed as the process of getting tasks accomplished with and through people. There is such a vast amount of growth in the hospitality field that the demand for qualified managers continues to exceed availability. In the foodservice area of the hospitality industry several entrepreneurs enter the field as owner/operators with no managerial experience at all. Some entrepreneurs have a desire to generate a profit and see the foodservice industry as a low capital investment avenue. Other entrepreneurs like working with food or enjoy working with people and think that the opportunities for business ventures in the foodservice area are easily available. The problem is that in most cases these individuals do not have the required managerial skills that are necessary to manage a business. Managerial and interpersonal skills are extremely important in the hospitality industry.

Inability to Control Operational Procedures

Managerial skills are important and control is a managerial function. Managers must have an understanding of an operation from a business point of view in order to make effective business decisions. It is important to have the interpersonal managerial skills to be able to satisfy the needs of guests and employees, but a manager must make sound business decisions in order to remain profitable and competitive. From a business standpoint, managers must be able to establish control standards based on operational acceptability and have the managerial skills to maintain the operation within those standards. Several hospitality operations may have had an outstanding business plan but once the plan was applied, the managerial skills were not in place to control the operation within the procedures and guidelines of the plan. This is especially true in the areas of leadership, predicting sales, maintaining accounting records, and procedures.

Competition

The hospitality industry boasts a fierce amount of competition. Unless an operation is able to find a competitive advantage, it becomes very difficult to survive. An advantage can be accomplished through service, quality, efficiency, differentiation, product, pricing, or a combination of these activities. As the world moves toward the twenty-first century, guests are constantly seeking as much value for their money as possible. All types of hospitality facilities and services must be able to develop a distinctive competitive advantage to entice guests to make decisions to patronize their facilities or services over some other. Some of the successful operations will be those that can differentiate themselves. Perception of value is going to play an extremely important part in the decision-making process. Mediocrity will not allow operations to survive in such a competitive industry. A mediocre operation with mediocre products or services will not be able to deliver sufficient sales for the operation to remain cost effective. There are many successful mom-and-pop type operations; however, a large number of such operations are only able to remain in existence because of the hours that the owner-operators are willing to put into the business. There are also a few franchise operations that are kept afloat in order to maintain market share, but eventually, even these operations will probably have to give into failure if the company as a whole is to remain profitable.

It is usually those hospitality operations that are able to combine service, quality, and efficiency on a consistent basis that will be profitable over the long run. Differentiation and pricing as a competitive advantage will only be able to carry an operation so far. Once other operations are able to compete in the uniqueness of an operation's product and deliver it at a comparable price, the competitive advantage is lost. The perception of value is more closely related to service and quality than price. In order to be competitive in the hospitality industry, one must develop a business plan for a product or service that fits a need. If an organization is willing to provide a quality product with outstanding service and can effectively control the operation, the organization can have a profitable business operation.

Employee Theft

The correlation between employee theft and the failure of business ventures has been well documented. However, theft becomes an even greater concern for those segments of the hospitality industry that deal with food and other types of amenities. Because the hospitality industry deals with products that are easily consumed, employee theft of these items is a monumental problem. The industry has a difficult time trying to control theft while at the same time making products available for easy delivery to guests to enhance guest service. Because of the small amount of profit generated by most hospitality operations, the endeavor to find a balance between servicing the guest while controlling inventory causes several facilities to meet with failure. With the increasing capabilities of technology, operations will have to instill sophisticated technological controls to enhance accountability.

Wrong Location

The location must fit the product. The demographics must be compatible with the operation in order for it to succeed. The public has become conscious of the importance of time. Because of the general economy, often it takes two members of a household to work to sustain a comfortable living standard. This has caused people to really value their time. Quality time has become a key phrase in our society. With the increase in the size of the population, travel to and from work is taking longer and longer. A business cannot expect guests to drive across town to purchase their products. At times, even the most loyal guests will choose convenience over taste. It takes a great deal of differentiation to get the public to drive any significant distance. Places such as Las Vegas continually attempt to provide differentiation to have guests travel there. While casinos are popping up all over the United States, Las Vegas provides a variety of shows that are unmatched anywhere else in the world. Without some true form of differentiation that is very attractive, the demographics must already be in place for an operation to succeed.

Even if the demographics are in place there are several other attributes of site selection that can prevent a business from being successful. For example, people like to build restaurants near other restaurants and other activities that generate traffic. If the market at that location is already saturated, a facility will only be able to share in the same amount of sales that are already there. A new operation would also have the difficulty of competing with established prices and services.

Accessibility is also an important factor in site selection. If getting in and out of a location is perceived as somewhat of a hassle, it could reduce the number of guest arrivals. Divided highways, access roads, and one-way streets must be considered when determining a location. In addition, parking as well as security must be priorities when selecting locations. All of these criteria are very important in the process of site selection. Research must be accomplished to make the wisest choice possible. It is difficult to break a lease, and in many cases an operation cannot afford the expense of moving to a different location. Several major companies have made costly mistakes in thinking that they had enough clout to open anywhere and people will just come, only to find that this is not true.

Wrong Concept

Some entrepreneurs go into business with a burning idea of something that they have always wanted to do. They feel that if they pursue the idea and do it well, guests will come. What may be the most important concept to an entrepreneur may not fulfill a need or there may not be a sufficient market to support that product or service. It is one thing to develop a business idea around a dream, but there is greater success in developing what the public would prefer. This has been the difference between the downfall or success of a vast number of restaurants. Some entrepreneurs succeeded in developing businesses that they always wanted. This can work if the product or service is perceived as a need to a certain segment of a market. On the other hand, numerous individuals have failed in trying to develop businesses that were only important to them. While everyone would like to be extremely happy in the work they do, if it is not fulfilling a need for the public, consumers will not exist. An entrepreneur may have a concept that he or she thinks is perfect, but before implementing that concept, an effort must be made to ensure that there is a market for it.

It is also wise to remember that in the hospitality industry concepts can overlap and an operation must be able to get a license to pursue the entire concept. If an organization establishes a restaurant and wants to sell the same alcoholic beverages that can be purchased in a local bar or tavern in the same vicinity, the question becomes whether the operation will be able to sell alcoholic beverages at that location. An organization may be able to get a license for a restaurant but not for alcohol, and this may reduce sales. For example, selling pizza without beer may not work. In other words, the concept of opening a dine-in pizza restaurant may be a great one; however, if beer cannot be sold, the operation may not be able to attract as many sales as necessary for the operation to exist. It is surprising how often companies have made this mistake. An organization must check on license requirements before attempting to open a business. If an organization fails to accomplish this, it may find that the business is failing because it cannot reach its projected sales. This is especially true once an organization begins to open different units. Zoning laws and licenses can be different from city to city, county to county, and state to state.

Inadequate Inventory Control

Several aspects of inventory control can cause a business to fail. Not knowing how much to order can result in stockout, which can cause guests not to come back. Having too much product in inventory can cause a product to spoil or deteriorate and have to be discarded. Even nonperishable products may begin to lose value in inventory as they become obsolete or outdated. Having too much inventory occupies space that could be utilized more effectively. Too much inventory on hand also ties up funds that could be used for cash discounts or just remain in the bank to draw interest. One of the major downfalls of too much inventory is the possibility that it will generate employee waste and employee theft. A business that cannot control its inventory will most often have financial problems because of waste or theft. Inventory is money and if the business does not control inventory, the business is not controlling money and the business will fail.

Poor Credit Practices

Most hospitality facilities accept credit cards, purchase orders, and other forms of noncash payments. Casinos may also extend other forms of credit. If poor business decisions are made in granting credit, a hospitality business can easily fail. Again, the hospitality business is very labor intensive. The waitstaff, house-keepers, game-room attendants, and other personnel must be paid. Accounts receivable cannot be used on payday. Businesses must have the cash on hand to pay employees while maintaining necessary reserves to pay for new products.

Too Much Personal Income

The amount of income to be removed from a business should be established in the business plan. Once this amount has been approved there should not be any dipping into the till. In planning a business, it should be understood that the normal life cycle curve illustrates that a business will have larger sales volume as it takes off. The curve also shows that this will taper off. However, some proprietors misread this start-up growth, thinking that it will last indefinitely and begin taking too much income from the business. When business begins to taper off there is no money available to sustain the business or to take advantage of cash discounts, let alone to pay hefty salaries to owners. Without capital to sustain the business, the business may face failure.

Wrong Attitude

In this text, attitude will be referenced several times. While a positive attitude toward employees and guests is important throughout any industry, it is vital to survival in the hospitality industry. A less than positive attitude will eventually reach the guests. Owner/operators must have a positive attitude toward the business, employees, and guests. Managers lead by example, whether they intend to or not. If managers or owner/operators convey a negative attitude, employees will eventually pass it on to guests. A negative attitude will drive guests away and cause a reduction in sales. One of the most difficult tasks for a business to accomplish is to turn around a trend of declining sales. This is especially challenging in the hospitality field wherein a business usually has such a small margin of profit. What it takes to increase sales is money and a positive attitude. Money is needed to advertise and to entice guests to come, and a positive attitude on the part of employees is necessary to get them to return. Without money and a positive attitude a manager may not be able to turn the business around.

Not Knowing Yourself

Many individuals would like to be owners or managers, and they will strive to reach these positions. In the hospitality industry a manager must be a people person. A people person is someone who possesses good interpersonal skills. As an owner or manager working in this industry, not only is it important to be a people person, it is also necessary to be able to think very quickly on your feet. A manager must be able to relate well with guests and employees while juggling a lot of other important activities at the same time. A manager cannot contribute less attention to any area without "dropping the ball" in another. For example, a manager cannot be overly concerned with a major problem in the kitchen and in the process be rude to a guest or an employee. A manager must be able to problem-solve and make decisions about any crisis without becoming unraveled in front of guests or employees. If an owner or manager is not a people person and is not competent enough to make required changes very quickly, the business will be in disarray. Once this happens, the business is doomed to fail. Only the individual running the show will actually know if he or she has the capacity and drive to accomplish these managerial activities whenever necessary. It is important to complete a self-assessment as to whether being a manager in the hospitality industry is something that one can handle. "To thine own self be true." The hospitality industry is one of the most rewarding industries in which to work, but only the individual will know if he or she has the desire and ability to keep a large number of activities under control at the same time. A manager is expected to do a large number of activities while giving guests and employees a genuine smile at all times. If a manager cannot perform all these functions, he or she will not be able to control the operation.

Unrealistic Expectations

Far too many individuals enter the hospitality industry and other forms of business with unrealistic expectations. It takes time to generate a profit from a business. Before going into business, it is wise to weigh the possibility of investing funds rather than going into business. The percentage of profit that is usually generated from a hospitality business, other than casinos, is not that large. Several investors enter the business with the impression that they will be able to generate a quick profit. Others enter because of the ambiance and the thought of walking around in a suit and tie and giving orders. They do not realize that there will be days when employees may not show up for work and they will have to cook food, make beds, or operate the cash register. These unrealistic expectations on the part of owners and managers can cause them to lose motivation and begin to give up on the business. Once this energy is gone from owners or managers, it becomes difficult to keep employees motivated. Lack of motivation in leadership positions contributes to lack of motivation in employees, which quickly becomes evident to guests and can cause a business to fail.

Lack of Planning

The majority of all businesses fail due to the lack of or incompetent planning. Developing a business plan does not mean quickly throwing something together for the purpose of trying to get a bank loan. It entails a vast amount of research and gathering information from other entrepreneurs. Every possible scenario must be considered. Far too many businesses in the hospitality field are not carefully planned. Several "Mom and Pop" type operations are designed around basic arithmetic, concentrating on the costs of preparing a product or providing a service and the amount at which those products or service can be sold. This is just a small part of preparing a business plan. The sad fact is that some large operations also neglect the importance of planning. One must deal with the type of competition, the amount of market share, and most of all, the question as to whether the product will fulfill a need in the market place. These types of activities take additional research and most entrepreneurs are in too much of a hurry when doing a professional analysis in this area. Several entrepreneurs have entered business ventures without a plan at all. Without proper planning, one will almost certainly fail.

Summary

Taking into consideration why so many hospitality businesses fail, this text attempts to provide managers with the pertinent information to prevent this from happening. By far, the most important element to the success of a business is to initially start with a sound business plan and try to stick to the plan once the business is in operation. There are four major segments in the hospitality industry: food, tourism, lodging, and entertainment. All of these entities must undergo constant monitoring and control. Elements that are used to evaluate these operations are the income statement and the cost-volume relationship. Uniform systems of accounts are usually adopted by most facilities as they allow for easier comparison of national standards.

When comparing national standards, items of most concern are prime cost items: food, beverage, and labor. The cost of these items and other controllable expenses must be constantly controlled if an operation is to survive.

By examining why some businesses fail while others are able to sustain themselves, managers and business owners can avoid some of the major pitfalls of business failure and can become successful.

Review Exercises

1. For the purpose of control, financial reports in the hospitality industry should be made available for evaluation:
   a. quarterly
   b. annually
   c. monthly
   d. as frequently as feasibly possible

2. Which of the following items can be used in an evaluation process?
   a. uniform systems of accounts
   b. national standards
   c. cost-volume–profit relationship
   d. all of the above

3. Three important attributes in managing the control function in a hospitality operation are:
   a. motivation, professionalism, and measuring
   b. effective time management, professionalism, and acceptance of responsibility
   c. scheduling employees, effective time management, and motivation
   d. acceptance of responsibility, motivation, professionalism

4. Controllable expenses account for at least _____ percent of the cost of managing the average hospitality operation.
   a. 20
   b. 30
   c. 40
   d. 50

5. If a manager practices time management on the job he or she would not:
   a. talk with guests
   b. fraternize with employees
   c. become involved with performance appraisals
   d. waste time training employees

6. When should management provide feedback?
   a. only when something goes wrong
   b. if an employee is doing something correct
   c. as soon after evaluation as possible
   d. b and c

7. A lot of new managers will become disgruntled with the industry because:
   a. the pay is not sufficient
   b. they do not want to relocate
   c. they do not have enough responsibilities
   d. they are unable to control their employees

8. The majority of all businesses fail due to:
   a. wrong attitude
   b. lack of planning
   c. unrealistic expectations
   d. poor credit practices

9. If a business is to sustain itself it should:
   a. fulfill a need
   b. hold down cost
   c. remain competitive
   d. all of the above

10. The steps in the control cycle should include:
    a. establishing controls
    b. informing employees
    c. evaluating performance
    d. all of the above

11. Describe why professionalism is so important in controlling an operation.

12. Describe the significance of the four-step control cycle.

13. Explain what activities can occur in the life cycle curve.

14. Explain why it is important to understand national standards.

Examination Type Problems

1. List five major reasons for business failure.

2. List two major activities that help businesses sustain themselves.

3. List the three important attributes that a hospitality manager should have in managing the control function.

4. What are the main segments of the hospitality industry?

Case Study

The Case Study Hotel is a 700-room conference center in the downtown area of a major metropolitan city. Within Case Study Hotel are various dining outlets. The Model is a fine-dining restaurant featuring continental cuisine with entree prices ranging from $12.95 to $24.95. It is open for lunch and dinner, seven days a week. You have just been hired as the manager of Model and you report directly to the food and beverage director. The revenue levels have been quite stable but the restaurant has been losing money. The food and beverage director has given you this position to see if you can turn the business around. You realize that there are two tasks you must accomplish as soon as possible. These two tasks are to evaluate the financial position of the business and to have a meeting with the employees. Address the following two questions pertaining to your actions concerning these two tasks:

1. List five items that you would evaluate to determine the financial position of the business.
2. List six items that you would discuss with the employees.

2
The Control Function

Learning Objectives

After completing this chapter, you should be able to:

- describe the benefits of a business plan.
- explain the importance of market research.
- describe the importance of differentiation.
- explain the importance of a mission statement to managers, employees, and guests.

- explain the importance of establishing goals and objectives.
- determine and explain the various steps of the control cycle.
- explain the four major concerns of purchasing.

For an organization to be successful the managerial function of control must be applied. For the purpose of this text, the definition of control will center around establishing standards to be followed; informing employees of these standards; comparing actual operational procedures against these standards; and providing feedback and taking corrective actions if necessary. This must be a continuous process. Standards cannot be established and forgotten. Management must continually monitor, try to improve, and control operational procedures in each area of the control cycle (see Figure 2–1).

    In order to establish controls for an operation the organization must first establish what business the organization is in. In other words, the business plan is the first step of the control cycle. This can be a difficult process since some organizations have diversified to the point that it is difficult to know exactly what is the main concentration of their business. Diversification can be advantageous, but the overall mission and purpose of a business must be known for employees to have a common purpose. It is difficult to determine what type of business some hospitality organizations are operating. For example, is Domino's in the pizza business, delivery business, or both? What attracts guests to purchase their products? What is more essential to their survival: getting the product out and delivered on time or preparing a quality product? Do guests prefer the quality of their pizza or the convenience of their delivery? The manager and the employees must know what business they are in so that they can establish mission, goals, and objectives accordingly. It is difficult to try and control an operation when the operation is attempting to be too versatile. Several restaurants that the public once thought of as hamburger places now serve so many different products that they are actually both full and quick service restaurants serving full menus. To enhance profitability, and for managers to be able to control an operation, employees and management must work toward the same organizational objectives and goals, which can only be established through a sound business plan and a well-designed mission statement.

Figure 2–1   *Control Cycle in Hospitality Operations*

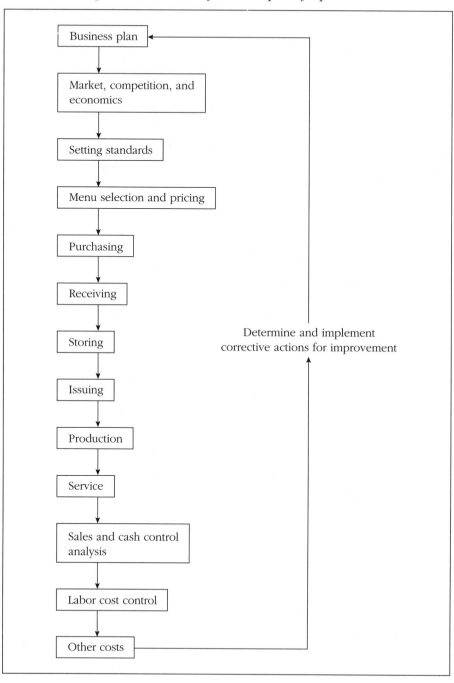

Business Plan: An Analysis of the Operation _____

Before developing a business plan an organization must complete its homework. Many business plans are doomed to fail before they are ever acted upon. An owner should not develop an impossible plan for an operation and ask a manager to control operational procedures. If a plan is not feasible an establishment cannot possibly work effectively. To be successful an organization must plan for success. When establishing a plan management has to know that they are fulfilling a need. Just because a facility is opened does not mean that guests are going to come or can even afford to come. If a concept does not fulfill a need or offer a certain amount of differentiation, there is no certainty that the concept will work. To have a successful operation an organization must start with a business plan that is feasible.

Therefore, the first step is market research to see if the concept will fill a need. In other words, determine whether the concept has a possibility of succeeding. Market research includes surveying demographics and location to establish whether there is actually a market for the product or service. This includes evaluating competitors and the market as a whole. Market research must be conducted before opening any business venture, or failure could be imminent. A manager cannot be expected to control costs if sufficient sales cannot even cover noncontrollable costs. Never build a house using cards if you want it to last. Anyone developing a business plan must complete their market research and interview as many target guests as possible before making any final decisions. No one can control cost if the business is not established to be operated cost effectively. Developing a business plan is not a simple process and the plan must be thoroughly thought out. This includes establishing a mission statement, goals, and objectives. In addition, the philosophy of the team concept, organizational structure, and departmentalization are all important.

Managers and owners must realize that even the most effect business plan can become out of date because of changing environmental conditions. Changes in customers, technology, competition, and internal factors such as the loss of key employees can cause a need for changes in the business plan. Managers must stay attuned to changes in the operation, the industry, and the market. If changes should occur that might have an impact on the business plan, then revisions should be made in the plan to adjust for these anticipated changes.

Mission Statement

Part of a business plan is the mission. It is important to have a mission statement that succinctly describes the nature and expectations of the business. A clear and concise mission statement can assist in providing direction for management and employees. A sound, well-understood, and acceptable mission statement provides several benefits. The three main contributions that can be derived from a sound mission statement for manager, employees, and guests are as follows:

1. It allows managers to have a benchmark for evaluating themselves and the operation. If the mission statement says that they are selling a

quality product with outstanding service, managers can assess whether this is occurring.

2. It provides employees common goals and objectives. In order to develop cohesive teams, employees must have common goals. If it is the goal of an organization to provide outstanding guest service, this effort will be far more successful when all employees are working toward that same effort.

3. It provides guests with the values, norms, and expectations of that organization. Guests identify with certain brands and franchises because of the expectations they have of those organizations.

Case Study Hotel's corporate mission has been developed in Figure 2–2.

Goals and Objectives

Goals and objectives must be written to support the business plan and the mission statement. Goals and objectives must be feasible and by all means costs effective. If not, they will neither gain the support of the manager nor the employees. Objectives must be set to maximize profit, but if they are perceived to be unreasonable, employees may become unmotivated and give far less than they are capable of performing. The employees may have the idea of "Why bother, I cannot achieve this anyway." If this perception is allowed to occur or persist, a situation can develop wherein employees become difficult to control. Goals and objectives should be written to motivate employees to want to control costs and succeed.

Figure 2–2   *Sample Mission Statement of the Case Study Hotel*

Case Study Hotel's Corporate Mission

To be recognized as the world's best first-class hotel organization,
to constantly strive to improve, and provide quality service to our guests,
our employees, and our shareholders.

To achieve this mission:

GUESTS
Quality services and products will need to be continually improved
to provide our guests with first-class experiences.

EMPLOYEES
Teamwork, involvement, integrity and commitment will be our motto for our eveyday operation.

SHAREHOLDERS
We pledge our utmost efforts to provide quality products and service for our guests
and a superb work environment for ourselves to achieve efficiency and hence
profitability to maximize the wealth of our shareholders.

Empowerment and Involvement: A Team Concept

To carry out goals and objectives a team concept of empowerment and involvement of employees is essential. Empowerment will lead to more involvement among employees and the development of a team concept. Goals and objectives are much easier to accomplish by a team than an individual. When employees work as a team they are more committed to the success of each other and the organization. Methods of controls and accountability are more acceptable as policies and procedures are more closely followed. Employees are more apt to work as a team when esprit de corp is in place. Japanese companies strive to develop teams within their organizations and this accounts for much of their success. When employees depend on each other and support each other, all policies run a lot smoother. In addition, less managerial and supervisory control is needed if teams are implemented properly.

Organizational Structure

Organizational structure is the presentation of the team relationship. Most hospitality operations are very flat. Even if the structure is multilayered, the general manager is ultimately responsible for all operational procedures. Usually a general manager in all hospitality establishments has the responsibility of implementing organizational policy and control procedures. Larger operations and especially franchises may have policy and control procedures established and handed down for management to implement. Because the industry is labor intensive, managers have the responsibility of overseeing that costs control activities are implemented and adhered to on a day-to-day basis. If an organization is large and has multiple units, the methods of controlling costs and the operating budget may be established at the headquarters. However, in all operational structures the unit manager is responsible for the implementation and supervision of control and accountability procedures.

Supervision of Departments

When the structure of a hospitality operation is large enough to have departments, the implementation of cost control activities can become the responsibility of department supervisors. Although departments can be instrumental in providing more stringent supervision of control factors and operational procedures, the general manager is still ultimately responsible. Problems can occur if departmental supervisors are not following correct procedures. Since supervisors are closer to day-to-day activities than are general managers, they are usually more specialized in their areas. Therefore, they can control and monitor daily operations of their departments in a more detailed manner.

The leadership of supervisors in directing their departments is very important. If they have a positive view of operation and support managerial cost control methods, all members of the department may be more supportive toward cost control procedures. On the other hand, if departmental supervisors are not concerned about supporting cost control activities they may sway department members in the same direction. Unconcerned informal groups may soon develop. This can happen in spite of how much a general manager may attempt to establish a positive example for all employees. Because of the importance of supervisory influences, managers must constantly reinforce the issue of cost control to their departmental supervisors. They may have to spend more time ensuring that the climate and culture of the organization is one of controlling costs. A general manager of a large operation cannot take the attitude that something as important as controlling costs will automatically be taken care of by supervisors because there is a manual for them to follow. The general manager will have to "manage by walking around" (MBWA). One department's disinterest in controlling resources can easily spread to other departments.

Japanese companies that have managers in different countries overseeing operational procedures will bring those managers back to Japan every year for a type of reorientation. They want to ensure that their methods of doing business and directing operational procedures will remain the same regardless of the location. They do not want managers doing their own thing. For this reason, managers of large hospitality operations need to have routine meetings and discussions to ensure that organizational culture is maintained.

Market, Competition, and Economics: An Analysis of the External Environment

After determining the internal situation a business needs to view the macroenvironment: the market in general, competition, and finally, how economic theories affect the control function.

Market

The hospitality market is so competitive that all operations are constantly looking for new advantages and niches. Just as one must conduct market research before opening a business venture, one must not forget the importance of conducting a marketing audit once the business is established. A marketing audit will force an operation to use a checklist to see how the business is performing and how it fares when compared to its competitors. Finding a means of staying competitive can be a difficult task. For most operations there are only two major avenues to pursue: differentiation or cost control.

If an operation can establish a form of differentiation and find a niche that is unique and appealing to guests, the facility may be able to capture a share of the market. Managers and business planners are wise to choose this approach. Even if the establishment has been in existence for a while, it is usually advantageous to develop some type of differentiation. Otherwise, why should guests frequent one facility over some others? Differentiation may be in the form of service, product, size of portion, or a particular theme. Differentiation is any activity or feature that will allow an operation to stand above the rest.

If differentiation cannot be attained, then one will have to look toward controlling costs better than the rest of its competitors. McDonald's has done an outstanding job of controlling costs to remain competitive. This can be a difficult means of obtaining a competitive advantage, but by operating efficiently and in a cost-effective manner, one operation may survive while others fail. In order for most operations to remain competitive they must be very effective at controlling costs.

Competition

To stay abreast of changes in the marketplace and to remain aware of what the competition is doing an organization must continuously scan the environment. Environmental scanning can be a time consuming activity because of the amount of information that must be evaluated to detect emerging trends and create scenarios. Social trends and a change in demographics can cause a decline in the demand for a particular product or service. If the competition is more in tune to these changes, they will react faster and capture a larger share of the market very quickly. Therefore, it is imperative for an operation to know who its competitors are, what the competitors are doing, and how these activities will affect the operation. An operation must constantly garner as much information about their competitors as possible. Not only must an organization read newspaper advertisements and flyers about the competition, they will occasionally have to visit the competition and purchase the competition's products to make a true, meaningful assessment.

Once there are any noticeable changes among the competition, an organization should evaluate several scenarios for dealing with the anticipated activity. For example, if another restaurant announces that it is planning a particular lunch special or sales that could reduce the amount of business for an operation, then the management of this operation should be prepared to counteract this strategy. It may want to offer a special or find some other means of dealing with the possible reduction in sales. It may also simply reduce the amount of production and thus the amount of labor to prevent a loss. However, by contemplating different scenarios, the operation would be prepared for adapting to the activity that the competition was planning. This is why continuous environmental scanning of the competition is so important.

At times an operation may want to assess or evaluate its own potential. One means is to perform an analysis of its strengths, weaknesses, opportunities, and threats (SWOT). Strengths and weaknesses pertain more to the operation's internal processes as compared to the environment, while opportunities and threats are more related to the external activities. For example, strengths could be those items associated with cost advantages, good competitive skills, product innovation skills, and so on. Weaknesses may lie in areas such as poor market image, lack of managerial depth and talent, and higher overall unit costs relative to key competitors. Potential opportunities may be in serving additional customer groups, entering new markets or segments, and expanding the product line; potential external threats could be raising sales of substitute products, slower market growth, and changing buyer needs and tastes. This analysis would help in assessing the status of the organization

Economics

The laws of supply and demand control the success or failure of an operation. If more hospitality ventures heeded the basic laws of supply and demand, many of them might not have attempted to open a business. There is only so much discretionary income in any demographic area; therefore, all operations have to share the market with other facilities that are already in existence and with those who may open after them. Many individuals enter business ventures in the hospitality industry with dreams of opening some type of outstanding moneymaking establishment. Without a superior form of differentiation, one will only be able to obtain a marginal share in the discretionary income of any demographic area. An operation cannot survive if the market share obtained cannot cover costs and generate a profit.

The basic laws of economics must also be considered when designing menus. Prices tend to rise when supply is limited, and prices tend to drop when supply is plentiful; therefore, a manager must plan accordingly. Heavy rains in California could damage lettuce crops, which would cause a shortage and the price would go up. Prices rise when demand is high and prices drop when demand is low. The law of demand states that people buy more of something at a lower price than at a higher price; therefore, the lower the price the greater the quantity demanded. These and other factors must be considered when writing and pricing menus.

Once an operation has an overall perspective it can then proceed to the other steps in the control cycle. Each of these steps is of equal importance. If one step is not followed, the negative impact can trickle down and affect the entire operation. The following is a brief discussion of each of the steps, which will be further expanded in subsequent chapters.

Setting Standards

Setting standards is an important step in the control cycle; and for this reason the process and importance of setting standards are explained further in Chapter 3. Without established standards employees will not have any direction for controlling costs and providing consistency to the operation. Standards must be established and met for an operation to fully utilize its resources. Even if an operation is successful, without standards the operation would have difficulty measuring its success. Standards are the cornerstone of maintaining consistency and cost control.

Menu Selection and Pricing

Once the analyses of the company and of the industry are completed, then the menu is next. Everything starts with the menu, as the menu lays the ground rules for all controls to follow. The menu is the blueprint of the facility. With a mission, a theme is set for the restaurant and the menu can then be developed to complement the blueprint. This is the same for hotels, mega resorts, clubs, and casinos. The importance of the menu cannot be overstated. Without a menu, the equipment needed cannot be properly purchased, the cost of food cannot adequately be projected, and labor cannot be precisely scheduled. It is difficult to imagine that even with the understanding of the importance of a menu, facilities are still opening without a detailed marketable menu. A menu must be developed before any other major decisions can be addressed.

With the menu determined, the amount and type of equipment can be purchased. One does not want to purchase unnecessary equipment. On the other hand, one also wants to purchase equipment that can handle the necessary capacity. Why purchase a deep-fat fryer if fried products are not on the menu? By the same token, if products are to be fried and the sales level has been projected, then what capacity of fryers are be needed? These and other decisions about equipment cannot be made without an established menu. With a shortage of equipment, quality control standards cannot be met and guest count will begin to decrease.

Since purchases can account for a large portion of total expenditures, without establishing a menu, a facility cannot accurately estimate the amount of food and supplies to be purchased and thus the cost of goods sold. Many facilities that fail can look back and say had they written a sound menu they could have predicted costs more accurately. Had they written a sound menu they would have seen that in the long run the business would have encountered problems. It is easy to see how a mistake in developing a menu can reverberate throughout the different areas of the business.

Just as correct product cost projections cannot be made without a menu, the same hold true for labor cost. The products on a menu and the equipment required to prepare those products along with the amount of service to be offered will determine the amount of labor required. Because the hospitality industry is so labor intensive, the cost of labor can range from 25% to 60% of sales. Thus, accurate projections are imperative.

The menu should dictate the location of the business and equipment for the business. The location, equipment, and type of service will then influence the amount of labor. All of these activities will affect the prices that must be charged to cover expenses and generate a profit. Therefore, the menu determines the standards for all activities. It would be difficult for any manager to control a business if an error occurred in establishing standards in any of these areas. All of these activities are extremely dependent on an effective menu. The entire concept of the menu will be discussed in detail in Chapter 4, while pricing will be expanded in Chapter 5.

Purchasing

Once a decision has been made to open a particular type of business, the type of product served, the quality of that product, and the type of service provided, along with availability, will determine what products are to be purchased at what quality and quantity. A major issue in purchasing is not to always purchase the cheapest product, but to purchase the minimum acceptable required quality. The key terms are "acceptable" and "required."

Because such a large percentage of the cost of operating a business is incurred during the purchasing process, controlling this process will often determine the success of a business. In the purchasing process, management is mainly involved with controlling four main issues: quality, quantity, time, and price.

To ensure that these issues are addressed properly the hospitality operation must have written standard purchasing specifications. Purchasing specifications should be written for every item that the operation intends to purchase as a direct means of carrying out its day-to-day functions. A foodservice operation must have written specifications for all food products; a lodging facility must have specifications for towels, sheets, and all other items. Purchasing will be explained further in Chapter 6.

Quality

To control cost one should try to prevent purchasing a quality above what is acceptable or required. If green beans are to be mixed into a stew to give it color, fancy green beans are not required as uniformity of length of cut is not material. On the other hand, if an operation is purchasing green beans to serve as a vegetable, color and uniformity of length may be concerns. If an operation is purchasing towels for a hotel, they may want to ensure that the towels have the quality to be able to endure over 500 washes; otherwise, they could end up purchasing towels more frequently and spending more resources.

Remember that written specifications for quality are essential in controlling costs, as mistakes in specifications can be costly. If a product is ordered for a large function and the product is to be received fresh at the last minute, and it is not delivered in the form, size, or shape that is required, the operation could lose both guests and revenues. For example, an operation does not want to receive 50 pounds of sliced American cheese when it actually needs grated mozzarella to make pizza. Items such as ham and cheese can come in a variety of shapes, form, and sizes. In order to control purchasing cost, the minimum acceptable required standards have to be met.

Quantity

To meet the needs of guests a business wants to ensure that products are always available. Stockout can cause an operation to lose guests. If guests go out of their way to a particular establishment to purchase a special product and the product is out of stock, the establishment may lose those guests forever. While an operation may want to control cost by purchasing the minimum acceptable and required quality, it also needs a reliable vendor that can provide the operation with sufficient quantity. Trying to ensure quantity may often result in purchasing a higher quality than one desires. Although this may be a last resort it can often be an issue that must be considered for the survival of the business.

Time

If a product cannot be obtained when needed, the business will have no product to sell. Be careful in selecting vendors that say they can deliver on all counts just to obtain the initial business. Always deal with vendors that can deliver products in a feasible amount of time. Timing is a two-sided issue. Not only does a business want products to be delivered on time, the products must also be ordered in a timely manner. Not ordering products on time can be costly and can substantially increase the cost of purchasing. Any time a vendor must make an unscheduled run to deliver to an operation it will normally cost the operation additional money. The use of airfreight or other special services and handling because products were not ordered on time can be very costly. When it comes to ordering products it is best to know the par stock—the level of inventory that should be maintained at all times. The amount of products on hand must be inventoried, then the difference between the amounts on hand and the amounts desired is ordered, unless there is a special occasion or event that could cause an adjustment in the amount desired. Mistakes can happen if a manager waits until the last minute to place an order, or if the vendor calls at the last minute to ask for the order. Any time a rush is made to place an order without checking the par stock, inventory, and special requirements there is always a chance of ordering too much or not enough. In the long run, rushing to place orders will cost the operation money. Whenever orders are being placed always remember that money is being spent and the survival of the business depends upon controlling these costs. When placing orders a manager must be in control and make the most cost-effective decisions.

Price

Quality, quantity, and time must be taken into consideration while attempting to obtain the lowest price possible. A manger wants to consistently obtain minimum acceptable required quality, in the right quantity, ordered and delivered in a timely manner, and at the lowest price. A manager wants these activities to occur on a consistent basis at the lowest possible price. Here, the key term is consistency. Vendors will often quote a lower price just to obtain the initial business or will make other promises to the operation concerning their ability to meet specifications and quantity standards. Once they have the contract, prices can often slowly increase and the quality and consistency can begin to deteriorate. Managers must constantly stay attuned to the market place to ensure that purchasing is cost effective. Purchasing is not a simple task, and remember, in most hospitality operations, purchasing accounts for over 35% of business costs. Because of this large percentage, managers must control the purchasing function of the control cycle.

Receiving

Once products have been purchased, the next step in the control cycle is to receive the products. The correct products with the quality that was specified and in the amount requested must be received on time at the price requested. To ensure that controls are implemented during the receiving process, the individuals receiving products must have a copy of the purchase request, the equipment for checking products, and the necessary training for receiving the products. Receiving personnel must have a copy of the specifications to ensure that the quality, form, shape, and size of the products are correct. Receiving personnel must also have a copy of the purchase request to account for quantity, timeliness of delivery, and the price that was negotiated. Unless the owner of the facility is receiving the products, it is important to realize that the person requesting the products, receiving the products, and preparing the products are not one in the same. If the owner is not performing the receiving function, these duties must be separated or collusion can occur.

Receiving personnel must have equipment such as thermometers to check temperatures of food products, as food should be rejected if it is not at the required temperature range. They should have scales to weigh products and be well advised of the numerous problems that can occur at this point in the control cycle. A pint of water weighs one pound. A truck driver can easily substitute a pint of water for 16 ounces of meat. If you take out one pound of meat and splash in 16 ounces of water and keep the carton on the refrigerated truck, by the time it reaches a facility an hour later, a manager will be signing for a case of meat plus one pound of ice crystals. If during the process of receiving products a case of meat is found with ice crystals, either water has been added as a substitute or the temperature of meat has been allowed to rise above freezing and has been refrozen. At any rate, the cause for ice crystals should be questioned. This is extremely important if ice crystals are found in seafood, as a guest could become very ill if the product has been defrosted and then refrozen. The receiving control function will be covered in greater detail in Chapter 7.

Storing

Products must be stored as quickly as possible to prevent deterioration and theft. Do not allow products to sit around, as items may become missing. In preparing items for storage, items must be tagged. Tagging entails the placing of a tag or tape on an item with the date received, cost of the product, weight or count, and any additional information that can be used in controlling the product. This makes the procedures of first in, first out (FIFO) easier to identify. Most importantly, tagging forces receiving personnel and storage room personnel to have to weigh and count products. Additionally, prices are placed on items during tagging. This is beneficial to the control element in two ways: management can improve the perception and understanding that products are actually money; and, it makes the inventory process easier because current prices will be readily available when taking and extending inventory.

For control purposes all products in storage should have a specific location in the storage room. The shelves should be labeled. This can also help in identifying high cost items so that they will not be placed close to the door for easy pilferage. Expensive items should never be stored close to the door of the storeroom.

Only authorized employees should be allowed in the storage area. Delivery personnel should never be allowed in the storage room. They may be tempted to remove items in empty cartons on their way out. Therefore, do not allow delivery personnel to store products and always keep storage areas locked whenever they are not in use.

Issuing

A requisition should be submitted whenever products are issued. In all facilities products should be signed for when they are removed from storage. If products are not signed for, they may come up missing and there would be no way of tracing them. The few minutes it takes to sign and date the removal of product from storage is a worthwhile endeavor to the control process. A requisition form should be used if the organization is large enough, but even the smallest operations need to record any item that is removed from storage.

Another important aspect of the issuing procedure that is often overlooked is products that have been issued but have not been used. Products that are removed from storage should be accounted for on some type of production sheet. Products that are not used should be returned to storage. Often products that are not used are allowed to go unaccounted for and they eventually end up missing or being written off. Managers must understand the importance of physically counting and comparing guest checks and the number of expensive items removed from storage to see if the items have been sold. This is especially true for large functions where products are paid for by the guest in advance. If a party of 500 ordered steak and paid for the guaranteed amount but only 450 people showed up, this does not mean that the other 50 steaks should go unaccounted for. The guest that paid for them can request to have them boxed to take home or the steaks should be returned to storage if they have not been cooked. They should not be given to employees. Giving food to employees is a bad practice since employees may begin to take leftovers without asking. After a period of time, they may even start generating leftovers through overpreparation. If this is allowed to occur, eventually managers will not be able to discern leftovers from other food products that are sold. Items that are issued but not used should be returned to the storeroom. The topics of storing and issuing will be discussed in Chapter 8.

Production

The production and preparation processes can be the most difficult step in the cycle to control. They will be explained in Chapter 9. All of the hard work of the previous processes can be lost if production is not at least adequate. The best quality of meat could have been purchased, received, and issued to the kitchen but if it is cooked too long or on heat that is too high, the product can be ruined. If spatulas are not used to get the remains out of can and jars, servings can be thrown away. If someone accidentally puts too much salt in a product, it can be ruined. If potatoes are allowed to remain in an automatic peeler too long, usable portions can be lost. If the ends of products such as carrots and onions are cut off too thickly, again portions can be lost. Through the course of a year these small amounts of waste can add up to hundreds of dollars. If a guest frequents a facility because he or she likes the taste of a particular item only to find the item to be different, the facility may lose that guest forever. To prevent products from becoming ruined during the production process an operation must use standard recipes to maintain consistency. Simply forgetting to add the proper garnish or using withered or dried out garnish can destroy the perception of value from a product. Preparation, production, and products must be monitored to ensure that kitchen personnel are not underpreparing—cheating guests and taking items home to use or sell. Occasionally managers have to weigh a serving of roast beef to ensure that the guest is getting the number of ounces that are prescribed by the recipes. Managers must inspect hotel rooms to see if all of the amenities are being placed and that housekeeping personnel are not taking items home. During the production process bartenders are placed in an advantageous position to waste and to steal products and money.

These wasteful and dishonest activities can cost an operation monetary resources through loss of sales and in replacement items. At times, one can identify a problem by just simply counting. Every once in a while managers must count the number of guests they have served and compare this to the number of products that are used. Managers are usually concerned with products going out the back door. It is right to be concerned about theft in this manner. However, be aware that a lot of theft occurs because of collusion between users, receivers, and delivery personnel; in some instances, products may have never entered the facility.

Collusion can occur through products never entering the facility or through delivery of a substandard product. If a receiving clerk orders an additional 20 pounds of steak each week and establishes an agreement with the truck driver to sell it elsewhere, the clerk can either falsify requisitions to account for the steak or establish an agreement with a cook to account for them. If management also agrees to take part in the collusion, it becomes even more difficult for owners to identify the theft. The best method to use in preventing collusion is to try to have all areas in the control cycle performed by different individuals. Management should make every attempt to allocate duties to as many different employees as possible.

Service

Controlling guest service can be a difficult task for managers because like the production process it is also labor intensive. Service will be discussed in Chapter 10. To control the service process it is important to have employees trained in the correct method of delivery and service. As stated earlier, controls rely to a great extent on perceptions. A manager must let it be known that poor guest service will not be tolerated. It is in this step of the cycle that a manager has another opportunity to lead by example. Employees must be made aware that it is far easier to get loyal guests to come back than it is to attract new guests. If sales are lost as a result of poor guest service, other costs can suffer. Labor and product costs must still be paid for. Poor service can cause sales income from a regular guest to be lost forever. Once sales drop, managers may not be able to meet their controllable and noncontrollable costs.

When operating a foodservice facility, guest checks must be monitored to determine which waitstaff personnel are not doing enough suggestive selling or may just be providing bad service. Managers should make an effort to reward employees that provide outstanding service. Positive behavior must be reinforced if it is to continue.

While trying to control guest service to prevent losing guests and sales, managers also want to ensure that their waitstaff is not going into business for themselves. In the foodservice industry, employees may try to go into business for themselves by simply using a guest check several times to order food or beverage items, deliver them to the guest, and pocket the money. In casinos it could be the substitution of coupons for tokens and selling the tokens. Clerks in travel agencies can collect the frequent flyer miles of their guests. Bartenders have an array of activities that they can perform, from bringing in their own bottles and selling shots from them, to simply short-pouring guests. Because production and service are so labor intensive, managers must try to implement sound control procedures. Personnel have to be aware that management is on top of things. Employees that never want to take a vacation or time off could have developed theft activities, and they may not want the difference in sales income to be observed during their absence. Managers may have to run the bar for an hour on a busy night just to see if the amount of sales increase substantially. Managers must monitor employees' activities. Often managers use "mystery shoppers" to keep employees honest. Honest employees are usually not disturbed by monitoring and evaluation.

Sales and Cash Control Analysis

Financial analysis and statements will be covered in more detail later in Chapter 11; however, the importance of controlling cash must be mentioned at this time. Cash control is essential to staying in business. Managers must have employees document why they think they may have been over or short. Managers should not become so lazy that they allow cashiers to deduct an over-ring or a void from the cash register. This task may be delegated to a supervisor in a large operation, but in any situation two people should be involved when a void or over-ring occurs. Additionally, a record of these activities should be maintained. Employees may be less apt to use this avenue to steal from the operation if they are aware that records are maintained. Using voids to steal can be a quick method for employees or managers to pick up $50 to $100 a week. By only using one large over-ring on a busy night an employee can pocket $50 or more. If a pattern occurs, find a new cashier; and in many cases, it may be advisable to find a new manager.

Power surges may occur in certain locations during rainy seasons or snowstorms and may cause equipment failure. Be sure to have back-up receipt books available so that any money received from guests during periods when cash registers or point-of-sale (POS) equipment is not operating can be entered into the system. Owners should be aware that a dishonest manager might cut off the power to registers during a busy fifteen-minute or half-hour period just so they can sell products during this period without having to enter them into the POS system. All orders taken when POS systems are not working should be entered later and the trail tape should be annotated to explain what has occurred. If there is a frequent occurrence of these types of activities, the manager or owner needs to start an investigation.

Labor Cost Control

Labor cost control and analysis is of the utmost importance to a hospitality operation. Training employees is a must and the importance of training to controlling labor cannot be overstated. Training and job rotation are essential to consistency, continuity, and survival of the business. Since the hospitality field is so labor intensive, extra concern must be given to controlling labor. Labor only has to be one or two percentage points out of line to cause a loss for the accounting period. Managers cannot afford to allow employees to clock in ten or fifteen minutes early or clock out ten or fifteen minutes late. One way of preventing this is through computerized equipment, time clocks, cash registers, POS systems, and so on. Another method is to have employees bring their time cards to the manager so that the manager can sign them in and out. If managers allow employee labor errors to go unattended, not only will employees clock in early and clock out late, they may begin to clock other employees in and out.

All overtime should be explained in writing to prevent managers from getting lazy with their scheduling. It will also reduce favoritism if it is occurring at the operation's expense. Managers should always complete a statement justifying overtime and should review time cards to see if it is the same employee. This could also identify other problems.

"Ghost employees" may also be a problem and this is especially true for isolated locations. Managers may carry relatives or friends on the payroll that may have never worked at the facility. In most cases these employees are carried on the payrolls for periods of less than a week. If their work period is extended much longer than a few days it may become too obvious. Management should account for all employees by position. If a manager has a large rate of turnover with employees working only short periods and then terminating, the situation should be investigated.

As technology improves, it will become somewhat easier for managers to maintain accountability for all resources. However, accountability will never be a full substitute for controls. It is always worth remembering that figures do not lie, but liars can figure. Whenever money is involved, there is always a chance that some employees and managers are attempting to circumvent the control system for their own gains. Owners and managers must implement controls and monitor the control system. Managers must instill an attitude among their employees that controlling costs is important to the survival of the business. Managers must consistently and routinely check, inspect, and monitor operational procedures if this attitude is to be implemented and accepted. Even with the best controls in place, without constantly monitoring the operational procedures owners and managers will not know if controls are being circumvented.

Other Costs

The ability to control the overall activities of an operation is by far the most challenging aspect of the control process. A manager can always match figures and balance books, but this will not pinpoint why the operation is having a decrease in sales. Keeping up with all of the details of day-to-day activities will cause a manager to be successful in controlling resources. For example, it takes approximately 40 pounds of roast beef to feed 100 people. A manager can order 40 pounds and the invoices and other accounting documentation may balance. The operation may have served 100 people and guest receipts will reflect this. However, just because all of these activities are balanced, does not mean that the guests actually received all or any of the 40 pounds of meat. This is the aspect of control that is difficult to manage. Ensuring that procedures are being followed is a difficult managerial task that must be controlled. If 100 guests are supposed to be served 6 ounces of roast beef but are actually getting 5 ounces, the cook is taking 100 ounces home. All of the figures may match and balance. The only way a manager may be able to detect this type of problem is because of a decrease in business. If this type of theft occurs, it is usually impossible to regain all of the unhappy guests that are lost. Guests may not complain about small portions, they just may not come back. A manager must stay on top of these control factors at all times. This is why this text presents a more realistic approach to hospitality control. Managers must be made aware that there are other activities that they must monitor even though all figures are balancing and the facility may be generating a profit. By controlling all costs, an operation can maximize the amount of profit that can be generated.

Mathematics in Control: Fractions, Decimals, Ratios, and Percentages

As discussed in Chapter 1, control involves numbers. Although advanced mathematics or calculus are not normally used in control, management has to deal with fractions, decimals, ratios, and percentages on a daily basis. A serving of pie is one-sixth, hence a fraction. The inventory of the house brand of vodka is 2.6, hence a decimal, signifying the operation has a bit over two and a half bottles on hand. In a particular hotel, each room attendant is responsible for 14 rooms, resulting in a ratio of 1:14. The food cost percentage quoted by a restaurant in a country club is 44%, thus a percentage. Numbers are expressed in one of these four means on a daily basis. Therefore, to be knowledgeable in control, one needs to be comfortable with manipulating such numerical expressions.

Fractions are most used in control when converting standardized recipes to accommodate a certain number of guests. They are widely used in portioning dessert items such as cakes and pies and are used in preparation, such as ½ cup of oil or ⅓ teaspoon of nutmeg. One will also find fractions when mixing chemicals for cleaning, such as ¾ cup of bleach. Fractions help bakers divide their dough mixture into equal parts. A fraction is one or more equal parts of a whole. If a cake is divided into eight parts, then one part of the cake is ⅛ and five parts are ⅝. Similarly, if a pie is divided into six parts, three parts are ³⁄₆, or half of the pie, while six parts are ⁶⁄₆, or the entire pie. The first number, or top part, of a fraction is known as the numerator; the last number, or bottom part, is known as the denominator.

Fractions in which the numerator is smaller than the denominator, such as ⅝, ⅜, or 2/7, are known as proper fractions; fractions in which the numerator is larger than the denominator are improper fractions. An improper fraction is essentially a whole plus a fraction, or a mixed number. For instance 5/3 is an improper faction that can be expressed as a mixed number of 1⅔:

3/3 + ⅔, where the numerators 3 and 2 total 5

Because 3/3 is really one whole the number should be expressed as 1 and ⅔ rather than 5/3.

Unlike factions that can be divided into many parts, decimals are based on the number 10. Decimal fractions, therefore, are factions that are expressed with denominators of 10 or multiples of 10, such as:

$$\frac{9}{10} \qquad \frac{27}{100} \qquad \frac{533}{1000} \qquad \frac{9873}{10{,}000}$$

However, instead of expressing these numbers as decimal fractions, a decimal point (.) is used. Thus, the numbers above can be expressed as: 0.9, 0.27, 0.533, and 0.9873. Therefore, half a bottle can be expressed as 5/10 or 0.5. To convert a decimal fraction into a decimal number first write the number in the numerator, then count the number of zeros in the denominator and place the decimal point according to the number of zeros. For example, to convert 9/10 into a decimal first write the number 9, then count the number of zeros in the denominator (the number 10 has one zero) and place the decimal point immediately to the left of the number 9 (which is one digit). To convert 9/100, again first write the 9. In this case there are two zeros in the denominator and only one digit (9) in the numerator. Thus, to place the decimal point according to the number of zeros, add one zero immediately to the left of the number 9 before placing the decimal, resulting in 0.09.

Decimal numbers go in two directions of the decimal point. To the left of the decimal is the one, or the unit, column. Each column moving left is an increase in the multiple of 10. For example:

Thousands	Hundreds	Tens	Ones/Units	Decimal Point
1000	100	10	1	(.)

If the column is moving to the right of the decimal point, each move is one-tenth of the number in the column to its immediate left. Thus, one-tenth of 1 is 1/10, one-tenth of 1/10 is 1/100, and one-tenth of 1/100 is 1/1000. Working with fractions is quite simple if one remembers to line up the decimal points and place whole numbers and decimal fractions in their proper columns.

A ratio is defined as the relative size of two quantities expressed as the quotient of one divided by another. Going back to the example of the one room attendant being responsible for 14 rooms, the ratio can be expressed as 14 divided by one, which results in a quotient of 14, or in the written form of 14:1

or 1:14. Ratios are widely used in staffing and food production. They are also used daily when the cleaning crew dilutes concentrated chemicals with water.

Of the four numerical expressions, the percentage is the most widely used in the hospitality industry. As mentioned, it is used to express rates such as food cost percentage, beverage cost percentage, profit margin, and the like. For those who are currently working or have worked in the hospitality business, a phrase such as "our labor cost of 48% is way out of line, we need to keep it under control" is common. Percent (%) means per, for, or out of each hundred. Thus, 75% of the guests means 75 out of 100 guests. The whole, in this case, is 100. As an example, 50-pound steamship round represents the whole. A few servings of the round total 5 pounds, representing a fraction of the whole. Expressed as a fraction, this is $\frac{5}{50}$, or reduced, $\frac{1}{10}$. To express a common faction as a percentage, the numerator is divided by the denominator, which becomes 0.1. Since percent means hundredths, the decimal will then be moved to the right two places when the percentage sign is used, resulting in 10%. Thus the fraction $\frac{1}{10}$ is 0.1 as a decimal and 10% as a percentage.

Because the function of control depends on results expressed in measurable forms, such as fractions, decimals, ratios, and percentages, the knowledge and comfort level in dealing with these numbers is crucial.

Summary

Performing an analysis of an operation can be an important process for a new manager. This allows for establishing a general business plan to see if goals and objectives are feasible and will aid in satisfying the ideals of the mission statement. An operation should continuously develop a team concept and empower employees. This will develop an organizational culture that will allow employees to have autonomy to achieve organizational goals and objectives.

Managers must anticipate factors in the market, competition, and economy that can affect operational procedures. Shifts in one of these three areas can often present danger or opportunity to a business. From menu selection to managing costs, each process or area of concern must be constantly evaluated. A manager has the greatest influence over profit generation and control within this process.

Review Exercises

1. The three contributions provided by a mission statement for managers, employees, and customers are:
   a. benchmark, common goals, and organizational values
   b. organizational values, benchmark, and training
   c. benchmark, common goals, and training
   d. leadership, common goals, and organizational values

2. For a business to be successful it is essential for it to be:
   a. feasible
   b. realistic
   c. as detailed as possible
   d. adequate

3. In order to establish controls for an operation, one must first establish
   a. what business one is in
   b. the organizational goals
   c. the organizational objectives
   d. all of the above

4. Empowerment will lead to more involvement among employees in developing:
   a. a team concept
   b. the accomplishment of goals and objectives
   c. a work setting for less supervision
   d. all of the above

5. Goals and objectives must be:
   a. feasible and cost effective
   b. ideal
   c. imaginary
   d. frequently changed

6. In most hospitality organizations, the organization structure is very:
   a. flat
   b. tall
   c. large
   d. small

7. A marketing audit should be completed:
   a. the first couple of days that one is in business
   b. before one opens the business
   c. after the business has been established
   d. as part of the original planning process

8. The control cycle begins with:
   a. setting standards
   b. receiving
   c. storing
   d. menu

9. Which basic law of economics must be considered when writing menus?
   a. prices tend to rise when supply is limited
   b. prices tend to rise when supply is abundant
   c. people actually buy more when prices are higher
   d. the higher the price the greater the quantity demanded

10. The menu controls all of the following except:
    a. equipment to be purchased
    b. the cost of labor
    c. managerial expertise
    d. site selection

As an entrepreneur of a 100-seat, fine dining, five-star restaurant, you are developing your new business.

11. Develop your mission statement.

12. Develop four goals for your restaurant.

13. Develop four objectives for your restaurant.

14. Explain the value of environmental scanning of the competition.

Examination Type Problems

1. List a factor that can affect market competition for a 300-seat family restaurant and explain how you would deal with it.

2. List four important factors associated with the storing of products.

3. What three factors must be taken into consideration while trying to obtain the lowest price?

4. Explain why service should be included in the control cycle.

Case Study

The Case Study Hotel is contemplating the opening of a medium-priced 100-seat casual dining facility. The hotel manager has just advised you that you will be the general manager of the new restaurant. You have full responsibility for establishing the theme and the type of business operation that will be implemented. Understanding the difficulty of the control function, establish a control cycle for this new restaurant. After the major steps in the cycle are determined, list two subitems for each of these major steps and explain why you believe that these subitems will help your new restaurant become successful.

3
Setting Standards

Key Terms

as purchased (AP)	objectives	standardized recipes
attainable	operational cost	standards
compromise	prime cost	support center
feedback	revenue center	turnover
hidden costs	servable portion	usable portion (UP)
labor intensive		

Learning Objectives

After completing this chapter, you should be able to:

- explain the concept of organizational standards and the purpose of establishing standards.
- describe the four major components in the overall process of developing standards.
- outline the eight major areas of setting standards for food and beverage operations.
- explain as purchased (AP) and usable portion (UP) as they relate to standardized recipes and costs.

- assess the importance of labor and equipment standards to the overall cost control process.
- outline the five major steps in any action plan of cost control.
- create a preliminary audit for measuring standards.

Outline

Guidelines for Standards
   Measurability
   Attainability
   Improvement
   Feedback
Relevancy of Standards

Setting Standards for Food and Beverage
   Operations
   Establishing Standardized Recipes
   Establishing Servable Portion and Cost
   Determining Range of Acceptable Cost
   Determining Labor Procedures and Cost

A standard is a model or method that serves as a basis for comparison. The purpose for setting standards is to control and measure the efficiency of production and the overall effectiveness of an organization. Setting standards in the hospitality industry involves determining the expected amount of sales income that can be derived from the utilization of a prescribed amount of resources. These resources include prime cost items such as food, beverage, and labor. In the case of casinos it also comprises the utilization of equipment. The objective of standards is to provide employees with direction and to allow for efficient business decisions and employee performance evaluation.

It is important for employees to have standards for an organization to be successful. Employees cannot be instructed to generate sales or reduce costs without being given specific parameters of what is acceptable or what is to be attained, and for commitment and motivational purposes, why it should be attained. All too often managers and employees are given a vague set of instructions and later they are penalized when these poorly stated objectives are not accomplished. In any type of business venture, especially in the hospitality industry that is labor intensive, standards must be set or proper cost cannot be determined. Just like objectives, standards must be measurable if they are to be used effectively.

Guidelines for Standards

What constitutes good standards? Standards must be established for all areas of an operation. This means standards must be set for all revenue centers and support centers. While revenue centers such as food and beverage operations and the gift shop may be responsible for sales, housekeeping and other support centers are also responsible for controlling labor and for the security and accountability of products. To be effective, standards must comply with the following four guidelines:

1. Standards must be measurable.
2. If standards cannot be attained, they should be reevaluated.
3. If standards are attained, the organization must determine if they can be improved.
4. Employees must receive feedback if the process is to work efficiently.

Measurability

Before the control process can be implemented, standards must be established. Standards, as with objectives, must be measurable. A manager should not be asked to increase sales without being provided with some type of guideline to see if the increase can actually be accomplished. To state that sales should be increased by 2% or 5% during the next accounting period would provide a manager with a means of measuring whether he or she would be able to accomplish the objective and then one could fairly evaluate the individual based on his or her accomplishments. The same can be said when employees are instructed to provide better guest service. How is that to be measured? If management says that it would like to provide better guest service so that the number of guest complaints can be decreased by 10% during the next month, then it is feasible to count the number of comment cards to see if the objective was met. Establishing measurable standards provides a systematic method to give feedback to employees. If standards are not stated in a measurable manner, the action taken cannot be compared.

Attainability

Besides being measurable and quantifiable, standards also need to be attainable. Standards that are set too high most likely cannot be met. A standard may have been set in such a manner that it cannot be feasibly accomplished with existing resources. The three methods most often used by owners when they cannot attain budgetary standards are to raise prices, reduce portion size, or lower the quality of the products. However, before making any such moves, management must ensure that lowering the standard will not be detrimental to the financial stability of the operation. Trying to meet a standard can be as simple as finding a substitute product or as complex as having to complete a marketing audit to establish the organization's position in the market place. However, once standards are set, the organization should try its best to meet the stated objectives.

Improvement

Just because standards are being met is not an indication that they cannot be improved. If a business is generating a profit they may be able to generate an even greater profit. If a business is making a 15% profit, without implementing evaluation control factors, management has no way of knowing if the operation should be generating 16 or 17%. Meeting an established standard may not be an indication of maximization. Several operations are generating a profit because of the location and uniqueness of product; however, because of lack of standards and control they are not maximizing their return on investments. Therefore, an operation should always look for methods to improve operational procedures and to reduce unnecessary costs.

Feedback

Employees must be made aware of their performance and that of the organization. Without proper feedback employees may perceive that either standards are not important or that their input into the organization is not important. Since perception creates reality, regardless as to whether standards have been attained, employees should be informed of the progress; and their opinions of how to improve operational procedures should be solicited.

Relevancy of Standards

When setting standards an organization must consider operating expenses and required profit for that particular facility. It is important to understand that standards must be based on operational expenses and anticipated profit for the facility for which the standards are to be implemented. There is a continuing debate concerning what should be the average food cost or labor cost of certain types of operations. While industry standards for prime cost percentages may not be that far off, they cannot account for all of the nuances of every operation. Two operations may be identical in many ways but can be very different in associated costs. For example, operations may differ in the following ways:

1. A facility may have been established long enough to own its own property and rent may not be a required expenditure.

2. Because of location and the job market, the cost of labor can be significantly different.

3. Menus for two different facilities could be the same but because of the demographics of the area, the popularity of menu items could be completely different. This would have a major effect on food cost percentage.

4. Food cost of seasonal items can be quite different in different geographical areas.

Because of these and other factors, standards for each facility must be based on the operational cost of that facility. Standards must also be set for the different areas in a facility. While small business operations may have a consolidated labor cost, a large facility may be more labor intensive in different areas. Without setting standards for each area, management would not know where standards were not being met. It is also imperative to remember that a percentage standard in any cost is only a guideline and does not reveal a lot of information concerning a business unless it is viewed together with a dollar value. Every business would like to have a lower percentage in costs. Just remember, the lowest cost percentage is always 0%; this also means that the business is closed. A business cannot be run effectively without some costs.

Setting Standards for Food and Beverage Operations

In the hospitality industry, food, beverage, and labor are considered prime costs. Most chain operations will set strict standards in percentages for these costs. In order to derive standardized cost percentages, they must be done correctly. To obtain food cost percentage, divide the cost of food by the amount of food sales. For example, if it costs $4.00 to produce a chicken entree that sells for $10.00, then the food cost percentage for that particular entree can be calculated as follows:

$$\text{Food cost \%} = \frac{\text{Food cost (\$)}}{\text{Food sales (\$)}}$$
$$\text{Food cost \% (chicken entree)} = \frac{\$4.00}{\$10.00}$$
$$= 40\%$$

To derive beverage cost percentage, use a similar formula and divide beverage cost by beverage sales. For example, if it takes $1.00 to produce a cocktail that can be sold for $4.00, then the beverage cost percentage would be:

$$\text{Beverage cost \%} = \frac{\text{Beverage cost (\$)}}{\text{Beverage sales (\$)}}$$
$$\text{Beverage cost \% (cocktail)} = \frac{\$1.00}{\$4.00}$$
$$= 25\%$$

This technique develops a percentage to compare to the standard. The mistake that is often made is that total sales are used to determine the percentage for food and beverage cost. The percentages must be derived by dividing food cost by food sales and beverage cost by beverage sales.

When establishing standards for food and beverage operations eight areas must be addressed, as shown in Figure 3–1. In addressing each of these areas, management must establish standards that meet the four criteria that were discussed: measurability, attainability, improvement, and feedback.

Figure 3–1   *Establishing Standards for Food and Beverage Operations*

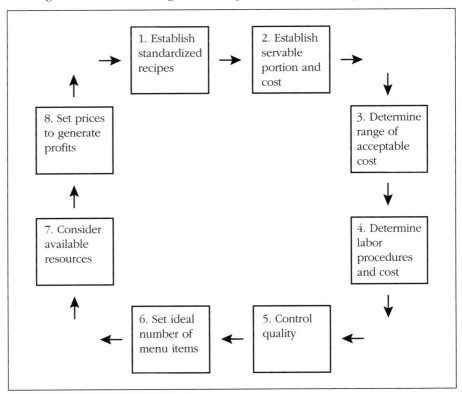

Establishing Standardized Recipes

Constructing standardized recipes is the basis of product consistency. Correct recipe development is essential to organizational policy of food and beverage operations. Management must develop a recipe for every food and beverage item that is to be sold. Without standardized recipes one can have unhappy or disgruntled guests and one cannot control costs. A typical standardized recipe includes the following categories:

- Name of recipe
- Yield
- Ingredients
- Prepreparation procedures
- Preparation method
- Portion size

A sample standardized recipe is shown in Figure 3–2. Some may also include diagrams of required equipment or preparation methods.

Figure 3–2 *Standardized Recipe*

Full recipe name: Smokey Joe's Split Pea Soup Prep pan/type: 10 qt stock pot
Short recipe name: Split Pea Serving pan: 10 qt stock pot
Source: Smokey Joe's Bistro Serving dish: 10 oz bowl
Manager: Greg Watson Portion size: 8 oz
Day/date: Monday/December 21, 1998 Cooking time/temp: 2 hours

Ingredients	Extended Quantity	Preparation Method	Time	Equipment
Number of portions: 30				
Prepreparation:		Gather all ingredients and equipment.	20 min	10 qt stock pot
Bacon, finely chopped	14 oz	Saute the bacon in the oil		
Canola oil	1.5 fl oz	Add onions and celery.		
Onions, yellow, chopped	18 oz	Saute until onions become transparant.		
Celery, chopped	6 oz	Add garlic and saute until aroma		
Garlic, chopped	1 tsp	develops; do not brown.		
Flour, all-purpose	4.5 oz	Add flour to make a roux.		
Soup base, chicken	6 oz	Add water and chicken base and bring to a		
Water	240 fl oz	simmer.		
Peas, green, split, dry	2 lbs	Add split peas and ham hocks.	1 ½ hrs	
Pork, ham hock, smoked	1 ¾ lbs	Allow soup to simmer for 1 ½ hours.		
Bay leaves	3	Add bay leaves and simmer for another half hour.		
		Remove ham hocks and discard bay leaves.		
		Clean hocks and return meat to soup.		
Preparation and holding procedures:				
Croutons	7–10/serving	Reheat soup properly. Portion soup with an 8 oz ladle into 10 oz bowl. Top with croutons.	45 min	8 oz ladel

Standardized recipes yield consistent quality and quantity. It does not matter if different cooks are on duty, if they use the same standardized recipe and follow the instructions, they should obtain identical products. Standardized recipes also dictate the exact amount of food required to yield the desired portions. Conversion of recipes for small groups to feed large banquets is important. If a standardized recipe for 8 is converted to feed 80, the conversion of all ingredients must be performed accurately so that the final product will still be of the same quality and within the actual food production cost.

Moreover, an operation can encounter a host of problems if standardized recipes are not used. Leftovers can become a major issue. Employees may overprepare to prevent running out of a product or to purposely create leftovers if they are allowed to take excess products home. Even if leftovers can be sold, there is always deterioration in quality that can be recognized by the guests. Thus, preventing waste is another reason why employees should know and understand the value of standardized recipes and how to use and convert them.

Establishing Servable Portion and Cost

Servable portion and cost must be established to determine the actual cost of an item. The as purchased (AP) price and the servable or usable portion (UP) price can be completely different; and this can change the overall costs to the operation.

To determine the servable portion and cost of an item, first refer to an established table on the estimated usable portion of any produce or meat item or calculate an estimate. Figure 3–3 provides a list of AP and UP information on some produce items. For instance, 100% of lettuce cannot be used for production. In this case, according to the USDA data, 5% (about an ounce) is lost in one pound of lettuce. Thus, if two pounds of servable portion is needed, then approximately two pounds and two ounces of lettuce will need to be purchased to allow for the 5% loss. The amount of loss can vary at different times of the year because the quality of the product may change.

AP and UP become more important when dealing with high-priced items such as meat. Which is more cost effective for turkey sandwiches: uncooked turkey breast that has 82% yield, or 18% loss factor, or a more expensive cooked turkey roll with 95% yield? Although AP and UP calculations will be explained in more detail in the chapter on purchasing, it should be noted that these numbers may vary, depending on staff skill levels. Therefore, management may wish to perform its own AP and UP calculations.

Determining Range of Acceptable Cost

Once AP and UP are determined, management has a cost factor for that particular item as long as the recipe and other procedures remain the same. A standard must be established for acceptable amount and range of allowable food cost. Because of the sales mix of a menu, an approximate cost percentage of food can be established. An increase in food cost or percentage may not

Figure 3–3 *As Purchased versus Usable Portion Analysis*

Yield from Fresh Vegetables		
Vegetable	Waste (% = oz per lb)*	AP Quantity Needed To Yield 1 Pound of UP
Cabbage	20% = 3.25 oz	20 oz
Carrots	20% = 3.25 oz	20 oz
Celery	11% = 2 oz	18.25 oz
Cucumber	3% = 0.5 oz	17.75 oz
Garlic	13% = 2.25 oz	18.50 oz
Lettuce, iceberg	5% = 1 oz	17 oz
Onion	10% = 1.75 oz	18 oz
Pepper, sweet bell	18% = 3 oz	19.75 oz
Radishes	10% = 1.75 oz	21.50 oz
Spinach	28% = 4.5 oz	22.50 oz
Tomato	9% = 1.5 oz	17.75 oz

Source: Calculated from data in *USDA Agriculture Handbook.*
*Rounded up to the next 0.25 oz

be cause for alarm if accompanied by a sufficient increase in sales; however, management still needs to examine the bottom line. An apparent standard must be set if an operation is to monitor food cost on a frequent and routine basis. The procedure for establishing cost standards to maximize income will be discussed in detail in later chapters.

Determining Labor Procedures and Cost

Another area that must be considered when developing standards for an operation is labor cost. Standardized recipes may enable a facility to monitor and reduce labor cost, and because turnover is extremely high in the food service industry, an owner/operator must always have labor cost and the turnover rate in mind when establishing recipes. Standardized recipes may enable management to use more unskilled employees without a reduction in quality; and these employees are easier to replace should management lose staff through turnover. Whether employees have the skills to prepare a product or whether the composition of the menu will allow employees the time to prepare all of the products must be addressed. When setting standards for the preparation of products an operator must be aware that the kitchen can be a dangerous environment in which to work if employees begin to rush. Standard must be set to get the job accomplished with the safety of the employees as well as productivity in mind.

Quality Control

Standards must be assessed to ensure the highest quality of products and service to all guests. If standards are generated solely with profit in mind, an operation could end up providing poor quality and service. Intense focus on the guest is one of the foundations of total quality management (TQM). The expectation of generating a profit is why a business venture exists; however, an operation's first objective must be to stay in business before it can be able to generate a profit. Quality products and services can lead to greater profits. An organization could face failure if it allows profit-driven motives to override quality and service standards. One reason why organizations such as Coca Cola and McDonald's have been able to survive and thrive in a competitive market is because they have done an outstanding job of placing quality and service ahead of making a profit.

Setting an Ideal Number of Menu Items

Placing too many food products on a menu can easily cause an operation to lose sight of goals and expectations. As the number of menu items increases, so does the possibility of spoilage, waste, and theft. Not only can a business lose money because of spoilage, waste, and theft, but there is always a chance of reduction in quality. Reduction in quality can have a negative effect on sales and financial performance. When deciding how many items should be on a menu, remember that there must be a balance of different tastes and selections to allow for a profitable sales mix; therefore, the number of items on a menu should be kept to a minimum yet should compensate for taste, profit, and maximum sales.

Available Resources

The amount of available resources must be taken into consideration when developing standards for any type of business venture. A business must have the equipment and labor skills to develop products. Only a certain amount of resources are available in these areas and every effort must be made to understand the capacity and capability of each before standards can be developed. Certain items cannot be placed on a menu and certain items cannot be prepared because of limited resources. If available equipment can only process a set amount of products, an operation can only expect to generate that amount and can only expect to generate a certain amount of profit.

Setting Prices to Generate Profits

After standards have been established, prices for products and services can then be determined. The correct pricing of products and services and the different methods of determining prices will be addressed in detail in Chapter 4. Prices can be extremely difficult to change without irritating the guests, therefore this topic must be given a great deal of consideration. The bottom line is that standardized recipes for food and beverage products will allow for efficiency and consistency, which are of the utmost importance when trying to predict cost and control cost.

Setting Standards for Labor

Determining the amount of labor used to provide a service or prepare a product will assist in pricing the product or service correctly. A labor standard must be set for all services and production, especially for the production or delivery of those activities that may consume a vast amount of time. If a product or service involves a great deal of preparation, a standard labor time for developing that product must be established.

The preparation of some products can be labor intensive, and it is important to understand the amount of time required so that the price will adequately reflect the amount of resources expended. Similarly, it is critical to include additional time for other factors, such as removing items from storage, as all of these procedures in the production process can consume a great deal of time. Guests can become dismayed if it takes a long time for room service to be delivered. Travelers are usually tired and want service as soon as possible. Standards should be established to inform guests that a certain maximum or minimum amount of time will be required before the product or service can be provided. Time and motion study is one method used to set such standards. The entire process of setting labor standards will be discussed in detail in Chapters 13 and 14. When standards are set and effectively communicated to the staff, then proper costs can be estimated and optimal service can be provided.

Setting Standards for Equipment and Supplies

Proper equipment standards can enhance the menu and enable employees to maintain other standards. Standards should be set as to which piece of equipment should be used for cooking and serving each item. Equipment not only includes large implements such as ovens, coolers, and freezers, it also encompasses smaller objects such as serving utensils, china, glasses, and tableware. These smaller yet important items must be selected to add color, height, and appeal to menu items and, at the same time, to help render proper portions. For example, a kids menu may have fresh homemade ice cream as a dessert item, beautifully arranged in a sundae glass. According to the recipe, the serving size is 4 ounces, or half a cup. The item has been correctly priced and properly marketed with table tents. All costs have been meticulously calculated. However, due to an oversight, the operation does not have the right size ice cream scoop. The waitstaff, therefore, use a #16 scoop for the ice cream. Since one scoop looks lost, the waitstaff piles the ice cream high to make it more appealing. In this scenario, the standard in recipe and cost are set. The equipment standard, however, is not. Because of a wrong scoop to help yield a 4 ounce portion, the cost of the item increases. Due to a bigger portion, the gross margin has decreased, and so do the profits. Therefore, proper equipment is essential. This issue is equally important in beverage operations. If the wrong type of glassware is used for serving a beverage, the taste of the drink can be diluted. The cost of the beverage also increases due to the amount of mixer used to fill up the glass. The recipe of the beverage has also changed.

A sound business plan should establish the specific type of equipment that is required for an operation to function effectively and efficiently. Standards in equipment include identifying the correct intended use of the equipment and utilizing the capacity of the equipment; therefore, when building a restaurant, it is always recommended that a menu be established before equipment is purchased. An operation cannot afford to purchase equipment only to find that the equipment is not right for the menu or that the equipment cannot handle the capacity of menu items. If buying an existing restaurant, remember that menu items must conform to the equipment in the existing kitchen; otherwise, the menu may have to be rewritten. However, when the menu changes, so does the mission and concept of the business. Also, it may not be easy to return equipment if it is not the correct item for the task. Therefore, it must be established beforehand that a specific piece of equipment is capable of providing the service in which it is intended.

Once the correct equipment has been selected for the facility, standards for usage must be put into place in order to maximize the capacity of the equipment. This is an area that is often neglected by owners and managers. A standard may be established that a particular piece of equipment may not need to be turned on if a smaller piece of equipment can perform the same task. Equipment should not be purchased if a cost-value analysis demonstrates that a product or service can be obtained more effectively through some other source. For example, management should not purchase a machine to shampoo carpets if cost analysis demonstrates that it is more cost effective to use a janitorial service. This is true with equipment and all types of convenient foods. There may not be a need for a meat slicer if a prefabricated quality product is less expensive than the cost of preparing the product yourself.

A standard may be set for controlling the time in which different pieces of equipment should be turned on. Plate warmers and food warmers need to be turned on by a hotel banquet breakfast crew when they arrive at work. This ensures that breakfast items that will be served on a hot plate and that will be stored and transported in a heated container will be served hot. On the other hand, a kitchen's breakfast crew may not need to turn on the deep-fat fryer for the French fries for the lunch menu until late morning. If all of the equipment is turned on at one time, it may cause a power surge. Some utility companies charge an additional fee for this surge. Some kitchen personnel are used to coming in and turning on all the grills, ovens, deep-fat fryers, and the like, so that they will be hot when needed. Not only does this create a possible danger of accidents, it is also a waste of energy and may reduce the life of the equipment. Besides waste, if a piece of equipment is turned on and not used, or if it is left on by the previous shift, dangerous situations could arise. Energy and replacement costs may be reduced if standards are established for equipment usage. Therefore, standards for the utilization and maintenance of equipment are extremely important in preventing accidents and for maximizing equipment use.

Equipment and supplies must be conveniently located to maximize the efforts of time and motion. Labor is a major cost factor for the hospitality industry. In a casino, management would want to position a piece of equipment, such as a change machine, to maximize the utilization of that piece of equipment.

Standards should be set to maximize a return on investment from each piece of equipment. In a hotel, management would want to position equipment in a guest room for easy access and aesthetic value. In food and beverage operations, management is not only interested in the accessibility of the equipment but also in the ease of cleaning the equipment. If an employee has to walk from one end of the kitchen to another to get two products to complete a certain task, the possibility of moving one of the products should be evaluated. For example, one of the most obvious scenarios is when the cashier or a person in the front of the establishment has to go to the back to get a takeout container because a guest may want takeout or wish to take home some leftovers. Many restaurants do not position these containers near the area where they are most requested. Guest service is lost during the process of going to the back and having guests wait.

Standards should also be established for the utilization of supplies. The misuse of supplies can be a hidden cost in a hospitality establishment. Specific supplies should be delegated for specific tasks, and employees need to be aware of these procedures. If employees are allowed to wipe up spills with tablecloths or cloth napkins, they may incur stains that cannot be washed out and these items will have to be replaced. Utensils can be thrown into the trash along with cups and saucers if employees are not instructed to be careful when removing dirty dishes and flatware from tables. These products can be extremely expensive to replace in some fine dining facilities. There should be standard procedures established as to how these products are to be handled.

Figure 3–4   *Publications for Industry Standards*

Industry Segment	Publication	Publisher
Hotel	*Hostitality Directions*	PricewaterhouseCoopers L.L.P.
Hotel	*Trends in the Hotel Industry* and *Lodging Industry Wrap-up and Forecast*	PKF Consulting
Hotel	*U.S. Lodging Almanac*	Bear, Stearns & Co. Inc.
Restaurant	*Restaurant Industry Operations Report*	Deloitte & Touche and the National Restaurant Association
Club	*Club in Town and Country*	PKF Worldwide

Industry Standards

As discussed, standards for each operation will differ depending upon a number of factors. One can always compare one's operation to another to see if one is operating well. However, management needs to compare "apples to apples" and "oranges to oranges." There are a number of hospitality industry publications that management can obtain to assess the business (see Figure 3–4). These standards are often subcategorized by sales volume, asset value, or geographical location so that comparisons become meaningful.

Action Plan

After standards have been established, they must be implemented and routinely measured and compared. Corrective action must be taken and these processes must be evaluated. Without following through with these accountability procedures, standards may be established but never fully implemented. Therefore, five major steps guide the action plan:

1. Implementing standards
2. Measurement of standards: the audit
3. Feedback
4. Corrective action
5. Improvement

Implementing Standards

Numerous facilities have outstanding policy and procedure manuals, but they are not being used. As an owner/operator, one must ensure that standards are being implemented. This means actually becoming involved with day-to-day operations. Most importantly, to implement standards is to ensure that owners/operators and management lead by example. Whenever one becomes involved in day-to-day operations, one must always follow correct procedures and standards. Do not cut corners in front of employees as you will compromise the standards. Once a manager compromises a standard, or allows a standard to be ignored because of short-staffing or any other reason, the standard will become unimportant. Standards must be implemented and constantly reinforced.

Measurement of Standards: The Audit

Once management has implemented standards, it must measure performance to see whether standards are being met. It is important to constantly and routinely measure standards. In the hospitality field, as in any other business, if management waits until the situation is totally out of hand, it will be not be able to make an adjustment without affecting quality and service. If management allows labor costs to exceed the average during a slow period, such as in the early part of the week, the operation may suffer with having to run a high labor cost percentage during the weekend when the volume of business may be heavier. Therefore, management must constantly evaluate daily operations to avoid surprises and situations that it may be unable to correct.

Two qualifications must be met to measure standards. First, the individuals who measure the standard must fully understand what the standard is and how it is to be measured. For example, when performing an inventory count are products such as condiments on a guest table, crackers in a salad bar, or opened containers counted as part of the ending inventory, or should this consist only of the items in the storage areas? If these products are counted by an individual one week and another individual the next, food costs may be incorrect. Different people follow different procedures: one may count and weigh everything and another may only count and weigh items that are in the storeroom. Therefore, the person measuring the standards must fully understand what the standards are and how the standards are to be measured. Second, standards should be easy to measure or they may not be measured frequently enough. Utensils, equipment, and accounting documents must be made available to follow correct procedures and they must also be available for quick and easy measurement. Employees and even management often complain about the time involved in measurement. It is far more important for a business to spend the time to check standards frequently to ensure that they are being met rather than to deal with an irate guest who may complain about a portion size or a product that has not been prepared according to set standards.

The best way to measure is to perform an audit. An audit is simply a set of standards for the various areas of a business. Part of a rooms audit may contain standards of how a room should be cleaned and arranged; a part of a food and beverage audit may consist of the proper receiving and storing of food items. Standards for receiving food items may include questions such as:

- Are separate receiving records maintained?
- Are all deliveries checked against the written purchase order/price/brand/size?
- Are bottles checked for leakage or breakage—verify bottles count?
- Who is the receiving agent?
- Have all invoices been entered—items, price, units?

If all standards are arranged as items of an audit, then measuring standards will simply be completing a checklist with some simple analyses. As mentioned, the easier management makes the procedures for others to use and follow, the more these procedures will be used and followed.

When measuring and comparing standards, management must bear in mind that they are to compare activities that represent the same attributes. When comparing accounting figures, management has to ensure that they are comparing accounting periods against accounting periods of identical lengths. For example, if management compares one month's sales with another month's, they would have made a mistake if the first month had four weekends and the second month had five. Since the bulk of hospitality sales are generated on the weekend, one month can look outstanding when compared to another. If management uses accounting periods that begin on the same day of the week and extend for four weeks, all expenses and sales are more apt to be accurately compared. Otherwise, make sure that the analysis does not simply compare dollar value but also common size percentages.

Feedback

Once standards have been measured, management should then compare the results to see if standards have been met and communicate the results back to the performers—the employees and managers. This must be done routinely and frequently to promote good work habits and reinforce the importance of standards and feedback. It also allows for timely correction.

Corrective Action

After comparing performance to set standards management must take corrective action. A small variance may not require any action or may only require monitoring. On the other hand, a major deviation requires immediate attention and correction. In most hospitality organizations, fluctuation in standards will occur in areas of prime cost—food, beverage, and labor. In casinos, it may also be a result of equipment misuse.

If the problem is in the food or beverage area, it may be the result of faulty inventory, overportioning, or even theft. Employee theft or guest theft can increase food cost. Or, it may be the result of a price increase that management did not account for or was unaware of. Whatever the cause, it must be corrected or adjusted.

If an inconsistency develops in a labor standard, then records, schedules, and sales must be reviewed. A labor problem could be the result of improper scheduling or could be the result of an intentional ploy by employees to generate more hours. For example, management cannot afford to allow employees to clock in 10 to 15 minutes early or stand around the time clock talking before clocking out, thereby adding time to their schedules. Some hospitality facilities have several hundred employees and even small quick service operations may have 20 employees or more. Adding this amount of time to a time sheet can cause labor cost to increase immensely.

In casinos a malfunctioning piece of equipment may not generate the profit it is supposed to generate. Because management anticipates a certain amount of income per machine or floor space income will be lost if a machine is not functioning properly. For example, a guest may walk away from a slot machine if he or she keeps dropping a coin in and it falls right through without crediting for a play. This problem can be as simple as a dirty coin mechanism. However, if not corrected, the operation will continue to lose money on your investment of floor space.

Once management establishes that a standard is not being met, the problem must be corrected. A change in operational procedure has to be made to ensure that standards can be met. Changing the standard must always be viewed as an action of last resort. If the survival of the business is based upon a certain set of cost percentages, standards may not be changed easily. One of the purposes for establishing standards is to anticipate the financial production of the business. If the margin of profit is not sufficient for survival, a change in standard is not an option. Therefore, it is best to reevaluate the process rather than to try to adjust the required outcome.

Improvement

If standards are met, management should see if it is possible to improve the standards to operate at maximum efficiency. Complacency will not challenge employees and may prevent an operation from being as competitive as it should. In the hospitality industry standards often provide an organization with a competitive advantage.

Once a standard has been altered or upgraded it must be evaluated to determine if the change was feasible. This is a systems approach, as changing standards in one area can cause problems in another. Implementing activities to reduce theft may slow down the operating efficiency of guest service. For example, it takes additional time for an employee to obtain permission to cash a personal check or to obtain a key to get a particular bottle of wine, and an operation can end up with an unhappy guest, which may result in a reduction in sales.

Because a change in one area can affect the outcome of another area, it is essential to require employees to provide feedback and to stay attuned to guest comments. Standards can provide direction for an organization, and their implementation must be pursued if an operation is to be successful.

Summary _____

Standards must be established in order to provide direction for employees and to establish a basis for control. The purpose for setting standards is to be able to control and measure the efficiency of production and the overall effectiveness of an organization. Setting standards in the hospitality industry involves determining the expected amount of income that can be derived from the utilization of a prescribed amount of resources. Establishing standards provides an operation with the ability to determine the amount of resources that will be utilized and the results that can be anticipated.

Standards must be established for all areas of an operation, including revenue centers and support centers. To be effective, standards must be measurable and attainable. Feedback must be provided to ensure that standards are working effectively, and it is pertinent to constantly determine if standards can be improved.

When setting standards, an organization must take into consideration the operating expenses and required profit for that particular facility. Standards must aid an organization to cover all costs, both prime and hidden. It is essential to establish standards for all resources—food, beverage, labor, equipment, and supplies.

If food, beverage, and labor standards are to be met, equipment and supplies must be located to maximize the efforts of time and motion. Additionally, proper equipment can enhance the products offered and help maintain the prime cost. For food and beverage areas, equipment can maintain portion sizes, taste, and aesthetic appeal; for other areas of the operation, proper equipment is essential in reducing repairs, maintenance, and replacement costs.

After standards have been established they must be implemented and routinely measured and compared so that necessary corrective action can be taken. An operation cannot function effectively without proper standards.

Review Exercises

1. All of the following are major components in developing standards except:
   a. standards must be measurable
   b. standards should be established by the employees
   c. if standards cannot be attained, they should be reevaluated
   d. if standards are attained, the organization must determine if they can be improved

2. The purpose of establishing standards is to:
   a. allow customers to know what is on the menu
   b. inform employees what is on the menu
   c. inform employees how to prepare menu items
   d. give variety to the menu

3. Standardized recipes:
   a. establish quality and consistency
   b. reduce the cost of menu items
   c. permit the use of unskilled workers
   d. allow items to be prepared from scratch

4. Determining servable portions cost:
   a. allows a manager to know the exact cost of items
   b. helps in determining the selling cost of items
   c. informs management exactly how much to order
   d. all of the above

5. Why is it important to convert standardized recipes correctly?
   a. to save trip to the storage room
   b. to reduce the cost of a product
   c. to prevent overpreparation
   d. c and d

6. If standards are not attainable owner/operators have a choice of trying to:
   a. raise prices
   b. reduce portion size
   c. purchase lower quality
   d. all of the above

7. Once standards are being met, management should:
   a. give employees a raise for maintaining and meeting standards
   b. try to improve cost by raising the standards
   c. try to provide better service by lowering the standards
   d. ensure that each standard is cost effective

8. Why can costs differ in two franchised facilities that are identical in size and menu?
   a. one facility may have to implement additional security
   b. because of location and the job market, the cost of labor can be significantly different
   c. because of the demographics of the area, the popularity of menu items can be completely different
   d. all of the above

9. Standards must be established for the sole purpose of:
   a. generating a profit
   b. providing quality products and service
   c. trying to stay in business
   d. b and c

10. Standards must be established for the utilization of equipment because:
    a. management must know the capacity of their equipment
    b. management can determine when to turn on equipment
    c. equipment can be purchased before writing the menu
    d. a and b

11. What is the purpose of establishing standards?

12. Describe the importance of standardized recipes.

13. Explain how as purchased (AP) and usable portion (UP) relate to standardized recipes and costs.

14. Describe the four major components in the overall process of developing standards.

Examination Type Problems

1. List the eight major areas to consider when setting standards for food and beverage operations.

2. List categories that a typical standardized recipe includes.

3. Describe the significance of labor and equipment standards to the overall cost control process.

4. What are the five steps in the action plan of cost control?

Case Study _____

After setting a control cycle for Model and helping your friend by giving him advice on his new restaurant, you are ready to set some standard measurements for Model. You fully understand that standards will help you assess the efficiency of your restaurant.

As mentioned in previous chapters in this text, standards for the receiving function can include questions such as:

- Are separate receiving records maintained?
- Are all deliveries checked against the written purchase order/price/brand/size?
- Are bottles checked for leakage or breakage—verify bottles count?
- Who is the receiving agent?
- Have all invoices been entered—items, price, units?

Given the situation of your restaurant within the Case Study Hotel, various areas warrant a separate section of an audit. For a start, your general manager would like to concentrate on these six areas:

1. Food production
2. Food purchasing
3. Labor–waitstaff
4. Labor–kitchen
5. Labor–utility
6. Customer comment cards

Prepare three audit questions for each of the above areas.

4

The Menu as a Cost Control Tool

Key Terms

a la carte	limited menu	site selection
cyclical	magic number	table d'hôte
demographics	major events	truth in advertising
labor skills	off-hour menu	variety and appeal

Learning Objectives

After completing this chapter, you should be able to:

- discuss the importance of the menu in site selection and demographics.
- discuss the importance of the relationship between menu and equipment requirement.
- discuss how the labor market, weather, and major events can affect the determination of menu items.

- describe the importance of variety and appeal when developing menus.
- discuss factors involved in truth in advertising when establishing menus.

Outline

Factors to Consider When Designing
  Menus
    Site Selection
    Demographics
    Equipment
    Prices
    Food Products Availability
    Labor Market
    Major Events
    Competitors
    Number of Menu Items

Structure of the Menu
    Menu Item Placement
    Appetizers and Soups
    Salads
    Entrees
    Starches and Vegetables
    Desserts and Breads
    Beverages
Types of Menus
    A la Carte
    Table d'hôte

Once a mission statement has been developed and a decision has been made as to what type of business will be established, the menu can then be written. The menu of available products and services is the driving force behind all types of businesses. The foodservice industry uses menus to list products and services available to the public; other types of businesses may use brochures or other methods of presenting products and services. It is essential that menus be developed with care. Managers have to be aware of the control factors that must be considered when designing menus; therefore, this chapter deals with the considerations and constraints in menu planning and the control process.

Factors to Consider When Designing Menus

Designing a menu is the first activity to be considered in the control process. Because the menu is essential to the foodservice industry, it acts as a blueprint and selling tool for the entire operation. The menu must be thought of as the primary control document for the business. Decisions made when constructing the menu will determine the financial success or failure of the business. Since the menu is the instrument that acts as a standard for the entire operation, menu activities must be controlled in order to maintain that standard. When controlling cost, it is best to understand that any money saved in purchasing goes directly to the bottom line; therefore, a great deal of thought must be given to the selection of menu items. The menu must be developed so that money is not wasted in the purchasing of menu items and in the initial development of an establishment. Because the menu is the primary document for controlling an operation, the following factors must be taken into consideration when writing the menu:

- Site selection
- Demographics
- Equipment
- Prices
- Food products availability

- Labor market
- Major events
- Competitors
- Number of menu items

These factors are essential since the majority of them are part of the external environment in which an establishment will have to operate its business.

Site Selection

Site selection alone can often determine the success of a business operation. Whether products can be legally sold or prepared at a particular site or whether the customer base would accept the product or services offered must be considered. License requirements to open an establishment or whether the operation will be able to sell alcoholic beverages should be researched. Numerous operations have invested money and then discovered that they would not be able to open a business as originally planned because a license could not be obtained. Since a return on investment in a business venture is usually based on an operation succeeding in the long run, it is important to discover whether there are plans for rezoning or reconstructing the area in which the facility will be constructed. Accessibility, safety, and security of employees and guests are of the utmost importance to the long-range success of an operation. With ample planning these and other types of costly mistakes can be avoided.

Demographics

The demographics of the area must be compatible with the type of menu that is planned. A pizza parlor with an arcade may be an ideal project for an area where there are several schools and a lot of children and young adults. However, to open this type of establishment in a retirement community could be a major mistake. If planning to open a facility in a business district with the expectation of a large volume of lunch business, first make every attempt to research the soundness of the corporations and businesses within that area. If a major corporation plans to close a facility, slow down development, or phase out a product, a major change in demographics could occur. Not only should the most cost-effective menu for the demographics be established, but research must also ascertain whether an anticipated change in the demographics already exists. Downsizing has become a common occurrence in today's business environment; therefore, an organization must investigate the long range stability of the market.

Equipment

Equipment should not be chosen based on what is normally found in a typical foodservice operation. Just because the restaurant down the road has a rotary oven does not dictate that your operation must also have one. The types of equipment used in different types of operations can vary greatly. There are a vast number of institutional operations of considerable size that do not have stoves or hot tops. Equipment selection should be based upon the type of food to be prepared, how much is to be prepared, and the quality that is expected. Purchasing equipment that is not required ties up capital that could be invested in other areas.

The amount of volume that is anticipated can determine the required capacity or durability of a piece of equipment. Numerous operations, especially the smaller ones, make a major mistake in trying to use noncommercial refrigerators and other types of household kitchen equipment in commercial facilities. Menu items and the anticipated volume of business are essential elements in planning for equipment. The type of equipment available will determine the type and amount of business you can accept. To plan for a certain number of baked items with an insufficient amount of oven space will cause a delay in service that can result in a possible profit reduction. The capacity of equipment must be known before accepting an order. Equipment has to be purchased to satisfy the quality, quantity, and consistency of the menu.

Prices

Prices must be established to cover cost and generate a profit. The type of establishment and the location of the establishment will play an important part in determining the level of prices. Prices must be thoroughly evaluated before they are applied to a menu, because prices cannot be raised easily without incurring guest dissatisfaction. Prices should also be established for sufficient profit to account for hidden cost. Regardless of how efficient a business plan may be, there are always unexpected repairs and other occurrences; therefore, an operation should be careful when establishing prices to account for unexpected expenses. Methods for establishing prices will be discussed in more detail in Chapter 5.

Food Products Availability

In developing a menu, it is important to ensure that the food products for that menu are going to be consistently available and affordable. Some products may be more expensive during certain seasons. The increase in prices when products are out of season could significantly increase food cost during those periods. If seasonal price increases are not accounted for, an operation may not be able to cover expenses. If possible, try to include seasonal and local products in the menu as they can be inexpensive at certain times of the year.

The weather can affect the availability and sale of certain products. Guests may seek some products come rain or shine; however, certain products may take a downturn when it rains. Other products may sell better in cold weather than in hot weather and vice versa. Therefore, menu items and prices must account for the fluctuation in sales during these periods. An operation could fail if it does not have a menu with a sales mix that accounts for certain changes in sales. Possible changes in sales volume must be accounted for when establishing the operational budget and when setting prices. A long stretch of bad weather can have a negative effect but can be predicted for certain times of the year if an operation plans accordingly. Businesses have failed because they did not plan for fluctuations in sales due to changes in the weather.

Labor Market

When constructing a menu, it is essential to be aware of the levels of skill required to prepare menu items. An operation also needs to account for wage rates within the labor market. Do not develop a menu that requires skilled labor if it is not available or if the price of labor is too expensive. The cost of labor in certain geographical areas can be much higher than in others. An operation may have to pay higher wage rates if it wishes to retain employees and prevent excessive turnover. Unionism can also add a new dimension. Because labor cost is one of the prime costs of running an operation, evaluation of the job market and the cost of labor must be completed before opening a facility.

Major Events

The number of major events in an area can affect the financial success of a business. If sales increase substantially during such events, an operation initially may want to set lower menu prices to provide a possible competitive advantage during other times of the year. If sales decrease during these events then the difference in sales must be accounted for when establishing prices. Major events can have a negative or positive effect on a hospitality operation. Event planners often fail to include local businesses in the planning process and because of this businesses may have a decline in sales. Contingency plans, therefore, must be developed and the staff must be informed as to how to deal with these fluctuations.

Competitors

The number and type of competitors are additional factors that affect the development of a menu. When developing a menu, an operation must consider its own costs and still be competitive. Move with caution when establishing menus and evaluating competitors. Every operation is unique and a menu should have some level of differentiation that will generate a profit. Competitors must be considered and evaluated but they should not be the sole factor in the construction; the menu must fit the demographics and generate a profit.

Number of Menu Items

For the most part, it is advisable best to keep menu items to a minimum. Problems lie in trying to prepare too many products in an effort to generate profit. The "magic number" of menu items is the number that can be safely controlled and will still maximize guest satisfaction and profit. Too many menu items will often lead to waste, theft, and decreased quality. A manager has to balance guest satisfaction, sanitation, labor skills, service required, and profit to determine the magic number. An operation may have to carry certain items that may not be as profitable as others, but items should not be carried on the menu if they cannot be safely prepared, safely held, and safely served. Employees must be able to prepare all items without losing quality. The menu should establish the nature of the business, and if the operation is relying on a particular form of differentiation, too many menu items can detract from that competitive advantage. Once a menu has been implemented, management should periodically perform a menu analysis to determine if the menu allows control procedures to be met.

Structure of the Menu

In discussing the structure of a menu, the emphasis is on control and not so much the production, nutritional, or aesthetic value. A menu must be designed to enhance profit while allowing for effective sanitary and monetary controls. Some of the most successful facilities are those with limited menus; other facilities have been successful with menus consisting of a large number of items; and still other facilities have been successful through serving large portions. In most cases, the structure of the menu depends on the preferences of the guests in the area. As more and more guests face time limitations in their daily lives and are more aware of nutrition, it is becoming increasingly difficult for new operations to succeed by using large portions as a means of competition. The possibility of changing menu prices may also have to be a concern in the physical structure of the menu. Since the menu will act as the selling tool of the operation, it will have to be structured with prices and eye appeal to attract guests.

Menu Item Placement

The manner in which items are placed on a menu is critical. A guest scans the menu for a minute or two and places an order. Because guests have only a short period of time to make a decision, restaurateurs place items that make the most dollars for the operation in conspicuous spots on the menu. Figure 4–1 shows three menu–eye motion diagrams for a single-page menu, a two-page menu, and a tri-fold menu.

As the diagrams demonstrate, the eye normally travels from the middle section of a menu, then moves right, and then left. In addition to eye movement, boxing menu items, printing them in a different font or size, putting icons next to them will all draw a guest's attention to those items. A sports bar may put football icons next to its most profitable items during the football season and may change those icons to basketballs during the basketball season to attract more attention. A restaurant that serves barbecued items may thematically box its most profitable items with ropes and fences rather than with plain lines. These are just a few ways to make a menu more appealing and catch the attention of the guests. It has also been found that if a menu lists a group of items under one category, say, entrees, guests tend to order the first or last item on the list. Thus, items that have the highest selection rate benefit the operation if they also earn the most profit. Therefore, to maximize this natural eye movement, operations should list items that have the highest profit first or last rather than in the middle of the list.

Figure 4–1 *Menu–Eye Motion Diagrams*

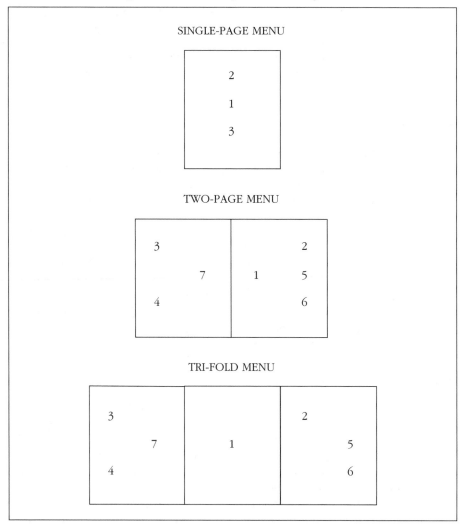

Appetizers and Soups

When selecting appetizers and soups, for a menu, managers should remember that it is more profitable if patrons consume an entire meal. Just as hunger can cause a state of dissatisfaction, overindulgence can do the same. It is a good idea to offer slightly smaller portions of appetizers and soups, so that guests can fully enjoy the rest of their meal. Many facilities make the portion sizes of appetizers and soups so large that they become a meal in themselves. Returning guests may not order these products because they do not want to be full and not be able to enjoy the entrees or because they do not want to waste food. Worse still, returning guests may simply order an appetizer, which is normally priced less than an entree. Either way, sales are lost.

On the average, soup served as an appetizer should not be more than six to eight ounces. An appetizer should live up to its name to tease the appetite of guests. If soup is served as an entree, then perhaps a twelve to sixteen ounce portion would be good. If shrimp scampi is served as an appetizer, two to three jumbo shrimps or five to six mid-size shrimps are plenty; five to six jumbo shrimps with some vegetables and starch would make a great entree. An operation would benefit from reducing the size and price of appetizers and soups in order to sell more of them rather than have patrons reluctant to purchase these products.

Salads

After meats, salad items can be the most costly to produce. Because of the perishability of produce, these items cannot be stored and re-served as easily as other products without losing their freshness. The ordering and inventory of salad products must be controlled. In numerous cases employees waste salad dressing by placing too much dressing on salads. Now that guests are becoming more health conscious, this presents even more of a problem as guests send back overdressed salads, which then have to be discarded. Not only does too much dressing cause a waste but it can also turn off the guests. The temperature of salads is also important. If cold salads are not served chilled, they lose their crispness and appeal, and this could lead to dissatisfied guests. Lettuce that has turned brown on the edges should not be served. This may seem like a small detail to some, but it serves as a huge turn off to guests, who will also begin to wonder about the freshness of the other products that you are serving. Waste leads to lost revenue, and unhappy guests lead to lost sales. These seemingly small details are what cause costs to get out of line. No matter how well a manager balances the numbers, if he or she cannot maintain control over these minor details, money will be lost.

Entrees

The delivery, production, and portioning of entrees must be designed not only to please guests but also to maintain control. Always pre-portion food products for easy control and maintenance of consistency. Counting and comparing sales to inventory may provide sufficient control over pre-portioned items; items that are not pre-portioned need to be monitored to ensure that guests are receiving the correct amount or designated weight. Entrees account for a large percentage of food costs; thus, portion sizes must be monitored. Managers must consistently observe and monitor products as they leave the kitchen and as they are served to the guests to see if portions are correct.

Starches and Vegetables

Because of the short cooking time that is usually required for starches and vegetables, they should be prepared in small batches to prevent leftovers. Leftover starches and vegetables can often be used in other products, and contingency plans should be developed for their possible utilization, otherwise an inexperienced individual may discard the products. If leftover products have been maintained at the proper temperature and can be utilized during the next meal period, a manager saves the operation a few pennies. A manager always leads by example; if employees see management waste products, they will waste even more. Managers are usually most concerned about throwing away leftover meat products but the same concern must be given to all food items. In saving leftover items, the first concern must be for the safety of the guests. If the products are safe, they can be used.

Desserts and Breads

Temperature and eye appeal can have a lot to do with the acceptability and sales of salads and this is more so for desserts and breads. If bread is served hot or warm, the freshness of the product is accentuated and the product becomes far more acceptable to guests. Because bread is often the first product that guests consume, if it is hot or warm and pleasing, it can set the tone for the acceptability of the rest of the meal. Many operations do not realize the importance of this small detail. Managers should prevent the sale of bread that is cold to the touch. However, this may not apply to the temperature of sandwich bread. Bread for a cold sandwich should be cool to the touch. As for desserts, items such as brownies and apple pie are preferable served warm. Remember that the two most important scenes in any performance are the opening and the closing. Warm bread or a chilled shrimp cocktail provides a great beginning; warm pie or firm ice cream provides a satisfactory closing. The psychology of a meal is extremely important as you are fulfilling a need. Strive to satisfy guests, as this may lead to return visits.

Beverages

When trying to control cost and generate profit from beverages, the question becomes how much is too much. The public has become more aware of the importance of consuming fluids and of the effects of alcoholic beverage consumption. Most beverages are served in much larger containers than in the past. While an operation wants guests to purchase these products and perceive a good value, one should not let guests overindulge. This is true for nonalcoholic beverages as well as for alcoholic beverages. Waitstaff should always ask guests if they want more iced tea rather than fill glasses without asking. Not only does this increase waste, but it may cause guests to become full and not purchase desserts or other products. Also, most coffee drinkers can tell when coffee is not fresh. Since this is part of the closing act of a meal, always ensure that the coffee is hot and fresh. Never serve coffee in a chipped or stained cup and saucer. This type of presentation generates a negative memory of what may have been an otherwise great experience. If coffee is overfilled or spilled into the saucer, make it a policy to replace the cup and saucer. Guests should not have to worry about dripping coffee on their clothing because of poor service. A great finish is important to any meal.

Enough cannot be said concerning the service of alcoholic beverages. While the contribution margin is great, operations should concentrate on market selection rather than quantity. It is far better to develop one or two unique drinks that may yield an outstanding contribution margin than to try to sell additional drinks. The key is to inform the waitstaff of the types of drinks that you would like to sell.

Types of Menus

A la Carte

Types of menus are discussed here from the perspective of the control problems that can be associated with each. An a la carte menu separates side items from entrees. For example, chicken fried steak is listed in the entree section and the starches and vegetables are listed separately (see Figure 4–2). An a la carte menu can create a control problem if certain side items are prepared and not

Figure 4–2 *A la Carte Menu*

ENTREES

Grilled Chicken Breast Beurre
Stir Fried Beef
Blackened Catfish
Osso Bucco Milanaise
Chicken Fried Steak

STARCHES

Rice Pilaf
Wild Rice
Mashed Potatoes
Fried Sweet Potatoes
Baked Potato
Twice Baked Potato

VEGETABLES

Seasoned Mixed Vegetables
Sweet Peas
Broccoli Florets
Cut Corn
Corn on the Cob
Glazed Carrots
Zucchini
Yellow Squash

---

ordered; therefore, it is a plus if guests do not mind waiting for the preparation of items. Moreover, providing several choices of side dishes can be time consuming and labor intensive. Each operation must be aware of the amount of space on the steam table when planning to provide guests with a large selection. Some restaurants create unsanitary conditions by trying to prepare and hold too many food products.

Table d'hôte

A table d'hôte menu, often known as a set menu, offers an appetizer and soup and/or salad with the entree (see Figure 4–3). The price of the meal also usually includes dessert and either tea, coffee, or a nonalcoholic beverage. While this sometimes presents a greater value to guests, the table d'hôte menu generates control problems because it increases the size of the window for theft. When an operation continuously serves a large number of the same products, some kitchen personnel may be begin to skim portion sizes and take products home since they have already been accounted for during the serving period. Managers must monitor portion sizes at all times. It is important to trust employees, but it is also important not to create a situation that makes theft easy. Management must demonstrate to employees that items will be monitored by spot-checking against standards.

Limited Menu

The concern with cost control in limited menus is that of maintaining cost standards and quality. Three guest expectations of a limited menu are speed, consistency, and quality. When an operation chooses a limited menu, guests expect good and consistent products to be served quickly. The ability to accomplish this is critical to the survival of quick-serve restaurants. Managers must meet these three expectations while staying within the cost standards established by the operating budget. On the positive side, limited menus lend themselves to the ease of accountability of products.

Cyclical Menu

Cyclical menus, if written correctly, can aid in planning the control of leftovers. This type of menu makes the planning for the utilization of leftovers, which should be a part of all meal systems, much easier. A small portion of items can be prepared for the next meal to roll over certain unused products. For example, if roast beef is served at one meal, hot roast beef sandwiches can be served the next meal as a supplement. Leftover spaghetti sauce can be revived as chili the next meal and leftover pasta can be used in soups. These items should be prepared in small amounts, as unused leftovers should be discarded after the second meal usage. A cyclical menu allows management to control the flow of products in this manner. It is always best to change the makeup of leftover products. Leftover pork may be best cut up and served in pork fried rice. If cyclical menus are written with this process in mind, it will reduce the amount

Figure 4–3   *Table d'hôte Menu*

Appetizer

Quiche Legume
A light vegetable quiche topped with pesto

Soup

Mushroom Fantasia
A creamy concoction of wild
mushrooms with a touch of sherry

Salad

Insalata del Oro
Mixed greens with carrots, pine nuts,
olives, and prosciutto. Served with a
honey mustard vinaigrette dressing.

Entrees

Linguine del Mar
Linguine served in a spicy marinara sauce, topped with
shrimp, mussel, scallops, and crab meat
$20.95

Pollo Parmigiano
Tender chicken breast filet lightly sautéed in a Parmesan crust.
Served with fettuccini Alfredo and grilled vegetables.
$18.95

Veal Nocturne
Roast loin of veal served with cream peppercorn sauce.
Accompanied by linguine and mixed squash.
$24.95

Dessert

Italian Ices
Raspberry, mango, or lemon-lime

Dinner prices include appetizer, choice of soup or salad, entree, and dessert.

---

of waste that is often difficult to account for with regular menus. Utilize leftovers as specials with a regular menu. While a manager should always try to forecast properly and control production so there will not be any leftovers, it is inevitable that, from time to time, business will have less than projected sales and leftovers will result. Thus, cyclical menus can allow for the planning and utilization of leftovers in advance. Figure 4–4 shows a sample cyclical menu.

Figure 4–4   *Cyclical Menu*

Monday	Tuesday	Wednesday	Thursday	Friday
Chef Salad Tray or Salisbury Steak or Steak Fingers w/ Gravy Mashed Potatoes Carrot Sticks-n-Dip Chilled Fruit Fruit Juice Multigrain Roll Milk	Super Sack or Breakfast for Lunch: Pancakes Scrambled Eggs Sausage Pattie Hash Browns w/ Catsup Assorted Fruits Fruit Juice Homemade Biscuit Milk	Chef Salad Tray or Footlong on Bun w/ Chili or Hamburger on Bun w/ Trimmings Chuckwagon Fries w/ Catsup Chilled Fruit Fruit Juice Milk	Super Sack or Taco Salad w/ Trimmings or Taco Roll w/ Sauce Spanish Rice Beans a la Charra Chilled Fruit Fruit Juice Milk	Chef Salad Tray or Cheese Pizza or Sausage Pizza Italian Corn Salad Pizzazz Chilled Fruit Fruit Juice Milk

Off-Hour Menu

Off-hour menus are an excellent tool for increasing sales and for assisting managers in controlling the utilization of labor. Off hours, such as between 2 and 5 p.m., can be an excellent time to cater to senior citizens. Most senior citizens do not like to eat late or to be out after dark. Special menus and special prices during slow periods can be an excellent time to market to these valuable guests. Many of these individuals belong to clubs and organizations, which could lead to additional business. Off-hour menus can also provide managers with a means of utilizing lunch leftovers and employees that must remain on duty during usual slow periods. Off hours are excellent times to feature specials or signature products. An off-hour menu should consist of products that are quick and easy to prepare. Most guests that order from these menus do not want to spend a lot of time or money; therefore, controlling time and labor becomes a major concern when using these menus.

Other Considerations

Menu Index

Menu indexing can be used to evaluate and establish which items are most appealing to guests. Also known as a sales mix or menu engineering, a menu index tracks the sales of each menu item. This process aids in future planning and can assist management in determining which items should be removed from the menu or should only be placed on the menu at certain times. This can be effective in controlling leftovers. Even though a facility may be successful and may have been in operation for a long time, it is still a good business practice to index the menu from time to time because the demographics of the area may have changed over time. With a change in demographics, demand can diminish for even the most popular items.

Nutrition and Health

As guests become more aware of eating healthfully, managers need to develop menus that provide guests with a selection of healthful items. The control process is to ensure that kitchen personnel are aware that these food items are prepared in such a manner as not to change the advertised sodium, calorie, and fat contents. These production processes only used to be a concern in health care facilities and nursing homes, however, this is no longer true. Low-sodium and low-fat menus can be developed for most foodservice operations.

Even some airlines have developed healthful menu alternatives. Instead of a ham and cheese sandwich with potato chips, Continental Airlines serves a 99% fat free sandwich with carrot sticks. As of July 1, 1998, Continental offers 26 special meals, including 10 that meet special dietary needs such as lactose free, gluten free, and high fiber.

Managers have to ensure that recipes are adhered to during preparation. Kitchen personnel should follow standardized recipes so that the waitstaff can inform guests what ingredients are included in products, as some guests are lactose intolerant, some cannot eat shellfish, and others need to reduce their sodium intake or are allergic to monosodium glutamate (MSG). If a guest asks whether one of these products is in a particular food item, it is essential that the waitstaff respond correctly. Managers must stress this area of control to kitchen personnel and waitstaff. Waitstaff must be informed of any substitutions of ingredients as well. A manager does not want someone to become ill from eating at his or her facility.

Meal Periods

Meal periods and hours of operation must be established to maximize sales and to maintain a competitive position. Products must be prepared in such a manner that they can retain their freshness throughout the meal period. Particular attention must be given to operations with cafeteria service to ensure that products are safe and retain their fresh appearance. Certain sauces and gravies must be stirred constantly, and special attention must be given to meat products, as they will dry out or lose appeal if they are allowed to sit too long on the service line. Managers must control personnel toward the end of meal periods to ensure that they do not break down the serving lines and start cleaning up too soon. Cleaning up and breaking down too soon is a disservice to guests and acts as a turn off to last-minute guests. While managers want to maximize the utilization of labor, they do not want to lose guest counts in the process. Managers must be even more alert in controlling this process during the last serving period of the day. Employees should not be allowed to clean equipment, such as grills, early. If a last-minute guest comes, he or she should not be told that the grill has already been cleaned and thus certain items cannot be prepared. The established meal period must be followed. In many cases managers are guilty of instigating these activities.

Sanitation and Safety

Sanitation and safety must be viewed by management as an ongoing concern. Management may be able to put off repairing a particular piece of equipment that is not being used, but any flaw in sanitation and safety should be dealt with as soon as it is identified. A manager often has to be tactful in this area when dealing with employees. While no employee should be caused undue embarrassment, on-the-spot corrections must be made any time there is a breach of conduct or procedure in sanitation and safety. Managers lead by example, therefore managers must be alert that sanitation and safety are observed during extremely busy periods or during large special events. Employees will perceive that if certain procedures are acceptable during busy periods then they are acceptable any time. Many managers lose control of procedures by trying to reduce labor hours during busy times and are surprised to find that guests are willing to wait to have something done correctly.

Safety hazards should be dealt with immediately. Not only is there a possibility of someone being injured, but an injury can lead to additional problems. If a guest becomes ill or injured, it may lead to dissatisfaction and worse still, bad publicity or lawsuit. Employee injury can lead to absenteeism. In either circumstance, illnesses and injuries can cause the facility to suffer. Employees must be trained in the proper handling of food and equipment. Food must be kept safe for consumption. Proper procedures and supplies must be used when operating and cleaning equipment. Operating procedures, cleaning procedures, and the supplies for cleaning equipment and facilities must be made convenient for employees to use. All employees should receive training in sanitation and safety, and the procedures learned should be practiced and constantly reinforced.

Variety and Appeal

A manager must control complexity when creating a menu to incorporate variety and appeal. Foods must be paired and placed to provide good eye appeal and a perception of value. A manager should prevent the mistake of serving a meal that solely consists of white-colored food, as it has no eye appeal. If the starch is mashed potatoes with cream gravy, and cauliflower is the vegetable, while baked fish or skinless chicken breast is the entree, needless to say, the meal looks bland even if it tastes marvelous. This mistake occurs more than one may think. How often is a dark-colored frosting, such as purple or navy, used to trim a cake? This is fine if the colors are for a specific holiday, such as when green and red are used for Christmas, otherwise, guests are somewhat turned off by dark blue or purple frosting. Cake trim should always be pastels or bright primary colors whenever possible. Managers with inexperienced personnel will constantly have to be on the lookout for these mismatches and keep employees informed of acceptable procedures.

Truth in Advertising

It is management's responsibility to ensure that menu items are in fact what they are advertised to be. To avoid misspelling the names of products, an occurrence often associated with alcoholic beverages and imported products, names should be taken directly from product labels. Many food products originate in different countries and the spelling of some products may be totally different from the way they are pronounced.

Emphasis must also be given to correct specifications. If you have ice cream listed on the menu, then that product must contain sufficient fat to be considered ice cream. By weight, ice cream should have approximately 8 to 12% nonfat milk solids. Many soft-serve products do not have sufficient fat to be referred to as ice cream. Brandy can only be referred to as brandy if it is made from grapes. If any other fruits, such as peaches, are used, the name of the fruit must be listed. For example, a product made from peaches should be referred to as peach brandy. If an operation advertises a product as Maine lobster, then the lobster must come from Maine. This is another reason why a facility should purchase products only from reputable sources. Red fish is often substituted for red snapper; scallops are often made from the fins of stingray. Practices such as these are unethical and should be avoided. It is also wise to remember that in naming mixed products, the item that is the largest portion of the product should have its name placed first. A menu should list "beans and ham," not "ham and beans," on the menu if beans are the largest quantity of the mixture. While products, such as pork and beans, that have been around for a while can still be advertised in this manner, new products should not.

Labor Production Capabilities

Labor skills must also be taken into consideration in developing menus. Employee skills are essential if an operation is to control the consistency of products and service. In the majority of the hospitality industry, people are the business. Standard recipes, policies, and procedures must be placed in writing, as this will allow for the training and hiring of lesser skilled workers. Because there is a vast amount of turnover in the industry, labor skills can affect the construction of a menu. If consistency is to be maintained a manager should not develop a menu that is overly dependent on the skills of one or two employees. The labor market must be taken into consideration so that if an employee decides to terminate his or her employment, the function of the operation will not be affected.

Equipment Capacity

Just as labor skills must be considered in maintaining consistency, the capacity of equipment is also pertinent. If a banquet for a large number of people is booked, a manager must be aware of the capacity of the production equipment before committing to a particular menu. If several baked products, such as potatoes, chicken, and special desserts, are requested, the operation may not have the oven space to handle the demand. This applies to steam kettles and other equipment. One of the most difficult meals to prepare fresh for a large number of people is chicken in the basket. Because this meal tradition-ally consists of half a fried chicken and French fries, a facility may be unable to provide both of these items fresh, in the requested volume. It may appear to be a simple meal, but it requires a large fryer capacity that an ordinary kitchen may not have. An awareness of equipment capacity can prevent man-agers from overcommitting themselves. An operation can easily lose a great deal of future business by not being able to satisfactorily fulfill a commitment to a large group. Negative word of mouth from a large group can devastate fu-ture business.

Space Usage and Allocation

Space costs money and the utilization of space, therefore, must be maximized. One concern a manager should have is to allow guests to sit in their own com-fort zones. It is fine to section off part of a dining room if it is saving labor be-cause of the distance traveled by the waitstaff. At the same time it is also im-portant to try to allow guests the advantage of selecting their own seats. People have different comfort zones, and comfort can have a lot to do with how much a person is able to enjoy a dining experience. If a manager sections off a cer-tain area to speed up service or to save on utilities, it may be cost effective, but to do this just as a matter of convenience is not smart. If there is extra space in a facility, see if the space can be utilized more productively. It is not cost effective for an operation to pay rent and air conditioning on an area that is not being utilized. Also, try to prevent areas that are not being used from becoming "junk rooms," as these areas may harbor rodents and other unwel-come pests.

Kitchen Layout and Design

The layout of a facility must take into account time and motion of people and equipment. A facility should be evaluated for bottlenecks, potential accident areas, and time and motion. A bottleneck that is causing a delay in production may only require the relocating of a piece of equipment or a change in proce-dures. Most bottlenecks either waste labor or cause a potential hazardous situ-ation for food or employees. Evaluate the layout to try to retain a smooth flow of production and procedures. Request feedback from kitchen personnel on how equipment or products can be relocated to give the workflow better con-tinuity. Employees who are actually performing the tasks may have excellent ideas for increasing productivity and service.

Service Capabilities

As equipment has capabilities and limitations, so do service facilities and service personnel. A facility may not be able to sell certain products because of its in-ability to hold the product until serving time. The correct procedures for serv-ing should be known as well as the proper containers and utensils used. Serving safe food is the most important control function and should always be a major concern of management. Although generating a profit is an ongoing objective, serving food that is safe must always be at the forefront.

Computers in Menu Planning

Computers can play a major role in helping to control the menu planning process. Available software can convert recipes, suggest substitute products, list calorie values, cost-out products and portions, and assist in maintaining inventory and in ordering products. For large health care facilities, the use of computers for developing menus to satisfy dietetic controls is a must. Not only can the computers break down the calorie value of products and recipes, they can quickly provide changes in values if products have to be substituted.

From a cost control standpoint, computers can be a valuable aid in tracking the cost and utilization of products. While there is no substitute for physically counting products, computers can provide assistance to reduce the number of physical inventories and can maintain a flow of accountability.

A computer can aid but cannot replace the brain for controlling costs. Controlling costs remains a managerial function that must be given a lot of attention; however, computers can make the tasks of control and accountability much more easy and accurate.

Summary

The menu acts as a blueprint for a hospitality operation. Because the menu is so important to the survival of an operation, procedures for maintaining the consistency of this document must be controlled.

Site selection, demographics, equipment, labor, and all other facets of the operation are dependent on the menu. The structure of the menu must be developed for marketing the operation and designed so that food products can be produced and served with maximum quality. Each type of menu has its own unique set of circumstances that must be controlled. Managers are responsible for selecting menu items that will be acceptable to the public and will generate maximum profit.

While generating sales and controlling costs, managers must ensure that nutritional and sanitary standards are maintained. A variety of products should be developed to complement the goals and objectives of the operation, and sanitary conditions, quality, and service must not be allowed to decline in the process of generating a profit.

When developing menus, concern must be given to the capacity of equipment and the capability to serve the products. A manager must control quality and consistency throughout the production process. Any decline in quality or consistency can cause a reduction in sales.

Plans must be developed to anticipate changes in business events, and computers should be used as a tracking device to ensure accountability through the operational process.

*Review Exercises*_____

1. Major decisions that must be taken into consideration when writing a menu include all of the following factors except:
   a. labor market
   b. weather
   c. uniforms
   d. prices

2. A problem with the site selection process may include:
   a. rezoning
   b. construction
   c. licenses
   d. all of the above

3. The demographics of an area can change quickly if:
   a. the weather changes
   b. a nearby corporation moves
   c. a school opens
   d. a and c

4. All of the following statements pertain to the purchasing of food service equipment except:
   a. noncommercial items are inexpensive and will save money in the long run
   b. purchasing equipment that is not required ties up capital
   c. the volume of business must be anticipated
   d. purchases must be made to satisfy quality, quantity, and consistency

5. Which of the following must be considered when establishing price?
   a. cost coverage
   b. the location of the establishment
   c. unexpected repairs
   d. all of the above

6. Which of the following is extremely important in establishing a menu?
   a. products should be available for a diverse market
   b. products should be available for dieting
   c. the changing of price of seasonal products should be accounted for
   d. there should be some type of meat-free dish on the menu

7. Labor is an important element in the construction of a menu because:
   a. there are so many menu items
   b. all restaurants require cooks that are highly trained
   c. labor is a large portion of the costs
   d. the menu dictates the type of labor skills required

8. The weather in an area can have an effect on the sale of certain products if:
   a. it is too cold
   b. it is too hot
   c. it rains a lot
   d. all of the above

9. Which of the following statements concerning major events is true?
   a. major events always cause a reduction in sales
   b. major events always cause an increase in sales
   c. major events can have a negative or positive effect on sales
   d. all of the above

10. Which type of menu is better for the planning of leftovers?
    a. cyclical
    b. off-hour
    c. a la carte
    d. all of the above

11. From the different types of menus discussed in the chapter, choose two types and develop a menu for each type. List three problems that could occur in trying to control the production, holding, and serving of each menu.

12. List five factors concerning the importance of demographics and site selection when designing menus.

13. Develop a list of at least five food products that may vary in supply and demand during certain times of the year.

14. List five major events that occur in your area, and explain how any two of these events may have a positive or negative effect on: 1) a full-service hotel; 2) a limited-service hotel; 3) a full-service restaurant; and 4) a fast-food restaurant.

Examination Type Problems _____

1. List five considerations and/or constraints that could be associated with the development of a cyclical menu.

2. Explain the importance of developing a menu index.

3. Name four concerns associated with selling, serving, and controlling beverages.

4. Why are variety and appeal in menu design so important, and what are some activities a manager can control to ensure these?

Case Study _____

While you are effectively operating the Model Restaurant at Case Study Hotel, your friend called you for some advice. He is a manager of a small 150-room hotel in a business community that does not have a foodservice facility. He has just been informed by his supervisor that the hotel will purchase the lot next to the hotel property and build a freestanding restaurant for the hotel guests and the community. The facility will seat approximately 300 guests. Your friend has been given the task of developing the menu for the facility, and he is seeking your general ideas and suggestions for the following activities:

- Type of menu and items: What and why?
- Hours of operation: What and why?
- Required kitchen equipment: What and when should they decide?
- Other questions he should ask his boss.

5
Pricing

Learning Objectives

After completing this chapter, you should be able to:

- explain the reasons for setting prices.
- explain factors that can affect menu prices.
- establish the break-even point and the amount of profit or loss.
- precost menus to determine contribution margin.
- discuss cost and pricing of nonfood and nonbeverage products or services.
- discuss the use of ideal, or standard, cost.
- explain the informal and formal approaches to pricing.
- describe computerization in the hospitality industry and discuss its role in cost control.

The face of the work force is constantly changing. There are far more women in the work force than in the past. One of the reasons for this is the increasing number of dual-income households. Because two members of a household are having to work, more and more individuals are willing to pay for services, and due to this increase in the work force, prices for these services have somewhat decreased in importance. Prices must still be reasonable, but service and quality have become far more critical. People have become busy and they are more interested in having products when they want them and at the quality that is expected. Therefore, some individuals place price as the third priority in their shopping patterns. People who once shopped according to price, quality, and service now have a more demanding life style and are interested in service, quality, and price. Convenience has become far more important, than price, this is evident in the increasing number of foodservice operations that provide delivery service. Price is important, but in this global marketplace, people expect to be able to purchase products whenever they want them.

Factors That Affect Menu Prices

In establishing prices and attempting to generate a profit, an operation generally relies on one ore more of three pricing methods: profitability by selling in volume, keeping up with the competition, and prestige. All operations attempt to establish prices to maximize gains and to minimize losses.

Setting Prices: Volume for Profits, Competition, and Prestige

Setting prices for volume to generate profits is the most common determinant for setting prices. The majority of operations, including most large chain restaurants, establish prices to meet this objective. Using volume as a competitive strategy, prices can be established to generate a profit over the long run. The majority of quick-service restaurants operate on a sales volume maximization basis.

A large number of operations establish prices comparable to the prices of the competition; however, establishing prices simply to compete is always dangerous. Other operations go for the cream of the market, a method known as prestige pricing. This type of pricing is designed for quality, assurance and exclusiveness. Exclusive operations may be found in large cities or expensive resort areas.

Demographics and Types of Services

The demographics of an area, the level of service, and the products being served all have an important role in determining prices. An area's demographics include but are not limited to population, household income, age, occupation, and the like. In addition to the demographics of an area, three levels of service are instrumental in determining prices: quick service and cafeteria style; basic table, or midlevel, service; and luxurious, or elegant or fine-dining, service.

Quick-service or volume-intensive restaurants normally price foods with a small amount of markup. The intent is to generate revenue through volume and cost control. These types of facilities normally have the lowest prices. They keep prices low by using convenient types of prepared products, thereby reducing waste as well. Additionally, these facilities keep down the cost of labor by using unskilled employees with a minimum amount of training. Quick-service restaurants are difficult to control because the margin of profit is small and the employees are often newcomers to the foodservice field.

Basic table, or midlevel, restaurants have more full-time employees and generally have more choices on their menus. These restaurants are difficult to control because of the number of employees and menu items; therefore, they often use a great deal of strategy in developing their prices. Most quick-service restaurants are chain restaurants and prices are relatively consistent between operations and competitors; however, some operations may have several different price ranges and may adjust more to the demographics of their guests. One of the major control problems for these types of restaurants is the large volume and variety of products in inventory. Theft and spoilage must be constantly monitored.

Luxurious, or elegant or fine-dining, restaurants illustrate the fact that an operation can actually establish any price as long as the perception of value is acceptable. A fine-dining restaurant has to be located in a city in which a sufficient population base can support the prices that will be charged. Usually only large cities can support these types of operations; guests may visit a fine-dining establishment for a special occasion, but it takes more than this to support these operations over the long run. Some of these facilities do not have to advertise as they are in business to acquire the elite of the market place. These facilities must deliver impeccable service in order to maintain their market share. The concern for service and quality far exceeds price. While prices for fine dining are usually easier to establish than for the other two styles of service, controlling service and quality are the managerial concern.

Break-Even Analysis

As mentioned, there are many factors that affect menu pricing. However, from a strict break-even analysis standpoint, prices must cover all costs and must generate a profit for a business venture to be successful. The three cost factors that need to be considered are:

1. Fixed costs, which remain constant despite increases or decreases in sales volume
2. Variable costs, which usually increase as sales volume increases and decrease as sales volume decreases
3. Total costs, which is fixed costs plus variable costs

When establishing prices, the break-even point must be calculated. Break-even is a relationship between profit and volume.

Classification of Costs

All costs must be classified as either fixed or variable; however, not all costs are so easily defined. Such costs are known as semivariable, or mixed, costs. Labor cost is one example. If a restaurant only has five guests for lunch, it cannot only schedule one person to seat the guests, wait on them, prepare the food, collect the sales amount, bus the table, and do the dishes. There is a minimum amount of fixed labor involved. This is also true for a hotel; it does not matter whether there is one guest or a hundred guests, a minimum number of front office personnel has to be staffed. A minimum number of fixed staff members can efficiently deliver services up to a certain extent, but when the number of guests increases, the number of staff members also has to increase. This is the variable portion. When calculating break-even, semivariable, or mixed, costs must be established as either variable or fixed. The owner/operator will have to determine which items are to be placed in which category. Items that are generally categorized as fixed costs are:

- Rent
- Interest
- Depreciation and amortization
- Insurance
- Real estate and personal property taxes

Items that may be categorized as variable costs are:

- Labor
- Food
- Beverage
- Supplies
- Employee meals

- Employee benefits
- Utilities
- Maintenance

Reflected in a profit and loss statement, these items would appear as in Figure 5–1.

Figure 5–1 *Fixed and Variable Costs Classification*

Profit and Loss Statement		
SALES		
Food	$434,365.00	72.00%
Beverage	166,243.00	28.00%
Total sales	600,608.00	100.00%
COST OF SALES		
Food	$172,020.00	28.64% - VC
Beverage	24,203.00	4.03% - VC
Total cost of sales	196,223.00	32.67%
GROSS PROFIT	$404,385.00	
CONTROLLABLE EXPENSES		
Direct wages	$156,158.25	26.00% - VC
Vacation accrual	9,609.75	1.60% - FC
Management salaries	15,015.25	2.50% - FC
Employee meals	1,501.50	0.25% - VC
Employee benefits	12,733.00	2.10% - VC
Utilities	12,012.00	2.00% - VC
Maintenance	9,609.75	1.60% - VC
Local advertising	9,009.00	1.50% - FC
Entertainment	7,808.00	1.30% - VC
OCCUPANCY EXPENSE		
Rent	$30,030.50	5.00% - FC
Interest	3,003.00	0.50% - FC
Depreciation and amortization	17,417.75	2.90% - FC
Insurance	6,006.00	1.00% - FC
Real estate and personal property taxes	10,811.00	1.80% - FC
NET PROFIT OR (LOSS) BEFORE TAXES	$103,660.25	17.26%
TOTAL VARIABLE COST	$396,045.50	
TOTAL FIXED COST	$100,902.25	
TOTAL COST	$496,947.75	

Formulas

After all of the financial information has been identified as sales, variable costs (VC), and fixed costs (FC), an operation can easily determine its break-even point. There are several formulas for determining break-even according to the type of information provided. A quick way to establish break-even is to use the following formula:

$$\text{Break-even} = \frac{\text{Fixed costs}}{1 - \dfrac{\text{Variable costs}}{\text{Total sales}}} \quad \text{or} \quad \frac{\text{Fixed costs}}{1 - \text{Variable costs percentage}}$$

1 − Variable costs percentage is also known as the contribution margin (CM) percentage, thus termed because sales "contibute" this amount to cover all expenses other than those that are classified as variable.

Therefore, the shorthand formula for break-even is usually stated as:

$$\text{Break-even} = \frac{\text{FC}}{1 - \text{VC\%}} \quad \text{or} \quad \frac{\text{FC}}{\text{CM\%}}$$

Contribution margin is the difference between sales and variable costs. For example, if a room is sold for \$100 and the variable cost associated with selling that room is \$20, the contribution margin is \$80 (\$100 − \$20). If a seafood entree is sold for \$18 and the variable cost associated with the production and sale of the entree is \$7, the contribution margin is \$11 (\$18 − \$7). In the example of the hotel room the contribution margin percentage can be calculated as follows:

$$\text{Contribution margin percentage} = \frac{\text{Contribution margin (\$)}}{\text{Sales (\$)}}$$
$$= \frac{80}{100}$$
$$= 80\%$$

The contribution margin percentage for the seafood entree can be similarily calculated:

$$\text{Contribution margin percentage} = \frac{\text{Contribution margin (\$)}}{\text{Sales (\$)}}$$
$$= \frac{11}{18}$$
$$= 61.11\%$$

It is important to understand that once an operation reaches break-even, the additional sales do not result in 100% profit. This mistake is often made when establishing the amount of profit or loss after the break-even point has been determined. Profit cannot be generated until an operation passes break-even; however, all sales made after reaching the break-even point do not flow through the income statement and become pure profit. Profit is the difference between costs and sales that are generated after break-even is reached.

For managers to be able to control operational procedures, they must have an awareness of their break-even point. This will help during budgeting, forecasting, and in day-to-day decision-making. Use Figure 5–2 as a guideline to correctly determine break-even and the amount of profit or loss for an operation. A problem that exists when establishing break-even is that few operations account for all of their variable costs. Even though a manager may use break-even to evaluate an operation's pricing structure it is extremely important to remember that an operation must attempt to have a margin of profit for hidden costs. The larger the menu, the larger the number of employees, the larger the size of the operation, and the greater the possibility for hidden costs.

Hidden Costs

Hidden costs and their important role in cost control will be mentioned throughout the text. Hidden costs are legitimate business costs; however, in many cases they have not been identified by management as additional costs.

Figure 5–2   *Steps in Determining Break-Even*

Using the information from Figure 5–1:
1. Total sales were $600,608.00.
2. Variable costs were 65.94% (or 0.6594) of total sales.
3. Fixed costs were $100,902.25

Step 1
Total sales × Variable cost percent = Variable cost
$600,608 × 0.6594 = $396,045.50

Step 2
Total sales − Variable cost = Contribution margin
$600,608 − $396,045.50 = $204,562.50

Step 3
Contribution margin ÷ Total sales = Contribution margin percent
$204,562.50 ÷ $600,608 = 34.06% (or 0.3406)

Step 4
Fixed cost ÷ Contribution margin percent = Break-even
$100,902 ÷ 0.3406 = $292,248.53

Step 5
Total sales − Break-even = Sales above or below break-even
$600,608 − $296,248.53 = $304,359.47 above break-even

Step 6
Sales above or below break-even × Gross profit percent = Profit or loss
$304,359.47 × 0.3406 = $103,664 profit (approximate due to rounding)

Hidden costs can exist as a result of numerous activities. During the planning process of a business, hidden costs are often not addressed; in fact, they are overlooked in the majority of all business plans. Not accounting for hidden costs can be a significant problem in the hospitality industry due to its labor-intensive structure, slim profit margin, and dramatically fluctuating market. Hidden costs can be defined as any activities that increase variable costs or unexpectedly reduce sales, which can reduce profit. For break-even to be as accurate as possible a small percentage should be included for hidden costs. This small percentage should be determined by management and should be viewed as variable costs.

It is a mistake to think that hidden costs do not exist in the hospitality industry. If there is a vast amount of rain in California and the lettuce crop is damaged, lettuce prices could quadruple. If an operation is highly dependent on lettuce for food products this situation could cut deeply into profit. A manager has no control over this type of event. If a manager runs out of lettuce during a busy shift and has to purchase some at the local grocery store and pay a higher price, the operation will incur additional costs. This type of situation can occur because of a lack of planning or because of an unexpected increase in sales. Either way, this situation will develop a hidden cost and will cut into profit.

Precosting the Menu

Precosting is essential to establishing the correct price and menu mix. Precosting has to be completed before prices are established in order for the operation to be able to generate a profit. It is at this point when all aspects of producing an item must be identified. Management must know the costs of ingredients and labor for all products. Several menu items can be far more labor intensive than others and these products must be identified so that accurate contribution margin can be determined. Seemingly minor details, such as presentations and garnishes, can add costs to a specific product. This is why menu construction is so important. A menu should be strategically designed to enhance sales by directing guests to items that management prefers to sell, those that have been priced with the greatest contribution margin. When developing menus, management and owners have to remember that most guests want the staff to provide suggestions as to which items to choose. This makes precosting and constructing a menu to enhance sales even more important. One way of ensuring that precosting is as accurate as possible is through the utilization of standardized recipes.

Standardized Recipes

Standardized recipes are essential in developing the correct price for menu items. An operation must be aware of exactly what it takes to produce a product. This can only be done if recipes are standardized and strictly followed; however, trying to get personnel to consistently follow recipes is a constant battle for most managers. By using standardized recipes an operation will know exactly how much it costs to prepare an item and how many individuals can be served from that particular recipe. Advantages in using standardized recipes include:

- Consistency
- Controlled labor cost
- Effective scheduling
- Predetermined product cost

Consistency of taste, texture, and presentation is important to the success of an operation. Many foodservice operations are based on special products or recipes. These operations may be successful because of the uniqueness of the products; however, standards still must be established for the products, and the procedures for developing such products must be placed into writing. Additionally, because standardized recipes provide clear directions, management can train employees with fewer skills and thus create a more controlled labor cost. The chef need not be present at all times because employees are trained according to directions on standardized recipes. This offers greater flexibility in scheduling. Because the ingredient amounts are clearly printed on standardized recipes, the exact product costs can be calculated easily. If there is no standard that specifies how much rice is needed to yield 100 4-ounce servings, inexperienced kitchen personnel may cook more than is needed. In such cases, products are wasted and costs increase.

To accurately establish prices, management must have a realistic idea of the cost of generating a product. This is why it is essential to use standardized recipes so that the cost of developing recipes will be consistent. To establish the cost of a standardized recipe management uses the market price of each ingredient, extends the cost of that ingredient in the recipe, calculates a total cost, and divides that by the number of recipe servings to obtain the unit cost per serving. Table 5–1 is an example of a standardized recipe that has been costed out.

Table 5–1

Chopped Steak		Approximately 50 Servings	
Ingredients	*Amount*	*Market Price*	*Extension Cost*
Ground chuck	14 lbs	$1.15 per lb	$16.10
Onions	3 lbs	.15 per lb	0.45
Garlic	½ oz	1.52 per lb	0.047
Salad oil	½ cup	.70 per qt	0.087
Bread crumbs	2 lbs	.36 per lb	0.72
Milk	1½ pts	1.65 per gal.	0.309
Whole eggs	8	.84 per doz	0.56
Pepper	¼ oz	1.18 per lb	0.018
Salt	1 oz	.16 per lb	0.01
Total cost	$18.301		
Cost per serving (yield)	$ 0.366		

Specialty and Discount Items

Pricing specialty and discount items can present an opportunity to generate a profit. If an operation can create a specialty from a low-cost or seasonal item, the item could result in a large contribution margin. This has been accomplished with onions, inexpensive cheeses, and all types of beverages. A specialty item can be created just by making an item appear substantially different. Managers should try to develop specialty items as differentiation can create competitive advantages. Specialty items can be created simply by using special food presentation containers or fancy delivery method. Once an item becomes a specialty, the price can exceed the average selling price for that item. A banana wrapped in a tortilla, fried, served on a plate with chocolate syrup and two scoops of ice cream cannot cost much. However, with spectacular presentation, this can be sold in restaurants as a specialty dessert with a price of $3.50 to $9.00, depending on the locale of the restaurant and the type of service.

Discounts can also be a source of generating sales, and they can provide a challenge for setting prices. Discounts are usually in the form of cash, trade, or quantity. In the foodservice industry, discount items can present an opportunity to sell items as loss leaders to generate sales in other areas. For hotels, discounts may generate longer stays; for the travel and tourism industry, discounts may generate a larger guest count. Discounts usually involve a reduction in sales price. A discount may be implemented to eliminate leftovers or to sell products that may lose their value if they are allowed to remain in storage. On the other hand, discounts can be used as a promotional technique. Every opportunity should be looked at from a standpoint of generating a profit. A manager must be careful when reducing prices to ensure that it will be cost effective in the long run. When discounts are designed to generate sales a manager must take into consideration that other variable costs could also increase. Trying to control and balance costs and prices can be a difficult task.

For the foodservice industry, there is always a danger in using a loss leader. A loss leader, or a product that may be sold at a price cheaper than cost, may not be cost effective in the long run. Reducing a price below cost on one item may not generate enough sales on other items or generate enough continued business to cover the additional variable costs. A guest can only purchase a limited number of products when going out for a meal. A loss leader at least will need to cover the price of the product. It is wise to remember that anytime sales are substantially increased, variable costs are apt to increase simultaneously. Because discounts usually reduce the price of products, variable costs must be considered. Therefore, evaluating and controlling costs and pricing of discounts can take a great deal of planning.

Costs of Nonfood and Nonbeverage
Products or Services

While pricing and costs of food and beverage items are important, this book concentrates on food, beverage, and labor cost controls. Prices must also be established for other profit centers in the hospitality field that also house food and beverage products. These operations may have a food and beverage facility but they must also establish prices to cover other services provided. Some of these types of operations are hotels, country clubs, and private clubs. Hotels and clubs price their nonfood activities as well as their food and beverage operations.

Rooms

Room prices usually yield a larger profit margin for a hotel operation than food and beverage prices. The costs involved in maintaining the lodging side of hotels can often be less expensive than running the food and beverage operations. In the past, numerous hotels would make more money from their restaurants then they would make from their rooms division. Dining in hotels was often an exquisite experience. While this is still true in many European and Asian hotels, the trend has changed dramatically in most hotels in the United States. The vast majority of hotels generate far more profit from their rooms divisions than their restaurant operations. While they still expect their restaurants to generate a profit, it is a much smaller percentage. With the addition of casino operations, the percentage of profit for rooms divisions often decreases. Rooms must be priced correctly, and many major operations even employ yield management for establishing prices to maximize profit.

Membership Dues

As another means of generating revenue, membership dues must be properly rated. Dues are often used by country clubs and private clubs to limit access and to help cover the costs of other activities. If a country club wants to establish a fine-dining facility but does not have a sufficient number of guests to cover all costs, the club may pass on this additional cost as dues. In some cases, food items cannot be priced high enough to generate a profit for the limited number of clientele that frequent the facility. Controlling costs in these facilities often depends to a large extent on how high dues can be set without resulting in a decline in membership. One of the main problems with controlling cost in facilities that charge a membership fee is that members usually charge meals and pay at the end of the month. This reduces the amount of cash flow and prevents the club from taking advantage of money saving practices such as cash discounts on purchases. Also, while the club is waiting for end-of-the-month receivable from members, midmonth payrolls must still be met; therefore, balancing cash flow activities can be a difficult procedure for club managers to control.

Ideal Cost

To effectively deal with the cost issue, operations need to develop ideal, or standard, cost. All efficient operations have a standard cost, which is the ideal cost of products or services. Standard cost is compared with actual cost in order to determine operational effectiveness. For example, if all standards for a particular menu item are met during the control process of purchasing, receiving, storing, production, and service, then the cost that has been established for that item should be met. If for some reason a standard was not met during the control process, then the actual cost for that particular item may not meet the standard cost that has been established.

Ideal Cost versus Actual Cost

An operation must attempt to have actual cost meet ideal cost as closely as possible. This can be difficult because of spillage, butcher's cut, shrinkage, and so on. However, every effort must be made to maximize the utilization of each product to try and reach its serving potential. By maximizing the serving potential of a product, the actual cost of the product comes close to the ideal cost. If a bottle of bourbon should cost an operation $6.00 and the operation is able to obtain the maximum number of shots from that particular bottle, then the sales from that bottle will yield the expected ideal cost of generating those sales. However, if spillage or evaporation is allowed to occur, or free drinks are allowed to be poured and not accounted for, then the sales are less and this increases the costs percentage of making those sales. Management must make every effort to evaluate standards so that standard cost can be established. Ideal cost provides management with a yardstick by which actual cost can be measured.

Tolerance to the Variance

Tolerance to the variance between actual costs must be established so that management will know what and when to monitor and when to take action. If the standard beverage cost is 26% and it goes up to 26.9%, there may not be a need to take action, but there may be a need to monitor the increase. On the other hand, if the standard beverage cost has been established at 26% and for the past two accounting periods the costs were 27.5%, an operation may not be able to tolerate this amount of increase and action must be taken. Every organization differs in the amount of cost fluctuations that can be tolerated. Standards must be set, and the amount of change that can occur before corrective action has to be taken should also be established. A small change within some organizations can be devastating if the reason for the change is not evaluated quickly. Changing the standard to the lower variance must always be seen as a last resort. Efforts must be made to reach potential cost. In food and beverage operations, 1.0 to 1.5% are normally deemed tolerable variances.

Approaches to Pricing _____

There are numerous approaches to pricing items on a menu. Developing menu prices is a time-consuming task and must be performed with long-range planning in mind. Remember, menu prices must cover all costs and generate a profit; thus, the time and effort involved in establishing prices are worth the investment. Some form of menu engineering must take place before prices are established. Menu engineering is a means of evaluating current and future menu pricing, menu design, and menu content in order to maximize profit. Menu engineering focuses on guest demand, menu mix analysis, and the contribution margin of each item on the menu.

It is important to perform menu engineering because menu prices can be difficult to change. A manager must be careful when setting and changing prices, as guests can become disgruntled when they realize that prices are being raised. It is best to change prices when new menus are printed. It is more noticeable and unprofessional to use tape or correction fluid on menus to change prices. Professionalism is essential to the perception of the guests. A manager may want to remove a product from the menu due to increases in costs but may want to bring it back as a special at a later date with a higher price. Another method is to enhance the appearance of the product and give it a different name and price. Raising prices is never easy, but it must be done eventually, and managers have to find ways of raising prices without lowering the perception of value.

BCG Matrix

When evaluating the menu mix or revenue centers of a hospitality organization, the BCG matrix can be used. The portfolio matrix developed by the Boston Consulting Group in the early 1970s was used to plot an organization's strategic business units on a two-by-two matrix. Hospitality organizations can use the BCG matrix to plot their business activities. A hotel or casino can plot their different revenue centers, or foodservice operations can plot the different products on their menu. In the two-by-two matrix the horizontal axis represents market share, and the vertical axis indicates anticipated market growth (see Figure 5–3).

Figure 5–3   *BCG Matrix*

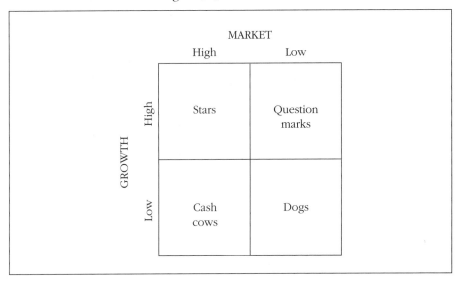

The matrix identifies four business groups, or in the case of a menu, four types of sales activities:

1. Cash cows (low growth, high market share). Products in this category generate large amounts of cash, but their prospects for future growth are limited.

2. Stars (high growth, high market share). These products are in a fast-growing market and hold a dominant share of that market but might or might not produce a positive cash flow, depending on the need for investment in a new plant and equipment or product development.

3. Question marks (high growth, low market share). These are speculative products that entail high risks. They may be profitable but they hold a small percentage of market share.

4. Dogs (low growth, low market share). This residual category does not produce much cash, nor does it require much. These products hold no promise for improved performance.

The BCG's research indicates that organizations that sacrifice short-run profits to gain market share yield the highest long-run profits (cash cows). So management should "milk" the cows as much as they can, limit any new cow investments to the minimal maintenance level, and use the large amounts of cash the cows generate to invest in stars. Heavy investment in stars should pay high dividends. Stars should eventually develop into cash cows as their markets mature and growth declines. The hardest decision usually relates to question marks. Some should be sold off or eliminated and others should be turned into stars. Question marks are risky, and management wants to have only a limited number of these speculative ventures. Dogs propose no strategic problems and they should be sold off or liquidated at the earliest opportunity. There is little to recommend their retention or further investment by the company. Money obtained from selling off dogs can be used to buy or finance question marks.

The BCG method has not been used much in recent years, as some organizations have found no correlation between increased market share and lower cost. Some organizations have also found that they cannot always divide activities into separate units. Also, some so-called dogs have shown consistently higher levels of profitability than their growing competitors with dominant market shares. Additionally, given the fact that a market normally has only one leader, more than half of all businesses fall by definition into the dog category. However, the BCG method is still a useful concept for evaluating revenue activities.

When evaluating a menu, most items can be placed into a two-by-two matrix. This can help management decide which items to keep, which items to promote, and which items may need to be rejuvenated. Of course, to make these decisions management must understand the contribution margin of each item.

Contribution Margin

As mentioned earlier, to evaluate the contribution margin it is accepted that each dollar of sales is divided into two portions. One portion must be allocated to cover variable costs associated with the item sold and the other to cover fixed costs and to provide profit. With this interpretation, the dollar amount remaining after variable costs have been subtracted from the sales dollar is defined as the contribution margin. When sales cover all variable costs and all fixed costs the amount remaining is profit, or break-even at the point wherein fixed costs are covered.

Management must be aware that when establishing the price of an item variable cost should never exceed price. When establishing menu prices, contribution margin must cover fixed costs, and when combined with all other items the price must provide an amount that will exceed break-even. This is why there is a danger in using loss leaders and cost leaders. A loss leader prices a product below cost; a cost leader prices a product at cost. These tactics are dangerous to a foodservice operation because a menu may not be able to regroup enough beyond break-even because customers can only consume a certain quantity of products.

Informal Approaches

One informal approach to menu pricing is to price items according to competitors' menus. This is often done by businesses that are entering the industry for the first time; however, simply trying to match the prices of competitors can be a major mistake. An establishment must be concerned with competitors' prices, but an establishment cannot allow competitors to dictate its own prices. Some operations attempt to follow the industry leader in pricing their products. This may be a poor plan, as the industry leader most likely has advantages, such as more purchasing power than other operations. Therefore, an operation may attempt to sell products at the same price as the industry leader without realizing that the ingredient costs can be significantly different.

Another informal approach is to charge what the market will bear. However, remember that prices have to be reasonable. If prices are totally unreasonable and if a competitor should enter the market with lower prices, guests will feel no loyalty to an operation and will leave. Establishing customer loyalty is essential to long-range planning and success. Guests must feel that prices are reasonable. What is reasonable may depend on the type of operation, the menu, the service, the demographics, and the availability of competitors.

Formal Approaches

Several methods are used in the foodservice field to establish menu prices. Most of these methods are closely related. For the purpose of this text, the four methods most commonly used in the hospitality industry will be discussed:

1. Derived food cost percentage
2. Pricing factor, or markup or multiplier
3. Combined food and labor cost
4. Actual cost pricing

When discussing pricing, the basic merchandising equation comes into effect.

> Selling price
> − Cost
> ―――――――――――――――――――――――
> Markup (gross profit or margin)
> − Operating expenses
> ―――――――――――――――――――――――
> = Net profit or net loss

When managers decide on a selling price, they have to know cost, markup, percent of markup, operating expenses, net profit, and percent of net profit desired. Cost is the price paid by the operation for the products. Markup, which is often referred to as gross profit or margin, is the difference between the cost of the products and the selling price. For instance, if the cost of an item is $1.00 and the markup is 75%, then the selling price is $4.00 ($1.00 × 100% ÷ 1 − 75%, or $1.00 × 100% ÷ 25%). The percentage of markup can be based on the cost percentage of the selling price. Markup must be large enough to cover operating expenses and have an amount left over for net profit. Operating expenses are expenditures, such as rent and utilities, involved in the daily cost of running an operation. Net profit is the amount of money that remains after operating expenses have been paid; the percentage of net profit is based on the selling price. When establishing price, the main questions are how much will products be marked up and what process will be used to determine this amount.

Derived Food Cost Percentage   A large number of facilities use derived food cost percentage to establish prices because it is simple and yet quite accurate. Management determines a desired markup percentage and the price for a product is obtained by dividing the dollar cost of the product by the desired percentage. If a product costs $2.50 and the desired percentage is 36%, the price is established by dividing $2.50 by 0.36, which establishes a menu price of approximately $6.95. This method of pricing is probably used more than any other as it provides an easy means for quickly establishing prices for all menu items.

Pricing Factor   The pricing factor, or markup or multiplier, method is closely related to the derived food cost percentage. When using this method, the established food cost percentage is divided into 100 to derive a factor. If an operation has a food cost of 40% they come up with a factor of 2.50. The raw food cost is simply multiplied by the pricing factor to establish the sales price. With a factor of 2.5, an entree that costs $3.00 has a selling price of $7.50. Like the food cost percentage method, this method is often used to establish menu prices because it is easy.

Combined Food and Labor Cost   Because the hospitality industry is labor intensive labor cost has to be considered when pricing products. This portion of cost is referred to as the prime cost. This is especially true with regard to large functions wherein the menu may include time-consuming garnishes and other decorative food displays. Using the combined food and labor cost method allows an operation to account for specific labor activities. If an operation wants

36% food cost and 28% labor cost, the combined food and labor cost is 64%. If the cost of a food item is $2.50 and labor cost is $1.50, the two costs are combined and divided by the combined percentage [($2.50 + $1.50) ÷ 0.64 = $6.25]. This procedure works well for operations that want to include food and labor costs in their selling prices.

Actual Cost Pricing   Actual cost pricing is a practical means of ensuring that a certain profit percentage is included in the pricing process. In the actual cost method, an operation combines the established food cost ($2.50), labor cost ($1.50), operating cost ($1.10), and percentage of required profit (10%) to arrive at the selling price:

($2.50 + $1.50 + $1.10) = $5.10 (combined cost)
$5.10 ÷ (1 − 10%) = $5.10 ÷ 90% = $5.70 (selling price)

The actual cost method allows an operation to account for profit. Viewing profit as an operating cost can be a sound business tactic.

Whichever method is used to establish prices, it is important to ensure not only that prices cover all costs but that prices also allow the organization to generate a profit. Profit can be lost if inadequate prices are originally posted; and trying to increase prices can be costly as well.

Rounding and Print Size

Whether prices are set informally or formally, two items are worth discussing here to ensure that operations maximize the prices that they set. The first item is rounding, which is especially useful in formal approaches that derive prices from numbers generated by formulas. Often, these formula-generated prices are not round numbers. Most rounding strategies suggest using $0.25 increments for menu prices under $5.00. For example, $2.27 may be rounded up to $2.50 or down to $2.25, based on an operation's projection of what guests will be willing to pay. Most rounding strategies suggest using $0.50 to $0.95 increments for menu items over $5.00.

The print size of the menu price also affects guests' perception of price. For example, guests may perceive $3.95 to be more expensive than $3.95; not because of the price itself, as both numbers are of the same value, but because of the differences in print sizes. Thus, on some menus the print size of the menu item and description is often larger than the print size of the price.

Costs, Pricing, and Profits _____

For a facility to operate in a cost-effective manner and maximize profit, it has to attempt to purchase quality products as economically as possible. While quality and consistency cannot be compromised, the lowest acceptable price must be sought. Once a product has been obtained at the best price possible, it must be priced effectively or all efficient purchasing activities are wasted. Most importantly, if a product is not priced correctly, then possible profit will be lost.

Correct Costing

It is essential to try to purchase products at the best price possible. The cost of purchases must be monitored to ensure that only minimum quality is being purchased, unless exceeding minimum quality will not incur additional costs. Product consistency and dependability may dictate higher costs, but the minimum cost should be pursued as the ideal. It is also vital to ensure that the cost of purchasing a product accounts for the servable amount of that product so that the correct price for the product can be established.

Accurate Pricing

Pricing cannot be accomplished haphazardly. Every attempt must be made to factor in all costs and to develop an effective menu mix. Analysis of the menu mix assists an operation in determining which items on a menu are being sold and in what relative proportions to the other items, and this allows an operation to identify guest demand for each menu item. Considerations must be given to menu mix and guest demand to ensure that prices are effective. The menu mix may allow an operation to spread cost around without having to establish unacceptable prices for certain products. Guest demand may also allow operations to charge substantially more for certain products. A balance must be accomplished in order to generate a profit and retain guests.

Appropriate Controls

Profit must be a major consideration when establishing prices. One of the major mistakes made by mom-and-pop operations and home businesses is to underestimate the amount of profit that is required for the effort and cost of investment. Considering the number of hours some small operations put into providing a product or service, the owners would be better off working for another facility. It is easy to underestimate the time, effort, and costs that can be involved in providing hospitality products and services. When providing guests with quotes for large functions, wherein setting up ballrooms and a great deal of equipment may be required, it is essential to account for a vast amount of labor. It is important to understand that labor costs not only entail the preparation of food products but also the serving of those food products. An operation may choose to charge a certain amount for the use of a banquet room or may simply add the cost of setting up a room to the price of the meal. Whichever pricing method is used, all required labor must be considered if sufficient profit is to be generated.

Computerization

Computerization can provide managers with a fast and efficient means of comparing standards to determine if controls are being met. It is essential in the hospitality industry to be able to evaluate and compare standards in a timely manner. This is especially true for labor cost. Adjustments in labor must be made quickly. By taking hourly cash register readings, a manager can often make cost-saving adjustments.

Spreadsheets

For multi-unit operations that may have to send financial information and other mathematical analyses to their corporate offices, computerization of this activity definitely reduces the possibility of error. When sending financial information via mail or courier, there is always a possibility that the package may be mishandled, misplaced, or lost. By using the full spectrum of spreadsheet programs, e-mail, and the Internet, an operation can prevent mistakes. However, do not forget the old adage "garbage in, garbage out." This is always a problem when an operation has two or more staff members making entries on spreadsheets and these people do not communicate. Mistakes and oversights occur far more often than the industry would like to admit and thus creates a waste in labor. With more accurate data, prices can be set to reflect all costs and the desired profit.

Databases

Database software as a control implement is greatly underused. Historical data on products, prices, sales, employees, and guests can be a valuable aid to an operation. The ability to index menu items and to see when and in what quantity products were sold can assist in production planning. Production planning can prevent waste and reduce the possibility of stockout. A manager can quickly determine when the costs of certain items were the lowest, and plan to take advantage of that rate in the future. This type of planning can help reduce food cost.

It is also essential to know the amount of sales and the costs of sales when certain employees are working. This is a control factor that is often overlooked. While all food service personnel do not waste or steal, many of them do. In many cases, if a manager should give the bartender a night off and run the bar himself, he may find a substantial increase in sales for that particular night. The same correlation can exist for food products and sales. By maintaining sales records and employees' schedules in a database, a manager may find that when certain employees are on duty, it takes a substantially larger quantity of some products to service a standard number of guests. While this can be a result of either waste or theft, the result is still a loss of income to the operation. A database program can quickly provide information regarding these events.

Historical files can be used as an excellent tool in providing guest services. Because database files can contain a vast amount of information, they can be used to anticipate guest needs. If a guest has not frequented an establishment for some time and yet small preferences are remembered, this will enhance guest loyalty. Everyone wants to feel special, and remembering that a guest prefers a nonsmoking room or likes a certain wine vintage can go a long way in retaining a guest. Remembering guests' birthdays and anniversaries is also important. Establishing and maintaining controls are important, but sales must also be generated. An operation is more apt to meet budgetary requirements and other control standards. When sales are generated; therefore, it is critical to maintain a solid guest base.

Database programs can provide comparisons and cross-references that are extremely beneficial to a manager in the hospitality industry, as he or she can quickly compare prices and evaluate the cost of a particular menu mix. This will aid in establishing effective prices. Profit maximization of menu items can be obtained through effective prices.

Proprietary Software

Proprietary software is another means of establishing control and consistency. Through proprietary software an organization can tailor information to fit their requirements. This type of software prevents breakdowns in the control system when managers are transferred or rotated between units. One of the most important features of proprietary software is that control features can be built into the system to protect the organization.

It is important to remember that computerization is not a substitute for management actually observing operational activities. Figures may balance, but only through physical observation can management determine if an operation is maximizing the utilization of resources. A manager must ensure that guests are receiving the quality and the quantity they are paying for and with the required amount of service.

Summary

Numerous activities can affect menu prices. A manager should be conscientious in trying to develop the most cost-effective prices. A menu should be precosted and standard recipes should be developed to ensure consistency over the long run. If consistency in purchasing, receiving, storage, production, and serving is not maintained, established prices cannot be effective in producing a profit. Specialty and discount items can be priced to increase sales, to take advantage of seasonal items, and can help in preventing loss through possible waste and spoilage.

Nonfood and nonbeverage items and other profit centers must also be priced correctly. Room rates and membership dues can enhance the overall revenue of an operation. The price of rooms can be adjusted for special events and periods to increase revenue. Membership dues can be adjusted to balance costs as long as increases only occur on an occasional basis.

Actual cost should be as close as possible to ideal cost. The amount of tolerance from ideal cost should be minimized. Different approaches to pricing must be evaluated in order to account for an amount of tolerance and to maximize pricing efforts. Costs and pricing have to be thoroughly evaluated and balanced if profits are to be maximized.

The availability and affordability of computerization and software should encourage management to go on-line to save time and increase accuracy. However, management must also be advised that computers do not eliminate the need for routinely taking a physical count of products and other resources. Often, figures may not relate what is actually occurring in the business and evidence of a problem may only become visible through a reduction in guest count.

Developing prices takes time and must be viewed as one of the most essential elements to the success of an operation. Prices must be as accurate as possible to cover all costs. Hidden and unexpected costs can be a major problem for new establishments.

Review Exercises

1. Customers' priority used to be price, followed by quality and service; now:
   a. price only has to be reasonable
   b. price is still the most important
   c. quality is not the most important
   d. price, quality, and brand name are the most important

2. What are the two main concerns when establishing menu prices?
   a. prices must be consistent and cheap
   b. prices must not change during seasons or increase during the accounting period
   c. prices must cover all costs and generate a profit
   d. prices must reflect the quality and availability of menu items

3. A menu must be precosted in order to determine:
   a. the popularity of items
   b. contribution margin
   c. the necessary quality of products
   d. when items will be available

4. Which pricing approach do mom-and-pop restaurants most often use?
   a. informal approach
   b. formal approach
   c. combined food and labor cost
   d. actual cost pricing

5. One of the major problems associated with posting noncomputerized spreadsheets is:
   a. accounting for credit memos
   b. comparing prices
   c. double payments
   d. inspecting quality

6. The formula for attaining the break-even point is:
   a. fixed cost divided by 1 minus the variable cost percentage
   b. variable cost divided by 1 minus the fixed cost percentage
   c. fixed cost divided by sales
   d. variable cost divided by 1 plus the fixed cost percentage

7. One of the main reasons for using proprietary software is:
   a. it can be purchased at any computer software facility
   b. it is easy to learn
   c. it is far less expensive than most software
   d. it can be used to implement additional control

8. One of the best methods for changing menu prices is:
   a. tape the new price over the old price
   b. remove the item from the menu and bring it back at a higher price
   c. use correction fluid to cover the old price
   d. only change the dollar amount

9. When establishing break-even an item that may be identified as a variable cost is:
   a. labor
   b. rent
   c. interest
   d. insurance

10. Specialty items can increase sales through:
    a. differentiation
    b. the use of cheap products that are sold at a higher price
    c. the use of special servicing utensils
    d. all of the above

11. Discuss the three types of services that affect menu pricing.

12. Explain the four formal approaches to pricing.

13. What are some examples of hidden costs and why are they important in menu pricing?

14. The food and beverage director of Hotel Premiere has estimated sales of $80,000 for the month of April. His estimated payroll is $30,000, overhead is $8,000, and food cost is 25%. What is the break-even point in dollars?

15. As follow-up to question 14, if the average check is $25.00, how many guests does Hotel Premiere have to serve to break even? Also, what is the profit at the $80,000 sales level?

16. Identify four advantages of using standardized recipes.

17. Discuss the role of computerization in menu pricing, especially the use of spreadsheets, databases, and proprietary software.

Examination Type Problems _____

1. Name and define each of the informal and formal approaches to pricing.

2. What are some demographic factors that affect menu pricing?

3. Define ideal cost and explain how one would use the concepts of ideal and actual costs to ascertain the health and effectiveness of a hospitality operation.

4. Give five examples of mixed costs and explain why they cannot be purely fixed or variable.

5. If the average guest check is $12.00 and the variable costs are 25%, what is the number of guests that a bar and grill needs to serve to cover their annual fixed cost of $250,000?

6. Fantasia Hotel has a monthly fixed cost of $100,000, average daily rate of $100.00, and an occupancy percentage of 65% with 80 rooms. What is the break-even point (in number of rooms) in March with 31 days if its variable cost is 30%?

Case Study

Case Study Hotel notices that weekends in the summer are normally not their high demand times. Therefore, to practice pricing correctly and to maximize profits, it is planning to offer weekend packages to their guests by serving dinner on Friday, three meals and tea on Saturday, and breakfast and lunch on Sunday. The target guests are mainly honeymooners and couples on a retreat away from the kids. The owner would like to offer wine with lunch and dinner. He would like to see a food cost of 35% to 40% and a beverage cost not to exceed 20%.

First, design the menu for the Friday night opening dinner. List an appetizer, soup or salad, entree, and dessert. Then write a standardized recipe for the entree and research the costs to produce the entree. Finally, determine the selling price if the entree is ordered as an a la carte item with a 35% desired food cost.

6

The Purchasing Function

Learning Objectives

After completing this chapter, you should be able to:

- explain the importance of establishing specifications.
- explain why an operation should try not to exceed its specified level of quality.
- explain why it is important to establish the needs of an organization.
- describe purchasing alternatives.
- explain the importance of establishing purchasing strategies.

- determine the standard yield of a product.
- determine cost per servable pound.
- explain the need for comparing brands.
- explain the need for comparing purveyors.
- explain the overall importance of the purchasing function to the bottom line.

In controlling cost during purchasing, organizations must look at the differences between commercial and consumer acquisitions. Most small hospitality operations do not fully understand the major difference between commercial purchasing and consumer purchasing. Because this difference is often not accepted or even considered, most managers assume that they have a great deal of familiarity or expertise in the purchasing process as they make various personal purchases on a daily basis.

A consumer point of view is often characterized by a shopping basket philosophy of purchasing. Consumers normally have no power to influence price, the method of marketing, or the manufacturer chosen by the supplier's management because consumers' total business is a small portion of the supplier's total sales. However, this is not true when purchasing for most hospitality operations. The purchases of most hospitality operations are large in volume, and in many cases, very specialized. Due to such volume purchases, large sums of money are involved, and therefore commercial buyers may have more bargaining power than an individual consumer. While this is good news for commercial buyers, there is also a lot of room and incentive for errors and collusion. Because of the vast amount of money that suppliers spend to attract buyers and the possibility of collusion, managers must understand the intricacies of maintaining control over purchasing.

The Importance of the Purchasing Function

Managers of any business venture must understand the importance of controlling the purchasing function. Not understanding the impact of the adage "it is not how much you make, it is how much you spend" has been the cause of numerous business failures. If an operation only nets about 5% profit, in theory the operation needs about $1000 in sales to net $50. It is difficult to generate $1000 in sales, not to mention the costs involved in generating $1000 in sales, such as wear and tear on the facility. If $50 can be saved in the purchasing process, then the savings can go straight to the bottom line. The difficulty of generating a profit is only one of the reasons why the purchasing function is so pertinent.

Because the purchasing function is so important to the survival and success of an operation, managers, purchasing personnel, and receiving personnel should be well trained. The purchasing task is one aspect of training that is normally omitted from most management training and development programs. Managers are usually given training that pertains to operational procedures and then they are required to purchase millions of dollars of products a year without having any training in this area whatsoever. Managers are left at the mercy of the purveyors with whom they do business. They are expected to control a function for which they have not received any training, a function that is one of the main sources of business failure.

Companies and owners should ensure that their managers are aware of the importance of the purchasing process and that their managers have an in-depth knowledge of the products and equipment that they will have to purchase. Managers should be made aware of product sources, prices, seasonal quality, and possible substitutions. Company owners must realize that when purchases are made, managers are spending company money. Thus, it is prudent to correctly train managers.

Controlling the Purchasing Function

In controlling the purchasing function, the first task a manager should accomplish is to identify the items that are essential to the operation of the business. This will prevent tying up resources by purchasing products that are nice to have but are not absolutely necessary. Items that are essential to an operation are purchased on a regular basis. Changes in prices of products purchased in large quantities over an accounting period can cause a significant shift in controllable expenses. A manager should ensure certain specifications for products that are ordered on a continuous basis. As stated in Chapter 2, specifications should include: quality, quantity, time, and price.

Specifications on Quality

It must be pointed out that quality is relative when discussing the purchasing function. An operation should only purchase products at the level of quality that meets the specifications of the menu or that the operational plan requires. To purchase at a level above the required needs must be viewed as a waste of resources. Hamburger patties made from prime cuts of meat will only be tough and expensive. Just because a raw product costs more does not mean that the final product will be of greater quality. Beef from older animals, which is normally sold at a cheaper price, actually enhances the flavor of soups and stews. Vine-ripened tomatoes are more expensive and deteriorate faster than tomatoes that are designed for shipping; therefore, vine-ripened tomatoes should not be requested if they are to be cooked, as this may not be the most economical tomato sauce. If managers are not made aware of these details, they are apt to waste money during purchasing.

Many factors must be taken into consideration when writing specifications for quality. Some of the most important factors are:

- Color
- Shape, form, or length
- Age
- Desired ripeness
- Size
- Brand
- Region

Informing the purveyors what color is needed is an extremely important factor for certain products. White pepper rather than whole black peppercorns is preferable in deviled eggs. For apple pies, a particular type of apple is important but the color is not; however, if the apples are used in fruit baskets in guestrooms, then color and size are important. Candied apples require a particular shape, size, and color.

A manager must also be careful when ordering a product in a different form than is usually required on a routine basis, such as an item for a special event. If a facility receives a special order for lunch and intends to make sandwiches it would be problematic to receive 50 pounds of cherry tomatoes instead of sandwich tomatoes because the type of tomato was not specified. The purveyor may think the order is the standard order that is used for the salad bar. These types of mistakes occur more often than one may realize.

Processed meats can come in an array of sizes, weights, and shapes. Turkey can come in forms from franks to whole birds. When ordering these products special care must be taken to review the recipe to acquire the most appropriate and cost-effective form.

Too many managers in charge of foodservice operations do not realize the intricacies of ordering specific types of food items for specific products. Any type of potato cannot be used to make quality French fries, just as any type of potato cannot be used for quality baked potatoes. The key is a quality or standard acceptable product. For managers to be able to control costs, a sufficient amount of sales must be generated. If the wrong food item is used, an operation may serve a product that is below acceptable standards. Poor quality products can cause guest dissatisfaction and eventually a decrease in sales.

A restaurateur once said that he was able to reduce food cost by a wide margin by simply looking at the specifications. The restaurant he managed was a midscale, table service restaurant. Shrimp cocktail was a popular appetizer item, and the manager was to discover why: six jumbo shrimp were used for the portion; six jumbo shrimp weigh approximately half a pound, so the $4.95 price was a real bargain. The food cost for the six shrimp was over 50%, and this did not include costs for the cocktail sauce, garnishes, and crackers and butter that are served with the appetizer. A miscalculation such as this can hurt the profitability of the operation.

Managers are urged to evaluate products to best fit their needs at a price they can afford. They must learn as much as possible about products and test items to determine initial quality and holding quality. Some products have to be consumed immediately, but if they must be held for a period of time, such as for large functions, they will begin to deteriorate in quality very quickly. The wrong type of baked potato is one of these items.

Product brands are also important in quality specifications. You may receive more usable weight in a number 10 can from one brand of whole tomatoes than you would from another. Can-cutting or tests and value analysis must be done. If one or two more servings can be obtained from one brand as compared to another, and a large number of servings of that product is served per week, this can become a major savings over a period of time.

When ordering alcoholic beverages, region and age of the product can reflect a major difference in taste and price. Be sure to order the correct product, especially if it is requested for a particular function. Do not try to pass off sparkling wine for champagne, or bourbon for whiskey. If the request is for rum and Coke or bourbon and Coke do not automatically substitute another cola without letting the guests know. The same goes for mayonnaise and salad dressing. These products have distinctively different tastes. Substitute items may be less expensive, but the taste and the quality of the final product can also suffer through such substitution.

Controlling quality during the purchasing function takes a great deal of attention to detail. The amount of money that can be saved during the purchasing function is truly worth the effort. Not only can money be saved for the operation but managers can also save themselves a great deal of stress by not receiving the wrong product at the last minute before a major function. When guests book functions in advance they expect everything to be prepared correctly. Major functions provide an excellent opportunity for generating new business.

Specifications on Quantity

Just as quality must be balanced between too high or substandard, the same holds true for quantity, where it may be too much or not enough. The ideal situation is to sell every portion of every product and have just-in-time inventory. Regardless as to which purveyor is selected, quantity must be available so that stockout will not occur. This is one of the main reasons why the lowest bid may not always be the most acceptable bid. A vendor may be able to supply products with the desired quality all of the time, but to properly operate a facility, the quantity and quality must be present consistently. It is not wise to buy the same products from different vendors simply to equalize costs, as vendors are less willing to provide the desired quantity when an operation consistently places only small or partial orders. Additionally, the operation ends up spending more time than necessary dealing with vendors. Unless hospitality operations have developed specific strategies for purchasing procedures, there are apt to be mistakes in the purchasing process.

Specifications on Time and Price

Specifications of time and price are equally as important as quality and quantity. Different quality products purchased in different quantity at different times, can vary in cost. Specifications on time include three aspects.

1. An operation has to be able to order products when desired, not at the convenience of the vendors.
2. Vendors must have products available when an order is placed to avoid stockout or substitutions.
3. Vendors must be able to deliver products at the specified time.

Prices depend on quality, quantity, and time specifications. Price fluctuation is a way of life in purchasing and the law of supply and demand will always apply. In certain seasons, some food items will be in abundance and the cost of those items will be more reasonable. At other times, if the supply of such products is relatively scarce and the demand is still high, hospitality operations will have to pay higher prices to secure the product. Therefore, it is imperative that a purchasing agent is aware of new products, the availability of the products that the operation uses, and the price structure of different purveyors. Price specifications are most important when purchasing through a bid process. Most purveyors are honest and supply purchasing agents with accurate price lists; however, some vendors may initially bid a low price to meet a price specification then raise the prices a bit at a time after they have obtained returning business. Thus, it is the purchasing agent's responsibility to ensure that price specifications are followed.

Purchasing Strategies

To control costs as effectively as possible, managers and purchasing agents must develop strategies to protect their organization. Strategies allow all personnel who perform the purchasing task at any level to know what is expected by their organization. Staying within the framework of the strategies will allow the organization to control and reduce costs. Not developing strategies can lead to wasted opportunities, overspending, and financial difficulties for the operation. Overspending can occur in business just as it may occur with personal spending. Certain strategies must be practiced so that the opportunity costs of making decisions can be maximized to the benefit of the organization.

When establishing strategies for purchasing, a manager must first identify the needs of the organization to prevent excessive purchasing and subsequent profit loss. Needs must be specifically defined to prevent waste and control costs. In the hospitality industry some facilities are a long distance from their corporate offices, and supervisors and owners may not frequently visit remote facilities. A list of specific needs can allow a manager to obtain approval by proxy for additional, indirect purchases, which can further reduce the amount of wasted resources.

After the needs of an organization are defined, a manager should establish purchasing strategies to control cost. Following are some strategies that can help control cost during the purchasing function:

- Maximizing Purchases
- Comparing Purveyors
- Comparing Brands
- Comparing Yields
- Taking advantage of cost-effective discounts
- Using unit pricing to compare packages
- Purchasing safe amounts of inventory
- Purchasing labor-saving products
- Comparing cash to credit
- Comparing interest rates
- Reading and understanding contracts
- Being aware of "good deals"
- Dealing with reputable sources in an ethical manner

Maximizing Purchases

To maximize purchases managers must evaluate all available options. Is there a possibility to do co-op buying with another unit member in the same town or vicinity, or is it possible to establish co-op buying with other hospitality operations? Although facilities within an industry must be competitive, competition should not prevent a facility from saving money during purchasing functions. Purchasing in large volumes usually provides additional purchasing power, which may enable operations to obtain products that are common to both facilities at a lower cost. Purchasing in volume also precludes the purveyor from having to make several trips to the same area. Operations can improve their bargaining position by helping to cut the sellers' costs. When buyers implement effective purchasing processes, sellers provide better pricing and service.

Comparing Purveyors

Purchasing managers must be aware of supply and demand as they relate to their purveyor. Because of their purchasing power or specialization, some purveyors may be able to obtain certain products at a much cheaper cost than other purveyors. This, among other reasons, is why an operation must compare different purveyors' prices, quality, service, and consistency. Although obtaining the lowest price is the driving force behind most purchasing decisions, a manager must compare purveyors, as the lowest price may not provide quality and consistency in the long run.

Purveyors' operational standards also need to be compared. If a purveyor does not practice good sanitation habits, a buyer can get dry goods and other products that are close to deterioration or that may be infested with insects or harmful levels of microorganisms. A purveyor's transportation method of delivery has to be evaluated to discern whether it provides timely delivery and is able to maintain products at the required temperature from delivery to storage. Managers must understand the significance of making comparisons, as many extenuating circumstances can make price a less significant factor. An operation can lose guests because of poor quality, stockout, and lack of consistency. Although state and federal regulations help control vendor activities, all vendors must be evaluated and compared carefully.

Comparing Brands

Just as there is a need to compare purveyors, brands must also be compared. When purchasing solely by brands, an operation can often waste a lot of money. Managers have to compare similar products to see whether they fit their needs and whether they provide the same quality and utilization of purpose. An operation may be able to use an alternate brand if it fits the required purpose and provides the desired quality. Often products have to be taste-tested to determine which provide the most desired taste.

In some cases raw products need to be carefully prepared not just for taste but for their holding ability. If holding a product is not a major concern, then a specific brand may not be a requirement. In banquets and catering, however, products are often held in warmers for service at a later time. Certain brands of potatoes can be held a lot longer than other brands of potatoes once they are baked. Some brands of potatoes make superior French fries as compared to other brands. Therefore, it is essential to know a product's intended use to determine which product should be ordered.

Not only is it necessary to determine whether a specific brand is required, but a price analysis must also be obtained whenever possible. The theory that "you get what you pay for" is not always true. One can purchase numerous different brands of aspirin with a large range of prices, only to find that they are basically the same products whether they are name brands or generic. Brands may provide consistency but only need to be used if required. An operation that only uses brand products may limit its choices of purveyors, which could lead to higher prices.

Comparing Yields

It is essential to know the standard yield that will be received from particular items. Knowledge of standard yield allows a manager to order the correct amount of products and to discern whether the pricing of a product is correct. The as purchased (AP) weight of products can be totally different from the usable portion (UP). Production loss from trimming and/or cooking can increase the cost of servable portions. For example, a 9-pound pork loin costs $4.85 per pound. A total of 15 ounces is lost in boning and trimming and an additional

24 ounces are lost through shrinkage during the roasting period. The cost of a 3-ounce serving can be calculated as follows:

$ 4.85	Price per pound
× 9	Pounds as purchased (AP)
$43.65	Total cost

Per-ounce price AP: $4.85 ÷ 16 = $0.3031
3-ounce portion cost: $0.3031 × 3 = $0.9094, or $0.91 (rounded)

16	Ounces per pound
× 9	Pounds purchased
144	Ounces purchased

144	Ounces purchased
− 39	Ounces lost (15 ounces from boning and trimming and 24 ounces from shrinkage during roasting)
105	Usable portions (UP) ounces

$43.65	Total cost
105	UP ounces
0.415	Cost per ounce of cooked meat

$0.415	Cost per ounce
× 3	Ounces per serving portion
$1.245	Cost per 3-ounce serving

Accounting for production loss, the cost of a 3-ounce serving is $1.25 rather than $0.91, a difference of 37.36%.

Taking Advantage of Cost-Effective Discounts

The majority of households in the United States understand the importance of discounts. For instance, if one takes advantage of the numerous coupons included in the local Sunday newspaper, the savings will more than offset the cost of the paper. Similarly, vendors sometimes offer discounts to hospitality facilities when marketing a product. A manager does not want to be so set on a particular brand that he or she never takes advantage of a discount. Some discounts may not be cost effective due to the nature of the product or due to the volume required to qualify for the discount; but, if a discount is indeed cost effective and an operation is not locked into a contract for a certain product with a purveyor, it may be smart to take advantage of the discount. Although a discount may be financially advantageous, one must still ensure that quality and consistency are maintained.

Using Unit Pricing to Compare Packages

When evaluating brands or other products, the unit price should be used as comparison. This is similar to the AP and UP example discussed earlier. From one package or container to another, one may pay one or two cents more per ounce for the same product. The amount of daily utilization also plays a part in the decision-making process. At times, it is important to use a convenient size of a product even if it is more expensive, as the amount of labor saved by using a convenient size can offset the cost of a more expensive product. For example, four 1-gallon jugs of salad dressing are used for banquets, while individual bottles are used for the restaurant. To purchase individual bottles to then be poured in bowls and placed on banquet tables just does not make sense. It is often more expensive per ounce and is more labor intensive opening individual bottles than opening a 1-gallon jug. This is why an operation must ensure that labor and utilization are also considered when evaluating unit pricing.

Purchasing Safe Amounts of Inventory

Storage and the amount of money that can be tied up in inventory are two major concerns when evaluating discounts and unit pricing. A vast amount of inventory increases the possibility for waste, theft, and deterioration; however, an operation does not want to be confronted with the problem of stockout, as this can cause an operation to lose guests. The situation that every organization must strive for is to have just enough inventory to prevent stockout situations. There are several methods of stocking inventory, including just in time, economic quality ordered, and simple par levels. The par stock level method is a useful tool for most hospitality operations.

Par stock level is the level of inventory per item that is needed to operate effectively until the next order. Par stock level is established to prevent the presence of too much inventory and to prevent stockout. It also has to be established for the average guest count and usage of products. In Figure 6–1 a restaurant is trying to determine an optional par level for an 8-ounce frozen chicken breast. The restaurant orders every Wednesday for a Thursday delivery. On the average, it sells 30 chicken entrees per day. If a 5% safety margin is desired, the restaurant will need to order 110.25 pounds per week as the par level.

Figure 6–1   *Setting Par Level for Frozen Chicken Breasts*

Step 1
Amount used per week
30 orders × 7 days = 210 orders

Step 2
Set a level of safety, such as 5%
210 × 5% = 10.5 orders

Step 3
Establish par level
210.0   Orders estimated use
+10.5   Orders safety margin
——————
220.5   Orders, or 221 8-ounce pieces

Par stock may differ during certain times of the year; therefore, products that do not sell nearly as much during certain months need to be identified. An abundance of products allowed to sit in inventory is money that could have been generating interest in a financial institution. Therefore, if an operation deals with a large volume of a product and during certain times of the year sales of this product are reduced, the inventory level should also be reduced. With regard to foodservice operations, a reduction in quality of a product may occur during slow sales periods, which may prompt further reduction in the inventory of a particular product.

Purchasing Labor-Saving Products

Whenever a purchasing decision is to be made, a value analysis must be completed to determine what effect the purchase will have on labor. For example, should an operation purchase a slicer and invest in labor costs to have sliced carrots on the menu or should it purchase sliced carrots from a produce distributor? The hospitality industry is a labor-intensive industry and lowering the cost of labor can often provide an operation with a competitive advantage. The type of equipment purchased and even the placement of equipment can increase or decrease the cost of labor. If the quality of a product or service will not be affected, then the quality of the equipment and how it will affect labor cost should be primary concerns. The types of products and equipment available are important in assisting a manager in cost control.

Comparing Cash to Credit

When making purchases, an organization must decide whether to pay cash or to use credit. Operations must bear in mind that a lack of working capital is one of the main reasons for business failure within the hospitality field. Quite often purveyors allow an operation 15 to 30 days to pay an outstanding invoice without charging any interest. While late charges or interest should be avoided, an operation should always try to hold funds as long as possible to accumulate bank interest. Additionally, if an operation is able to use its cash to generate more profit than the cost of the interest, then paying on credit may be cost effective. Whenever an operation uses credit instead of cash, the situation must be weighed carefully. The opportunity cost of using cash or credit should be well understood. An organization usually pays a higher price over time when something is purchased on credit or may receive a discount if cash is used.

Comparing Interest Rates

If an operation decides to use credit, then the amount of interest that the operation has to pay must be carefully examined. Research must be completed to determine whether it would be more advantageous to use the credit offered by the purveyor or whether it would be wiser to borrow the funds from a financial institution. Additionally, the length of credit terms must be evaluated. A company may be able to obtain a lower rate if the funds are to be used for a limited period of time. Because interest rates can change it is important to evaluate the rates and the availability of money.

Reading and Understanding Contracts

Because interest rates and the availability of money can fluctuate, individuals signing contracts should be well informed. Personnel should not sign contracts or sign for products unless they are authorized to do so and fully understand the terms of the contract. All too often in the hospitality field, anyone that is available when products are delivered will sign for the products. Because of this poor practice, products are sometimes not properly inspected or are received when not ordered. Some sales personnel may attempt to take advantage of inexperienced managers by stating that an operation can "sample" a product for a certain period of time free of charge; however, the managers are not informed that they will be charged if certain contract stipulations are not met. Other unethical activities can occur if managers allow anyone to sign for products or if managers sign contracts that they do not understand.

Being Aware of "Good Deals"

Receiving products that have not been ordered and sampling or testing products can cost an organization money. Always be aware of deals that appear to be too good to be true, as they usually are. Because hospitality managers deal with a large number of employees and guests, some unethical salespeople may be able to catch a manager off guard during a time when he or she is too busy to think rationally and can often persuade a manager to purchase or try products that the operation does not need. Managers should insist that salespeople make appointments, as many sales personnel purposely visit facilities at inopportune times just to take advantage of the moment. Managers must take the attitude that when in doubt, it is better to say no than to make a mistake. Any money wasted during the purchasing process, no matter how small, can affect costs, and thus profits.

Dealing with Reputable Sources in an Ethical Manner

When it comes to the purchasing function, there is much room for unethical conduct on the parts of both sellers and buyers. Purchasing personnel at all levels must be made aware that they must protect the interest of the company at all times. Because of the ease of misconduct and collusion in this area, policy and procedures should be implemented to try to limit unethical activities. Additionally, a code of ethics should be in writing, as people often need a foundation to fall back on when there is a gray area involved. Employees should be aware that they should not participate in questionable situations.

Other business organizations, personal contacts, and government agencies can assist in making good business decisions of all kinds. With the increasing amount of technology available comes a steady production of money-saving, time-saving, and labor-saving devices; and trade shows can provide a wealth of information concerning such devices.

Before making purchases of any kind, a manager should talk with as many business contacts as possible. Any additional information that can be obtained pertaining to vendors, equipment, or products often can prevent an organization from making costly mistakes.

Reports of government organizations and other private organizations should be reviewed before making any major purchasing decisions. Independent testing organizations, such as the Underwriters Laboratories (UL), should be used. The UL is a business organization that tests products for electrical and fire safety. Items that pass its tests are authorized to display the UL symbol. Foodservice operations should look for equipment that has been approved by the National Sanitation Foundation (NSF), an organization that provides sanitation classification. Organizations such as these assist a facility in purchasing reputable products.

Once purchasing strategies have been established, management must ensure that the established strategies are implemented. Purchasing strategies are standards that must be controlled in order to control purchasing costs and to make an organization profitable in the long run.

Purchasing Systems

Along with establishing strategies, cost control in purchasing involves the consideration of some basic alternatives. Every purchasing situation usually has one or more possible alternative. Alternatives revolve around the following questions:

- Is it possible to make the item instead of purchasing the item?
- Is it necessary to purchase a particular brand?
- Is it possible to delay the purchase?
- Should the item be paid for in cash?
- Who is the most reliable supplier when considering price, quality, consistency, and service?

Purchasing Directs

Directs present a problem for owners and managers of large facilities, as these items are usually inexpensive and do not go into storage. Directs can be specialty items that are purchased for a particular function and are put into production as they are received. The items are paid for, but because the items are immediately utilized, they are not entered in the inventory book. If the products are not totally utilized the excess can easily be wasted or taken by employees. Directs can be food items but can also be office supplies or other dry goods. Quite often kitchen personnel or managers order products for personal use and state that the items were used as garnish or for some other type of unaccountable usage. Because directs are not put into storage the accountability for such items can be lost quickly. This is why it is essential to establish which items should be purchased on a regular basis.

An additional problem with purchasing directs is the utilization of corporate purchasing cards, which are credit cards issued by an organization to individuals who perform purchasing functions. Corporate purchasing cards are used to reduce administrative costs for low-dollar direct items. While administrative costs can be reduced there is a certain amount of risk and loss of control associated with the cards. In an attempt to control the utilization of purchasing cards, some organizations have limited the number of transactions per card, type of transactions, and value of transactions. Even by implementing these types of restrictions, it is difficult for corporations that are spread out over large geographical distances to maintain control over the utilization of such cards; therefore, ensuring that the cards are not misused really becomes a managerial control issue at the local level.

Buying Methods

Controlling cost during purchasing is essential to maintain cost overall and to maximize profit. Buying methods must be evaluated to determine which is best for the operation and for the products that are required. Some buying methods that should be evaluated are:

- Cost-plus buying
- Bid buying
- Stockless purchasing
- Standing orders
- Co-op buying
- One-stop shopping

Cost-plus buying is a competitive means of purchasing products. This method of buying allows the buyer to pay for products at an agreed upon percentage above what the supplier paid for the products. Cost-plus buyiny is usually only available to large operations and is not always a preferred method of suppliers, as they have to provide cost information to buyers. However, it provides buyers with a better understanding of the cost of products.

Bid buying is usually less attractive to suppliers than cost-plus buying. While cost-plus buying allows buyers to see the supplier's cost of a product, bid buying may actually enable a buyer to obtain the lowest price. In bid buying a hospitality operation publishes a written notice of the desired product. This notice usually includes the specifications, amount required, and other details. Sellers reply in writing by stating their price and conditions of sale. Bids are usually opened in public and the lowest bid may be awarded the contract. Bid buying often calls for long-term price agreements, which can be a disadvantage to suppliers. This is especially true for the produce market, as weather conditions can cause tremendous fluctuations in produce prices. Once a bid has been accepted managers should watch for "low balling" in which a supplier may present an initial low price to obtain a bid and later try to increase price or reduce quality.

Many international companies as well as local companies use stockless purchasing. This method of buying is often used to purchase large quantities of products, and the shipment is either delivered in its entirety or placed in storage for the supplier to deliver requested amounts as needed. This form of forward buying can be convenient in overseas areas or for operations that have their own commissaries. Stockless purchasing can be used if a buyer anticipates that the price of a specific product is about to increase substantially or that a product may become limited.

Standing orders are a convenient way of purchasing products and passing some of the labor cost of taking inventory and stocking onto the seller. With this method a driver stops by the facility, takes an inventory of products, and brings the level of products back to the agreed upon par stock. This method is usually used for meat, bread, and the like. From a control standpoint, management must continue to evaluate par level as well as monitor the freshness of products. In addition, security becomes a concern whenever individuals are allowed access to certain areas.

Co-op buying is not often used because of the competitiveness of the industry. However, operations located in small towns that use the same suppliers should consider co-op buying to try to reduce cost. Co-op buying allows several small operations to band together to increase their purchasing power in order to obtain lower prices. Establishing such a purchasing system may take a lot of coordinating, but if the end results reduce cost without reducing quality, then the decision to use co-op buying should be evaluated.

Hospitality operators are becoming used to the convenience of one-stop shopping. One vendor providing all products reduces the cost of ordering and the amount of paperwork that must be maintained. It is also cost effective in reducing labor and paperwork in receiving. However, there are disadvantages to this process, including a loss of flexibility in product selection and lack of product comparison. Therefore, what a hospitality operation actually pays for in one-stop shopping is convenience. Managers should still compare prices with those of other vendors so that prices can be negotiated with the main supplier.

Purchasing Furniture, Fixtures, and Equipment

The purchasing of furniture, fixtures, and equipment is a difficult area to control. Although it may appear that these nonconsumable items do not pose a major control problem, it is simply not true. Because of the larger cost of these items, the control of these items represents a challenge to managers and owners. It has been on the news that high-ranking government officials purchased furniture for their homes using the government's budget. When it comes to purchasing these large, expensive items, a manager must be concerned with quality but must also have an even greater concern as to why the items are being purchased. Not only can inferior products be purchased but usable products can sometimes be intentionally disposed of to warrant the purchase.

It would be an extremely expensive venture if a district manager controls five or six operations and convinces the owners to change tables, chairs, or lighting. Replacement of such items can also open a multitude of opportunities for theft, collusion, and other unethical activities, which may include:

- Replacing or discarding usable equipment
- Discarding equipment with salvageable parts
- Improperly disposing of old equipment
- Intentionally breaking or marring equipment
- Discarding easily repaired equipment
- Purchasing substandard equipment

It is just as important to account for old equipment as it is for new equipment. All too often old equipment is stacked in a storeroom or simply thrown away. If a piece of equipment is purchased to replace an older piece that is still usable, the older piece should either be sent to another unit so that it can be utilized or sold to a used equipment company. Unless some type of trade-in has been agreed upon, old equipment should not be given to the delivery personnel who are delivering the new equipment as an easy way of disposing of it. Delivery personnel who offer their services usually take the equipment and sell it to a used equipment company for cash. Equipment must be properly disposed of and any monetary value from the equipment should go back to the operation.

Equipment can be intentionally marred or made inoperable. Managers may pursue this avenue in order to get a new piece of equipment, and employees may make a piece of equipment inoperable because they do not want to use the equipment or clean the equipment. The need to purchase expensive items must be well documented by the manager who is making the request. The same holds true for the repair of these items.

Equipment repair is also a form of purchasing. The same efforts must be made to ensure the best option. It behooves owners to find out if the repairs in question are necessary and what company will actually make the repairs. One way to prevent substandard repair service is to employ service contracts so that an official company with the right credentials bids on the contract and makes the repairs. Other bids should be kept on hand to ensure that the most cost-effective repair company is used.

Inexpensive Purchases

It is obvious that the cost of major purchases must be reviewed because of the financial investment involved, but do not think for one moment that inexpensive purchases do not warrant concern. Because products in the hospitality industry are easily consumed by all, they present a particular problem for theft, and managers cannot afford to take the attitude that some purchases are insignificant. All purchases are important—some are just more expensive than others.

Summary

The purchasing function is extremely important. Any money that is saved during the purchasing process goes directly to the bottom line. Because of the importance of the purchasing activity, managerial training programs should place more emphasis on this aspect during training.

Before purchases can be made, an organization must establish the needs of the operation, and then purchasing strategies should be established to provide guidelines for all individuals who will be involved in the purchasing process. Concern should be given to the maximization of purchasing, the importance of comparing purveyors and brands, and the advantage of discounts. Additionally, unit pricing, the amount of inventory, labor-saving devices, and considerations of financing must be analyzed. The significance of ethical conduct must also be established. This becomes increasingly important when purchasing expensive equipment or when having equipment repaired.

Managers must also be aware of several alternatives that will be presented during a purchasing decision. These alternatives should be evaluated, and managers should be restricted from purchasing any products that are not necessary regardless of the expense.

Mangers have to be trained to understand how closely related the purchasing function is to generating a profit. If money is wasted through purchases, it will take a vast amount of sales to offset the loss. Also, mangers must be aware that theft and collusion have the greatest possibility of occurring on a large scale within the purchasing function.

Review Exercises

1. When purchasing products, what method(s) can be used to reduce cost?
   a. co-op buying
   b. purchasing in volume
   c. comparing purveyors
   d. all of the above

2. What method of theft is more apt to take place during purchasing and is difficult to detect?
   a. ordering the wrong size
   b. ordering a lower quality
   c. underpurchasing
   d. overpurchasing

3. In a foodservice operation, who should be involved in deciding the specifications of the products?
   a. chef, manager, and receiving clerks
   b. chef, manager, and servers
   c. chef, receiving clerks, and servers
   d. manager, chef, and storeroom clerk

4. What document should be used to retrieve items from the storeroom?
   a. invoice
   b. receiving report
   c. requisition
   d. credit memo

5. How many requests for bids should be obtained when purchasing large quantities of products?
   a. none, as this is not necessary
   b. at least 1
   c. at least 2
   d. at least 3

6. When purchasing fresh fish, what is the most important concern?
   a. size
   b. quantity
   c. quality
   d. price

7. Which factor(s) should be considered when pricing products?
   a. transportation
   b. time
   c. brand name
   d. all of the above

8. If a guest requests a bottle of alcohol that the restaurant has sold out, the manager should do one of the following except:
   a. send an employee to a liquor store
   b. contact the vendor
   c. explain to the guest that they are out of stock
   d. ask the guest if he or she will accept a substitute

9. Before using a convenience product, management must:
   a. test the product
   b. ask vendors questions about the product
   c. perform a value analysis
   d. give samples to guests

10. The UP price is usually _____ the AP price.
    a. the same as
    b. higher than
    c. lower than
    d. incomparable to

11. From the list of purchasing strategies discussed in this chapter, describe five of them and explain how you would ensure that the purchasing process is accomplished using those five strategies.

12. Describe how cooking and trimming can increase the price of a product.

13. Make a list of five topbrand items and compare these items with other lesser known or generic brands.

14. List five specifications that may be required for apples used in a recipe for fruit compote.

15. Define and explain five buying methods that maximize the purchasing function.

16. Name one method of collusion that could be used between purveyors and managers during the purchasing function.

Examination Type Problems

For the following examination questions, assume that you are the owner of a 300-seat full-service restaurant in a medium-priced hotel.

1. Make a list of five purchasing strategies that you would implement for your manager to follow.

2. If a request was submitted to you for the purchase of an automatic potato peeler, what actions would you take before approving the request?

3. Name two aspects of purchasing that provide an opportunity for collusion.

4. What action would you take before changing brands of a product that your kitchen uses in large quantities on a weekly basis?

5. What items entering the kitchen might be considered directs?

6. List three purchasing situations for which you may require a value analysis to be completed before making a decision.

Case Study

The Case Study Hotel has a lounge that sells alcoholic beverages to guests. As the restaurant manager you are also responsible for the lounge. You have submitted a request for new chairs for the lounge and would also like to offer complimentary finger food during happy hour twice a week. You believe that the present lounge chairs, though they are in good repair, are uncomfortable, so guests do not stay very long. You also estimate that more people would drop in after work on Monday and Thursday if they could have free snacks with their drinks.

You realize this is a simple request but you also realize how the purchasing function can affect the bottom line.

1. How would you secure the specifications for the lounge chairs and what would those specifications be?
2. Knowing that the finger foods are provided as free items, write a menu of finger foods for one day and determine the general quality specifications of such items.
3. What purchasing method would you use for the furniture and the finger food? Explain.

7
Receiving

Learning Objectives

After completing this chapter, you should be able to:

- explain the importance of the layout and location of a receiving area.
- understand the importance of training personnel in the receiving function.
- establish a list of equipment that is a necessary part of the receiving process.
- provide an example of the procedures that should be used in the receiving process.
- list the basic forms and documents that should be used during receiving.
- establish procedures for handling credit memos.

- describe activities that safeguard the receiving process.
- describe methods that can be used during the receiving process to examine the quality of different products.
- explain why delivery times are essential to an operation.
- describe procedures to be used when collusion is suspected.
- explain the importance of the evaluation and receipt of nonfood supplies.

The Receiving Process: An Overview

Once the needed products have been purchased for an operation, the next step in the control cycle is to ensure that the correct products are received and meet the specified quality, quantity, delivery time, and price. To control the receiving process, the individual receiving products must have the necessary paperwork and documentation, the equipment, and the necessary training for receiving the products. Receiving personnel must have a copy of the specifications to ensure that the quality, form, shape, and size of a product are correct. They must also have a copy of the purchase order to compare the quality, quantity, and the price that was negotiated. The receiving process makes a portion of an organization's assets vulnerable. It is important to understand that the person who requests the product, receives the product, and stores the product are usually not one in the same. These duties must be separated or an operation's control standards may be compromised.

Even when ordering products from the most reputable suppliers, one has to be aware that some delivery personnel attempt to "go into business" for themselves. From time to time receiving personnel must examine the second and third tiers of steaks in a case to see if substitutions have occurred. The truck driver may have placed the higher quality product on top and switched some of the others. A driver can do the same thing with tomatoes and other produce, placing bruised products on bottom layers. Always lift crates to check if juice is seeping through. Every effort must be made to protect the welfare of the operation.

A useful control tool for individuals receiving products is the requisition of credit memos. Managers understand that when they go to a bank to cash a check, they should count the money issued by the teller and expect accountability if the amount is short. Yet these same managers review thousands of dollars worth of products and never bother to count anything. For many hospitality managers and employees, products do not equate money, and this attitude is often displayed when deliveries are short. Receiving personnel have to be aware that all products should be treated the same as money since they represent an expenditure by the operation. If one cashes a check and is given less than the amount of the check, one would expect to receive the rest of the funds or documentation as to why the remainder was not given. Yet when a delivery person is short a case of a product and says that he or she will bring it next time, hospitality managers often accept this without documentation, even though the undelivered product may be worth hundreds of dollars. Any time a product is rejected or a delivery is short, managers should request that the driver sign a credit memo for that particular item. When the driver leaves, the manager should call vendor to inform them of the credit memo and the circumstances involved. It is not good practice to file a credit memo with the purchase request or the invoice. A credit memo should be filed separately or kept in a file folder on the desk so that it is not forgotten. After the shortage or discrepancy has been corrected, the credit memo can be placed in the regular files.

Storerooms in hospitality facilities are full of products that were mistakenly received and cannot be used. If the wrong size product is delivered or if a product was ordered by mistake, try to return the product to the vendor for credit. Also, try to sell any equipment that will not be used. The longer an asset is not used, the more it becomes unusable due to age. Old equipment takes up valuable space and does not make money for the operation. Another option is interunit transfer in which another facility of the same operation may make use of unwanted equipment or inventory. Interunit transfers allow franchises that are in close geographical proximity to utilize each other's resources more effectively and efficiently. For instance, if Unit A is short of a case of French fries, it can call upon Unit B, which carries the same types of inventory, and request an interunit transfer of a case of fries. In this manner, the same quality product can be guaranteed and the unit that is short will not have to pay premium prices at local grocery stores. The accounting department simply does the paperwork and deducts the cost of the case of French fries from the cost of goods sold from Unit B and charges the cost to Unit A.

Most importantly, do not sign for or receive products that were not ordered. Check all products against the purchase request. Compare specifications, quantities, and prices. If all aspects of the delivery are satisfactory and everything checks out, sign for the products. If the operation has established a particular time for deliveries to be made and they are not delivered at the prescribed times, this should be discussed with the driver and the supplier. Receiving personnel should not receive deliveries when they do not have the time to properly inspect all products. Products represent valuable financial resources and must be treated with the same amount of concern as money. Making sure of the exactness of products is a step in the operational control cycle that cannot be understated. This point in the receiving process is where a great deal of theft and mismanagement occur. Theft may occur in an operation because of incapable or dishonest receiving personnel, delivery personnel, collusion between the two, or managers who just do not take appropriate measures to ensure that receiving is done correctly. If other establishments do a better job of inspecting and receiving products, delivery personnel may give them better quality products, because poor quality products will be noticed and rejected during the receiving process. If items are ordered in bundles of 40 or 50, such as towels, receiving personnel can count one bundle, weigh that bundle, and have a measurement to quickly compare the rest of the bundles. If no attempt is made to account for items, and delivery personnel discover this, every delivery may end up missing one or two items from each count. Taking one or two items, such as a steak, towel, or sheet, from a case can cost an operation hundreds of dollars a year. No business can survive this type of consistent leakage.

Layout of a Receiving Area

The layout of a receiving area must be operational and designed for control, security, and convenient access to storage areas for efficiency and the prevention of product deterioration. Because of the costs of products, receiving must be given a great deal of priority. It is essential that delivery hours be established for times when receiving personnel have ample opportunity to inspect products before signing for them.

Large operations receive products in large quantities, therefore management may want to have surveillance cameras strategically located so that the receiving area can be monitored. Many operations use surveillance cameras now that such equipment is becoming more affordable. Employers are finding that the presence of surveillance cameras can act as a deterrent in preventing theft. Most employees are less apt to steal or abuse property and products because of the presence of surveillance cameras. If a facility is of significant size, then a surveillance camera may be cost effective. It is one of the leading methods of trying to reduce theft and maintain security for products, employees, and guests.

Training Receiving Personnel

It is essential that receiving personnel be highly trained in the expectations and specifications of products received by a hospitality facility. It is bad business practice that most hospitality operations do not understand the importance of having trained personnel involved in the purchasing and receiving functions. The industry spends a great deal of money to train managers in operational procedures; however, the training of managers in the basics of purchasing and receiving products has been overlooked. In hotel operations alone, about 40% of all income goes back into purchasing in the form of inventory and other direct operating expenses. Receiving personnel should be able to recognize products, the quality of products, and the different grades of products. If receiving personnel are not trained, then some delivery personnel, as well as vendors, may take advantage of these operations. The majority of all business personnel are honest individuals; however, mistakes occur and receiving personnel must be able to protect the interest of the hospitality organization. Large operations usually have qualified receiving personnel; small operations often allow anyone to sign for products when they are delivered. Even small operations should ensure that individuals signing for products should have at least a basic knowledge of the products that the organization receives. Personnel must be trained to ask certain questions pertaining to the origin of products. Items such as shellfish and certain produce can have different levels of usefulness and can vary substantially in price depending on their origin.

Receiving Equipment

Receiving personnel must have the proper tools and equipment to work quickly and store items expediently. Such equipment should remain in the receiving area. Because of the need to store and secure products as quickly as possible, receiving personnel should not have to run back and forth to the kitchen and other areas to locate thermometers and other pieces of equipment. If personnel have to search for equipment, there are times when products stay unsecured too long or are allowed to deteriorate. At a minimum, receiving personnel should have the following equipment: thermometers, scales, rulers, knives, and clippers.

Receiving personnel must have thermometers to check temperatures of food products. The temperature of all refrigerated and frozen products should be checked to see if they have thawed. Food should be rejected if it is above the required temperature.

Scales are required to weigh products to verify their accuracy. Weighing products is of utmost importance, especially in today's computer age. A computerized label that indicates that a box of meat weighs 56.38 pounds may not be accurate. Computers make mistakes, just as human beings do. A computerized label is not 100% guaranteed. In some cases, weighing products is not enough, they should also be counted. If an operation ordered 150 two-pound lobsters, it behooves the receiving agent to count and weigh the merchandise. Even if only one lobster is missing, the food cost will be wrong.

Receiving personnel must also have rulers. Items such as tomatoes, apples, oranges, and potatoes must be the size you ordered or kitchen personnel may have to double portions to make up the difference. Correct size is important as well as using items for garnish. Rulers are also used to measure the thickness of fat on cuts of meat.

Knives should be available to cut into samples of produce to see if they have been affected by bad weather conditions, especially if temperatures have reached freezing. Lemons, limes, and peaches in particular should be cut and examined.

Clippers or other appropriate tools should be available to open cases. Frequently, expensive kitchen knives are used to open cases, and as a result of this, the tips of fine knives are often broken.

Procedures Involved in the Receiving Process

Receiving personnel must pay attention to detail during the receiving process as prices of certain products can vary from shipment to shipment. Fresh produce presents an ongoing problem because constant changes in the market not only affect price but supply and quality as well. Additionally, packing practices differ throughout the country and items can actually fall below their grade before they are delivered. For this reason receiving personnel must be concerned with the condition of the product when it is delivered and not just the grade of the product that was ordered.

Receiving personnel should be prepared to receive items, which means that they should have purchase orders and specifications available. Invoices received from the delivery person should be compared to purchase orders, and any discrepancies must be noted up front. After all products are received the shipment should be signed for, and the forms should be forwarded to the purchasing office.

Blind Receiving

Blind receiving is not used as frequently as it should be, as it is an excellent means of ensuring that receiving personnel have to count or weigh products. When using blind receiving, the areas on the receiving report that contain item quantity, description, and comments are left blank, requiring that receiving personal identify, count, weigh, and evaluate products (see Figure 7–1). Prices can also be omitted so that receiving personnel have to ensure that prices are correct for the products received.

Blind receiving is one method of implementing correct practices, but professionalism during the receiving process is a much more effective means of keeping employees honest. Professionalism and attention to detail should al-

Figure 7–1   *Blind Receiving Report*

Quantity	Item Description	Comments	Unit Price

Supplier _____

Date _____
Delivery Date _____
Salesperson _____

ways be at their highest levels whenever conducting any business activity that involves money. All activities must be documented and product transfers should be signed for to prevent any misunderstanding concerning what occurred during a specific transaction or delivery.

Forms and Documents Used during Receiving

Once a delivery arrives, all necessary forms should be reviewed for any discrepancies in price, quantity, or quality. If the delivery differs from the purchase request, it should be questioned at this time. This may prevent a waste of time and resources in unloading and having to reload the delivery because it was rejected even before further inspection. If no problems are noted upon arrival, then the products can be unloaded and inspected. All forms should be completed after inspection. Forms and documents that receiving personnel should have on hand are:

- Standard purchase specifications
- Purchase orders
- Delivery invoices
- Credit memos
- Receiving reports
- Tags

Standard purchase specifications should be available for quick reference by receiving personnel. Although receiving personnel may be extremely familiar with certain items, specifications should be on hand, as some items may be ordered infrequently or for special occasions. Additionally, the chef or management may change specifications and receiving personnel may not be as familiar with these changes. Figure 7–2 is an example specifications sheet.

Another important form is the purchase order (PO), which is used to indicate what deliveries are expected, to record the products ordered, and to standardize the information about those products (see Figure 7–3). The quantity and quality delivered should be compared to the purchase order and receiving report.

Any discrepancies should be annotated on the invoice, which the delivery person should initial. Credit memos should be issued for shortages. Once the delivery is evaluated to be satisfactory, the individual responsible for receiving the products or services should sign the invoice, a copy of which is given to the delivery person to confirm that products or services have been received and accepted. The receiving report should be completed at this point. The receiving report provides the accounting department with a detailed breakdown of what has been received on a daily basis (see Figure 7–4).

After a delivery has been accepted, products should be tagged and placed into storage as quickly as possible. A tag is a card that records the price of the product, the date it was delivered, and other pertinent information such as

Figure 7–2   *Specification Sheet*

Ingredient #	Description	Group	Vendor	Product Code	Pack Size
75	Onions, white, raw, jumbo/ea	Produce	A	75	Case/50#
178	Tofu, raw, hard, red	Produce	A	178	Case/12#
204	Fish, grouper, 2–15# avg, raw/oz	Meat	B	***	Pound
211	Fish, salmon, Atlantic, 6–8# avg, raw/oz	Meat	B	***	Pound
221	Oysters, raw, select/ea	Meat	B	***	Case/100
235	Chicken bones, raw/oz	Meat	C	***	Case/40#
240	Turkey, tom, raw, 16–20# avg/oz	Meat	C	***	Pound
248	Crab, stone, claws, raw, 6–8 ct/oz	Meat	B	***	Pound
267	Beef, ground, fine, chuck, 80/20	Meat	C	11369	Pound
305	Peppers, chili, cascabel, raw	Produce	A	305	Pound
317	Tortilla, corn, white, 3"/ea	Grocery	D	***	Case/12
348	Jelly, grape	Grocery	E	4184461	Case/6
398	Tea bag, iced, (96) 1 oz	Grocery	E	4202255	Case/96
425	Oil, canola	Grocery	C	68368	Case/2
504	Pepper, black, ground, pure	Grocery	E	5229323	Case/6#
524	Chocolate, dark, shavings	Grocery	F	***	Bag/4.4#
561	Cream, vanilla, pastry/oz	Grocery	F	***	Case/13.5
576	Cookie dough, chocolate chunk/ea	Grocery	E	2392355	Case/200
615	Tortellini, cheese/ea	Grocery	E	1614072	Case/800
622	Peas, sugar snap, frozen, stir-fry	Grocery	E	1399013	Case/12
708	Chorizo/oz	Meat	C	***	Case/2
726	Quail, semi-boneless, European-style/4 oz	Meat	C	***	Case/24
739	Shrimp, headless, shell-on, 50/60, frozen/oz	Meat	B	***	Pound
787	Fish, snapper, raw, skinless, fillet	Meat	B	***	Pound
797	Frog legs, raw, jumbo, 2/3 pp/oz	Meat	B	***	Pound
815	Pork, ham, cured, whole, 9–11# avg, oz	Meat	C	***	Pound
832	Pork, ham, prosciutto/oz	Meat	G	832	Pound
849	Lettuce, kale, green/head	Produce	H	849	Case/24
999	Fondant, prepared/oz	Grocery	E	9378365	Case/50#

Date_____ Page_____

Units per Pack	Amount	Measure	Price per Packs	Units	On-hand Packs	Units	Actual Value
50	1.00	Pound	25.00	0.50	0	12	9.01
12	1.00	Pound	0.00	0.00	3	9	42.63
1	1.00	Pound	5.95	5.95	15	0	89.25
1	1.00	Pound	2.90	2.90	6	0	17.40
100	1.00	Each	9.95	0.10	0	10	0.00
40	1.00	Pound	6.00	0.15	0	2	0.50
1	1.00	Pound	0.85	0.85	13	0	11.05
1	1.00	Pound	6.99	6.99	3	0	20.97
1	1.00	Pound	1.29	1.29	10	0	12.90
1	1.00	Pound	3.25	3.25	4	0	13.00
12	1.00	Each	0.15	0.01	1	0	0.15
6	1.00	No. 10 can	28.20	4.70	0	1	4.70
96	1.00	Each	14.76	0.15	3	0	44.28
2	2.50	Liter	29.41	14.71	2	0	58.82
6	1.00	Pound	33.08	5.51	0	1	5.52
1	4.40	Pound	24.21	24.21	3	0	72.63
1	13.50	Pound	32.50	32.50	1	0	32.50
200	1.00	Each	30.84	0.15	1	0	30.84
800	1.00	Each	22.50	0.03	3	0	73.26
12	2.00	Pound	30.00	2.50	0	1	2.50
2	5.00	Pound	21.90	10.95	1	0	21.90
24	1.00	Each	45.41	1.89	5	0	227.0
1	1.00	Pound	6.15	6.15	4	0	24.60
1	1.00	Pound	10.65	10.65	6	0	63.90
1	1.00	Pound	4.75	4.75	5	0	23.75
1	1.00	Pound	2.19	2.19	104	0	232.5
1	1.00	Pound	5.55	5.55	6	0	33.30
24	1.00	Each	16.80	0.70	2	6	34.09
50	1.00	Pound	23.45	0.47	1	0	23.47

Figure 7-3 *Purchase Order*

Date _____ Acct Code _____ Dept _____ Order Date _____
Company #1 _____ PO # _____
Company #2 _____ Del. Date _____
Company #3 _____

Item #	Qty.	Description	Co. Quotes 1	Co. Quotes 2	Co. Quotes 3	Item Cost	Item Total
1							
2							
3							
4							
5							
6							
7							
8							
9							
10							
11							
12							
13							
14							
15							

Subtotal
Shipping
Tax
Total

Special Instructions:

Purpose & Benefits:

Dept. Manager _____ Date _____   Purch. Manager _____ Date _____

Dir. of Finance _____ Date _____   Dept. Head _____ Date _____

1-Business Office   2-Originating Dept.   3- Purchasing

Figure 7–4   *Receiving Report*

Supplier _____   Date _____
         _____   Delivery Date _____
         _____   Salesperson _____
         _____

Quantity	Item Description	Comments	Unit Price
12 cases	Juice, tomato		11.99
4 cases	Mayonnaise	Heavy duty	17.25
6 cases	Milk, nonfat, dry		53.70
1	Puff pastry dough	Sheet/12	25.51
12	Soup base, chicken		62.42
2	Sugar substitute		14.89
13 pounds	Ham	Round	19.37
9 pounds	Turkey breast	Smoked	26.91
6 cases	Butter, 90		53.49
36 cases	Butter, solids		122.06

count or weight. Figure 7–5 shows an example of a product tag for meat. Tagging aids in first in first out (FIFO) procedures, which help prevent food deterioration. Less food spoilage also assists in maintaining sanitary conditions in storage areas. Placing prices on product tags expedites the inventory process and may reduce theft as well, as employees may be less apt to steal items when they know that management is able to quantify them. Price perception can often reinforce the concept that food is money.

Figure 7–5 *Meat Tag*

No. 15900

Cut _____

Value _____

Weight _____

Date _____

Procedures for Handling Credit Memos

The proper handling of credit memos is essential to preventing waste and theft within the operation. Storerooms throughout the hospitality industry are full of products that cannot be used because someone ordered or accepted the wrong product or the wrong size.

Credit memos should be requested under the following circumstances:

- The wrong product is delivered
- A product that is on the invoice is not delivered
- The total amount of a requested product is not delivered
- Ao product is rejected for any reason

Do not allow delivery personnel to say that they will bring credited products or a credit memo on the next delivery. Too often, managers are in a hurry or become so familiar with delivery personnel that they accept promises of delivery without documentation. Figure 7–6 is an example of a credit memo.

Credit memos should be handled in the following fashion:

1. Request a credit memo from the delivery person.
2. Make sure the form is accurately completed, why the credit memo was issued.
3. Request the signature of the delivery person.
4. Annotate the credit on the invoice so that the business office does not make payment for the product.
5. Give a copy of the credit memo to the delivery person and place a copy in a separate folder.
6. Store the remaining delivery.
7. Call the delivery company to make them aware of the discrepancy.
8. Attach the credit memo to the invoice and forward it to the business office for payment after the purveyor delivers the credited product or in some way satisfies the discrepancy.

Just as it is important to request a credit memo when a product is rejected or not delivered, a product that is delivered by mistake should also be reported to the purveyor. An operation should receive the products that it pays for, but

Figure 7–6 *Credit Memo*

☐ Pickup Order Only
☐ Pickup and Credit Order
☐ Credit Only (No Pickup Required)

Date _____

Sold To _____

No. 45215

Customer Number	Invoice Number	Original Invoice Date

Product Code	No. of Cases	Packaging-Size-Description	Package	Price	Amount

Approved By _____

Customer Signature _____

Date _____

at no time should it keep any product that is not recorded on the invoice. If a product is delivered by mistake, it should be properly stored and the incident should be reported to the purveyor as soon as possible.

Safeguarding the Receiving Process

Products are vulnerable during the receiving process. A great deal of concern is given to the storage and transportation of products; however, there are as many opportunities for theft and deterioration during receiving than any other time in the control process. Because most deliveries are made to the backdoors of kitchens or on loading docks, the temperature of frozen and refrigerated products can rise rapidly during the summer months. This is why products, especially frozen foods and other perishables, must be checked and stored as quickly as possible. Additionally, this is why deliveries should only be made when receiving personnel have time to properly receive the products. Inventory should be taken before deliveries are made so that the correct number or amounts of products can be ordered. This inventory process is also a good time to organize the refrigerators and freezers for storage of the new products. Products should not be allowed to sit on the kitchen floor while storage facilities are reorganized.

When products are being received, there is a window of opportunity for theft by kitchen personnel, passersby, and delivery personnel. Only individuals involved in the receiving process should be in the area where products are being received. Delivery personnel should not be allowed to enter storage areas. This is a common mistake made by numerous facilities. There is nothing to prevent delivery personnel from placing one product into storage while removing several other products on their way out. All operational procedures must be practiced in a professional manner, as products represent money and must be treated as such.

Examining Products for Quality

Even the smallest mom-and-pop operations should examine products for basic quality and determine whether products have been mishandled. If the bottom of a case of berries or any other type of produce displays a lot of moisture then the products within the case should be checked for overripeness or spoilage. If the delivery person should drop a case of eggs, carefully examine the product or simply reject the case, as the eggs on the bottom could be broken. Because bruising occurs easily in products such as bananas, pears, and apples, crates containing these products should be set down gently. Managers often forget that fresh produce is a living organism and therefore loses its quality rapidly through handling. Any frozen fish that is going into the freezer should be checked to see if the temperature is at least still below 10°F. It is extremely important that fish and other meats not be refrozen to prevent possible food poisoning. Frozen products should be examined for ice crystals, which may indicate that a product thawed and was refrozen or that a splash of water could have been added to adjust for the difference in weight. Dated products or color-coded products should be checked to ensure freshness. Even though a facility may have a reputable supplier, the delivery person may switch older items with newer items for clients with whom they are in collusion.

Accepting products that are not usable increases the amount of food cost for an organization. If substandard ingredients are used, an operation can develop a product of poor or unacceptable quality, and this may cause a facility to lose return business. There are times when suppliers will be out of a product or may have to substitute a product; however, any changes in cost, quality, or quantity should be discussed with the manager before the product is accepted.

Following is a list of some commons foods that all full-service restaurants purchase from time to time. The list provides guidelines to help receiving personnel evaluate these products for quality and freshness.

FRUIT

Apples—color is important to usage. Look for decay, internal browning or breakdown, bruises, sunburn, spray burn, or any type of insect damage. All crates should display the count or diameter.

Bananas—present a major problem because if they have been refrigerated the ripening process has been stopped. Bananas should appear fresh, firm and plump, and have good peel strength. They should be examined for size, degree of maturity, and overripeness.

Berries—will show deterioration by stains under the bottom of their crates. It is important not to purchase berries too far in advance and to purchase only what is needed. Receiving personnel must be careful to look for whole clean berries and not accept berries that are overripe.

Cherries—share basically the same characteristics as berries and should be checked for worms and shriveling.

Grapes—near maturity have the best quality. Shriveling indicates that grapes are old. Seeds should be brown and not green. Grapes that are fully ripe should have stems that are green, not brown. When a bunch of grapes is shaken few grapes should fall off the stem.

Lemons and limes—should be judged by cutting the fruit and tasting it.

Melons—can be very expensive during certain times of the year, therefore care must be taken to ensure that the best product possible is received. It can be difficult to discern ripeness. Softness at the blossom end is usually the best indicator. A cleanly broken stem scar, with no trace of stem, is a full slip, which indicates that the melon was ripe when picked. If the stem is still attached, the melon should be rejected, as it will not ripen or be of best flavor. Watermelons should be yellowish in color on the bottom. A hollow sound when the watermelon is thumped can indicate ripeness.

Pineapples—need to be checked carefully, as they do not become sweet until the last two weeks before ripeness. They should be evaluated for a distinct orange-yellow color with fully developed, waxy, bright surface squares and a slight whiteness at the base. The fruit should have a dry bottom, good plumpness, and appear heavy for its size.

VEGETABLES

Asparagus—is one of the more expensive traditional vegetables, therefore additional attention should be given during receiving. Asparagus should have an approximate 2-inch white, woody portion that draws moisture from wet moss on the bottom of the crate, which protects the quality. Asparagus that has too much white stem should be avoided. It should be a bright green color and have closed, firm, compact tips that snap or break with ease.

Beans (green or wax)—should snap with a distinct, clean break without strings. There should be evenness of maturity and shape with few tails. Tough or stringy beans should be rejected.

Broccoli—should be fresh, clean, deep green in color, and have compact buds. If broccoli is wilted, or is flabby with yellow leaves, it should be rejected. The base trim should be even and excess leaves should be removed. Broccoli should be inspected for cabbage worms and gray plant lice.

Brussels sprouts—well-trimmed, hard, compact, bright, cabbage-green sprouts should be accepted. Sprouts should be rejected if leaves are yellow or wilted or if heads have burst. If sprouts appear dirty and smudgy on the outer leaves, there may be plant lice. Additionally, products must be examined for worm damage.

Cabbage—is susceptible to worms. Look for decay, yellowing of leaves, and broken or burst heads. The stem should be rubbed to see if it is dry. If the stem is not dry, there is an indication of rot. Excessive softness can indicate poor quality and high waste.

Carrots—should not be less than 3 inches long and all should be close to the same diameter of not less than ¾ inch. Carrots should not be flabby, wilted, soft, or shriveled and should break with a crisp snap.

Celery—should be tested for crispness by bending a stalk until it snaps. A preferred stalk is 6 inches or more wide. Wilted or yellow leaves indicate excessive age, and excessively dirty celery should be rejected.

Corn—should have silk that is brown and not green and husks should be fresh and green, not dry. The husks should be pulled back and the corn should be punctured to see if there is plenty of juice in the kernels. If there is no juice or if it is pasty, the corn may be old and should be rejected.

Cucumbers—should be fresh, shiny, waxy, crisp, of medium size, and dark green in color. Cucumbers should not be withered or shriveled or have a tough rubbery flesh.

Peppers (sweet)—come in an assortment of colors. Peppers that are shriveled or excessively soft should be rejected. Crispness can be detected by puncturing a pepper with a thumbnail. Discoloration or sunken areas may indicate decay.

Potatoes—are usually purchased in large quantities and the place of origin often determines their usage. If it is necessary for the supplier to provide a substitute, then receiving personnel should be aware of what type of substitution can be made based on the intended use of the product. The Russet Burbank from Washington, Oregon, or Idaho is usually the best potato for baking, mashing, and deep-frying.

Tomatoes—should be selected based on flavor, firmness, internal characteristics, color, and size. Shape can also be an indication of quality. Tomatoes should be smooth and free from decay, freezing, bruises, cuts, sunburn, scars, disease, and insects.

MEAT

Meat products generally involve more control than other products, and receiving personnel need to be more aware of order specifications. Meat quality is a composite evaluation of flesh color, texture, moistness and firmness, and the degree of ossification of the bones. Receiving personnel should know the grades of meat, the different categories of marbling, and the significance of the color of fat and other factors, especially with regard to expensive meat. The National Association of Meat Purveyors' guidebook for meat cuts and quality is an excellent source for meat specifications.

Delivery Times

Deliveries must be scheduled for times that are convenient for the operation. This prevents deliveries from arriving when receiving personnel are busy with other tasks. Having a set time for delivery also ensures that storage facilities are prepared to receive deliveries. In so doing, the possibilities of deterioration and theft of products can be reduced. Additionally, some purveyors may provide incentives for accepting products at off times. Most facilities have the same time demands, but if an operation is willing or able to receive products at times other than peak periods, then incentives or discounts may be negotiated. Delivery times should be posted outside the facility for delivery personnel.

Procedures for Suspicion of Collusion

There may be times when employees are approached by delivery personnel or other individuals to misappropriate funds or products or misuse services; other times, employees may simply become aware of acts of collusion within an organization. Individuals are more apt to understand the consequences of unethical or illegal activities when managers or owners issue written procedures concerning such activities. If an organization places policies in writing, it appears more obvious to all that the operation wants certain procedures to be followed and that it will not tolerate certain activities or conduct. An organization should draft written policies with regard to the following:

- What procedures should be taken if collusion is suspected
- How collusion affects the bottom line and the entire organization
- What acts are considered collusion
- What action will be taken against individuals involved in collusion
- How silence can be construed as acceptance of collusive acts

An organization may be able to reduce the amount of unethical practices by issuing a written code of ethics and written guidelines for employees to follow in the event they suspect any unethical practices. Additionally, if employees realize that what affects the bottom line also affects promotions, raises, and job security, they may prevent other employees from pursuing unethical practices.

Monetary amounts of gifts and the type of gifts that can be accepted should also be explained to prevent managers and employees from compromising their positions. While all situations cannot be covered, employees should at least have written guidelines of the most common activities. Explaining expected behaviors in writing strengthens their importance in the minds of the employees.

It is imperative that employees be aware of the consequences of their actions. Rules need to be established and should be adhered to by all. In cases of theft or collusion an operation needs to implement "hot stove" types of disciplinary action, which are designed for situations that will not be tolerated even once; the disciplinary equivalent of touching a hot stove and getting burned. For example, if an employee is caught stealing, he or she will be terminated. Also, employees need to be aware that not reporting suspicious activities may be construed as condonation of unethical practices.

Management must realize that most hospitality facilities operate with a small margin of profit; therefore, if theft or any other unethical practices are allowed to occur, the facility may be forced into business failure. Control in all aspects of operational procedure must be consistently practiced if an organization is to maximize its output.

Nonfood Supplies

There are several concerns associated with receiving nonfood supplies. One concern is that some cartons remain in storage for some time, and roaches are great hitchhikers; therefore, cartons should be opened outside if possible. Paper goods present a particular problem because roaches attempt to lay eggs among goods such as napkins and paper towels. If infested products have to be thrown away or cause an operation additional cost for extermination, this takes away from the bottom line.

Another major concern of receiving nonfood products is the outright cost of certain items. While food products can be expensive, equipment and cleaning supplies can be more so. Be sure that a purchase order accompanies all equipment received and that the product was in fact ordered by the facility. An additional problem is that managers may be scammed or coaxed into purchasing unnecessary products.

Controlling resources is difficult when there are so many possibilities of wasting or losing funds. Professionalism in the receiving process can assist managers in keeping tabs on expenditures and in ensuring that expenditures for resources are yielding maximum results. Receiving personnel must be knowledgeable, loyal, and professional in order to protect the welfare of the organization.

Summary

Receiving involves checking deliveries for quality and quantity and comparing them against the purchase order. An important aspect of the receiving process is to ensure that the quantity, quality, and price of products received are what the organization requested. Once it is established that these comparisons are satisfactory, products must be secured as quickly as possible to prevent deterioration and theft. Correct and appropriate records need to be kept. It is critical for an organization to employ knowledgeable receiving personnel. Training is vital, as even the best specifications will be useless if receiving personnel do not know how to inspect products and do not understand the importance of inspecting products. For the receiving process to be as effective and efficient as possible, the layout of the area must be designed for control, security, and convenience.

Receiving personnel should have the necessary equipment to perform their duties. Large and small operations should have specific procedures for the receiving process. Personnel should be familiar with all receiving documents and should know how to process credit memos.

Receiving personnel must be aware of their responsibility in safeguarding products during the receiving process. This includes inspecting products for deterioration and protecting them against theft. This can only be accomplished by scheduling receiving for times when personnel are available to carefully inspect and receive products.

An organization must operate as a team in order for all functions and processes to work efficiently. Receiving personnel are expected to be knowledgeable and use this knowledge to the benefit of the organization. Honesty is a primary attribute for receiving personnel and for those employees that have access to the receiving area. If any employee suspects that a dishonest act has occurred, he or she should be able to report this without fear of retribution. Employees may only report these activities if they understand how theft affects the bottom line and the security of their employment.

Review Exercises _____

1. Credit memos should be used during receiving for all of the following except:
   a. to identify price increases
   b. to account for a shortage in products
   c. to account for products that are rejected
   d. to account for missing products

2. Tagging can be used for all of the following except:
   a. to record prices
   b. to record a transfer
   c. to record the date a product was received
   d. record the time a product was received

3. An interunit transfer is used:
   a. by purveyors to account for missing products
   b. to transfer a product from one unit to another in the same company
   c. to transfer products back to the purveyor
   d. to act as a purchase request from purveyors

4. When a case of bananas is delivered and they are dropped by the truck driver, receiving personnel should:
   a. check the products before signing for them
   b. reject the bananas
   c. make sure the bananas are cleaned before serving them
   d. use them as quickly as possible

5. A case of frozen steaks being delivered has ice crystals in it. This could be an indication that:
   a. the steaks may have been allowed to reach a temperature above freezing
   b. steaks may have been removed and replaced with water
   c. the steaks may have been in storage for a long time
   d. all of the above

6. During the process of receiving there is a possibility of theft by:
   a. delivery personnel
   b. kitchen personnel
   c. someone passing by
   d. all of the above

7. If the storage room contains unusable equipment or products, management should try all of the following except:
   a. transferring it to another unit
   b. returning it for credit
   c. selling it
   d. giving it to an employee

8. It is not a good receiving practice to:
    a. sign for products before inspection
    b. check all products against the purchase request
    c. check all prices
    d. none of the above

9. A kitchen knife should not be used to:
    a. to open cartons during receiving
    b. to slice meat
    c. to dice meat
    d. to chop vegetables

10. Nonfood supplies such as paper goods and equipment:
    a. do not need as much inspection as perishable items
    b. can be signed for as soon as delivered
    c. should be opened outside because of roaches
    d. do not require a purchase order

11. Make a list of five products of which you would want to inspect the bottom of the crates to ensure quality.

12. List at least five methods that can be used by receiving and delivery personnel in collusion.

13. List two produce products and two meat products and list the specifications necessary when ordering these products.

14. List the necessary steps in handling a credit memo.

Examination Type Problems

1. Explain the importance of tagging.

2. List two food items that require a count upon delivery.

3. List five items that have to be measured during the receiving process.

4. What could be an indication that a product had been allowed to thaw and was refrozen?

Case Study

As a manager of Model, you do not directly order or receive food items. The purchasing director and the receiving agent at Case Study Hotel have both been in their positions for a good number of years and they both are nice to their colleagues. One night, while you and your spouse were dining at an upscale restaurant, you observed that the receiving agent at the Case Study Hotel was having dinner with the driver who delivers meat products to the hotel. You recognize that particular driver because you became suspicious when you saw him remove a case of food from the freezer and place it in his delivery truck a week or so ago. At the time of the incident, you informed the receiving agent and he told you that the driver had previously delivered the wrong product. He also told you that you should pay more attention to your own duties and not concern yourself with other areas. As they finished their meal, you observed that the delivery person paid for the meal and gave the receiving agent a white envelope. You become even more suspicious and concerned. Following are three different plans of action:

1. Report the situation to higher authorities.
2. Do nothing unless you observe another similar situation.
3. Forget about it and pay more attention to your own tasks, as suggested by the receiving agent.

Discuss the pros and cons of each plan and recommend one.

References

Kotschevar, L. H., & Levinson, C. (1988). Quantity food purchasing. Third edition. New York: Macmillan, Inc.

Stefanelli, J. M. (1997). Purchasing. New York: John Wiley & Sons, Inc.

Warfel, M. C., & Waskey, F. H. (1979). The professional food buyer. Berkeley, California: McCutchan Publishing Corporation.

8
Storing and Issuing

Learning Objectives

After completing this chapter, you should be able to:

- describe the six factors that must be considered when establishing a storage facility.
- describe the ideal factors associated with cold storage.
- explain some of the problems associated with the storage of beer.
- explain how the copies of a requisition form should be distributed.
- describe how an operation develops a reorder point.
- describe the perpetual inventory method.
- explain the importance of physical inventory.
- explain the importance of accounting for products after they are issued.
- describe the correct method of storing products in a storage facility.

The Storage Function

Storage needs can vary according to the type of operation the storage facility must support. A fast-food facility with a limited menu has different storage needs than an establishment that provides a full-service menu. Operators of large establishments and franchises often find it financially advantageous to purchase in large amounts at discounted prices and warehouse the merchandise until needed. Regardless of the size and requirement of the facility, from a control point of view, products must be stored as quickly as possible to prevent deterioration and theft. Management cannot afford to allow products to sit around, as items will begin to come up missing. Proper storage is important to accountability, security, and quality retention.

Proper storage procedures are important because food products are constantly deteriorating and becoming outdated. Additionally, inventory represents a large cash value, therefore a great deal of concern must be given to the storage and issuing of products. When establishing storage facilities and procedures, six important factors must be considered.

1. Location and layout of facilities
2. Temperature and humidity control
3. Organization and placement of products
4. Dating and pricing stored products
5. Recordkeeping
6. Security

These six factors must be of concern when initially establishing a storage facility and continuous attention must be given to them if control procedures are to be maintained.

Location and Layout of Facilities

The location and layout of the storage facility should allow products to be quickly stored upon receipt. The layout should ensure that all functional activities can be accomplished efficiently without the possibility of damaging products. Whenever possible, the storage facilities for both perishable and nonperishable products should be located between the receiving area and preparation area. This allows for efficiency of time and motion activities and enhances a smooth flow of production procedures. Because of labor expense, it is not wise to waste a great deal of time in trying to receive products from the storage area. Many additional factors influence the layout and design of the storage area, but time and motion should also be given a great degree of consideration.

There are three basic types of storage facilities in the hospitality industry: dry storage, cold storage, and freezer storage. Storage facilities should be designed for easy access and cleaning and to allow for sufficient air circulation to prevent stagnant off-odors and to allow for uniform ventilation. This also applies to refrigerated areas. Windows in the storage area should not be clear, as direct light is detrimental to many different products.

Temperature and Humidity Control

Temperature and humidity can help maximize the life of food products while in storage. The factors involved in maintaining proper internal conditions include temperature, storage containers, shelving, and cleanliness. Food life can be maximized when products are stored at the correct temperature and humidity. The food controller and storage personnel should check the temperature gauges periodically to make sure the appropriate temperatures are maintained. Dry storage is usually maintained at a temperature of 50°F to 70°F.

Storing foods in appropriate containers can help protect products from moisture as well as from insects and vermin. Most of the time, staples are purchased in airtight containers and should be stored in that manner. However, some items are purchased in unsealed containers, often paper bags, boxes, and sacks, which are susceptible to attack by insects and vermin. Such products should be transferred into tightly sealed containers. For both raw and cooked perishable items, care should be given to storing them in whatever manner will best maintain their original quality. In general, cooked foods and opened canned foods should be stored in stainless steel or plastic containers that can be sealed.

Storage facilities should be cleaned on a regular basis. All too often they are only cleaned when an employee has free time. Cleanliness should be enforced in storage facilities to protect products from spoilage, insects, and odors. In refrigerated facilities cleanliness prevents the accumulation of spoiled food, of which even small amounts will give off odors and may affect other foods. In storeroom facilities cleanliness discourages infestation by insects and vermin. Regular extermination can prevent rodents and vermin from reaching population levels large enough to cause damage and disease.

Separate facilities for storage of different classes of foods should be maintained whenever feasible. Cold storage is the preferred temperature for most perishable products. Eggs, butter, meats, fruits, and vegetables are held more safely at a temperature between 30°F and 45°F, the temperature that is actually referred to as cold storage. It is important to remember that once food is removed from cold storage, it is not good practice to return them to cold storage. Freezer storage is kept at a temperature of 0°F or lower. Most products that are placed in freezer storage should not be held for more than three months and many products cannot be held this long. Freezer products should not be held for more than one year to avoid freezer burn.

Produce items need air to stay fresh longer. Thus, produce should be placed in storage that allows air to circulate as much as possible. Items such as potatoes, onions, oil, and dairy products can absorb odor from apples, and apples can absorb odors from other stronger products. Bananas should be stored at 50°F. Grapes should be stored at 32°F to 40°F. Freezing damages grapes. If grapes have a dull, dead color and the stem pulls out with the meat or brush attached, freezing may have occurred.

Proper temperature is also important in maintaining the shelf life of non-perishable products. Storage facilities for staple commodities or dry goods should generally be room temperature. Although the degree of risk is not as great with these type of products, it should be remembered that all foods are ultimately perishable, and food life is maximized by proper temperature and proper humidity. Maintaining proper temperature and humidity for cold storage, dry storage, and freezer storage is essential to maximizing the storage life of products. If storeroom personnel are in doubt as to what temperature or humidity is best for the retention of certain products, they should ask their vendors. Figure 8–1 lists recommended storage temperatures for certain products.

Figure 8–1   *Recommended Temperatures for Product Storage*

Items	Recommended Storage Temperature
Apples	32–36°F (0–2°C), 90–98% relative humidity
Avocados	Unripe: 45–50°F (7–10°C), 85–95% relative humidity
	Ripe: 32–36°F (0–2°C), 90–98% relative humidity
Bananas	Mature green and ripe: 60–65°F (16–18°C), 85–95% relative humidity
Cantaloupe	32–36°F (0–2°C), 90–98% relative humidity
Carambola	45–50°F (7–10°C), 85–95% relative humidity
Dates	32–36°F (0–2°C), 90–98% relative humidity
Feijoa	45–50°F (7–10°C), 85–95% relative humidity
Fresh-cut fruits	32–36°F (0–2°C), 90–98% relative humidity
Grapefruit	45–50°F (7–10°C), 85–95% relative humidity
Melons	60–65°F (16–18°C), 85–95% relative humidity
Passion fruit	45–50°F (7–10°C), 85–95% relative humidity
Artichokes	32–36°F (0–2°C), 90–98% relative humidity
Baby vegetables	Beets, bok choy, carrots, cauliflower, corn, kohlrabi, leeks, turnips: 32–36°F (0–2°C), 90–98% relative humidity
	Soft shell squash: 45–50°F (7–10°C), 85–95% relative humidity
Broccoli	32–36°F (0–2°C), 90–98% relative humidity
Cabbage	32–36°F (0–2°C), 90–98% relative humidity
Chinese long bean	45–50°F (7–10°C), 85–95% relative humidity
Endive/escarole	32–36°F (0–2°C), 90–98% relative humidity
Fresh-cut vegetables	32–36°F (0–2°C), 90–98% relative humidity
Herbs, fresh	All except basil: 32–36°F (0–2°C), 90–98% relative humidity
	Basil: 45–50°F (7–10°C), 85–95% relative humidity
Mushrooms	32–36°F (0–2°C), 90–98% relative humidity
Peppers, chili	45–50°F (7–10°C), 85–95% relative humidity
Potatoes	60–65°F (16–18°C), 85–95% relative humidity

Organization and Placement of Products

Products should be placed in storage in a manner in which the most frequently used items are located closest to the entrance; however, if possible, place expensive items some distance from the entrance to deter theft. Placing frequently used items close to the entrance reduces the time required to move needed foods from storage, which reduces labor costs over the long run. Additionally, the storeroom must be maintained in such a manner that each item has its own location and should be placed in the same location at all times. This permits easy access, as personnel become familiar with the location of products and assists storeroom personnel in maintaining inventory by using first-in first-out procedures.

First-in first-out (FIFO) procedures dictate that new deliveries should be stored behind the quantities already on hand. This enables old items to be used before newer items, which helps reduce the possibility of spoilage or infestation. All products should be stored eight inches above the floor and shelving in refrigerated facilities should be slotted to permit maximum circulation of air for perishable foods. Solid steel shelving is usually preferred for nonperishable products. Food products should not be stored on the floor at anytime.

Beverages and food should be stored separately, if possible, as the humidity, temperature, and security concerns for these products can be quite different. Alcoholic beverages can deteriorate quickly. Because of the sensitivity of alcoholic beverages, thermometers should be used in both dry and refrigerated storage areas. The cork in wine bottles and the labels on alcoholic products can deteriorate because of humidity. Wines are also sensitive to vibrations and this must be a concern when storing expensive products. In addition, locking all liquor, beer, and wine storage areas may deter pilferage.

Managers have to ensure the rotation of beer in storage, as beer does not mature with age. Beer begins to deteriorate as soon as it is processed and placed into containers for retail. Regular beer should be stored at a temperature of 40°F to 70°F and draft beer should be stored between 36°F and 38°F. As with all perishable products, it is imperative that first-in, first-out procedures are used with the storage of beer.

Dating and Pricing Stored Products

Because storeroom personnel must tabulate prices on all requisitions and prepare the storeroom for inventory, tagging products is essential. All products must be dated and have prices placed on them or on their containers as soon as they are received. This portion of the receiving process is essential for storeroom personnel to maintain accountability in a consistent manner. Additionally, since storeroom personnel are responsible for extending the cost of each requisition, placing prices on tags, bin cards, or containers makes this process much easier.

There are numerous benefits to placing dates and prices on products. Storeroom personnel can be helpful in drawing management's attention to an increase in costs. Dating assists storeroom personnel in rotating stock, and placing prices on products assists with inventory and determining food and beverage cost. Placing dates and prices on products may also reduce theft, as employees may be less apt to steal a product if it reflects some type of accountability, and if employees know that products have to be accounted for, they may realize that there is a greater chance that they would be caught.

Recordkeeping

The types of products received by hospitality operations usually fall into two categories: directs and stores. Directs are usually inexpensive perishable products that are frequently purchased for immediate use (e.g., fresh produce, baked goods, and dairy products). Directs are issued the moment they are received, so no storage record of these items is kept by receiving or storeroom personnel. Products that have a longer shelf life and will not be used for the delivery day's function are referred to as stores. Stores usually consist of staples, alcoholic beverages, meat, and other items that may be in storage for a while. For accountability purposes, these foods are considered part of inventory until issued for use and therefore are not included in cost figures until issued. A system must be implemented to account for stores until they are issued.

In foodservice operations, directs are charged to food cost when they are received. These food products are put in a refrigerator or freezer in the kitchen and are intended to be entirely used in the course of the day's food preparation. There are times when an establishment purchases more than a one-day supply of some directs. This may be done to obtain a cheaper price or to simplify recordkeeping. When ordering more than a one-day supply of directs, management must ensure that there is some means of accountability and storage of these products. The same holds true if the entire amount of a product is not used during the day that it has been requested for use. There must be accountability for excess amounts of these products. They should be returned to the vendor, if feasible, or they should be given to storeroom personnel for further accountability.

Some type of tracking procedures must be in place to ensure that the amount of directs requested is actually used. This is an important control procedure that is often overlooked. If 500 lobsters are ordered for a specific function, there must be some means of checking to ensure that all 500 were actually prepared and served. Often, beginning and ending inventory forms are filled out on a per-shift basis to account for the usage of higher priced items. Although most directs are not expensive items, it is necessary to implement tracking procedures for such items to prevent leakage in the control process.

Maintaining and completing records is essential to proper control of products in storage. Whenever a product is required from storage, a requisition should be submitted to storage personnel. Figure 8–2 is a sample requisition form. If the item is not in storage or has to be replaced to bring items back up to par, a standard purchase order should be used. Orders placed in person or over the telephone should be confirmed on a purchase order. One copy of the purchase order should go to the vendor, a second copy should go to the accounting department, a third copy should go to the receiving clerk, and a copy should be kept on file in the storeroom or by the person that originated the request. The receiving clerk, who should be a representative of the accounting department, must receive all products. Once the receiving clerk is satisfied with the quantity, quality, and price of products, he or she should record the quantity and description of the goods on the receiving sheet. The clerk then places

Figure 8–2   *Sample Requisition Form*

Food Storeroom Requisition

Date:_____   Date Needed:_____   Dept.:_____   Dept. Mgr.:_____

Qty. Ordered	Ingredient #	Description/Item	Qty. Issued	Unit Cost		Unit Total	

the products in storage, if necessary, or notifies the department that ordered the products. The invoice should be sent to the auditor in the business office.

Security

Security of products represents a major challenge for all hospitality operations because the hospitality industry deals with products that are easily consumed. For this reason several tasks must be divided among different individuals. Inventory of the storeroom should not be completed by storeroom personnel only. Two people make a better control team when taking inventory. One person can count and call out the amount while the other person records the amount in the inventory book. This not only cuts the time of inventory taking but also reduces the temptation of stealing. Closing off the storeroom during the inventory process is another option. Also, no products should be issued during the inventory process to reduce chances of error or stealing. For control purposes a storeroom should be locked and only should be accessible in the presence of the storeroom clerk for specific periods of time during designated hours. When the storeroom is closed it should be locked and the one key should be in possession of the storeroom supervisor. Other than for inventory purposes, no one except storeroom personnel should have access to the storeroom. A storeroom must be treated exactly like a bank vault. There should be accountability for all products that go in or out. Products should never be allowed to leave the storeroom without a requisition and a signature. Sloppy or relaxed procedures make the control system ineffective.

Items in storage should always be placed in the same location. This not only facilitates access by storeroom personnel but may reduce theft by preventing an employee from hiding an expensive item behind less expensive items for later removal. Designated storage spaces also reduce the risk of errors in counting during inventory. If the same product is stored in several locations, the possibly of theft is greatly increased. Additionally, every effort must be made to store expensive items as far as possible from the door of the storeroom to prevent quick and easy access for theft.

Surveillance Cameras Products should never be left unattended or stored in such a manner that would permit pilferage. Once deliveries have been received, products must be moved to the appropriate storage facility as quickly as possible because products are vulnerable to theft between the receiving and storing periods. Because this is such a vulnerable period, managers must ensure that products are moved to storage areas at optimum times. Obviously the amount of security should increase with the value of the items being stored. Because of the decreasing cost of video surveillance equipment, many operations, especially larger ones that have more receiving and storage areas to monitor, have taken the additional precaution of installing closed-circuit television cameras to keep various facilities under observation. These cameras can be directly linked to an operation's security department.

Once items are in storage appropriate security must be maintained at all times. Employees must not be permitted to remove products at will, even in the smallest mom-and-pop operations.

Keys For control purposes, procedures for the distribution of keys should be in writing. Such procedures must be established to keep the number of keys to a minimum. Management should authorize only the number of keys deemed appropriate for efficient operation and maximum security. If there is more than one key, or more than one person has access to a single key, it is advisable to have a sign-in and sign-out log. Another, albeit more expensive, suggestion is to change locks frequently to minimize the possibility that unauthorized persons may obtain and use duplicate keys. Also, it is important to change locks when a worker with access to the storeroom leaves the employ of the operation.

Electronic locks are also available. These locks have key pads that require a code, a swipe card, or similar means to open the lock. In addition, the electronic mechanism records the time that the locks were opened and by whom, often revealing an employee's inappropriate access or activities. One restaurateur discovered that his chef opened the storeroom door at 4 a.m., as the electronic mechanism registered the chef's authorization code. Electronic security systems have also become more affordable; therefore, it may prove beneficial for operations to consider the use of such technologies.

Retina Identification   A procedure in which a computer identifies an individual by scanning the retina, the light-sensitive membrane that lines the inner eyeball, may eventually make keys obsolete. Research has shown that retina identification is far more reliable than fingerprinting. With the adoption of this new procedure management will be able to control access to storage facilities and other areas with far more security than with the use of keys. Retina identification may be the wave of the future for controlling all types of resources.

The Issuing Function

The issuing function is vital to the success of the control process. Two main sets of procedures apply to issuing. The first set of procedures pertains to the process itself, movement of products from storage facilities to the production area or area of usage. The second set of procedures pertains to the record-keeping associated with determining the cost of the products that are issued. Accountability of these two procedures in the issuing process must be monitored or products may not go where they are intended to go and there may not be any record of issue or usage.

Process

For control measures to work properly, the process must start with a requisition form, the key form for accountability in the issuing process. Requisitions should always be used to obtain products from storage. A product should not be issued unless a requisition is received. A member of the operation initiates the process by listing on a requisition form the items and quantities needed from the storeroom. The supervisor of the department in which the products are to be used should review the requisition and check to see if each item is genuinely required in the amount listed. If the requisition is approved the supervisor signs it and gives it to the storeroom to fill the order. Requisitions should be maintained on file to ensure that control procedures can be evaluated.

Requisitions should be submitted in advance to enable storeroom personnel to prepare orders without having to rush. This allows banquet and kitchen personnel to anticipate needs and plan for production. To aid in the utilization of labor and costs control, definite times for issuing products from storage should be established so that storeroom personnel are able to perform duties in addition to issuing. These additional duties include cleaning the storage rooms, refrigerators, and freezers; maintaining stock on shelves; rotating stock to ensure FIFO procedures; and recordkeeping.

Storeroom personnel are responsible for extending the cost (i.e., the total dollar value of issued items) of each requisition. A requisition is extended by

Figure 8–3   *Completed Requisition Form with Cost Extensions*

Food Storeroom Requisition

Date: <u>May 10, 19XX</u>   Date Needed: <u>May 25, 19XX</u>   Dept.: <u>Banquet</u>   Dept. Mgr.: <u>D.J. Jones</u>

Qty. Ordered	Ingredient #	Description/Item	Qty. Issued	Unit Cost		Unit Total	
80 lbs	219	Chicken breast, boneless, skinless	80 lbs	6	88	550	40
3 ea	325	Ribeye (whole)	3 ea	50	00	150	00
2 box	004	Chicken tender	2 box	5	00	100	00
1 box	214	Mini quiche	1 box	15	00	15	00
5 lbs	159	Chorizo	5 lbs	5	52	27	60
10 lbs	245	Snapper	10 lbs	2	00	20	00

entering and multiplying the unit cost of each listed item by the number of units issued. This is why items are tagged upon receipt and the unit cost of each item is marked on each container. A file or inventory book must be maintained for all items in storage. As prices of items change, the most recent purchase price is listed in the perpetual inventory file. This assists management in determining the cost of goods sold.

Once the requisition has been filled and signed by the receiver, storeroom personnel should forward one copy of the requisition to the accounting department so that the cost of products used by each outlet can be easily identified and computed. The other copy should accompany the filled order to the department that originated the requisition so that records can be kept and to ensure that the products requested were filled correctly.

Requisition Forms

Figures 8–2 and 8–3 are examples of blank and completed requisition forms. A requisition form is a means of documenting requested products and helps determine the actual cost that should be charged. This is especially helpful for large operations that have different outlets.

Requisition forms are not solely used in food and beverage outlets. For instance, all housekeepers or room attendants should fill out requisition forms so the director of housekeeping can determine if products are used correctly.

Inventory

The increasing pressure on operations to manage inventories efficiently demands significant changes and improvements to traditional inventory management methods. This need is magnified when considering that material purchasing and inventory management often are areas governed by intuition and gut feelings. Indeed, making inventory decisions in this manner can be costly to an organization with inexperienced managers.

Par Stock

Before money should be invested in inventory, par stock level should be established. Par stock level, or simply par, is the amount of product that should be on hand between one delivery and the next. The par stock for certain items may have to change according to product demand and available delivery times. Items that are in season may be more in demand and the par stock level may have to increase as a result. If the time between delivery dates is decreased, the par stock level may decrease. Because of the positive and negative factors concerning the amount of inventory, par stock levels must be evaluated from time to time to see if the amount held in inventory is sufficient. When establishing par stock levels, management has to consider the relative quantities of each item used.

Before ordering products for par stock, the cost of carrying products in inventory must be evaluated. The ideal situation is always to keep inventory at a minimum. At times it may be convenient to purchase large amounts to obtain reduced prices; however, an analysis must be completed to ensure that carrying such a large amount in inventory will still be cost effective. The amount of business and the frequency of turnover of specific items are factors that affect the amount of products to be carried. Completion of a sales analysis allows management the opportunity to observe variations in demand. With regard to purchasing in large amounts, analysis may show that a significant difference between present prices and probable future prices may not be true in all cases. Whenever goods that are not needed for immediate consumption are purchased, interest on the money invested, insurance, cost of storage, labor, and possible waste or loss must also be taken into consideration.

Order Quantity

After a needs assessment has been completed and par stock level is determined, products can be ordered. As products are consumed they must be replaced by additional orders. The point in the storage cycle where additional products need to be ordered is referred to as the reorder point. Establishing the most effective reorder point is essential in controlling the amount of products in storage. The reorder point is the number of units to which the supply on hand should decrease before additional orders are placed. Before a reorder point can be established for any item, it is necessary to know both normal usage and the time needed to obtain delivery. If products are essential to operational procedures, a safety level must also be developed to allow for delivery delays and for possible increased usage. The reorder point in the perpetual inventory method is equivalent to the desired ending inventory in the periodic method. Because purveyors are not willing to sell less than a case of certain products, management must be aware of these products before ordering and be prepared to stock products by the case. Once par stock and safety levels have been determined, an operation can determine the amount that should be ordered each time the quantity of a particular item decreases to the reorder point. The following example shows how to calculate the reorder quantity to bring inventory back to par stock:

$$
\begin{array}{rl}
40 & \text{Par stock} \\
- \; 10 & \text{Reorder point} \\
\hline
= 30 & \text{Subtotal} \\
+ \; 5 & \text{Normal usage until delivery} \\
\hline
= 35 & \text{Reorder quantity}
\end{array}
$$

In the example, 40 cases of a product are needed as the par stock and the reorder point is set at 10 cases, therefore, the required subtotal is 30 cases. However, knowing that 5 cases will normally be used once the order is placed but before it is delivered, a safety margin of 5 cases needs to be added to the 30 cases, which brings the total reorder quantity to 35 cases.

Periodic Inventory

The most commonly used method for maintaining inventory of nonperishable items is periodic inventory. Periodic inventory allows management to determine the amount of money that can be tied up in inventory, as products are ordered based on the amount needed on hand until the next order date. The calculation for this method is as follows:

> Amount required for the upcoming period
> −Amount presently on hand
> +Amount wanted on hand at the end of the period to last until the next delivery
> _____
> =Amount to order

Although the majority of hospitality operations use this method, periodic inventory presents a potential problem in that the amount required and the necessary safety level are not usually as well thought out as when using perpetual inventory and dealing with par stocks. Additionally, managers often get in a hurry and ordering is done haphazardly. The amount on hand must be known; however, in many cases, managers are overwhelmed with other duties and do not check inventory reports or take a physical count of products. Many business failures may be attributed to inexperienced managerial personnel misunderstanding or misusing this method. A manager who orders more products than are needed not only creates an opportunity for waste through overordering but through possible theft by employees as well. On the other hand, if a manager orders less than is needed, products will not be on hand to meet the demand of the guests and this will cause guest dissatisfaction.

Perpetual Inventory

Some organizations employ a perpetual inventory system because it carries the potential to eliminate the need for frequent physical inventories; however, this may not be true for hospitality organizations. Because of the perishability of products and the amount of theft associated with these products, hospitality operations must take frequent physical inventories. Perpetual inventory is not an entirely inefficient system for hospitality operations, although the perishability of items along with the vast amount of turnover makes it prudent to have frequent physical inventories. A perpetual inventory system can help to ensure that quantities purchased are sufficient to meet anticipated needs without being excessive. This method operates like a checking account in that products, as funds, are subtracted from a set balance, or inventory; therefore, it is a convenient method of decreasing the possibility of stockout or overabundance of inventory. However, for the purpose of control, management must physically count products on a periodic basis.

In the perpetual inventory method the amount of products purchased is recorded, and as items are issued for use, the amounts issued are also recorded. The amounts recorded must reflect the movement of items into and out of storage. By following this procedure it is possible to examine the perpetual inventory records to determine how much of an item is in stock at any given time. When a physical inventory is taken, management can quickly determine if a product is overstocked, understocked, or missing. Information maintained in the perpetual inventory records includes the name and address of the supplier, the most recent purchase price for an item, par stock, reorder point, and reorder quantity.

Inventory Management

For the purpose of control, a physical inventory is a must. Physical inventory is the most commonly used inventory control method in the hospitality field. Generally taken at the close of an accounting period, physical inventory requires that a physical count be made of each product in stock. It is best to have a list of products on hand before taking inventory so that items will not be omitted. Products should be listed in the inventory book or log in a fashion that reflects their location in the storage facilities. This way, the individuals taking inventory can work in a logical manner, which facilitates a procedure that can be long and arduous, depending on the number of products in inventory. Two employees should take physical inventory. One person should count the products, and the other person should record the amounts in the inventory log. Once quantities are determined for each item, total values can be calculated. Physical inventory can aid in cost calculation in that once the closing inventory amount is determined, the amount consumed can be calculated.

> Opening inventory
> +Purchases during the accounting period
> =Total available for use
> −Closing inventory (number of units still available)
> =Amount consumed

There are at least five possible ways of assigning values to products in inventory: actual purchase price method, first-in first-out method, weighted average purchase price method, latest purchase price method, and last-in first-out method. Each of these accounting methods may provide a different amount of inventory value at the end of any given period. For control procedures to work effectively, management must establish and consistently use one inventory value method. Which method of inventory valuation is used may depend on whether the prices of a certain products fluctuate a lot. If prices are somewhat fixed, which method is used for valuing a closing inventory will not be as significant.

The actual purchase price method, as its name suggests, entails using the actual price of the inventory to determine the total value. This method is the most accurate but is also the most time consuming. For this method to work, each item in inventory must have its own price. For example, if there were two deliveries of canned tomato juice during a particular accounting period and the prices of these two shipments differed, then one price was marked on some cans of juice while a different price was marked on others. The actual purchase price method calls for storeroom personnel to add up all the price tags on all the items to obtain the total.

The first-in first-out method, which reflects the latest prices of goods, is a preferred method in the hospitality industry. First-in first-out means that the first of a particular item in storage (i.e., the oldest item) should be the first one used or issued from the storeroom. In so doing, the rotation of inventory is guaranteed. Take for example ABC Barbecue, which has an ending inventory of 10 pounds of brisket from the last inventory/accounting period. During this accounting period, ABC bought brisket four times. At the end, 8 pounds were left. The prices associated with the ending inventory and the four purchases are shown in Table 8–1.

Table 8–1

	Pounds	*Price per Pound*
Beginning inventory	10	$3.50
First purchase	20	$3.50
Second purchase	25	$3.75
Third purchase	30	$3.95
Fourth purchase	5	$3.99
Ending inventory	8	

The first-in first-out method indicates that, since the first amounts of brisket that ABC purchased were used first, the remaining 8 pounds have to be from the latest purchases. The last purchase was only 5 pounds, so 3 more pounds are needed to make up the remaining 8 pounds. These 3 pounds had to come from the next to the last purchase, which is $3.95 per pound. The amount of ending inventory is calculated in Table 8–2.

Table 8–2

Pounds	*Price per Pound*	*Extension*
5	$3.99	$19.95
3	$3.95	$11.85
Total		$31.80

The weighted average purchase price method consists of figuring out an average price and using that as the price of the ending inventory. Using the same information about ABC Barbecue as an example, the first step is to extend the figures (see Table 8–3).

In this case, there was a total of 90 pounds of meat worth $337.20. Thus the average price per pound is $337.20 divided by 90, or $3.75 (rounded). If 8 pounds are left as the ending inventory, the value is $3.75 multiplied by 8, or $30.00.

The latest purchase price method, also known as the most recent price method, is probably the simplest method in that the latest price is used to value the amount of inventory on hand. This method follows the assumptions that the

Table 8–3

	Pounds	Price per Pound	Extension
Beginning inventory	10	$3.50	$ 35.00
First purchase	20	$3.50	$ 70.00
Second purchase	25	$3.75	$ 93.75
Third purchase	30	$3.95	$118.50
Fourth purchase	5	$3.99	$ 19.95
Total	90		$337.20

right amount of inventory is purchased and that inventory rotation is being carried out so that the products in storage should all be from the last purchase. Using the sample data from ABC Barbecue, an ending inventory of 8 pounds of meat and a latest price of $3.99, the value of the ending inventory is $3.99 multiplied by 8, or $31.92.

The last-in first-out method, the least utilized in the hospitality business, uses the earliest prices as the method of valuation. This method is not widely used because it is based on the assumption that the last inventory items purchased will be used or issued from the storeroom before others and, therefore, does not allow for inventory rotation. Using the same set of data from ABC Barbecue, the value of the ending inventory can be calculated. As this method dictates that latest purchases be used first, the 8 pounds of brisket that are left have to be from the beginning inventory; therefore, at a price of $3.50 per pound, the ending inventory results in a value of $3.50 multiplied by 8, or $28.00.

Inventory Turnover

Controlling inventory entails having sufficient supplies of products available for use when needed. The difficulty of inventory management is trying to balance the difference between too much and too little. Excessive inventory can present several problems, including:

- Spoilage, because food must be held too long before being used
- Excessive capital tied up in inventory
- Higher than necessary labor cost to handle the greater amount of food
- Greater than necessary space allocated to storage
- Unwarranted opportunities for theft

To avoid these problems a facility should assess its inventory turnover rate. Inventory turnover rate can be calculated as follows:

$$\frac{\text{Cost of products sold for the period}}{\text{Average inventory}}$$

If the cost of food sold for the year is $50,000 and the average inventory for the year is $1000, then the inventory turnover is 50. This means that the inventory in general is changed 50 times per year. There are 52 weeks in a year, so an inventory turnover of 50 means that it usually takes slightly more than one week for old inventory to be used and new inventory to arrive. Most operations use this single inventory turnover figure for the entire inventory; however, some operations find it useful to calculate separate turnover rates for different categories of products. For example, the turnover rate for steaks may be calculated separately from other meat items, and the turnover rate for spirits, beers, and wines may be separated from other beverages. Generally, the accepted turnover rates for products can vary greatly due to the type of product. Perishable products are expected to have a much higher turnover rate than nonperishable products.

Trying to determine and maintain the correct amount of inventory is a challenge for all businesses. Because of the cost of maintaining inventory a manager must continuously evaluate usage and projected sales. Even the most comprehensive manufacturing, planning, and distribution management systems have yielded disappointing results in controlling inventory dollars. The traditional measure of inventory performance—inventory turns—does not adequately serve the materials managers of the 1990s. With the amount of competition in the hospitality industry a more effective means to measure inventory performance and to control the amount of products in inventory is an ongoing quest. According to Robert Morris and Associates, the median inventory turnover for fast-food restaurants with sales of $25 million and over was 35% (a ratio of 31.9) during the period of October 1, 1996 to March 31, 1997.

Unused Products

While storage, inventory, and issuing are important components of the control process, it is essential for management to know what happens to products once they are issued. Even if all of the numbers balance and products are accounted for from the point of receiving to issuing, a manager has the additional responsibility of ensuring that the products are used for the purpose in which they were intended. Another important aspect of the issuing procedure that is often allowed to go unaddressed is products that are ordered but not used. Products removed from storage should be accounted for on some type of production sheet, and products that are issued but not used should be returned to storage. All too often products that are not used are unaccounted for and eventually end up missing or being written off. Managers must understand the importance of physically counting items and comparing guest checks to the number of items removed from storage to see if the items have been sold. This is especially important in regard to expensive items and large functions wherein products are paid for upfront by a guest.

Bar Codes

Bar coding is a method for tracking products through an operation. Bar code systems emerged from industrial, warehouse, and materials handling applications. The concept of bar coding is that uniform symbols on items facilitate control and tracking measures, reduce labor costs, and increase inventory precision.

Bar codes are printed on bundles of products or on product labels or packaging. With the bar code method, a company assigns a number to every asset to be tracked and uses software to generate tags encoded with the particular item's identification number. The number then links each item to its electronic file, which contains information such as purchase date and cost; the person to whom the equipment is assigned; location; vendor; and any warranties, upgrades, or license agreements.

Bar codes can be altered to meet the specific needs of foodservice operations. Dealers can generate bar codes that are used to track items internally. When the manufacturer provides bar codes, dealerships adapt them to their particular internal system. In this manner, all inventory that comes in and out of their facilities is uniformly scanned, tracked, and stored.

2-D bar coding is one of the more accurate means of maintaining control of the flow of products. 2-D bar codes such as PDF417, MaxiCode, and Data Matrix are examples of technology that require only minimal real estate on the inventory unit. They pack up to 2500 characters into printed symbols measuring 1 square inch or smaller. The data then can be scanned at a workstation and almost instantaneously displayed on a local terminal.

A conventional bar code acts as a unique identifying license plate for inventory. Only a small number of characters can be printed in this linear format before the bar code becomes too long for practical use, and once that bar code is scanned, a computer-resident database must be accessed to obtain any details about the inventory. In contrast, 2-D symbologies are intended to be small, stand-alone databases. While there are several ways to encode data in such a compact format, there are two generally accepted types of 2-D symbologies—stacked symbologies and matrix symbologies. 2-D bar codes are still in the early stages of acceptance by industry, but there is little doubt that they have a significant future.

Summary

Proper storage is important to accountability and quality retention. Items in storage must be tagged to facilitate first-in first-out (FIFO) procedures, and most importantly, to force receiving and storage room personnel to weigh and count products. Placing prices on items during tagging is beneficial to the control element in two ways. Prices on items improve the perception and understanding that products are actually money and they ease the inventory process.

For control purposes all products in storage should have a specific location in the storage room. Shelves should be labeled and prices should be placed on the shelves. This aids in the FIFO process because items are not placed behind other items and forgotten. Procedures such as this also speed up the inventory process, aid in sanitation of the storeroom, and help in identifying high cost items so that they will not be placed close to the door for easy pilferage.

Delivery personnel should never be allowed in the storage room, as they may be tempted to remove items on their way out. Therefore, only authorized employees should be allowed in the storage room and storage areas should be kept locked at all times.

Products should only be issued when a requisition has been submitted, and products should be signed for when removed from storage to maintain accountability. Without these controls products can come up missing with no way of tracing them. The few minutes it takes to sign and date the removal of product from storage is a worthwhile endeavor to the control process. Even the smallest operations need to record any item that is removed.

It is important to point out that once products are issued, the management function of control is not finished. Products that are not used should be returned to storage personnel who should either hold the products for reissue or return them to the vendor for credit. Management must understand that just because figures may balance it does not mean that the process is successful. It is only through constant observation and feedback from guests and employees that management can be assured that controls are functioning properly.

Review Exercises

1. With regard to physical inventory, it is important from a control point of view that:
   a. it is performed by at least two people
   b. it is done once a month
   c. it occurs during the middle of an accounting period
   d. it includes items that are on order

2. Which of the following is a method of assigning values to an inventory?
   a. last-in first-out
   b. first-in first-out
   c. actual purchase price
   d. all of the above

3. Excessive products on hand can cause the following problem:
   a. the price of the item may increase
   b. the item may become limited on the market
   c. excessive capital is tied up in the inventory account
   d. all of the above

4. Inventory turnover rate can be calculated by:
   a. multiplying the amount of inventory by sales
   b. dividing the cost of products sold by the average inventory
   c. adding the ending and closing inventory amounts
   d. dividing sales by the average inventory

5. Which of the following is important when establishing a storage facility?
   a. location
   b. recordkeeping
   c. type of inventory
   d. only a and b

6. Which of the following is a benefit of placing dates and prices on products?
   a. the vendor is known
   b. it assists in rotating stocks
   c. management knows when to reorder
   d. all of the above

7. Products received by a foodservice operation normally fall into two categories:
   a. directs and stores
   b. directs and perishables
   c. stores and perishables
   d. frozen and dry

8. Stores are items such as:
   a. canned goods
   b. flour
   c. sugar
   d. all of the above

9. Par stock is
   a. the amount that is ordered for a new restaurant
   b. the amount on hand between deliveries
   c. determined by the vendor
   d. the amount on hand during a promotion

10. Which of the following is a major issue regarding storing:
    a. security of products
    b. linen products
    c. bulk items such as flour and sugar
    d. time of delivery

11. What are the procedures for distribution of a requisition?

12. How would you establish the par level for flour if 10 pounds are used on a daily basis and you receive deliveries every five days?

13. List five ways in which bar codes may be used to support the control function of a foodservice operation.

14. What control procedure(s) would you use to ensure that physical inventory will be taken accurately?

Examination Type Problems _____

1. What formula is used to determine inventory turnover and what are some advantages of performing this calculation?

2. What formula is used to determine the amount of products consumed during an accounting period?

3. In operating an upscale steak house, in what fashion should products be stored in the refrigerator?

4. Explain how a requisition is extended and the importance of this activity.

Case Study _____

The storeroom manager of the Case Study Hotel told you that one of your cooks came to him at 9 a.m. and requested a 2½ pound can of coffee. The cook said that they just ran out of coffee and they were still serving breakfast and the dining room was packed. The storeroom manager asked him for his requisition and he said he did not have time to fill one out and would try to have the shift supervisor sign it, as this was an emergency. The storeroom manager told you that this individual had the same problem a couple of weeks before with a different item. At that time the cook told him that he would get a requisition completed right after breakfast, but two days passed before he gave the storeroom manager the requisition. As the restaurant manager, write out the process of proper requisition and present it to your staff so that such incidents will not happen in the future. Please outline the process point-by-point from assessing the needs of the restaurant to receiving the products from the storeroom manager.

References _____

Forger, G. (September 1996). 2-D bar codes: More options, new ways to manage inventory data. *Modern Material Handling, 51,* 37–39.

Keough, J. J. (February 1997). Vendor managed inventory takes center stage. *Industrial Distribution, 86,* 13.

RMA annual statement studies. (1997). Philadelphia: Robert Morris Associates.

Zalud, B. (May 1996). Asset tracking embraces printing, tour improvements. *Security, 33* 63–64.

9

Preparation and Production

Key Terms

contingency menu
leftovers
pilferage
production errors

production schedule
recipe conversion
recipe yield
sales history

standardized recipe
substitution
time series
working factor

Learning Objectives

After completing this chapter, you should be able to:

- list ways to prevent waste during production.
- explain the importance of forecasting to the production process.
- describe recipe conversion procedures.
- explain the importance of using measuring devices during production.
- explain how to arrive at the food cost for a product.
- explain why only one person should be in charge of preparing a product.
- explain how production errors can increase costs.
- explain the significance of production control to cost, time, and perception of value.

- explain why it is important to have a production schedule.
- explain the cost relationship in substituting products.
- describe effective ways to use leftovers.
- understand the importance of a contingency menu.
- list the essential factors that should be listed on a kitchen production worksheet.
- describe the importance of correct tools, equipment usage, and maintenance.
- describe ways in which pilferage can occur during the production process.

Outline

The preparation and production process begins with standardized recipes of products listed on the menu. As discussed in Chapter 3, standardized recipes provide instructional information to production personnel and information to management for determining the cost of products. A correctly written recipe provides all the necessary standards for ingredients, measurements of products, methods of preparation, cooking temperature, cooking time, portion size, amount yield, and equipment. If products are prepared according to standards listed on a recipe, a consistent product will be achieved and guest satisfaction can be enhanced. Standardized recipes establish standard yield and consistency and help control costs effectively.

The production process should not generate any type of waste, if possible. When meat such as chicken and turkey is cut up, trims such as fat, skin, and bones that may otherwise be discarded should be put into a stockpot. Small servings of products can be used in soups or to provide color or garnish other products. Small scrapes of dough can be used to make bread sticks or pastry sticks. Leftover toast can be used to make croutons. Spatulas are a must for a foodservice operation. Without them, servings of items such as mayonnaise, mustard, salad dressing, ketchup, tomato paste, and most items that are prepared in mixing bowls can be wasted. Every effort must be made to completely use all of every product. In short, carefully planned and executed preparation and production can save the operation a lot of money.

Employee Training

When preparing items for serving or cooking, waste can easily occur if employees are not properly trained. All production employees should be trained in the techniques prescribed by standardized recipes, including the slicing, dicing, and trimming of products. Portions can be lost if personnel are allowed to use their own discretion in making preparation decisions. Employees must be trained to chop, slice, or dice products according to the specifications in the standardized recipes. Chop generally means to cut the product into small pieces about the same size, while dice usually means to cut into small cubes of ¼, ⅓, or ¾ inch. Employees must be shown the differences. If carrots are to be sliced, the thickness of slices must be dictated along with how much is to be eliminated from the top and bottom. If apples or potatoes are to be peeled, employees should be monitored to ensure that they are not removing too much of the product itself with the peel. Employees often become lazy when peeling these types of products. They may find it easier to remove a large amount of the product than to remove only the skin. It is important not only to train personnel about proper procedures but also to monitor or observe as well.

Forecasting in Production

In a hospitality operation the ideal scenario is that the last serving of a food product is served to the last guest in line. Everyone understands the difficulty of attaining this, however, every effort must be made to try and reach this point of efficiency when projecting the volume of production. Forecasting sales is extremely difficult, but hospitality operations must make these types of business decisions on a daily and weekly basis. Projecting sales in the hospitality industry is crucial to cost control, as certain items cannot be placed back into inventory. Decisions must be made regarding production and personnel as well as other components of the business. This type of planning requires forecasting business volume. Forecasting is usually based on what is occurring at present and what has occurred in the past; therefore, time is considered one of the most important factors in managerial decision-making. Because time is so important, statistical inferences concerning the future include a variable or set of variables based on past and current events. When forecasting, a hospitality operation may want to use a time series, which is a sequence of measurements for a variable or composite of variables arranged in chronological order of their occurrences. Therefore, forecasting of sales is usually far more successful in preventing overproduction and overstaffing when organized procedures are used rather than gut feelings. Additional information concerning forecasting procedures will be discussed in Chapter 16.

The importance of forecasting cannot be understated; however, few operations understand the importance of maintaining a sales history. There are several benefits in maintaining an accurate sales history. For control purposes, a sales history can provide two invaluable types of information. First, management can evaluate previous sales projections to help determine future projections. Second, just as important from a control point of view, management can evaluate sales trends when certain employees are working. A sales history can help management identify certain trends in sales for different meal times, days of the week, and seasonal activities. This can prevent the overutilization of labor and overproduction. If specific production personnel or bartenders are stealing, a sales history often reflects a reduction in sales or an increase in costs when these employees are on duty. Even if employees are not stealing, a reduction in sales may indicate that they are not as effective in suggestive selling and guest service as other personnel. Most operations basically use their sales history for the purpose of forecasting, but other trends, such as an employee's job performance, can also be examined.

Determining Portions and Food Costs

Production errors can occur as a result of not accurately projecting the correct amount of yield. Products can be priced incorrectly if management is not aware of the true usable portions of products. Some products have a much lower percentage yield than the amount purchased. If the amount required is not projected correctly, then the wrong price for the product may be listed on the menu or quoted to guests for functions. Some products have to be trimmed and portions may be lost during cooking because of shrinkage. The formula for deriving the correct yield is as follows:

$$\text{As purchased amount} = \frac{\text{Usable portion}}{1 - \text{Waste percentage}}$$

If management would like to serve 300 6-ounce portions of pork loin and 30% of the portion is lost during trimming, cooking, and portioning, then the amount that needs to be purchased can be calculated:

$$300 \text{ people} \times \frac{6 \text{ oz}}{\text{person}} \times \frac{1 \text{ lb}}{16 \text{ oz}} = \frac{300 \times 6 \text{ oz}}{16}$$
$$= 112.5 \text{ lbs (usable portion)}$$

$$\frac{112.5}{1 - .3} = \frac{112.5}{.7} = 161 \text{ lbs (as purchased amount, rounded)}$$

Production personnel should draw 161 pounds of pork loin from storage to ensure that 300 people will receive 6 ounces each. The amount required to serve 300 guests (161 pounds) differs significantly from the amount that would be anticipated without determining usable portion (112.5 pounds); therefore, it follows that costs also differ. Mistakes in portioning can be costly, as prices, once quoted or printed, cannot be raised.

Understanding food cost when developing products is essential. The contribution margin of a product and other cost factors are important. Additionally, in order to price products correctly, the cost of developing those products must be known. To determine the cost of a standardized recipe, the ingredient costs are totaled and a per-unit cost is calculated. For example, when preparing a recipe that yields 100 servings, all ingredient costs are added to obtain a total cost, and then the total is divided by 100 to determine the cost of each portion served. Food cost should be determined for each item on the menu. If food cost is not known, a product can be underpriced, and this can be costly to an operation over the long run. Also, always use as purchased amounts to price recipes accurately.

Recipe Conversion

Standardized recipes provide consistency in developing quality products. Recipes are usually developed for specific amounts of yield; therefore, it is frequently necessary to modify the standard yield of a recipe to accommodate a larger or smaller number of projected sales. To maintain consistency, recipes must be converted as accurately as possible. If recipes are converted haphazardly, waste is apt to occur and in some cases the entire product may have to be discarded. If an operation employs unskilled cooks, management may want to convert recipes and indicate the number of portions to be prepared rather than allow inexperienced personnel to convert them. Preconverted product amounts can save time and prevent mistakes in production.

Standardized recipes are usually developed to produce yields of 25, 50, 75, or 100 servings. Because an operation cannot afford waste, it must forecast as accurately as possible the number of portions to be served. Before converting a standardized recipe, all of the items in the recipe must be reduced to a common denominator and a working factor must be developed. In other words, if a recipe contains measurements in both pounds and ounces, all pounds should be changed to ounces. Once the amounts of all the ingredients have been changed to the same measurement, the quantity of each ingredient is multiplied by the working factor, and then all ingredients can be changed back to usable measurements.

To develop a working factor in cases in which the desired amount of the product is greater than the amount yielded by the standard recipe, divide the standard yield of the recipe into the amount desired. For example, if the yield of a standard recipe is 50 and the amount required is 400, the working factor is calculated as follows:

$$\frac{400 \text{ (amount required)}}{50 \text{ (recipe yield)}} = 8 \text{ (working factor)}$$

The amount required is 8 times the yield of the standard recipe; therefore, the quantity of each ingredient in the recipe should be multiplied by 8 to establish the correct amount of ingredients to be used. The working factor is a whole number in this example; however, sometimes the working factor can result in a mixed decimal fraction. For instance, if a standard recipe yield is 50 and the amount required is 440, the working factor is calculated as follows:

$$\frac{440 \text{ (amount required)}}{50 \text{ (recipe yield)}} = 8.8 \text{ (working factor)}$$

The amount required is 8.8 times the yield of the standard recipe; therefore, the quantity of each ingredient in the recipe should be multiplied by 8.8 to obtain the required amount.

If the amount required is less than the amount yielded by the standard recipe, only a portion of the original yield is needed. First, form a fraction by

Figure 9–1   *Recipe Conversion*

Ingredients for 8 Dozen Dinner Rolls	Ingredients for 5 Dozen Dinner Rolls
10 oz granulated sugar	6 ¼ oz granulated sugar
10 oz hydrogenated shortening	6 ¼ oz hydrogenated shortening
1 oz salt	⅝ oz salt
3 oz dry milk	1 ⅞ oz dry milk
4 oz whole egg	2 ½ oz whole eggs
3 lbs 12 oz bread flour	2 lbs 5 ½ oz bread flour
2 lbs water	1 lb 4 oz water
5 oz yeast, compressed	3 ⅛ oz yeast, compressed

placing the amount desired over the amount yielded by the standard recipe. Then reduce the fraction to find the working factor and multiply the quantity of each ingredient in the recipe by the fraction to obtain the desired amounts. If a standard recipe yields 50 servings and 25 servings are required, the working factor is calculated as follows:

$$\frac{25}{50} = \frac{1}{2}$$

The quantity of each ingredient in the recipe should be multiplied by ½.

Food service personnel must be accurate in converting recipes. While the conversion steps are simple, a mistake can be costly. With regard to the recipe in Figure 9–1, a mistake in converting measurements for yeast, salt, or sugar easily make the product inedible. If not enough salt is used, the rolls may not turn golden brown on top and may burn on the bottom; too much salt can kill the yeast and the rolls will not rise. If there is doubt about the accuracy of a conversion, it is best to have it reviewed.

Measuring Devices

Employees must be trained to use and understand all the different measuring devices. Although most employees know what a scoop is, they may not know the equivalent weights and measures of the different sizes of scoops. The correct utilization of measuring devices aids in preventing waste through overusage and can prevent ruining a product because of an incorrect measurement. It is often said that cooking is an art and baking is a science. On the contrary, cooking is also a science. By not correctly measuring ingredients during preparation, a product can become too spicy, too salty, or too greasy. Changing the composition of a product can often cover a mistake during the cooking process;

Figure 9–2   *Sample Conversion Table*

Fraction	1 Tablespoon	1 Cup	1 Pint	1 Quart	1 Gallon	1 Pound
1	3 tsp	16 tbsp	2 cups	2 pints	4 quarts	16 oz
⅞	2 ½ tsp	1 cup less 2 tbsp	1 ¾ cups	3 ½ cups	3 quarts plus 1 pint	14 oz
¾	2 ¼ tsp	12 tbsp	1 ½ cups	3 cups	3 quarts	12 oz
⅔	2 tsp	10 tbsp plus 2 tsp	1 ⅓ cups	2 ⅔ cups	2 quarts plus 2 ⅔ cups	10 ⅔ oz
⅝	2 tsp (scant)	10 tbsp	1 ¼ cups	2 ½ cups	2 quarts plus 1 pint	10 oz
½	1 ½ tsp	8 tbsp	1 cup	2 cups	2 quarts	8 oz
⅜	1 ⅛ tsp	6 tbsp	¾ cup	1 ½ cups	1 quart plus 1 pint	6 oz
⅓	1 tsp	5 tbsp plus 1 tsp	⅔ cup	1 ⅓ cups	1 quart plus 1 ⅓ cups	5 ⅓ oz
¼	¾ tsp	4 tbsp	½ cup	1 cup	1 quart	4 oz
⅛	½ tsp (scant)	2 tbsp	¼ cup	½ cup	1 pint	2 oz
¹⁄₁₆	¼ tsp (scant)	1 tbsp	2 tbsp	4 tbsp	1 cup	1 oz

however, some products can easily become inedible if a mistake is made, especially during baking. Any mistake can cause a facility to lose time and money. Unskilled personnel frequently have a difficult time converting measurements. Tables like those in Figures 9–2 and 9–3, laminated and taped to the wall or put in a folder, give employees the necessary tools to do their tasks better.

Figure 9-3   *Weights and Measures for Scoops*

Scoop Size #	Measurement in Tablespoons	Approximate Weight
6	10	6 ounces
10	6	4–5 ounces
12	5	2.4–3 ounces
16	4	2–2.5 ounces
20	3	1.74–2 ounces
24	2 ⅔	1.5–1.73 ounces
30	2	1–1.5 ounces

Production Schedule

A production schedule or cook's worksheet for controlling cost is essential in maintaining consistency and in preventing production errors. A production schedule enables management to maximize and estimate the utilization of labor, equipment, and other resources. If many baked items need to be prepared for a meal, an operation's baking facilities may not be able to support the meal. The same can be said for a deep-fat fryer and other equipment. A production schedule assists managers in identifying these problems so that alternative plans can be made. Also, management is able to conserve labor hours by scheduling personnel only when needed, or if personnel are on a regular work schedule, by assigning other tasks when production is not being done.

Figure 9–4 shows the minimum information that should be included on a production schedule. Management must be specific when stating what is to be prepared, what method of preparation is to be used, and how much is to be prepared. To achieve the expected outcome, products must be prepared according to specific instructions. If a manager only lists fried chicken on the production sheet and the recipes for both traditional fried chicken and southern fried chicken are the same with just a few additional steps for the southern fried chicken, the outcome of the product may differ from what was intended. Misunderstandings can be prevented by being specific.

Cost control is an important factor when making decisions as to what is to be prepared and how much should be prepared; therefore, management must ensure that all leftovers and perishable items in storage have been taken into

Figure 9–4   *Production Schedule*

Item to Be Prepared	Method of Preparation (per standardized recipe)	Amount to Be Prepared	Shift	Personnel	Amount of Leftovers	Items Returned to Storage
Carrots	Peel and julienne	40 lbs	1	Ricky		
Rice	Cook in oven	15 lbs	1	Ricky		
Cheddar cheese	Cut into 1-inch cubes	20 lbs	2	Bill		
Tenderloin 7-up	Trim and cut into 6-oz portions	40 portions	2	Jack		
Russet Potatoes	Wash and wrap in foil	40	2	Bill		

consideration. Also, specifying who should prepare the product may reduce the possibility of errors and waste during the production process. The production process centers on preparing, cooking, and holding food. If a specific person is not responsible for each product, a breakdown in one of these steps can occur. Unless a product has to be completed at different times by different personnel or shifts, only one person should be responsible for preparing a product. The possibility for error increases if two or more individuals are involved in preparing the same product. An ingredient could be added to a product twice, or one individual may assume that another person is going to take care of a specific procedure and it may never get accomplished. If one person completes a production task from beginning to end, there is less chance of a problem occurring. If a product such as chicken salad is to be prepared and the ingredients are allowed to stand at room temperature for too long while shifts change or while personnel decide who is to add which ingredient, a guest could become ill from consuming the salad. Additionally, management would know who should be consulted if a product is not up to standards or if the required amount was not prepared.

A production sheet should record how many servings of a product were leftover. Recording leftovers is essential to the control of the production process. If a large amount is leftover the product may have been unappealing to guests or overpreparation may have occurred. Recording the information may provide management the ability to evaluate why leftovers exist. Additionally, management should note any meals that were rejected or exchanged as this assists in accountability of production. If a guest sends a steak back, management wants to be able to account for that particular product and note the reason for the incident.

Management should ensure that the production schedule is posted early enough in advance to provide personnel an opportunity to draw products from storage and to organize their work tasks. Some items may have to be drawn from storage the day before to be thawed under refrigeration. Items that are not used and do not need to be used as leftovers should be recorded on the production sheet and returned to storage. If items are not returned to storage properly, they may eventually be misplaced or stolen or have to be discarded.

Production Errors and Waste

As mentioned, standardized recipes are developed to ensure consistency in quality and accuracy in projecting costs for products. If an operation loses consistency, it may experience an increase in cost and a decrease in guest count. Managers should keep an eye out for basic production mistakes, as a loss of quality may indicate that standardized recipes are not being followed. It is easy to discern when an item such as brown gravy has an incorrect grease to flour ratio, or when black spots in the gravy indicate that the roux was cooked on heat that was too high. Management must also watch to see if servers or cooks are placing too much dressing on salads. These are problems that managers should identify, evaluate, and correct.

Every effort must be made during the production process to prevent waste. Although an operation may have outstanding specifications for products and may order quality products, it means little if production personnel do not respect the value and costs of those products. Half a serving of a product wasted on a daily basis can add up to more than 180 servings a year. If this product is a vegetable item that sells for $1.25 per serving, this accounts for a loss of $225 per year.

Communication

Production errors can quickly crop up if there is a breakdown in communication. It is essential that production personnel be made aware of changes that affect production. For instance, if personnel were not informed of an increase in guest count, an embarrassing situation could result because not enough food was prepared. If the number of guests decreased substantially but the original amount of food was prepared, products may have to be thrown away, and the cost may not be recouped because advance notification of the change in guest count was given to the operation, although management failed to notify production. Constant communication between management and production personnel is vital to successful cost and waste control.

Meat Products

Meat products present special production problems because they constitute a major part of food cost and are very perishable. Temperatures for cooking meats must be strictly observed in order to develop standardized products. Temperatures that are too high reduce the size and yield of a product and make the meat less tender. If chicken is fried in grease that is not hot enough the product will not become golden brown and will absorb a lot of grease. On the other hand, if the grease is too hot the chicken will become golden brown but may not be completely cooked inside. If fried chicken is too greasy, guests may send it back to be replaced. If chicken is not completely cooked, a guest may send it back or may unknowingly eat it and become ill. Incorrectly prepared products culminate in lost money and dissatisfied guests.

With regard to boning and removing meat from bones, employees must be shown what is expected, as waste can occur when boning a product, just as when peeling products. Trimming meat can also cause waste. If too much meat is cut off, the yield decreases and food cost increases.

Salt can also ruin meat products. Employees must be trained not to salt meat before placing it on the grill or directly on heat, as salt makes protein tough. Inexperienced cooks often think they can improve the taste of a steak by putting salt and pepper on it before placing it on the grill. What actually happens is they take an expensive piece of meat and make it tough.

The incorrect slicing of meat can also make a quality product undesirable. Guests may find it unappealing when an expensive piece of meat is made tough by slicing it with the grain instead of across or against the grain. An operation may lose guests because of inferior quality, and over the course of time, even minor errors and small amounts of waste can add up to a large loss in revenue.

Production Control

Production control has to be maintained if food cost is to remain within cost standards. If recipes and cooking times are not followed expensive portions can be lost, which increases food cost. Cooking vegetables in too much water causes the dissipation of nutritional value as well as portions. If meats such as spareribs, ham hocks, or baked chicken are overcooked, portions can be lost due to meat falling off the bone. In many cases, additional portions have to be prepared as a result of overcooking, and this wastes time as well as money.

Management must be aware that the public has standard perceptions of consistency, taste, and appearance of certain products. If the taste, consistency, or appearance of a product differs from the norm, a facility would be wise to identify the product as some type of house specialty. For example, a potato salad that does not have the appearance of most standard potato salads can be given a specialty name. If the chef's name is Bennet, it could be called Chef Bennet's special potato salad. This would prepare guests for the perceptual difference and may actually improve their perception of value.

Cost Relationship in Substituting Products

Foodservice operations are always looking for ways to reduce cost and increase profit. To increase profit an operation can select from four activities.

1. Reduce quality
2. Reduce portion sizes
3. Increase prices
4. Substitute products

Any of these activities may affect quality and the perception of value. Guests are apt to identify a reduction in quality quickly. There is a difference between substituting products that simply have a cheaper cost and substituting quality. Guests will notice that a cut of meat is tough because of a change in quality or that portion sizes have been reduced. If an operation begins to "play games" with prices, the laws of supply and demand will begin to take effect and guest count may decrease. Therefore, the least threatening of the four cost-control factors is to try to substitute an ingredient with one of the same quality but a lower price. Examples of this would be to use walnuts instead of pecans in bakery products and to cook with conventional tomatoes instead of vine-ripened tomatoes.

When the cost of some products become too expensive, an all-out change in the menu or substitutions may have to be made. This is always a possibility with a regard to produce. Prices in the produce market can change quickly due to events caused by nature. If the menu features asparagus, which is normally considered an expensive item, management may substitute a different vegetable. This type of change may go unnoticed, especially if they are temporary. If handled with care, management may use substitutions from time to time to bring costs back in line. Conversely, management must ensure that production personnel do not intentionally substitute products to try to cover up pilferage. Substitutions should only be made with the consent of management and there should be a valid reason for the substitution.

Contingency Menus

It is important for production personnel to have contingency menus. Contingency menus are necessary to prevent the development of leftovers. There are times when an increase or reduction in the amount to prepare may not suffice. Major events and other situations can cause a vast increase or decrease in guest count, and thus may require a different menu. If the guest count increases significantly, the equipment in the facility may not be able to handle the regular menu. If the guest count decreases significantly it may not be cost effective to prepare certain items. Management should anticipate major annual events and develop contingencies for food production and labor volume to control cost. If the operation depends upon some type of seasonal product, contingency menus should be available, as the lengths of seasons vary from year to year.

Utilization of Leftovers

Even though management may attempt to forecast food sales as accurately as possible there are still many uncertainties that cannot be anticipated. A vast decrease in projected guest count can cause a full-service facility to end up with a great deal of leftovers. It is management's responsibility to prevent the waste of leftovers. Four factors must be considered when dealing with leftovers.

1. Leftovers must be used at the next meal or as soon as possible.
2. Leftovers must be heated to an internal temperature of at least 165°F without interference in the heating process.
3. Management should change the face (composition) of leftovers.
4. Management should never attempt to offer leftovers a second time.

Because improperly handled leftovers carry potential dangers, management must not allow the sole aim of reducing food cost to influence their decision to serve questionable products. Because food is always deteriorating, leftovers should be served at the next meal. The longer food is held, the greater the possibilities for further deterioration, contamination, and bacterial growth, which could make someone ill. Because of potential health risks, leftovers should always be reheated to at least 165°F as quickly as possible. For safety reasons and prudent and ethical management, controlling cost should never be an overriding factor in using leftovers.

If leftovers are served as the same product, they may lack the consistency and quality that guests expect; therefore, management should develop plans for changing the face of leftover menu items. Grilled pork chops can be turned into smothered pork chops. If not enough pork chops remain to make this change worthwhile, the meat can be chopped and used in pork fried rice. Because items made with leftovers are not usually featured on the menu, they may have to be offered as specials. Changing the face of products can expand the menu and may provide greater sales appeal to guests. Proper utilization of leftovers can assist in maintaining food cost; however, there are limits to using leftovers and once items have been reused they must be discarded. Leftover items must never be carried over to a third meal.

If there are leftovers at the conclusion of a meal, management has the additional responsibility of determining whether the kitchen overprepared. Leftovers are normally the result of a decrease in the amount of anticipated sales; however, not paying attention to the production sheet and overproducing can also cause leftovers. Management must also ensure that overproduction did not purposely occur. If management establishes a policy that employees can eat leftovers or take them home, employees may intentionally overprepare products. Fast-food operations, requiring that some items are always prepared to ensure fast delivery, are often confronted with this problem. Management has to evaluate why leftovers occurred and attempt to eliminate the problem.

Tools, Equipment, and Maintenance

Just as measuring devices are important to proper production procedures, so are other tools and equipment. Without the proper tools and equipment, it is difficult for production personnel to comply with control standards. Additionally, production personnel are apt to take shortcuts if they have to search for the correct tools. Taking shortcuts and using inappropriate or malfunctioning tools can result in incompleted tasks or injury to personnel. Dull knives cause far more accidents than sharp knives because dull knives require more exertion to cut. Employees often break expensive kitchen knives by using them to open cans and crates, to separate frozen meat, and to cut bands on cases. Personnel should be trained to properly use tools and equipment. When equipment is expected to outperform its capabilities or if employees are allowed to abuse equipment, it will become costly for the operation. Maintenance must be routinely done and not viewed as tasks to be completed because there is nothing else to do. Documentation as to how equipment should be cleaned and what type of cleaners should be used must be readily available or employees may use incorrect procedures or cleaning compounds. Schedules that dictate how, when, and who should clean a piece of equipment must be posted.

Pilferage

As stated earlier in the text, the most vulnerable time for products to be stolen is during the receiving and storage periods. During this period products are out in the open and anyone passing by has access to them. Also, collusion between delivery personnel and receiving personnel may prevent products from ever actually entering the facility. Once products are placed into storage, and storage facilities are given the necessary security, the probability for pilferage decreases. However, as soon as the production process begins, incidents of pilferage, waste, and fraud are highly possible. The production process presents opportunities for theft to a large group of employees.

While there is a possibility of theft throughout the control process, it is during the production and serving process that a manager must really understand the techniques of control. Far too many managers believe that if numbers balance from purchasing through production, then the control process has been completed. Most students are indoctrinated with this process in mind. If input equals output, then all is okay. This is far from the truth when dealing with consumable products. If operations constantly lose profits because of pilferage and a subsequent increase in costs, managers may eventually lose their jobs and foodservice facilities may fail.

Managers must ensure that cooks and servers are not eating, giving away, or stealing food products. Managers must follow and strictly enforce company policies with respect to these activities; otherwise, these activities can quickly get out of hand, which has been the reason for business failure in numerous foodservice operations. An operation should not establish any kind of policy—either written or understood—that allows employees to consume or take home food leftovers. Not only may employees attempt to generate leftovers, but it may become difficult for management to identify which products are real leftovers and which products are purposely generated leftovers. Food products must be treated and respected exactly like money. At times, management can identify a problem simply by counting and comparing products. Every once in a while, a manager needs to count the number of guests and compare this count to the number of products that have been consumed. A manager must remember that balanced figures do not obviate the need for an occasional physical count of products.

Management must practice some fundamentals concerning the prevention of theft by production personnel. Managers should observe employees carrying large handbags and gym bags as they can be used to remove products from the preparation area. Employees taking trips to their cars in the parking lot should be monitored. It is wise to have a designated smoking area away from parked cars so that employees will not have a reason to go to their vehicles. Trash must be checked from time to time to ensure that employees are not mistakenly or intentionally discarding flatware or carefully wrapped food products to be retrieved at the back door. Policies must be established for employee meals and how much food is considered the "tasting" of food by production personnel. Locks must be changed whenever an employee who has keys to any part of the facility is terminated or resigns.

Beverage Production Control

The beverage department is one of the most profitable areas in a hospitality operation. The contribution margin for beverages far exceeds the margin provided by food or other products. Many operations, including quick-service restaurants, are able to reduce prices on other products because of the contribution margin of beverages. While iced tea is probably the leader in generating the largest contribution margin in most establishments, operations that sell alcoholic beverages may have numerous items with outstanding margins. Because the contribution margin for alcohol is fairly large, the production process of beverages is important to the success of an operation. In most full-service restaurants, food accounts for about 78% of sales, and alcohol accounts for about 22% of sales with far less labor cost. Although controlling beverage production is not as difficult as controlling food production, the possibilities for the misappropriation of funds in beverage operations are far greater. A successful beverage operation requires a great amount of control during the production process. Important aspects of the beverage production process are showmanship, consistency, and control.

Showmanship involves the style bartenders use in preparing and merchandising products. Because of the rising concern for responsible drinking, bartenders cannot attempt to increase sales through volume. Thus, the only way is either through an increase in prices or control in costs. Therefore, merchandising and showmanship may offset an increase in the price of drinks. During the showmanship process, production must be monitored to ensure that there is no overpouring or spillage of products, that standard recipes are being used, and that control procedures and standards are being met. For proper showmanship and merchandising the correct glass must be used for each drink. A scratched or chipped glass should never be used as it takes away from presentation and is a potential hazard. The correct swizzle sticks, napkins, and coasters should be used and fresh garnishes are a must. Bartenders should not use garnishes that are wilted or turning color. Any products that may detract from merchandising or showmanship should be replaced or avoided.

Consistency in beverage operations is important to taste and the perception of value. Guests like to know that every time they order a drink, the product will have the same taste and consistency. If products are not consistent, guests may complain or may not order an additional drink. Consistency is obtained through the use of standard recipes, measurements, and portion control tools such as shot glasses and jiggers. Consistency also enables bartenders to prepare drinks to the established quality and cost requirements. Consistency of quality does not present as much of a problem for beverage operations as for foodservice operations. A basic difference between alcohol and food is that, by law, alcoholic products themselves usually have a consistent quality. Therefore, when purchasing alcohol there is not as much concern for controlling quality. However, when preparing drinks quality is extremely important. Customers like each drink to taste the same regardless of the facility. With the exception of specialty drinks, the average highball contains 1 to 1½ ounces of liquor. If a hospitality operation establishes shot standards that differ from the norm, then the established standards must remain constant. Consistency must be a priority in order to satisfy customers' perception of value.

The large contribution margin of alcoholic products and the anticipated income make it essential that management monitor all beverage operations. Because of the increased availability for theft by bartenders and waitstaff, beverage operations can be one of the most difficult areas to manage. The potential loss of income, possibility of theft, and the fact that alcohol is highly regulated pose problems. The beverage license of an operation could be jeopardized if regulations are not followed; therefore, the control and monitoring of alcohol is a necessity. Ways by which bartenders may erode the profits of an operation will discussed more in detail in Chapters 10 and 11.

Because alcohol is the most regulated product in the hospitality industry, the amount of control for alcohol is increased. Not only must management ensure that bartenders do not bring in their own alcohol to sell, there is always the possibility of state inspectors finding a bottle of alcohol that does not have a state seal or sticker. To prevent this and other problems the same control procedures for food should be applied to beverage production. As with food products, a requisition should be used to request any products from storage and all products must be accounted for at the end of the production process. Management should ensure that the amount of liquor at the bar at the beginning of a bartender's shift is accounted for at the end of the shift.

Empty bottles should be accounted for to ensure that state regulations are followed and that the refilling of bottles does not occur. To control inventory, empty bottles should be brought to the storage room any time a replacement bottle is required. However, this should not be the end of the control of empty bottles. State requirements for empty bottles should be implemented by storeroom personnel. In some states the law requires that empty bottles be broken and not simply thrown into the trash. If empty bottles are not accounted for, bartenders may refill them with their own alcohol, as the empty bottles would already have a state or organizational sticker or marking.

As long as tasks behind the bar cannot be separated, monitoring bartender activities will continue to be a priority. In no other position in the hospitality field is an employee responsible for taking and preparing guest orders, determining the amount of money that should be collected, collecting the money, and ringing up the sales into the cash register. Without feasible separation of these duties the beverage operation must be closely monitored. Management must occasionally work behind the bar to monitor activities as well as hire "secret shoppers" to monitor operational procedures. Management and secret shoppers should make sure that standard recipes and other standards are being followed and should note of any type of suspicious activity that may call for future monitoring.

Summary

Every effort must be made to prevent waste during the preparation and production phase. Standardized recipes, with specific procedures for measurements, weights, and amounts of yield, must be in place. The proper tools must be available to ensure that ingredients can be accurately measured during the production process. Equipment must be in place and maintained if the production process is to generate consistency and save labor costs. If personnel use equipment that is not appropriate for the task that needs to be accomplished, they may not maintain consistency and may also damage the equipment.

Forecasting has to be as accurate as possible to prevent the development of leftover products. Production sheets must be completed with the required yields, time of preparation, and the individuals responsible for preparing the products. If leftovers still meet the requirements for consumption, management should find a means of utilizing them as soon as possible to prevent further deterioration of the product.

Efforts must also be made to reduce waste through errors in production. If standardized recipes are not followed, mistakes in preparation and cooking will exist. Products may have to be discarded as inedible or because of a lack of appeal to guests. This can be the result of production errors or mistakes in recipe conversions. Recipe conversion must be taken seriously because discarding a large amount of a product that has to be remade will double the food and labor costs of that product. To further reduce the possibility of production errors, only one individual should be involved in the preparation of a food product. To prevent errors in production amounts, management may want to devise a contingency menu for certain occasions.

Accurate food costs of products have to be derived in order for products to be priced correctly. Additionally, portion control must be employed if standards are to be met. Employees should not be allowed to deviate from the standards. Management must realize that substituting a product or ingredient to reduce cost may reduce quality.

The public has a standard perception of consistency, taste, and appearance of certain products. If the taste, consistency, or appearance of a product is not perceived as the norm, guest count may decrease. Therefore, management must be trained to recognize and evaluate standard products. This is true even if the products are specialties of the facility.

The maintenance of consistency in products and portion control make the production process one of the most difficult steps in the control process. Pilferage must be prevented though accountability and attention to detail. During the production process, there are many opportunities for pilferage through substitution and incorrect portion sizes. Management must constantly observe production personnel procedures and guests reactions. All of the control procedures in the previous processes can be lost if products are not consistent and at least adequate. The best quality of a product could have been purchased, received, and issued to the kitchen, but if it is overcooked or cooked at a temperature that is too high, the product can be ruined. If spatulas are not used to get the remains out of cans and jars, servings can be thrown away. Too much salt can ruin a product. If potatoes remain in an automatic potato peeler too long, portions can be lost. Portions can also be lost if too much of the ends of products, such as carrots or onions, are cut off. During the preparation and production process, management must constantly monitor standards to ensure that consistency is maintained and waste does not occur.

Review Exercises

1. The first step toward ensuring quality products and dining experiences that meet or exceed guest expectation is:
   a. planning production
   b. developing service procedures
   c. ordering products
   d. preparing products

2. A production schedule reflects a forecast and is used to:
   a. set production goals for a chef and staff
   b. establish production standards
   c. list production techniques to be used in training
   d. inform production personnel of new recipes

3. A chef needs to prepare carrots for 400 guests. The portion size is 4 ounces per guest. If carrots have a waste percentage of 10%, what is the total edible portion that needs to be prepared?
   a. 300 pounds
   b. 200 pounds
   c. 400 pounds
   d. 100 pounds

4. Referring to question #3, what is the total purchased amount needed?
   a. 90.0 pounds
   b. 110.00 pounds
   c. 111.11 pounds
   d. 120.00 pounds

5. What is the working factor to convert a recipe if the standardized recipe is for 100 guests and the number of guests for a function is 500?
   a. 4.00
   b. 1.25
   c. 0.20
   d. 5.00

6. Which of the following is not necessarily pertinent information to be included in a production schedule?
   a. method of preparation to use
   b. amount to be prepared
   c. when food is to be prepared
   d. the name of the group the food is prepared for

7. Standardized recipes should be used in:
   a. restaurants in a hotel
   b. restaurants in a club
   c. foodservice outlets in institutions
   d. all of the above

8. What can sales history identify in forecasting for food production?
   a. guest counts or trends for certain meal times
   b. waitstaff performance level
   c. the working factor for recipe conversion
   d. how long the restaurant has been open

9. Which of the following can cause errors in production?
   a. day of the week
   b. temperature
   c. weather
   d. number of guests served

10. Which of the following is considered pilferage in the production process?
    a. cooks using a different measuring device
    b. cooks taking food home without permission
    c. cooks giving waitstaff food as part of employees benefits
    d. cooks not communicating well with the waitstaff

11. List five activities that can cause production errors.

12. List five ways in which pilferage can occur during production.

13. What is the working factor to convert a recipe of 50 to feed 220 guests?

14. In preparing the Mother's Day lunch buffet, you estimated a total guest count of 450. Of the 450 guests, you forecast that 200 would take the steamship round. The portion size for the steamship round is set at 4 ounces and the waste factor due to trimming and cooking is 25%. How much meat will need to be purchased for the buffet?

15. There is normally a 5% waste in cleaning iceberg lettuce. If 6 ounces is needed for each serving, how much lettuce will need to be purchased for a banquet of 60? If processed iceberg is $1.10 per pound and regular iceberg is $1.00 per pound, should you buy the processed lettuce? (Ignore the labor involved for calculation purposes.)

Examination Type Problems

1. Using the yield formula, determine how many pounds of beef ribs production personnel would have to request from storage to serve 200 6-ounce portions when 40% is lost through cooking and trimming.

2. Using the recipe conversion formula, convert the following recipe for dinner rolls from 12 dozen to 8 dozen.

   1 pound 4 ounces granulated sugar
   1 pound 4 ounces shortening
   8 ounces dry milk
   2 ounces salt
   5 ounces whole eggs
   6 ounces yeast
   3 pounds cold water
   7 pounds soft four

3. Describe four important procedures that should be adhered to when handling leftovers.

4. Give two reasons why only one employee should be responsible for preparing a product.

5. A standardized recipe calls for 10 pounds of julienned onions for making French onion soup. If the waste factor for onions is 10%, how many pounds of onions need to be purchased?

6. A conference group booked a banquet for 350 and has chosen zucchini as one of the vegetables. If 2 ounces of zucchini batonettes are served to each guest and the waste factor in preparing zucchini batonettes is 10%, what is the as purchased amount?

Case Study

As the manager of Model Restaurant, you are always concerned with controlling cost. You walk through the kitchen and see your baker making rolls for the day's business and he is not measuring his ingredients. This is the second time you have observed him not measuring ingredients and you talked to him about it the first time. You question him about it and he tells you that he has been making the rolls this way for over two years and that there is no need for a standardized recipe for rolls. The baker is a dependable and highly motivated employee. He is always willing to come in on call. However, he only works five days a week. You are concerned with the consistency of the products and the fact that when he is off for two days an inexperienced cook will have to prepare the rolls. You go back to your office and check the purchases of flour and you notice that there is a vast amount of waste in that product. You do not want to demotivate the baker but you would like him to measure the ingredients so that you will be able to maintain the cost of all products and so that you will be able to develop the same quality product when he is not working. What are some steps that you can initiate to have the preparation and production of rolls followed? Give five suggestions and explain the importance of each suggestion.

10
Service

Learning Objectives

After completing this chapter, you should be able to:

- explain the importance of service as a competitive advantage.
- describe guest expectations.
- describe the important elements of portioning.
- explain the need to control condiments.
- explain the importance of quality control as it applies to service.
- analyze the pros and cons of empowerment.

- describe why different types of service require different methods of control.
- describe the difficulties in controlling the back and front of the house.
- describe the need for departmental relationships.
- explain the importance of a POS system.
- explain some of the problems associated with beverage operations and control.

In the hospitality industry, differentiation and location are usually the major reasons why one operation is more successful than another. If an operation has a great location, it may have a captive market; if not, some form of differentiation is usually required for guests to select one service facility over numerous others. Dominos Pizza made several other pizza organizations realize the importance of service when they opened their speedy delivery service. Fast-food operations and other types of service operations maintain their share of the market by providing a drive-through service. Outstanding service, therefore, can provide a competitive advantage. In order to maintain this advantage, management must control the consistency of service. Service can be one of the most cost-effective means of maintaining and gaining a better share of the market.

Front of the House

Quality Control

All activities that occur in any business revolve around delivering quality products with the highest possible quality of service. An operation is apt to be more successful if their customers are satisfied. It is important to remember that customers have basic expectations and decide what constitutes quality service. Management may think that service is great, but guests may feel totally different.

Because the hospitality industry is labor intensive, employees are an operation's most important resource. The majority of managers in the hospitality field may say that guests are the most important constituent in a hospitality operation. For an operation to be successful, however, managers must realize that employees are an equally important, if not the most important, component of an operation. Because quality of service greatly influences guest perception, management must attempt to motivate all employees to deliver the highest possible quality of service. Outstanding service can make an average meal outstanding, and by the same token, poor service can make an outstanding meal distasteful. Substandard service or employees with negative attitudes can put off guests and dramatically reduce an operation's guest count.

The difficulty in motivating employees to provide outstanding service is even far greater in the hospitality industry than in other industries. Considering that the majority of employees in the hospitality industry only earn minimum wage and that the average annual turnover rate in many facilities is over a 100%, management has to be concerned with controlling the quality of service. Regardless of how much effort has gone into other aspects of controlling an operation, all is lost if employees fail to provide quality service. This is why managers must lead by example. If managers treat guests and coworkers with courtesy, employees are apt to emulate this. To control the service process, management must set an outstanding example when interacting with guests and train employees to attain a set level of expectations. Management must also constantly impress upon employees how important their presence is to the operation and how important the level of service to guests is to the success of the operation.

Guest Expectations

Guests have basic expectations for each level and type of service according to the type of facility. Patrons of a medium-scale foodservice establishment and patrons of a medium-scale beverage operation generally expect both operations to provide the same level of service, although guests in a beverage operation may expect to be able to talk and interact more with the bartender or other guests. Guests in an upscale restaurant expect outstanding service; guests in moderately priced facilities may only expect adequate service. This holds true for the hotel business. Guests in a resort hotel expect a much higher level of service than that of a budget hotel. Nonetheless, guests in any one of these types of facilities expect the following service features:

- Courtesy
- Timeliness
- Knowledgeability
- Accuracy
- Honest and ethical practices
- Cleanliness

Courtesy Employees must be taught to be courteous to guests. The old adage that the customer is always right has not changed. However, what employees may consider courteous over the years may have changed. Management cannot take for granted that employees know how to approach and address guests. Employees come from all walks of life and the guest base is usually extremely diverse. This is where the difficulty lies. Employees must not only be trained to be courteous to guests but they also must be trained to treat each guest as an individual. It is through flexibility that guests feel special and a server is able to meet their expectations.

A server should approach every situation with extreme courtesy. He or she should not use guests' first names unless guests request this type of familiarity. Servers should never embarrass guests, many of whom are at a facility for business meetings and dinners, by correcting the pronunciation of a word or dish on the menu. They should only correct a guest to clarify an order. Communication skills are an important part of courtesy. Guests should not have to repeat their orders or "test" a server by asking him or her to repeat what was said. Servers should maintain eye contact to avoid appearing aloof and to assure guests that they are paying attention and will not make a mistake with the order. A mistake in taking an order wastes the guests' time because the order has to be returned to the kitchen and it also costs the facility money because an additional product has to be made. It must also be pointed out that good posture is important as it displays a sign of attentiveness and respect, for oneself and for others. Management would be wise to look for these traits when interviewing prospective servers.

Timeliness   Timeliness and prompt service are important, as a high seat turnover rate during the course of a day's business generates more profit. Additionally, timeliness in service means that all the members of a dining party can be served at the same time. Staggered or slow service can entirely ruin an affair. Anytime an operation is busy management must instruct servers to inform the guests that it will take longer than usual to fill orders. Guests should be notified in advance to decide whether they have time to wait or whether they would prefer to patronize another establishment; they should not place an order and then find that it is going to take much longer than anticipated. Additionally, it is important for servers to look out for orders so that they can be delivered as soon as they are prepared to maintain product quality. Return business may decline if guests can see their orders waiting to be picked up while service people stand around talking.

To enhance timeliness, workstations should be established and equipment strategically located to reduce the time and motion needed to retrieve items. Handheld service terminals are becoming popular mechanisms for reducing time and motion and also reducing the possibility of mistakes in reading orders. The ability to electronically enter orders at the table prevents servers from having to walk back and forth to the kitchen or computer terminal.

Paying attention to detail can make the difference in whether service is perceived as quality service. Anything that wastes time can detract from a guest's perception of quality. If a guest waits to be served a particular product only to be told that the facility has run out of that item, the guest may become upset because the situation was not stated upfront. This situation is especially awkward if there are two or more people in a party and a guest is not told until the rest of the party is being served. Servers and production personnel must communicate to avoid breakdowns of this type. Stockout is bad enough, but not informing a guest right away is unacceptable. Servers must be aware of changes in menu items and should know which items on the food and beverage menus have the largest contribution margins. This way they can make suggestions to guests when a product is out of stock. This is also helpful when they are suggestive-selling or making recommendations.

Knowledgeability   Servers should be as knowledgeable as possible about menu items, their facility, and their surroundings. If a guest asks what the special is and the server has to find out, aspects of professionalism and quality are lost. Because of diet or health concerns, guests may enquire about the ingredients in products, and servers must be able to provide accurate information.

Servers must also be knowledgeable about surrounding facilities and current activities that might have drawn people to the restaurant or hotel. This makes guests feel that they made the right decision in choosing that particular facility. Servers should be aware of the closest banking facilities and automatic teller machines. They should know the location of the nearest post office and the number and name of the nearest interstate exit or highway exit.

Whenever a guest telephones for directions or hours of operation for the facility, anyone who answers the phone should be able to provide accurate information. All employees must be aware that guests begin to measure quality of service with first impressions. Whether it is a telephone call, driving into the parking lot, or entering the facility, perception of service always starts with the initial contact with an employee or the facility.

Accuracy Every effort should be made to ensure that a guest's order is clearly received, as this is an essential part of successful service. If a product has to be returned to the kitchen for any reason, time and service quality are lost. The time spent getting an order correct the first time is well worthwhile. Repeating orders back to guests is one way of doing this; however, servers should refrain from doing this unless they are unsure of what was said. The decision whether this method should be employed will have to be made based on the level of confidence that management has in its employees. Servers must be sure to clarify such things as cooking options to avoid mistakes. If a guest orders catfish and the facility provides different methods of preparation for catfish, such as fried and broiled, the server should enquire as to which method is preferred. Servers should not simply select the most common method of preparation or assume which method a guest prefers. Also, the possibility of substitutions should be made clear upon taking an order, as this provides a guest with more options and lets a guest feel that he or she is in charge. French fries may come with a dish according to the menu, but an operation may not mind substituting a baked potato.

Just as accuracy is important in taking orders, it is also important in providing the correct service when delivering products. Service personnel should know how the different products should be presented and served. An establishment must provide training classes, videos, or films to illustrate every service procedure that is expected. The proper methods of delivering products and retrieving empty containers should be addressed. It is useful to have these procedures on film because all employees may need to occasionally watch them, as even the best employees can develop bad habits over the years. Having films for new servers to watch also ensures standards. When training and reinforcement are assigned to an experienced employee, he or she may pass on bad serving traits to a new employee.

Not only must servers use correct serving procedures but they must also use the correct utensils. Under no circumstances should an operation use chipped china or glassware. Dinner plates should be replaced once the glaze begins to wear off.

Honest and Ethical Practices Guests expect honest and ethical practices from operations and servers. Guests like to know that products are wholesome and fit for consumption, and that leftovers are not retained at all costs. Guests do not want to worry about being overcharged, receiving incorrect change, or being victims of credit card abuse. While management hopes that all of their employees are honest, from time to time a mistake is made during the hiring process and a dishonest employee may be hired. Some employees may take money from the cash drawer or may upgrade tips on credit card receipts. If a server is constantly having problems making change or adding tickets, the server should be watched, counseled, then reprimanded, and even replaced if no progress is made, as guests may perceive an honest mistake as an attempt to cheat them.

Cleanliness   Guests' perception of cleanliness is crucial to the success of a hospitality facility. A facility must look and smell clean, and employees must reflect this in their carriage, dress, and hygiene. Clean and trimmed fingernails, tidy uniforms, well-groomed hair, and overall personal hygiene all reflect on guests' perception of cleanliness. How products, tools, and equipment appear also has a lot to do with expectations of cleanliness. If guests are observed wiping off their flatware or removing crumbs from their chairs before sitting down, management should be concerned. Dishes returned to the kitchen with a lot of food remaining may indicate that guests are unhappy with the food or the service. Management must remain aware of guest expectations and try to motivate employees to meet or exceed these expectations.

Portion Control

One may wonder why this topic appears in a chapter about service, especially since portion control was discussed with regard to food preparation and production in Chapter 9. The reason for including a discussion of portion control in this chapter is because waitstaff are responsible for many types of portioning in the service area.

Because of new equipment, technology, and storage methods, portion control has been made a lot easier for the industry than it was in the past. However, the perception of value still belongs to the guest. Servers should communicate with cooks and management if portions do not appear to be in accordance with standards or if a guest makes a comment concerning an insufficient portion. There are always some guests who complain unjustifiably, but if complaints become frequent, management must investigate the problem.

If standard portions are not followed, costs will eventually be out of line with budgetary expectations. Managers must periodically weigh portions and train employees to know what a standard portion of a product should look like. Trying to ensure consistency in portions can be difficult when slicing cold cuts, portioning roast beef, or even serving salad and salad dressing. Management must compare portions to see if the amount requested matches the amount served and must constantly monitor servings to see if guests are receiving the correct amount. Even garnish portions must be consistent. Serving sizes can be even more complicated in cafeteria lines where guests can see inequities in their servings as compared to those of others. Also, because some guests frequent an establishment on a regular basis they are apt to notice if there is a decrease in the amount they usually receive.

Management must monitor employees to make sure they are not shorting portions to pilfer products. The greatest amount of theft within a food service operation occurs through a reduction in portions. It is important to constantly monitor and evaluate the size of portions and to let cooks and service personnel know that portions will be monitored.

Managers have to ensure that cooks are not working in collusion with servers to try to gain larger tips through larger portions. If servers realize that they have some big tippers, they may persuade cooks to provide those guests with slightly larger portions or ask bartenders to pour larger amounts and split the tips. Bartenders may exchange drinks for food and tips with cooks and waitstaff. Adjustments for these factors can usually be found in decreased portions to other guests.

Controlling Condiments

Employees place small monetary value on items such as restaurant condiments and guestroom amenities (soap, shampoo, and so on) and often take these products home. Most employees do not understand that individually packaged or portioned items are expensive. Employees may not take large bottles of ketchup but will take the same amount in small packages without realizing that the amount in small packages that equates the amount in a bottle is far more expensive because of the individual packaging. Management may stand a better chance of controlling these items if they explain to employees that pilferage of these items substantially detracts from the bottom line. Signs may need to be posted in the back of the house to list the cost of these items and how stolen items can increase costs over the long run.

Airlines discontinued packaging sugar with flatware several years ago. It was easy to see how much sugar could be saved in a day by just asking passengers if they wanted sugar. Foodservice employees should also be trained to ask guests about these types of items. Many guests do not want ketchup with their French fries yet many fast-food operations place a large number of ketchup packages in each takeout bag. Also, when guests request order to go in full-service establishments, they should be asked when picking up the order if they require plastic flatware. In a majority of cases, guests are going home to eat and prefer to use their own flatware. When serving salads, the waitstaff should be instructed to ask guests how much dressing they would like. Too much dressing can ruin a salad as well as waste money.

Empowerment

The issue of empowerment is still not totally accepted by all managers because of the negative stereotyping of hospitality employees as unskilled and uneducated. The concept of empowerment is that management gives employees decision-making power. Of course, this power is not bestowed on employees as soon as they are hired. Training assists employees to make operating decisions on a daily basis so that they do not have to obtain approval from management in every decision. As employees become better educated, management will find that by increasing the decision-making discretion of workers, they will be able to provide a higher quality of service. Two factors may prompt managers to become more involved in empowering their employees. First, managers of hospitality organizations usually juggle so many tasks that they need employees to make quick decisions and realize that employees must have the ability to do so. Second, management realizes that employees may be more aware of the sensitivity of an immediate situation. If a guest is irate, the problem is best solved as quickly as possible.

Managers who advocate employee empowerment believe that it is cost effective in the long run. They think that employees become better educated through empowerment, and if cost control is explained to them, they will not abuse the privilege. Some managers assert that empowerment helps to motivate employees by making them an integral part of the organization, which aids in reducing costly turnover. Additionally, empowerment can enable the quick resolution of problems, which can heighten a guest's perception of value if a server is allowed to make a decision on the spot.

Managers who are against empowerment feel that the majority of employees in the industry are not capable or ready to make some decisions. Some managers think that employees will take advantage of empowerment and abuse it in certain situations. For instance, if employees are allowed to replace meals that are unacceptable without having to check with management, they may simply give meals to friends or relatives. Another reason for the rejection of empowerment by managers is the control factor. Many managers want to be involved in every decision and find it extremely difficult to delegate responsibility.

Whether management is for or against empowerment, the truth of the matter is that hospitality managers are required to perform a large number of tasks during any given day. If employees are not utilized to their fullest, micromanagement may cause numerous managers to leave the industry. The answer may be to try to be more selective when hiring employees, as management may have to rely on a certain amount of empowerment to control operations successfully.

Types of Services and Control

Different types of services require different controls. If a facility uses expensive china and silverware, the amount of concern over these products should increase. The same can be said for paper goods in fast-food operations. Fast-food operations use a large volume of paper goods and employees have a tendency to waste paper goods with the perception that they will be discarded anyway, so there is no need to be concerned with their conservation. However, if an item represents a major cost to that particular hospitality operation then control of that item becomes a major concern.

Full-menu table service restaurants usually have a major advantage over all other types of foodservice operations because these facilities usually sell alcohol, and the sales and markup of alcohol can substantially cover mistakes in other areas. The markup on alcohol is generally so large that it allows full-menu table service operations the ability to generate a profit. Wine sales in some of these facilities account for a large portion of sales. Because of the profit margin and cost of some of these wines, controls must be very tight. Some bottles of wine in upscale full-menu table service restaurants carry prices that exceed $10,000. Imagine the amount of security and control needed in these types of facilities. Also, the china, crystal, silverware, and meat products in some of these facilities make control procedures extremely important.

Limited-menu table service restaurants often have other control issues. Although these types of facilities may not have as many expensive wines and serving utensils, they have to be even more concerned with controlling cost because they do not have the luxury of selling a lot of expensive wines to cover other costs. These types of facilities have to focus more on portion control and food cost. Upscale full-menu table service facilities have a concern with food cost but not nearly the concern that a limited-menu table service facility has. Operations that have a limited menu usually have to maintain greater control on inexpensive items, as every item represents a large margin of cost. Fast-food operations have small margins of profit and therefore must implement a vast amount of control on all items. Full-service facilities can use an ABCD classification approach to controlling items and can place more control over certain items such as expensive wines. These items fall into category A, less expensive items that require less control fall into category B, and so on. A fast-food operation does not have to break down control of products in this fashion. Limited service restaurants face additional control problems in that they have younger, more inexperienced employees and far greater turnover.

Cafeteria-style operations may be the most difficult to control when it comes to portion standards, even though these types of facilities may purchase convenience foods, which may help in the production phase. The difficulty is that dishonest and/or experienced cooks and servers can manipulate products for pilferage. Also, servers who work on the cafeteria line may waste products by portioning too much or upset the guests by not portioning enough. Servers should inform management if they think that products are inconsistent or if guests reject products because of their appearance. Significant quality substitutions in a product will usually be noticed by servers and guests alike.

Suggestive Selling

Suggestive selling by servers is important to the success of any operation. Suggestive selling is one of the best methods of increasing sales and should be practiced by servers and all employees that have guest contact. The idea behind suggestive selling is to help guests recognize true needs rather than to sell them unwanted products. This is also true when attempting any type of upselling, which is an effort to encourage guests to purchase a higher priced or larger item. It must be remembered that these methods should respect the constraints of a guest's real needs. Servers must also be aware that suggestive selling may persuade a guest to try a product the next time; however, if a server sells a guest something that he or she does not like or cannot use, the potential for the guest purchasing a similar item the next time is substantially diminished.

Management's job of controlling guest checks and monitoring the sales of servers have been made more effective through the use of computerized systems. Managers need to know how much suggestive selling each server is accomplishing and whether servers are reusing tickets. It is difficult to detect if servers are stealing if they are working in collusion with kitchen personnel. This is a major problem with regard to lunch specials and buffets wherein the price of a meal is set and most guests order that same meal. The same guest check can be presented to kitchen personnel several times and can be presented to different guests several times. Management should question a server if a guest check stays open too long. Guest checks are a type of service control that cannot be taken for granted, as dishonest employees always try to circumvent any type of control measure.

A reduction in sales by a server can be the result of the server using the same guest check several times or it could be that the server is simply an inept or lazy employee. Managers in foodservice facilities must monitor guest checks to determine which personnel in their waitstaff are not doing enough suggestive selling or may just be providing bad service. Management has to talk with these employees and explain to them the importance of suggestive selling. Management has the task of trying to motivate all employees to provide the best possible service. Every effort must be made to reward employees that are providing outstanding service. Positive behavior must be reinforced for that behavior to continue. Management must reassess the employment status of employees who are not trying to enhance sales.

Serving Alcoholic Beverages

The quality of products is not as big an issue with regard to serving alcohol as it is with serving food; however, the control problems are paramount. Bartenders are responsible for producing, merchandising, and selling their products. It is difficult for an employee to be proficient at all of these tasks. Because of third-party liability and dram shop laws, operations must attempt to generate a profit through quality and service. Quantity should never be looked upon as a driving force to generate revenue, as responsible drinking becomes a concern. Bartenders have a great opportunity for producing and merchandising drinks and can be creative in trying to develop drinks that will enhance the size of a guest check. Bartenders should know which drink or drinks create the largest contribution margin for the operation. The expectation of bartenders by management is the same as for food servers. Additionally, bartenders are expected to be more attentive in remembering names of guests and their preferences of drinks and in being able to discuss current events. It would be wise for bartenders to read newspapers, magazines, and journals to stay abreast of current events. Although bartenders should not become involved in guests' conversations and should always avoid taking sides, it is helpful if they know what event is being discussed in case they are asked about it.

Beverage control must be implemented to ensure efficient and effective operational procedures, as there are many opportunities for a dishonest bartender to steal from an operation. Management has to be very selective when hiring bartenders, and references, including previous employers, should be checked, especially since they are going to handle money. Management must make every effort to protect the operation not only because bartenders have numerous opportunities to steal, but also because of third-party liability. Dishonest bartending practices included:

- Bringing their own bottles to substitute for the operation's inventory
- Overpouring for friends or to generate tips
- Short-shotting or underpouring
- Substituting call brands with well brands
- Underringing sales
- Adding water to alcohol products to fool the inventory process

- Leaving the cash drawer open
- Leaving the tip jar next to the cash register
- Padding the spill sheet
- Placing epoxy in jiggers
- Promotional abuse
- Voiding sales that were actually prepared

Bartenders usually do not choose only one of these activities; a dishonest bartender will probably use all available activities, all of which can take away from the bottom line.

If an operation does not place some type of identifying stamp on their bottles, bartenders may not hesitate to bring in their own bottles to sell. Placing identifying stamps on house bottles may at least slow this process down or deter bartenders from doing it at all. Bartenders who cannot bring in their own bottles may add a small amount of water to drinks or to the bottles. When they cannot easily perform these two types of activities they may simply substitute a cheaper brand or well drink for a call drink. This is a risky procedure because many guests know exactly how their particular drink should taste.

Dishonest bartenders may also overpour and underpour shots. They will overpour to try to generate larger tips. If a guest sees that he is getting almost twice as much per shot, he may not hesitate to make up for this by substantially increasing the tip. It is cheaper for the guest to leave a larger tip than to have to pay for additional drinks. Underpouring is normally done to conserve small amounts of alcohol for later use. For example, if a bartender short-shots three drinks by a quarter of a shot, then he or she can sell a three-quarter shot and keep the profit. Bartenders often have some means of keeping count by tallying swizzle sticks or by placing dimes or other coins in the cash drawer slot with bills. To under-pour shots with a certain amount of ease, some bartenders bring in their own stainless steel jiggers in which a small amount of clear epoxy has been placed in the bottom. This allows them to pour short shots right in front of guests and management without them ever knowing the difference. An operation may consider using an automated beverage system in which bottles of liquor are linked through hoses to a tabulating device. When a guest orders a drink, the bartender pushes a button or some other device and the right amount of liquor is dispensed and one drink is added to the liquor sales tally. If bartenders are allowed to free pour, it is quite difficult, if not impossible, to control standards.

Underringing sales can occur if bartenders are allowed to leave the cash drawer open. As there is no need to ring up sales, this is like having a license to steal. The same type of procedure can occur if bartenders are allowed to leave their tip jars by the cash registers. Bartenders can use their tip jars as a bank to take out sales that have not been rung and as a depository for money that is being collected through short shots or underpouring. Management must be observant of bartenders or cashiers that have a lot of expensive voids because in some cases the products may have been prepared and served. If a bartender runs a "Z reading," or a closing reading, an hour or so before the close of business, that last hour is pure profit for the bartender. Management must make sure that bartenders and servers do not have access to coupons or chits, as they can be easily substituted for cash at the time of a purchase or later when the cash drawer is being reconciled. Coupons and chits really open the door for unrecorded sales.

Back of the House

"Back of the house" does not simply mean the kitchen. Back of the house includes all functions that are normally out of the view of guests. Reservations, accounting, engineering and maintenance, and housekeeping are just some examples. Therefore, a good working relationship with the proper technological support is essential to provide the desired level of services.

Departmental Relationships

Departments must coordinate their activities for an operation to be successful. Every effort must be made throughout the organization to control cost. Lines of communication must remain open, as constant communication can prevent the possibility of breakdowns in services to guests. The entire organization must understand why guests frequent a facility. Guests are usually motivated by self-fulfillment and biological, social, and psychological needs. Servers are the individuals that must try to satisfy these needs. When guests enter a hospitality operation for food or lodging, they are usually hungry or tired, any one of which may cause discomfort. If there is a breakdown in communication in attempting to satisfy these guests, the server or front desk employee will receive the brunt of complaints. Therefore, all departments must interact to ensure that there is not a breakdown in expectations. For example, the kitchen may require expediters or food checkers to ensure that food products are acceptable and are delivered in a timely manner. When a guest is hungry and a mistake is made in the order, the guest does not care who made the mistake; he or she simply wants to be served. If a party arrives for a special event that was to have been set up and no one at the facility is aware of the situation, the entire occasion could be ruined for those individuals. Coordination and communication is the key to avoiding these types of problems.

Point-of-Sales Systems

With all of the managerial information that an effective point-of-sales (POS) system can provide, and with the reasonable prices of most models, every hospitality facility would be wise to invest in one of these systems for the purpose of control. Some POS systems can be linked to all areas of a facility. For instance, if a hotel guest decides to have breakfast before he checks out, a POS system that is linked to all areas in a facility will permit the close of the breakfast sale because the guest is still a registered active guest. As the POS closes the sale, the transaction is simultaneously posted to the guest's folio; therefore, when the guest checks out at the front desk, his breakfast charges have already been added to his total bill. However, in a slightly different scenario, if another guest decides to check out early to avoid the crowd and then finds that she has time to have a quick breakfast, a POS system will not allow the closing of the sale to a room charge because the guest is not an active guest.

POS systems easily maintain sales and inventory records and allow management to maintain waitstaff sales histories. If a POS system shows that the same individual has the lowest guest check average every week, and there is not a valid reason, this particular individual may have to be retrained or terminated. POS systems keep management informed of business and sales trends and can even extract certain types of sales from a broader base. For example, alcoholic beverage sales can be extracted from nonalcoholic beverage sales, and steak and lobster can be separated from other food products. The more items that can be extracted in a reporting system, the easier it is to detect mistakes or problems. The ability to extract this information and compare costs separately makes the purchase of this type of system cost effective.

The more controls that are built into the system, the more information the system can provide. Some systems that link bar operations may include types of drinks and brands used. Because prices can also be programmed into a system, there is less chance for error. Many operations find that POS systems can provide greater control for managing operations and thus allow management the ability to spend more time with guests.

Closing a Sale

The last impression is almost as important as the first impression. To develop a relationship with a guest and to generate return business, servers must make guests feel that their business is appreciated. It must be remembered that guests can take their business anywhere; therefore, all service personnel must be instructed to thank guests for their patronage. Every employee that guests see as they leave the facility should do this. This can add to a guest's feeling of satisfaction and may enable an operation to increase sales through return business.

Employee Theft

Theft by employees throughout the hospitality industry is a continuous challenge for management. While trying to control service to prevent losing guests and sales, management also wants to ensure that their staff is not going into business for themselves. In the foodservice arena, this may be as simple as a server using a guest check several times to order food or beverage items. In casinos, it could be an employee substituting coupons for tokens and selling the tokens. Clerks in a travel agency can collect clients' frequent flyer miles. Bartenders can perform an array of activities from bringing in their own bottles and selling shots to simply pouring short shots.

Because production and service are so labor intensive, management must try to implement sound control procedures. Personnel must be made aware that management is on top of things. Management may have a problem if some employees never want to take a vacation or time off, as these employees may not want management to observe any differences in sales income, which may indicate that the employees are stealing. Managers may have to run the bar for an hour on busy nights just to see if the amount of sales increase, or they may have to pull a cash drawer in the middle of a shift and replace it with a new one to see if someone is building a cash bank. All activities must be monitored and corrective action taken as quickly as possible. Once costs get out of hand it is difficult for a manager to regain control.

Summary

To control the service process, it is important to train employees in the operation's standard of delivery and service. Controls rely to a great extent on perceptions. A manager must let it be known that poor guest service will not be tolerated. Manager's must lead by example. Employees must be made aware that it is far easier to get guests to come back than it is to attract new guests. If sales are lost as a result of poor guest service, other costs will suffer. Labor and product costs cannot be paid if poor service loses guests. Once sales drop, an operation may not be able to meet its controllable and noncontrollable costs.

Dishonest activities practiced by service personnel must be controlled. A manager must monitor operations for such activities and may have to use secret shoppers to keep employees honest. Honest employees are usually not disturbed by monitoring and evaluation. Regardless of the efficiency of the interviewing process and the thoroughness of the references check, the hospitality field—with its easily consumable products—has to deal with its share of dishonest employees. Many outstanding employees have dedicated their careers to the hospitality industry, and yet many individuals take advantage of weak control systems.

Review Exercises

1. Which of the following do guests expect of service personnel?
    a. courtesy
    b. accuracy
    c. timeliness
    d. all of the above

2. Timeliness to a guest means:
    a. employees clock out at the assigned time
    b. servers deliver the products as soon as they are ready
    c. servers always get the drink order first even if a guest is ready to order the food item
    d. servers can answer all questions regarding the menu

3. Accuracy to a guest entails:
   a. an operation correctly getting the information and requests of a reservation
   b. an operation getting the information and requests of a reservation the quickest way possible
   c. servers knowing the names of all the guests
   d. servers smiling at guests at all times

4. Service personnel has influence over portion control in the following instance:
   a. when filling drink orders
   b. when putting salad dressing on a salad
   c. when getting bread, crackers, and butter for guests
   d. when cooking an entree

5. One of the best methods to increase sales by a server is:
   a. suggestive selling
   b. giving guests whatever they ask for
   c. selling the item that is the easiest to prepare
   d. padding the check with items that guests did not order

6. Good service in the beverage area includes:
   a. overpouring to keep guests happy
   b. giving complimentary drinks to guests
   c. getting the correct drink order to the guest in a timely manner
   d. diluting drinks so that guests will consume less alcohol

7. Good service is not important in which stage of the service cycle?
   a. when a guest first enters an operation
   b. when a guest is consuming the service or product
   c. when a guest is departing from the operation
   d. none of the above

8. Cleanliness as a service point for guests applies to:
   a. equipment used to prepare and serve the food
   b. personal grooming of the staff
   c. loading dock and trash storage area
   d. all of the above

9. The function of control is important in which type of operation?
   a. luxury
   b. midscale
   c. fast food
   d. all types of operations

10. Which action should a manager take if he or she suspects that a bartender is pilfering from the operation?
    a. terminate the bartender
    b. do not schedule the bartender and give him or her a leave of absence
    c. employ a trustworthy secret shopper to observe the bartender
    d. check the bartender's personal belongings when he or she arrives to work

11. Discuss why some managers are for empowerment and why some are against it.

12. List five methods to ensure that portion control consistently meets set standards.

13. List five attributes you would look for when interviewing an individual for a position as a server.

14. Explain how service can be used as a competitive advantage.

Examination Type Problems

1. List five expectations that guests have of servers.

2. List eight ways in which bartenders have an opportunity to steal.

3. Describe how servers can manipulate certain products in order to steal from the operation.

4. List three ways servers can use a POS system to enhance control activities.

Case Study

The Model Restaurant has been doing quite well and you are satisfied with its operating results. In the last month, however, with an increase in business, you have hired a few new staff members to cover this increase in sales. One evening, while you are visiting with guests throughout the facility, you notice that a guest has just received a prime rib that appears smaller than the 10-ounce portion listed on the menu. You stop by another table and ask the guests if they are enjoying their meals and one guest complains that his meal is not really hot. You also notice that a party of four has to ask for butter after receiving their bread. On your way back toward the kitchen, one of your regular guests tells you his meal tastes great. While continuing to make your way to the kitchen you observe two waiters leaning against the wall, smiling and talking.

At the end of the business day you analyze these activities. Make a list of issues that you would like to discuss with both your service and kitchen personnel and explain how you will handle each issue.

11
Sales and Cash Control

Key Terms

bank check card
bonding employees
cash bank
computerized systems

credit cards
debit cards
effective discount rate
guest checks

missing checks
overages and shortages
statement analysis formula
voids and overrings

Learning Objectives

After completing this chapter, you should be able to:

- list the items that should be included on a guest check accountability log.
- describe how to handle missing guest checks.
- describe the capabilities of a POS system.
- evaluate the advantages and disadvantages of a POS system.
- describe the three methods of payment or settlement of accounts and the convenience of each.
- explain the criteria an operation should consider when determining which credit cards to accept.

- explain different types of credit card fraud.
- design programs to prevent credit card fraud.
- explain why certain employees should be bonded.
- explain the disadvantages of a manual system.
- describe the differences between a credit card and a charge card.

Outline

Due to the competitiveness of the hospitality industry, cash control must be an ongoing concern of all hospitality operations. The margin of profit in the industry is not large enough to allow for any leakage. All efforts on other control measures will be wasted if cash can be easily stolen through sales, fraud, or pilferage. Cash control is essential if an operation intends to enjoy success and longevity. Management make employees aware of the importance of all cash handling procedures. When it comes to accountability, management must document why an overage or shortage on any type of cash transaction occurred. Management cannot become complacent and allow employees to perform managerial functions concerning the handling of cash. Also, management should not become so trusting that they allow cashiers to deduct overrings out of their cash registers or close out their own registers. In large operations, management may allow supervisors to void overrings, but even then, two people should be involved when voids or overrings occur.

Additionally, a record of these types of activities should be maintained. Employees may be less apt to use cash transactions to steal if they are aware that records are maintained. All theft is detrimental to an operation. When products are stolen, they are not available for sale. When cash is stolen out of sales, the products that were used to generate the sales in addition to the cash paid by guests to settle the payment have been consumed; therefore, stolen cash represents an even greater loss to an operation than stolen products. Management must attempt to install all necessary systems to secure and control cash.

Guest Checks

Guest checks used by employees are essential and should be viewed the same as blank checks. Without some form of control, employees may go into business for themselves, giving away food or selling food. For this reason alone, products from the kitchen or the bar should not be given to the waitstaff without some type of guest check or written request. Controlling guest checks is essential in maintaining accountability for sales.

Types of Guest Checks

Because guest checks are important control documents, those that can be purchased at a supply store should be avoided. Checks should be unique and developed specifically for an organization. Guest checks must be sequentially numbered for accounting and tracking purposes and should be printed on non-erasable paper, as this decreases the chances for substitution or alteration of checks. Point-of-sales (POS) systems and electronic cash registers can produce guest checks, which provides an operation with greater control.

Guest checks issued by an operation should be controlled with a sign-out sheet or a guest check accountability log. This sheet or log must list the check numbers, the dates the checks are signed for, the time of day when the checks are issued and returned, and a place for employees to sign checks in and out. Any unused checks should be returned at the end of the shift and the information should be noted on the sign-out sheet. As seen in Figure 11–1, management enters the name of the waitstaff, the shift worked, the beginning and ending numbers of the checks issued, and the date. Waitstaff is responsible for entering the time issued and returned, the numbers of any unused and missing checks, and their signatures. A program such as this highlights to your crew the importance of control and accountability.

At the very least, an operation should use a duplicate-check (dupe) system, which enables management to increase control over products as they are prepared and sold. A copy of each check is given to the production area that is to prepare the product. The copies are then placed in a locked container and compared to their originals at the end of the shift or the business day. With this process, an additional check needs to be written if a guest requests an additional food item. Some restaurants only use duplicates for expensive items, but they should be used for all items for better control. A security problem can exist when two separate checks are written for the same table and guests are allowed to present checks to the cashier and pay on their way out. Guests may pocket the more expensive check and only pay the less expensive one. For better accountability, anytime there are two checks for the same group, both checks should be annotated so that the cashier knows to look for two checks or more. Cashiers must make every effort to maintain strict control of checks that are presented to them by guests.

Missing Guest Checks

Missing guest checks should be viewed in the same manner as missing funds. Missing checks may have been altered or substituted. Management has no idea as to how much the transaction amount of the check might have been; however, this issue can be resolved through the use of a POS system. A POS system ensures the use of duplicates for control purposes and terminals can be set up for the waitstaff to place orders directly to the bar or the kitchen from the

Figure 11–1   Sample Check Accountability Log

Name of Waitstaff	Shift Worked	Sequence Numbers		Date	Time Issued	Time Returned	Sequence Number of Unused Check	Sequence Number of Missing Check	Waitstaff's Signature
		Beginning Check	Ending Check						

dining area. Even though management may make every effort to prevent the loss of guest checks, it may still happen on rare occasions. If it occurs too often, there may be a major control problem. Every organization should have procedures for dealing with missing guest checks, some of which may include:

1. Every effort must be made to determine if the check is in the facility. It could have been misplaced in the kitchen or folded in a menu.

2. The employee who is responsible for the missing check should write a statement as to the best of his or her knowledge of the whereabouts of the check.

3. Once it has been established that the guest check is not in the facility, the cash register tape, kitchen production sheets, or backroom printer should be checked to see if the amount of the order can be located; otherwise, all funds should be counted to estimate the amount of the check. Determining the amount of the check can help to determine the amount of the mistake or pilferage that might have occurred.

4. The sales record for that day should be annotated with the approximate amount of the check and the name of the employee who is responsible for the check.

5. The employee must be given a written reprimand, as there may be no way of determining the exact amount of funds that may have been lost. The employee should also be counseled on the consequences of a second occurrence.

6. If there is a second occurrence the employee should be given a final warning or terminated.

Management must provide written procedures to inform employees of the need to maintain security of their guest checks and the consequences of losing a check. Employees should also be asked to sign a form acknowledging that they are aware of the consequences. Employees perceive procedures and policies as more important when management takes the time to put them in writing.

Cash Register/POS Systems

Types of POS Systems

There are numerous types of POS systems available. The majority of systems can be programmed to handle any task that management requires, from maintaining a record of prices to linking departments. Some systems can track menu items and brands of beverages sold at the bar. Systems can usually be programmed to provide a daily menu mix, amount of sales, amount of inventory, and amount and cost of items consumed. The system can provide information on an hourly and daily basis. Some systems also perform time-clock activities as well as process authorizations for credit cards. Some systems are sophisticated enough to recognize reorder points and can generate purchase requests to bring inventory back to par stock level. Management must consider the present and future needs of the operation and should select a system that will allow the greatest efficiency in controlling costs.

Manual versus Computerized Systems

In this age of technology, with the costs of computer hardware and software decreasing to affordable levels, the benefits of computerized systems outweigh those of manual systems. Electronic cash registers provide some of the same capabilities as POS systems, but POS systems provide management with more capabilities to maintain control and reduce labor cost. POS systems perform activities faster and more efficiently. Following are some disadvantages of manually performing sales activities.

- Errors can occur as a result of misreading handwriting.
- Guest checks from food and beverage outlets may not be posted to portfolios in sufficient time before guests' departure.
- The possibilities for theft and fraud are much greater.
- Mistakes in arithmetic can occur.
- It can be difficult to evaluate sales performance.
- Management cannot compare readings against cash received.
- Checks used for payment by guests cannot be validated as quickly as they can with a computerized system.
- A trail tape is not available to compare sales and check for mistakes.
- Errors can occur because prices of items are not coded into key functions.

Clearly there is no longer an equitable comparison between manual systems and computerized systems. Even the least expensive computerized systems provide more controls and save management a vast amount of time, which makes them extremely cost effective. Additionally, because 70% of all transactions in fine-dining facilities are paid for by credit card, it is imperative that a POS system be linked to the credit card authorization process. If credit cards cannot be easily used or are not accepted, a facility is apt to lose some business. A manual system often delays employees, as they must wait for approval on credit cards.

Management should provide written procedures if a manual system is used for handling guest checks and other sales income. For instance, employees should be informed that pens—not pencils—should be used, and a single line should be drawn through mistakes rather than erasing them. This allows guests, managers, and auditors the ability to see what occurred. Even a manual system should include attaching a calculator tape to the final check to ensure that every effort has been made to prevent arithmetic errors. At the end of the shift, all checks should be accounted for before the employee who signed for the checks leaves. If a check is unaccounted for, the problem may be easier to resolve while the situation is still current.

A computerized system increases efficiency and reduces the possibility of lost checks. A server opens a guest check within the system by inputting his or her identification number and the guest check's serial number, although some POS systems automatically read the guest check number, thus bypassing the need to enter the serial number. Orders are placed in the system and are simultaneously relayed to the production area and printed on the guest check, thereby creating duplicate checks. An open guest check file usually contains the following:

- Location of the terminal used
- Server identification number
- Guest check identification number
- Time the guest check was opened
- Menu items ordered
- Method of preparation or special instructions for menu items
- Price of the items ordered
- Tax
- Total amount due

In a computerized system, items can easily be added to an open guest check, and because items are usually coded into different keys, there is less possibility for an error to occur when an employee is entering an order. Computerized systems provide management the ability to review a guest check at any time and to check voids or returned products.

Cash Banks

At the beginning of a shift, cashiers and often the waitstaff are given a cash bank. The volume of business usually dictates the amount of money in a cash bank. The amount and denominations of currencies that are in a cash bank should be listed on a cash register tape from the previous shift with the initials of the manager that verified the amount of the bank. Once the amount and denominations are verified, the employee using the cash bank must sign for it. Only the employee that signed for the cash bank can have access to it. When the bank is not in use, the cash drawer or container should be locked. Of course, when possible, a new cash bank should be given to the next shift so that any discrepancies or issues that may come up from the previous shift can be handled in a timely manner.

Even though an employee signs for a cash bank, management's responsibility for the transactions that occur from the bank do not end. Managers should constantly monitor cash sales; otherwise, employees may take money for a sale and say that the guest walked out or refused to pay, or they may collect money from a guest and destroy the ticket or take part of the money for a ticket and change the total on the ticket. If management does not show additional interest after the bank is signed for, these and other dishonest activities may occur. A cashier's log to record the day, date, outlet location, shift, and the amount that a cashier receives is helpful (see Figure 11–2). The cashier simply records his or her

Figure 11–2 *Cashier's Log*

Day	Date	Outlet Location	Shift	Amount Received	Cashier/Mgr's Name	Cashier/Mgr's Signature	Remarks

name, signs it, and notes any overage or shortage when the cash bank was given. Some restaurants require their waitstaff and cashiers to bring their own cash banks. Regardless of the cash bank supplier, it is imperative for management to follow and monitor sales and balance the banks to deter theft and mistakes.

Sufficient funds should be available in cash banks for cashiers and waitstaff to make change throughout a shift. This is important because mistakes can occur if cashiers and waitstaff begin to use their own funds or those of other employees in order to give correct change to guests. Cash banks should be stocked with currency denominations that are most suitable for the cost of products in the facility.

Following are some basic rules that should be followed when handling funds:

- Cash banks should be counted and signed for at the start of each shift.
- The drop box for extra cash should remain locked during each shift and cash drawers should be closed after each transaction.
- Bills over $50 should be placed underneath the currency tray to prevent easy access for theft.
- Cashiers and waitstaff should not attempt to complete two transactions at once.
- Cashiers and waitstaff should be aware of "change artists" who try to short cash banks by confusing employees.
- Personal funds of employees or management should never be used to make change.

Accounting for Overages and Shortages

At the end of each shift, employees who handle cash must verify the amount of funds in their cash banks and managers should take a reading from the POS system. Readings should never be given to an employee until the cash in the bank has been counted. If a reading is given to an employee before the bank is counted, the employee will be able to correct any overage or shortage without management being aware that a problem exists. This provides dishonest employees the opportunity to cheat guests and an operation without even having to maintain a count. Bartenders usually try to maintain a count whenever they are using short shots or some other method to generate funds for themselves; however, if they do not have to be concerned about the reading, they can simply deduct their profit from the cash bank before returning it to management. Some managers become so complacent that they allow employees to close out their own cash banks. This practice should never be tolerated.

Management should always be concerned about cash bank shortages, yet they should be just as concerned about cash bank overages. If a cash bank is over, a guest may have been shortchanged and may not have said anything, as he or she may not have thought it worthwhile; however, the guest may be offended, thinking that the operation is not well run and that the cashier is not trained, and may never return. If some guests are not concerned about keeping pennies from their change, a cash bank may be over by a few cents. Employees should try to prevent this by keeping extra pennies separate. Management should set a tolerance level to account for overages of a few pennies; however, management must be concerned if overages exceed more than a few cents. All overages and shortages should be documented for future monitoring. Figure 11–3 is a sample shift report in which overages and shortages can be recorded. Additionally, a facility's policies regarding overages and shortages should be included in the employee handbook.

Some operations use a three-step policy in handling overages and shortages. They may set a tolerance level of less than one dollar and any overage or shortage of more than five dollars is a major infraction and more than ten dollars is cause for a written reprimand. An employee who exceeds the amount of tolerance will be verbally counseled. Overages or shortages that exceed five dollars will be recorded in writing. An employee who exceeds the tolerance level three times will receive a written reprimand. An employee will receive a written reprimand if an overage or shortage of more than five dollars occurs a second time or if the discrepancy is more than ten dollars. Once an employee receives a written reprimand, he or she may be terminated if another incident occurs. Management must confer with its legal department to determine how to handle particular situations.

Processing Transactions and Deposits

Managers must ensure that all transactions are accounted for and that the cash register readings are reconciled with the daily summary report, credit card charges, checks, and guest checks. If for some reason cash, credit cards, checks, and coupons do not balance with the total amount recorded by the register or the POS system, management must check the readings for voids that may not have been reported or arithmetic mistakes. All cash receipts should be placed in a cash envelope and all vouchers and noncash materials should be placed in a shift envelope. There should be places on the outside of the envelopes to record the cashier's name, the amount of sales, the amount collected, and any overages and shortages. A deposit slip is completed, indicating the amount of cash and checks, and then the deposit is made according to the procedures of the operation.

Reports and Reconciliation

All activities should be compared and reconciled at the end of each shift and at the end of the day. Cash register balances should be reconciled with cash receipts at least once during each shift and all shift activities should be balanced at the end of the day. If transactions do not balance, managers must discern whether the cause is in the area of voids, checks, coupons, or stolen cash. Management should not leave the facility until all cash functions balance for the day's business.

Of course, reconciliation tasks do not begin and end on a daily basis. Because the hospitality industry is labor intensive and because the market fluctuates so much, all standards and variances must be evaluated and compared as frequently as possible to determine where costs are out of line. Funds or resources can be wasted if a problem exists and it is not corrected quickly. Weekly summary reports must be compared against budgeted projections to ensure that sales, labor cost, food cost, beverage cost, and all other activities are

Figure 11–3   *Sample Shift Report*

	Lunch	Dinner	Daily Totals
Day: Manager on duty: Cashier:			
Total payments	A	A1	
Payments previous shift	B	B1	
Tip less previous shift: A − B = C	C	C1	
Add ending open checks	D	D1	
Less beginning open checks	E	E1	
Gross Sales: A − B + (D − E) = F	F	F1	
Less taxes	G	G1	
Less charged tips	H	H1	
Net sales: F − G − H = 1	I	I1	
Total Sales: I + X = J	J	J1	
Credit card sales	K	K1	
American Express	L	L1	
Visa and MasterCard	M	M1	
Discover	N	N1	
Total credit card sales			
Hotel ledger charges	O	O1	
Department charges	P	P1	
Hotel room charges	Q	Q1	
Total hotel charges			
Cash reconciliation			
Travelers checks			
Large bills			
Twenties ($20)			
Tens ($10)			
Fives ($5)			
Ones ($1)			
Quarters ($0.25)			
Dimes ($0.10)			
Nickels ($0.05)			
Pennies ($0.01)			
Total cash receipts in drawer	R	R1	
Less beginning bank	S	S1	
Net cash	T	T1	
Total cash receipts	U	U1	
Less tips paid out	V	V1	
Net cash receipts	W	W1	
Cash over/short	X	X1	
Total receipts	Y	Y1	
Total number of cash receipts	Z	Z1	

as expected. Action must be taken immediately if there are any major variances. If variances are great, management must ask the following questions:

- Is the food or beverage cost percentage out of line because of price increases or because of theft?
- Is the labor cost percentage out of line because of a decrease in projected sales or are employees clocking in early or clocking out late to steal time?
- Are all controllable costs being efficiently controlled?

Fraud and Theft by Employees

Fraud and theft by dishonest employees can cause an operation to lose guests as well as income and trying to prevent these activities can be a difficult task. A vast amount of money is lost in the hospitality industry due to spoilage, leftovers, and unskilled labor, and when dishonest employees are added to the list, it is easy to understand why the industry is confronted with such a large amount of business failure. To reduce fraud, an operation must have a "hot stove rule" to send a clear message to all employees that management is serious about fraud, pilferage, and theft. Once dishonest employees are identified, they must be terminated.

There are numerous ways in which employees steal from an operation. Some dishonest employees, including managers and supervisors, use voids to steal. Voids can be a quick method to steal $50 to $100 by using only one large overring on a busy night. If a certain pattern of voids occurs, find a new cashier, and in many cases, a new manager. This outright stealing through sales presents a double loss, as employees steal the money and guests consume the products. The same thing occurs when an employee underrings sales.

Power surges or outages may occur in certain locations during rainy seasons and snowstorms; therefore, a facility must have backup guest checks so that money received from guests while cash registers or POS equipment are not in operation can be entered into the system later. Also, the trail tape should be annotated to explain why there was a time break in transactions. However, not all power surges have a valid explanation. Employees may cut off power to register systems during a busy fifteen-minute or half-hour period so they can sell products and keep the proceeds for themselves, as sales during this period cannot be entered into the system. This is why every power surge that occurs during business hours must be investigated. Frequent occurrences of this type of activity must be investigated by the manager or owner.

Following are some basic concerns about cash management and practices that may facilitate employee theft.

1. Managers become busy and give their keys to the POS system to an employee to take care of a managerial transaction. Managers must not allow employees access to their keys unless absolutely necessary, and in these cases, access should be limited and documented.

2. Managers sometimes allow the detail tape to run out and the continuity of transactions is lost, and with some systems, records of transactions are also lost. Managers should check the detail tape to ensure that there is a sufficient

supply before resetting the register. The detail tape should also be monitored from time to time to see if there are rings for no sale, voids, and guest check close-outs that are widely out of sequence.

3. Managers may use a key or a code to bypass alarms on cash register systems that are in place to alert management and employees that the cash drawer is being opened. Not only should alarms not be bypassed, but managers should monitor cash register operations as a regular part of their duties. Surprise cash register audits are a must to ascertain whether an employee is stealing from a cash bank.

4. Employees should not be allowed to cash personal checks at the facility where they work.

5. The cash register should not be used as an imprest fund, which is basically the same as petty cash in that money from the fund is used to pay for miscellaneous expenses and then the fund is reimbursed later. Small businesses often use funds in the cash register as petty cash and accountability eventually is lost.

6. Sales amounts that are rung into a register should be conveniently visible for guests.

7. Readings from a POS system should agree with the amount of cash received.

8. An employee who does not want to take a vacation or a day off may not want management to notice discrepancies in sales, which may indicate that an employee is stealing.

9. Cash registers should be emptied and left open when an operation is closed to prevent thieves from breaking into them and damaging the equipment.

10. A guest may pay with cash and an employee may pocket the money and say that a guest didn't pay his or her bill.

Bonding Employees

Management must be aware that dishonest employees can be detrimental to an operation and can cause an operation to fail. Cash control efforts are basically designed to maintain control of funds and provide security for funds. More importantly, cash control is designed to keep employees honest. There is little that can be done to prevent theft by individuals that are prone to steal. Dishonest employees exist regardless of how effective management's hiring practices may be. Even though management may make every effort to check references and verify past employment records, a thief can be difficult to detect.

The process of bonding protects an operation in cases of employee theft or when a subcontractor fails to complete a job within an agreed upon time. In hotel and motel operations, employees have opportunities to steal guests' belongings. The same holds true for credit cards, sales revenue, and other types of funds. To protect itself, a hospitality operation should bond employees who have access to large sums of money or have access to expensive property belonging to the business or to guests. Additional insurance can be purchased in case of theft of property. If operations depend on subcontractors to supply equipment or services, bonding can eliminate some of the liability in these situations. If the situation warrants, additional insurance can also be purchased to cover losses such as property, casualty, life, or workers' compensation.

Thoroughly screening employees helps prevent mistakes in hiring. Operations that have a large volume of cash transactions or that have large sums of money or expensive products on the premises should have employees bonded regardless of how efficient the screening process might be. Even though management may think that it has made the best hiring decisions, using secret shoppers and spotters is probably the best method of monitoring and assessing service activities. As managers attempt to implement controls, dishonest employees try to circumvent them.

Theft by Guests

Any type of theft presents a problem for a hospitality operation and will eventually affect the bottom line. Even if products are stolen instead of cash, products represent a cash value and will probably have to be replaced. Dishonest guests may steal from hospitality facilities. For example, guests may consume a large portion of a meal and then complain so they will not have to pay for the entire meal. Whenever guests do not pay for meals because of what may appear to be invalid complaints, management should take note of the individuals involved as they may try the same stunt again. Guests may also walk out without paying or they may pay with worthless checks or stolen credit cards. Management must ensure that all personnel are trained to try to prevent these mishaps. Cashier stations should be located near exits to prevent guests from leaving without paying.

Guests may steal property such as towels, bathrobes, ashtrays, coffee cups, flatware, and so on, and some guests may be more prone to steal products that feature a facility's logo; therefore, an operation would be wise to sell these products at cost to deter a certain amount of theft. Guests should be made aware that these products are available for sale at the cashier's desk or in the gift shop.

Some dishonest guests like to pay their checks at busy times in order to more easily cheat an operation. If a guest has a check of less than $10, he or she may flash a $20 bill in view of the cashier and then pay with a $10 bill. The cashier may give the guest change for $20 because the $20 bill is already recorded in the cashier's mind. These types of situations are difficult to prove, so cashiers must be trained in procedures for handling cash and must always be on the alert for scam artists.

Protecting the resources, image, and solvency of the hospitality organization must be an ongoing concern for managers. Management must implement control measures to prevent theft by employees, vendors, and guests. Employees must be informed that any type of theft will not be tolerated and they must be trained to perform their duties safely and effectively and to be alert for any type of dishonest activities. Procedures for handling cash, checks, guest checks, credit cards, and other resources should be in writing so that employees can read these policies and instructions and sign that they have read and understood them. If management establishes controls, emphasizes the importance of functions, trains employees, and sets the correct example a vast amount of fraud, waste, and abuse can be prevented.

Methods of Payment

When purchasing goods or services in the hospitality industry guests can use one of three methods of payment: cash, checks (personal, business, or travelers'), or credit cards. The method of payment used should be whatever is most convenient for or preferred by the guest, as method of payment often determines a guest's choice of facility or service. However, an organization's cash flow must also be considered when establishing which type of payments an operation will accept.

Cash and Checks

The advantage of cash is that it is universally accepted and it helps hospitality operations to maintain a good amount of working cash flow. Checks traditionally were used more than any other form of payment; however, the use of checks is now on the decline. Some facilities no longer accept personal checks because of the liability associated with them. To ensure that bad checks are not accepted, many hospitality operations have contracted companies that provide check verification and validation services. Electronic equipment is installed whereby an employee simply swipes the check through a machine to obtain validation. The acceptance of check payments by a business or organization for a specific function should be approved beforehand. This is important, as some nonprofit organizations are tax exempt and management must be sure to obtain their tax-exempt number. Travelers' checks are usually accepted even if a facility does not accept personal checks or credit cards. The near 100% replacement value on lost or stolen travelers' checks makes them a safe and convenient method of payment. If given a choice, most hospitality operations would prefer that guests pay with cash; however, from a control standpoint, most organizations and businesses prefer to make payment by check, as it is the most effective way for an organization to control output and maintain a record of payment.

Credit Cards

Credit cards provide guests with a method of payment that is similar in convenience to checks. When deciding which credit cards to accept, management must understand how credit cards work. A credit card company issues a card to a guest. The guest makes a purchase at a hospitality facility, and the hospitality facility sends the charge to the credit card company. The credit card company pays the hospitality operation, and the hospitality operation pays a percentage back to the credit card company. The credit card company bills the cardholder, and the cardholder settles the charges with the credit card company.

Types of Cards   All cards are not created equal. Visa and MasterCard are credit cards in which a cardholder receives a line of credit and interest is charged to the cardholder if the full balance is not paid off. Charge cards such as American Express require full payment at the end of a billing cycle of 20 to 30 days. The advantage of these cards is the unlimited ceiling on charges.

Bank check cards are becoming popular. A bank check card frees a cardholder from having to write a check, as the amount of payment owed to a facility is deducted directly from the cardholder's checking account. Because bank check cards are supported by cards such as Visa and MasterCard, facilities that usually do not accept checks now have the backing of a credit card. With regard to hotel stays, a hold is placed on the account for the number of anticipated days plus an additional amount to cover incidental expenses such as in-room telephone calls, movies, and so on. For example, if a guest checks into a hotel for five days and presents a bank check card, and if the room cost is $100 a night and the hotel's deposit policy for cash guests is the rate of the room plus $25 a day, the card holder's checking account will have a hold placed on $625 ($500 for the room and $125 for incidentals).

A debit card works differently from a bank check card. Debit cards are generally issued by a bank to be used at automatic teller machines. Many facilities do not accept debit cards; however, some banks have combined their bank check card and debit card and guests can use the same card for all transactions.

Which Cards to Accept?   When deciding which cards to accept, management must be concerned with three factors.

1. Availability and frequency of use of a card.
2. Cost or rate of a card. The pretax income of an average restaurant is about 4%, and a credit card company's charges further reduce this percentage.
3. Length of time it takes a credit card company to reimburse an operation.

Several other cost factors must also be considered, but these are the major concerns over the long run.

Management has a large number of cards to choose from, as there are now so many available. Additionally, the choice can be even more difficult if an operation is heavily involved in the international market. Although it does not hold a large share of the market, Diners' Club is considered the first modern charge card. In view of its name, it should also come as no surprise that the hospitality industry was involved in the inception of Diners' Club. Attorney Frank X. McNamara found himself in a restaurant with insufficient funds to pay his bill, and the idea for Diners' Club was generated. When American Express entered the market in 1958 it became the major competitor of Diners' Club in the hospitality industry. Bank of America in California introduced Bank Americard in 1960. The card was franchised to other banks and is now known as Visa. In 1970 Master Card and Master Charge merged into MasterCard International and became a competitor of Visa. Sears introduced Discover Card in 1985. The current leaders in the credit and charge card market, arranged in order of volume of cards in circulation, are Visa, MasterCard, Discover Card, and American Express.

Volume reflects availability. The fact that most cards, including Discover Card, which appeared in 1985, have passed more established cards such as American Express and Diners' Club in total volume indicates that guests prefer credit cards over charge cards. Therefore, when deciding which cards to use or accept, remember that credit cards are viewed as a convenient utility and that charge cards usually represent prestige. Patrons of a full-service, midscale restaurant or cafeteria expect the facility to accept credit cards; patrons of an upscale restaurant expect for the facility to accept credit cards and charge cards. Also, an operation must be aware that of all card transactions 59% are for retail purchases and 15% are for restaurant purchases, and that 73% of these purchases are made with Visa, MasterCard, Discover Card, or American Express. The type of card used by guests is often a perception of prestige. This is one reason why some guests use gold or platinum cards, as they indicate that a cardholder has graduated to a higher card level or credit line.

Although travel and entertainment cards such as American Express, Diners' Club, and Carte Blanche carry an annual fee, many businesses issue these cards to employees for expense account purposes, as these cards are usually accepted internationally. A hospitality operation may accept these cards because they provide marketing promotions, encourage business travelers to frequent the facility, and increases sales; however, these cards are usually more costly to a facility. Credit card companies receive most of their revenue in the forms of merchant discount rates and cardholder interest charges, while charge card companies such as American Express only obtain revenues from the businesses that accept their cards.

Factors in deciding which credit cards to accept—or whether to accept them at all—are the ability to increase sales, the ability to decrease losses that result from bad checks, and the cost of using credit cards, which is far less to an operation than the cost of travel and entertainment cards. Credit cards are also now accepted internationally. In deciding which card to accept from a popularity standpoint, Visa is used more often in restaurants than any other card. However, in the hospitality industry as a whole, travel and entertainment cards are widely used.

A facility should determine its target market, and the most widely held card of that target market should be evaluated for acceptance. Management's decision whether to accept a particular card must be based on feasibility and not solely based on what the competitors are doing. Before signing a credit card agreement, an operation must evaluate the cost of accepting a credit card to determine if using the card is cost effective; therefore, management must evaluate the effective discount rate. Figure 11–4 shows a statement analysis formula for business to evaluate the true cost of accepting a credit card.

Figure 11–4   *Statement Analysis of Credit Card Charge*

Required Information	Formula	Calculation
A. Annual volume of credit card sales	A = Given (e.g., $800,000)	
B. Average monthly volume of credit card sales	B = A ÷ 12	800,000 ÷ 12 = 66,666.67
C. Average number of credit card transactions per month	C = Given (e.g., 3150)	
D. Average check	D = B ÷ C	66,666.67 ÷ 3150 = 21.164
E. Discount rate	E = Given by credit card company (e.g., 2.5%)	2.5 ÷ 100 = 0.025
F. Statement fee	F = Fee given by credit card company ÷ B (e.g., $20)	20 ÷ 66,666.67 = 0.0003
G. Transaction fee	G = Fee given by credit card company ÷ D (e.g., $0.50)	0.50 ÷ 21.164 = 0.02369
TOTAL EFFECTIVE DISCOUNT RATE	0.0489, or 4.89%	

Once the effective discount rate is known, a hospitality operation should negotiate for the best possible offer. If management decides to go with Visa, they should contact at least three companies that handle Visa to try to obtain the best proposal for the operation. The merchant discount rates and fees of Visa, MasterCard, and Discover Card are about the same. These rates range from 1.75% to about 4%. Rates are usually based on processing and authorization procedures, average credit card transaction, and annual credit card volume. Rates for American Express are usually higher than rates for Visa, MasterCard, and Discover Card.

Processing Credit Cards   Processing a credit card refers to the manner in which a credit card transaction is completed. This procedure consists of three steps: handling, authorization, and settlement. The costs of each of these steps must be evaluated. Handling is the method in which a hospitality operation generates a sales slip for a guest. Authorization is the approval given by a credit card company and is required if the purchase exceeds the predetermined limit established in the credit card agreement. Settlement is the method in which a hospitality facility receives payment for a purchase. All of these activities can be processed electronically, which is the most effective way to control the transactions, reduce fraud and mistakes, and maintain cash flow.

Along with merchant discount rates, a facility must evaluate several miscellaneous fees for which it is responsible. These fees are in addition to charges involved in purchasing or leasing electronic equipment and processing fees and include setup fees, statement fees, programming fees, and charge-back fees.

Electronic Equipment   Unless a facility is very small and the volume of business is very small, from a control standpoint, using electronic equipment is the safest and most cost-effective method of handling, approving, and settling credit card transactions. Electronic equipment can be purchased or leased, and when selecting equipment, management should ask whether the equipment offers preauthorization, tip and server identification, as well as other features that meet the needs of the facility. Whether the equipment can be upgraded and what types of warranties are available are important questions. Issues concerning installation and maintenance should also be clarified.

Signage   Once a facility decides which card or cards to accept, guests must be made aware of their acceptance. Guests should not have to ask which credit cards a hospitality operation accepts. Signage should be displayed on the front of the facility and in the Yellow Pages. This is important because guests often make their spending or dining decisions based on whether an establishment accepts a particular credit card. Guests may pass over a facility because signage is not in view and they do not want to ask. Guests use credit cards because of the convenience, and if signage is not readily recognizable, then guests may choose another facility. All credit card companies provide signage and it should be used. Hospitality operations can place signage on windows, guest check trays, menu clips, plaques, counter displays, and so on. Care must be used when placing signage as guests need to be informed, but ambiance also needs to be maintained.

Credit Card Fraud   The majority of credit card fraud is a result of lost or stolen cards. Dishonest individuals often steal cards from the mail and may also fraudulently apply for credit cards through the mail. Most credit card advertisements state that a card has been preapproved and many individuals who receive such an advertisement consider it junk mail and throw it in the trash. A dishonest person can retrieve it from the trash, sign the name of the addressee, request a change of address, and in a couple of weeks, this person will have a credit card in someone else's name, which will enable him or her to use someone else's credit.

An employee can commit fraud even with all the controls provided by electronic equipment used for credit card approval. When given a card by a guest, an employee can run two credit slips and use one for the next cash transaction. Some employees may even run an invalid credit through the electronic equipment to credit their own accounts. Employees may also increase the amount of tips on credit card slips. This often happens in tourist areas, where employees have overheard guests say that they are just passing through, or in situations in which one person in a party pays for the entire bill with a credit card and the other members of the party leave a cash tip. If the additional amount is five or ten dollars, some guests do not complain because they believe that the money is less valuable than the time they would have to invest in trying to correct the fraud. However, those extra five- or ten-dollar amounts can easily add up as a lucrative pay supplement for a dishonest employee.

Management must make every effort to prevent credit card fraud and must insist that all purchases be processed through the electronic terminal. Credit card agreements and limits must be fully understood. Employees should be trained to observe expiration dates and to check signatures for discrepancies. Card companies do attempt to reduce fraud, but dishonest individuals work diligently to overcome security procedures.

Summary

The theft of organizational funds and sales revenues can cause a reduction in working capital and can lead an operation into business failure. The guest check is the primary source of maintaining control throughout the hospitality operation. Employees must be informed, in writing and during training, of the importance of guest checks and that the misappropriation of funds will not be tolerated. An organization should evaluate whether it is cost effective to use a POS system for controlling sales.

The three basic forms of payment are cash, checks, or credit cards. There are major differences between credit cards, charge cards, bank check cards, and debit cards. As the utilization of personal checks and currency decreases, hospitality operations have to consider the acceptance of some form of credit card. Once a decision is made to accept a particular card, management must then shop around to obtain the best possible proposal for the operation. Management has to be aware that the majority of guests who frequent fine-dining facilities pay for their meals with some form of credit card.

Review Exercises

1. Which of the following is not a common method of payment used in the hospitality industry?
   a. cash
   b. credit cards
   c. charge to a house account
   d. checks

2. A guest check accountability log should include:
   a. name of waitstaff
   b. sequence number of missing check
   c. waitstaff's signature
   d. all of the above

3. Which statement regarding computerized POS systems versus manual systems is not true?
   a. computerized systems are more economical
   b. errors in reading handwriting in manual systems can cause mistakes in orders
   c. sales performance reports are easier to compile using a manual system
   d. a trail tape is not necessary when using a manual system

4. What information can a POS system automatically include on a guest check?
   a. waitstaff or server identification number
   b. tax calculation
   c. menu items ordered and their prices
   d. all of the above

5. The amount of sales recorded in a POS system should equal:
   a. the total amount of cash, credit, and checks in the cash drawer
   b. the total amount of cash, credit, and checks in the cash drawer minus the beginning amount issued
   c. all voids
   d. the number of guest checks used that particular day

6. Which of the following is a good procedure for making change?
   a. bills over $5 should be put under the currency tray
   b. cashiers should try to complete multiple transactions simultaneously to service guests faster
   c. cashiers can use personal funds so that time will not be wasted in tracking down management for change
   d. the drop box for cash should remain locked during each shift

7. If the cash, credit card vouchers, checks, and coupons do not balance with the register reading, management must check:
   a. the quality of food
   b. the total amount of cash collected
   c. unreported mistakes or voids
   d. the deposit slip

8. The most important factor that a manager should consider when deciding which credit card to accept is the:
   a. effective discount rate
   b. statement fee
   c. cost of each transaction
   d. volume of business of the operation

9. The three steps in processing a credit card, in the correct sequence, are:
   a. settlement, authorization, handling
   b. authorization, settlement, handling
   c. handling, authorization, settlement
   d. authorization, handling, settlement

10. It is good business practice to bond:
    a. employees who handle cash
    b. all waitstaff
    c. employees who have worked at the operation more than five years
    d. all employees

11. Explain in detail the factors that must be considered when deciding which credit card or cards to accept.

12. Explain in detail two reasons why a guest check may be missing.

13. List ten methods that can be used to commit fraud during cash transactions.

14. List five reasons why a hospitality facility may want to use a POS system rather than a manual cash register.

15. Given average monthly credit card sales of $60,000 and an average number of monthly credit card transactions of 2800, calculate the effective discount rate of two credit cards. Company A offers a discount rate of 3%, a statement fee of $30, and a fee of $0.50 per transaction. Company B proposes a discount rate of 2.5%, a statement fee of $10, and a fee of $0.75 per transaction. Which credit card company would you choose?

Examination Type Problems

1. What three factors are used to determine credit card rates?

2. What are the three methods of payment and how does each benefit the guest?

3. Why is it important that some employees should be bonded?

4. The annual credit card sales of a restaurant are $500,000 and the average number of credit card transactions per month is 3000. Company X offers a discount rate of 2%, a transaction fee of $0.50, and a statement fee of $40. Company Y offers a discount rate of 3%, a transaction fee of $0.25, and a statement fee of $20. Which company's offer is better?

Case Study

One of the waitresses at the Model Restaurant is missing a guest check and this is the second occurrence this week. This waitress has been working at Model for about three years and has lost two or three tickets in the past. She is very efficient in her work and friendly toward the guests and you feel that a lot of local guests frequent the facility because of her presence and service. However, you also realize that you cannot afford to keep losing guest checks. Each time you talk with her about a missing check she always states that a guest must have taken it. As the manager of Model, establish a written policy of guest check control, including the following:

- The procedure for the issuance and return of guest checks
- The responsibility of employees regarding missing guest checks

12
Sales Analysis

Key Terms

contribution margin	guest count	popularity of items
formal communication	informal communication	publicity
guest comments	menu mix	seat turnover

Learning Objectives

After completing this chapter, you should be able to:

- explain the need for accessing information to be disseminated.
- explain why it is important to control information.
- explain why training must be an ongoing process.
- describe the importance of knowing the guest check average.
- explain why guests should be counted.
- explain why it is important to measure the length of time between seat turnover.
- describe the importance of perception in the pricing of a specialty item.
- understand why employees should be awarded for outstanding performance.

Outline

Pertinent Information
    What Information Do I Want?
    How Do I Obtain That Information?
    What Information Do I Want Other
       People to Know?
    How Do I Distribute Such
       Information?
Sales Analysis and Pricing
    Who Are the Target Guests?
    What Are the Type and Location of the
       Facility?
    What Are the Prices of Competitors?
    What Are the Costs of Preparing and
       Providing the Products or Services?
    What Amount of Profit Does Management
       Want to Generate?

Sales or Menu Mix Analysis
    Identifying the Contribution Margins of
       Items
    Identifying the Popularity of Items
    Special Sale Items
Waitstaff Performance Tracking
    Analyzing Items Sold
    Pointing Out Trouble Areas
    Additional Training
    Praises and Awards
Guest Counts
    Meal Periods
    Waitstaff Assignments
    Dining Areas
    Calculating Seat Turnover
    Forecasting According to Days of the Week

Pertinent Information

With today's technological advancement, information itself does not provide as much of a competitive advantage as it did in the past because computers and the Internet have made information readily available. However, if used correctly and in a timely manner, information still provides a strategic advantage and can assist managers in maintaining their competitive position. Managers who are willing to search for information concerning market conditions may be able to remain competitive by adjusting quickly to anticipate changes in the market place. With this information at hand, strategic plans can be developed to maintain or enhance market share. Management should address the following questions concerning the gathering and utilization of information.

- What information do I want?
- How do I obtain that information?
- What information do I want other people to know?
- How do I distribute such information?

What Information Do I Want?

Because there is so much information available, managers have to discern what information they really want. Information can assist managers in controlling operational procedures by enabling them to quickly analyze deviation from standards; however, too much information may bog down managers with data that are not pertinent to operational activities. Managers need information that will help them to perform their duties and to remain within budgetary constraints. If the information received is not going to assist managers in the performance of their duties and in running the most efficient and effective operation possible, then maintenance of such information may only take away valuable time. Management must complete an evaluation of costs and sales and have an understanding of what information can affect the control of these items. Therefore, sales reports, cost reports, and payroll registers are all essential information for good management.

How Do I Obtain That Information?

The majority of information that is used in most organizations comes from computer-supported applications such as database management programs. These programs allow managers the ability to look up answers or find the source of problems without having to dig through piles of paper. Managers are able to identify alternatives quickly, evaluate those alternatives, develop a list of contingencies, and select an alternative based on financial data. Management information system (MIS) has several definitions, but in practice, it is a system that provides management with needed information on a regular basis. Electronic cash registers and POS systems provide information in a systematic order, arrangement, and purpose, which is in agreement with the function of a management information system. An MIS presents information in a usable fashion and not just as raw data. In the hospitality industry, management needs information in an organized manner so that cost-control activities can be quickly enforced or put into place. The method in which information is received must also be consistent so that when management conveys information to ownership, upper management, or employees, everyone will understand what the information means.

Because the majority of information used by management in the hospitality industry comes from POS systems, efforts should be made to ensure that the system selected by an operation can provide information in the manner required. For example, a system should be able to store historical data so that management can forecast production and sales based upon such data. This would eliminate a number of decisions that are made by pulling numbers from thin air. Management in a cafeteria-style restaurant determine how much of each item on the serving line to prepare based on previous sales. Management does not have to go through files in a file cabinet, as this information can be obtained by simply entering the dates and the menu into the POS database. A computer gives a more accurate recommendation than that which would be obtained from manual projection. This heightens control by preventing leftovers, which may decrease controllable costs.

A number of publications that provide information about the hospitality industry were mentioned in previous chapters and a number of Internet addresses provide research data, statistics and averages, and news of the industry. For example, the National Restaurant Association's web site (www.restaurant.org) provides news, trends, and research data for the public. Many web sites are available for hoteliers as well. The appendix at the end of this chapter provides a sample list of web sites of hospitality associations and companies.

What Information Do I Want Other People to Know?

Controlling information is necessary. This does not mean that management should ever distort information or should lie to the public or employees. Honesty and directness are always best when dealing with employees and the public. However, because information is power, a company may need to control access to different pieces of information. Also, timing is important in the business arena and timing can influence the impact of a message. Timing of information can enhance its purpose. Additionally, dissemination of information should be limited as necessary to avoid information overload. When it comes to information, more is not always necessarily better. The theory that managers need all of the information they can obtain is far from the truth. Increasingly, the quantity of information might hinder the decision-making process. Managers can become overwhelmed with too much information and some of it may be of little value.

It is important for information to be relevant, accurate, complete, reliable, and timely; however, even if these criteria are met, it must be remembered that additional information comes with additional cost. Some individuals believe that new information is better and they will use the latest information to make purchasing or business decisions. They may want to purchase new equipment based upon new information, although it may be best to allow time for new items to be tested in the market place before making quick decisions. Therefore, upper management may not need to inform lower level managers about the possibility of purchasing new equipment until there is a need to get them involved, otherwise the move to purchase might be made too quickly.

Certain types of information need to be shared. It may be a good idea to inform employees of the costs of every piece of small wares in the food and beverage area. In doing so, employees will know that if they "accidentally" drop a spoon in the trash can and do not care to retrieve it, this act will cost the establishment a certain amount of money. Small mistakes and neglectful acts soon add up to big amounts. It may also be a good idea to inform employees when a certain goal of sales is reached. After all, it is group work that brings in the sales, not just the hard work of the managers.

There may be information about a company that management may want the public to be aware of and there may be information that may not be of interest or could be detrimental to an organization. Management may not want the public to know that the company is having financial problems or problems with products that do not pose a threat to the public. If the public knew this it could cause a decrease in sales.

Information can be used to gain a competitive advantage. Computerized systems can efficiently evaluate historical data, as opposed to evaluating information manually; however, in most cases, a competitive advantage gained by an information system will not be a permanent advantage because, as with all products and services, other organizations will either duplicate or improve on the methods.

How Do I Distribute Such Information?

Information that an organization wants the public to accept is that which is available as publicity. This is why the question "What information do I want other people to know?" is so important. Advertising provides an instant awareness of products or services and sales promotions can produce immediate guest response, but publicity has a much higher credibility rate as compared to other promotional techniques; therefore, hospitality operations use public relations as a means of getting information to the public. This type of information is apt to boast positive and cost-effective results, which can be achieved through outstanding service with follow-up thank-you notes sent to guests.

When disseminating information to employees, management may use different techniques. For control purposes, management may not choose to share with employees items pertaining to percent of profit from sales of certain products. However, management should keep employees informed through formal and informal communication techniques. By keeping employees informed, mangers can prevent resistance to changes and other activities that have a tendency to demotivate employees. For formal communication, managers can use organizational meetings or can include letters with paychecks. Meetings about guest comment cards give tremendous feedback to all parties involved. Managers can also use "the grapevine," as individuals who typically pass on information are easy to identify. The grapevine informs managers of concerns that employees might have and can be used to curtail rumors that may be detrimental to employee motivation.

Management can use advertising to distribute information and to attract guests. When advertising to increase sales, management must not use a shotgun, or random, approach. The public receives all types of junk mail that may never even be read. Management has to be selective so that advertising is addressed to the target market. Advertising must also be cost effective. Therefore, a sales analysis must be accomplished to monitor whether coupons or newspaper advertisements generate enough new guests to make such advertisements and promotions profitable. A neighborhood newspaper may be far more cost effective than the city paper. Radio is great for special events and for reaching the target market. Television commercials must be timed effectively to reach the desired market.

Sales Analysis and Pricing

Information provided through a sales analysis can assist managers in evaluating guests' preferences of menu items and numerous other services and activities to help in establishing prices. When prices reflect the value perceived by guests, satisfaction will follow. Management may find the following questions pertinent in generating this information.

- Who are the target guests?
- What are the type and location of the facility?
- What are the prices of competitors?
- What are the costs of preparing and providing the products or services?
- What amount of profit does management want to generate?

Who Are the Target Guests?

Knowing the type of guests who frequent an operation gives management an idea of the market's preferences, needs, and wants. While it is not always advisable to set prices according to what the market will bear, being aware of guests' spending patterns can assist management in pricing products appropriately. Knowing the guests also enables management to have a better understanding of the perception of value and the expected level of service. Additionally, if the ethnicity and demographics of patrons are considered, management can determine their eating and diet habits, which can boost sales.

What Are the Type and Location of the Facility?

The type and location of a facility play a large part in establishing a menu mix and prices. When developing a menu mix, pricing the menu, and considering the location of a facility, it is essential that management be aware of the controllable and noncontrollable costs. Rent can be very expensive for a facility located in a strip mall, in a downtown area, or in an office building. Therefore, menu prices may have to be set to cover the expense of a higher fixed cost. Prices in an upscale dining facility are expected to be high to attract a particular clientele. The demographics of an area are definitely important. Prices must be affordable to certain guests in the area and to certain guests outside the area, otherwise they may hesitate coming to a certain area because of the demographics. If an area is perceived to support high prices, the ambiance, products, and services have to reflect this. If the majority of a target market consists of students, then prices have to be affordable for that particular clientele. If senior citizens frequent a facility, then prices have to be geared toward individuals on a fixed income.

What Are the Prices of Competitors?

Management cannot afford to ignore the competition. Information must be gathered concerning the activities and prices of competitors in the vicinity. Factors such as industry growth and product and service differences can determine how intense rivalry will be among establishments in the hospitality industry. Prices must be based upon the expenses of the organization, but if competitors have prices that are much lower, management will have to find some means of differentiating its products or services. Competitors' new methods of production or delivery of products also have to be examined, as they can often provide a competitive advantage in lower pricing.

What Are the Costs of Preparing and Providing the Products or Services?

Knowing the actual cost of preparing and serving products can assist in determining the cost of goods sold, the amount of labor lost, and other controllable expenses. If sales analysis is to be completed as accurately as possible, then actual cost must be obtained. Actual cost provides a realistic figure of how much it costs to prepare and serve different items. The problem with determining actual cost in the hospitality industry is that the cost factors that are most often used are always average costs. However, the difference in average, potential, and actual costs can be enormous. Whether items are prepared for large banquets or are part of regular business, actual costs for producing such items need to be determined. This prevents the hospitality operation from losing money through incorrect pricing of a product or service.

What Amount of Profit Does Management Want to Generate?

When deciding upon menu prices management has to determine how much profit they would like to generate to have a sufficient return on investment. All too often, mom-and-pop operations view profit as the amount left after doing business. This can be disheartening when hidden costs are not accounted for and profits are small. Chain operations usually view profit as cost. By using this approach, an operation's required profit and sales goals can be predetermined.

If more small business operators used this approach, they would have a more realistic view of the possible success of their business from the beginning.

Sales or Menu Mix Analysis

Knowing what sells in an operation and knowing how much contribution an item can give an establishment can help harness desired profits. The concepts of contribution margin and popularity work together. After all, it would be problematic for a hotel if all of its guests prefer suites, which give the hotel a great contribution margin, but only 5% of the hotel's rooms are suites. Also, it may prove detrimental for a restaurant to retain a menu item that has not sold for the last five months, especially if the item is expensive to produce and the restaurant is maintaining an inventory to produce such an item, just in case a guest may order it one day.

Identifying the Contribution Margins of Items

Contribution margin is the dollar amount that remains after variable costs have been subtracted from the sales amount. Contribution margin can be the key to a successful menu mix. A sales mix has to be established to generate the maximum contribution margin that guests will accept and still perceive prices to be reasonable. The contribution margin of each item must be known in order to price menus correctly. The fast-food industry does an outstanding job of establishing the correct menu mix when developing sales promotions. More operations need to focus on contribution margin rather than the cost of the ingredients in the product. Inexperienced operators often make this mistake. Steak usually has a far greater contribution margin than chicken even though the food cost is vastly different. Figure 12–1 is a contribution margin analysis of a spaghetti dinner and a lobster dinner, which shows that it is indeed better to try to sell one lobster dinner than approximately eight spaghetti dinners.

Figure 12–1   *Contribution Margin Analysis*

	Lobster	Spaghetti
Sales price	$25.00	$3.75
Food cost	8.00	1.50
Contribution margin	$17.00	$2.25
Advantage margin	$17.00 versus $2.25 = 17 ÷ 2.25	
	= 7.56 times	

Identifying the Popularity of Items

Management has more success in selling items and in controlling cost when the popularity of items is known. This helps to prevent leftovers and aids in selling items that are more acceptable to the target market. This information is easily obtained from electronic cash registers or POS systems. Items that are not popular should be removed from the menu unless the contribution margins of the items are great or they are on the menu for balance, such as low-fat and low-calorie items. If an unpopular menu item is retained, efforts must be made to change the appeal of the product to make it more popular to a larger majority of guests. If the item entails high labor cost, then management may want to consider adjusting the production process, as the minimum wage law indicates that the cost of labor will probably continue to increase in the future. Management has to understand that the popularity of an item is relative and does not mean that retaining an unpopular menu item is not cost effective. If the markup on an item is sufficient or the contribution margin is large enough, then sufficient profit may be made on those occasions when the item is sold. For example, the markup on fine wines can be sufficient enough to keep them in inventory even if they are only sold occasionally.

Special Sale Items

Facilities always try to establish special sale items. This can work for some operations through the development of the sales mix. A restaurant may set low prices for special sale items; however, other items may be priced to offset the special sale items. Precautions must be taken when promoting special sale items because lost leaders—specially priced items that do not generate additional sales—may cause a facility to lose money in the long run. With regard to lost leaders, restaurants and grocery stores differ because, depending on the number of people in a dining party, few additional items are purchased in a restaurant to offset the price of a sale item. Also, it must be remembered that consumers are only mildly influenced by promotional pricing and that continued use of an artificially low price may give guests the perception that the product should actually be sold at the lower price. Price is always an indicator of how the guest perceives the product's quality and the quality of the operation. Hospitality operators must also remember that most guests have limits within which their quality of product perceptions vary directly with price; therefore products that are priced below the lower limit are perceived as cheap or of poor quality and products that are priced above the upper limit are perceived as too expensive or extravagant.

Waitstaff Performance Tracking _____

Any sales analysis would not be complete without tracking the activities of sales personnel. The waitstaff is the sales force in a hospitality operation. Although management and marketing may do an outstanding job of getting guests to come to an operation, it is usually the servers who enhance the size of guest checks with suggestive selling and who generate return business through good guest service; therefore, servers are extremely important to the success of a hospitality operation.

Analyzing Items Sold

By analyzing the items sold, management is able to obtain several important pieces of data. Management may find that some items should be removed from the menu. Management is also able to see what items are most attractive to guests, whether servers are aware of the items that have the highest contribution margin, and whether servers are attempting to enhance sales through suggestive selling or upselling. Through suggestive selling servers may persuade guests to select items with higher contribution margins, and upselling can increase guest check averages. The numbers of desserts or appetizers sold often is an indication of the amount of suggestive selling. If suggestive selling is applied the number of these products consumed should increase. When guests ask servers about menu items, servers must be aware of the contribution margin in order to make beneficial suggestions. Therefore, by analyzing the items sold, the effectiveness of the waitstaff can also be determined.

Pointing Out Trouble Areas

Waitstaff performance tracking can also point out trouble areas in the operation. Guest check averages may be down when a certain special is on the menu or when certain production personnel are on duty. Managers must talk with the waitstaff when they are not generating sufficient guest check averages. Managers may find that it is due to poor service of the waitstaff. According to the menu mix and the clientele mix, management should be able to estimate a guest check average and establish a standard based on the average. This is how management often projects sales for a given period. If waitstaff do not reach the average, it may be necessary to evaluate products, procedures, and personnel.

Setting standards in the hospitality industry involves determining the expected amount of sales income that can be derived from the utilization of a prescribed amount of resources. The number of anticipated guests should determine the number of waitstaff on duty. Additionally, each server is expected to generate an average income. Everyone is expected to carry his or her own weight. If a server consistently does not achieve a set standard, there may be a trouble point in the flow of procedures that may be preventing him or her from doing so. The objective of a standard is to provide employees with direction and to allow for efficient business decisions and employee performance evaluations. The purpose for setting standards is to be able to control and measure the efficiency of production, procedures, and productivity of personnel. A standard is a model or method that stands as a basis for comparison. If check averages are substandard then management must attempt to pin-point the problem.

Additional Training

A sales analysis can often indicate a need for training. Once a sales analysis is completed, management has to attempt to find any oversights or mistakes in procedures. Waitstaff and production personnel must be trained to meet the standards of the organization. Employees must be trained to meet guests' expectations and to increase sales. Individuals that consistently have the lowest guest check averages must be retrained or terminated. A business that makes 15% profit without an ongoing training program may be able to generate 16 or 17% profit by implementing an ongoing training program that assists management in improving techniques and all-around efficiency. Meeting an established standard may not be an indication of maximization. Training improves productivity as well as enhances the motivational level of employees. This is why training must be an ongoing process even if according to a sales analysis all activities appear to be within standards.

Praises and Awards

Employees must be made aware of their own performance results and the overall performance of the organization. Without feedback, employees may perceive that everything is all right, that standards are not important, or that their input into the organization is not important. Therefore, regardless of whether standards are being met, employees should be informed and their opinions of how to improve operational procedures should be solicited. Just because standards are being met does not indicate that they cannot be improved. If a business is generating a profit, management should investigate whether they can generate even more. Another reason why average check size and average number of guests served must be tracked and evaluated is that managers need to determine which members of the waitstaff have the highest average so that they can be commended. The best way to encourage commendable behavior is to show it is appreciated.

Guest Counts

Guest counts, otherwise known as covers, are closely related to sales levels, therefore, it is extremely important that management consistently monitor guest counts. From a control standpoint, this is important for several reasons. Managers can determine whether guest checks are missing or are being reused or whether some servers have far less guest checks than others do. The guest count should usually coincide with the number of entrees sold; however, employees should be made aware that managers are also going to do manual guest counts, as this may deter the possibility of theft. Guest counts are important in the following areas:

- Meal periods
- Waitstaff assignments
- Dining areas
- Calculating seat turnover
- Forecasting according to days of the week

Meal Periods

Guest count can be done on a daily basis; however, to be more effective, it should be done by meal periods to ensure that entrees sold and the number of guests coincides. A few guests may not order an entree but the majority will. By having an accurate guest count, managers can project labor usage and food cost and can forecast production sheets and employee work schedules according to the volume of business on certain days of the week.

Waitstaff Assignments

In addition to counting guests by meal periods, the number of guests served should also be counted by waitstaff, as this provides useful data for management. If one waitstaff member always serves 30 more guests than the other waitstaff, management should check into the situation, because the assignment of the stations may always favor that particular waitstaff member and thus he or she may serve more guests and thus receive more tips. If guests' satisfaction is high and service quality is not compromised, this indicates that the waitstaff is able to efficiently serve a higher volume of guests otherwise, adjustments may need to be made.

Dining Areas

Problems may be easier to identify by maintaining guest count by dining areas, especially if a POS outlet is used to place orders. A full-service hotel may have several dining outlets, and by monitoring the guest count of each dining area, improvements can be made in those outlets that are less frequented by guests.

Calculating Seat Turnover

Managers must know the number of seats and the capacity of equipment to plan for busy periods and to book and handle large functions. Guest counts can help management project how long guests may have to wait for a table. Seat turnover is derived by dividing the number of guests served during a given meal or period by the number of seats available. For example, if 300 guests are served lunch in a restaurant that has 150 seats, then the restaurant has achieved seat turnover times 2. If lunch is served from 11 a.m. to 2 p.m., then the average dining time for guests is estimated to be an hour and a half. Figure 12–2 is a sample seat turnover calculation.

Forecasting According to Days of the Week

Average guest count for certain days of the week is an essential piece of information in helping managers forecast sales, production, and labor hours. Trying to anticipate the amount of sales so that production and the utilization of waitstaff are maximized is an essential component in the cost control process. Average guest count for certain days of the week along with average guest check

Figure 12–2   *Seat Turnover Calculation*

Capacity seating	= 150
Guests served during lunch	= 450
Seat turnover for lunch	= 450 ÷ 150
	= 3 times
Guests served during dinner	= 300
Seat turnover for dinner	= 300 ÷ 150
	= 2 times
Total guest turnover per day	= Total guests served ÷ Total seats available
	= 750 ÷ 150
	= 5 times

can be used to anticipate the volume of sales and the production and waitstaff that it will take to support these sales. These figures can differ according to days of the week, meal periods, and menu items. Some facilities have a larger lunch guest count on Fridays due to the relaxed attitude of most individuals on Friday. However, some facilities may have a smaller lunch crowd on Friday than any other day of the week because some individuals work compressed work weeks or take off early for commutes, travel, or long weekends. Management should evaluate days of the week and the menus of those days separately when forecasting for future sales.

Items Sold

A realistic average number of items sold can be useful to an operation. This number can be used to prevent waste in production, to schedule labor, and to determine appropriate operating hours. The historical data of an electronic cash register or POS system can usually provide this information. If a computerized system is not used then guest checks can assist in verifying this information. Information from production personnel should be used to validate the figures. If a computerized system is not used, information from production personnel should never solely be used to establish the number of items sold, as production personnel could inflate the numbers to account for products that are stolen. In this case, production personnel should only verify the number of items sold and the number of items prepared.

Menu Mix Analysis by Meal Period

The menu sales mix by meal period assists managers in forecasting production and labor utilization. Management would like to place the least possible number of items on the menu so that the production process can be streamlined, thereby requiring less labor and having less waste. Placing too many food products on a menu can easily cause an operation to lose sight of its origins or goals. As the number of menu items increases so does the possibility of spoilage, waste, and theft, which can cause an organization to lose money and can cause a reduction in quality. Some concept restaurants feature a wide menu selection but limit the possibility of spoilage and waste of products by preparing the same ingredients in many different ways with a few basic sauces, herbs, and spices. The number of items on a menu must present a balance of different tastes and selections to allow for a profitable sales mix.

Item Placement on Menus

If management would like to increase orders of items that have large contribution margins, then these items may need to be relocated on the menu. Additionally, items that have low contribution margins may need to be relocated if they are taking up prime spots on the menu. When reading a menu, most guests look directly at the middle of the menu; therefore, this is where management should place items that have large contribution margins. It may also be profitable to take items off the menu, change their presentation, and bring them back as specials with higher prices that will generate larger contribution margins.

Signature Items

Signature items can provide differentiation. A specialty item that guests cannot find at any other location may attract additional guests. It is often thought in the foodservice industry that specialty products have to be inexpensive to attract guests. This is generally not the case and foodservice managers need to change their perception. If a restaurant features a 32-ounce steak as a signature product, this does not mean that the steak should be inexpensive. Guests may order a signature product for prestige or for the experience, and price may not be as much of a factor. When beverage operations sell drinks in particular glasses and allow guests to take the glasses, guests generally have paid expensive prices for inexpensive glasses. Therefore, specialty items can be extremely cost effective. Specialty products simply need to be marketed correctly. Because facilities determine their own house specialties, most specialty items are well marketed, and a certain clientele is motivated to purchase these products.

Other Useful Measurements

Guest Comments

Managers must seriously consider comments provided by guests. All positive and negative comments should be evaluated. Some people may unjustifiably complain, however, a dissatisfied guest can actually identify a significant problem of which management may not be aware. Too often, managers do not address guests' comments because they do not perceive them to be significant problems. Management must remember that perception of value belongs to the guest and that the level of service and quality of products are only as good as that perception. Comment cards should be read, and guests should be contacted if they raise valid issues and leave addresses on the cards. Guests normally do not leave addresses or phone numbers unless they think the problem is significant or something is really outstanding. Managers must also treat guest comments seriously when discussing them with employees. Management's reaction to comments may illustrate to employees the amount of concern that management has for guests and employees.

Management must be especially attentive to comments when any changes have been made in operating procedures or menu prices. Because a change in one area can often affect another area, it is essential to require employees to provide feedback and to be open to guest comments. Standards can provide direction for the organization but their implementation must be pursued if the operation is to be successful. Guest comments often let management know if standards are below expectations. Guest comments can also indicate if changes and improvements of problem areas are successful.

Per Person Average

The per person average provides management with the information needed for predicting sales, and in some cases, for rejecting functions. The per person average, or average check per person, is determined by dividing the total dollar sales for a period by the number of guests served in that period. The average dollar amount represents the average amount spent by each person. If sales can be more accurately predicted, labor and other controllable costs can be adjusted. If a manager knows that the check average for a given night is $25 with approximately 50 guests, he or she can make a more cost-effective decision based on this information. For instance, if an organization reserves the restaurant for that particular night for a party of 50 and the requested meal is $18 per person, the manager, given the per person average, knows that he or she should try to have the group select a slower night. If the manager cannot convince the group to select a slower night, he or she could subtly suggest a more expensive meal.

Food Cost Percentage

All percentages should be broken down into as many categories as possible and costs should be compared as frequently as possible. Sales analysis is apt to be more accurate and leakage, waste, and theft can be easier to identify, if items are separated into categories. This also allows managers to pinpoint problems before they become too costly to the operation. A standard must be established for acceptable food cost. Because of the sales mix of a menu, an approximate food percentage can be established. Although an increase in food cost may not be cause for alarm because sales may correspondingly increase, an apparent standard must be set if management is to be able to monitor food cost on a frequent and routine basis. It is essential when analyzing food cost percentage that food cost is compared to food sales and not to total sales. Food cost

Figure 12–3   *Food and Beverage Cost Percentage Analysis*

	Dollars	Percentage	Explanation
Food sales	$450,000	81.82%	450,000 ÷ 550,000
Beverage sales	100,000	18.18%	100,000 ÷ 550,000
Total sales	550,000	100.00%	550,000 ÷ 550,000
Food cost	$162,000	36%	162,000 ÷ 450,000
Beverage cost	20,000	20%	20,000 ÷ 100,000
Total cost	182,000	33.09%	182,000 ÷ 550,000

percentage is derived by dividing food cost by food sales and not food cost by total sales. This mistake is often made. For sales analysis to be correct, cost percentages must be derived correctly.

Beverage Cost Percentage

Beverage cost percentage is as important as food cost percentage. It is determined by dividing beverage cost by beverage sales rather than total sales. Alcoholic and nonalcoholic beverages should be accounted for separately and the cost percentage for each should also be determined separately. Alcoholic beverage percentage is determined by dividing the cost of alcohol by the sales of alcohol, the percentage for nonalcoholic beverages is added to food sales and is determined in the same manner. Figure 12–3 provides a sample food and beverage cost percentage analysis.

Summary

Sales analysis can be more accurate if information is provided in a usable fashion. Managers should not be placed in situations wherein they will be confronted with information overload. If the structures of organizations are flat, management will have to make a vast number of decisions and information overload can occur. Employees and guests should be provided with correct information and management should attempt to disseminate accurate and quality information that will be beneficial to all constituencies of an organization.

If an organization understands its target market, it can more effectively develop a menu mix that will have a sufficient contribution margin and sales to generate a significant profit for the organization. When developing a menu mix, managers must understand that contribution margin is a component of pricing that deals specifically with the profitability of each item.

Waitstaff performance must be evaluated to maintain control and to know which waitstaff members are doing an outstanding job of selling and which ones may need additional training. Management must constantly identify and reward individuals that contribute to the success of the operation if commendable behavior is to continue. Conversely, management must understand the importance of either retraining or terminating employees who are not helping the advancement of an operation. The success of the service industry depends more on service than the products that are being sold. Employees are important to the success of an operation and their performance must be monitored.

Guest counts provide information for an operation to forecast sales, production, and labor utilization. Management must occasionally count guests and compare this count with the reading from the computerized system to see if a dishonest employee is circumventing the system. Guest count is also helpful in booking future business, in determining seat turnover, and in informing guests of the average wait before seating.

The number of items sold per meal period reflects the popularity of items and provides management with information for forecasting. This information can determine whether production of certain items needs to be increased or decreased on certain days of the week. Management may also find that some items may need to be relocated on the menu or completely removed from the menu.

When completing a sales analysis, an organization must take into consideration the menu mix, operating expenses, and required profit for that particular facility. It is important to understand that the menu mix must be based on operational expenses and the amount of sales that are required for the continued success of the operation. There is continuing debate regarding the average food cost or labor cost of certain types of operations. Industry standards for prime cost percentages may not be that far off, but they cannot account for all nuances of every operation. Through sales analysis, management can compare sales, production, and workforce performance to established standards. Management can then evaluate the menu mix and implement control factors to ensure that the standards and quality of that menu are maintained.

Review Exercises

1. When gathering information, managers usually have all of the following concerns except:
   a. how much information is available?
   b what information do I want?
   c. how do I obtain that information?
   d. what information do I want other people to know?

2. When assessing the utilization of information, which of the following is true?
   a. an information system provides management with information in a usable fashion and not just as raw data
   b. the majority of information that is used in most organizations comes from computer-supported applications
   c. managers need information that will assist them in the performance of their duties and will aid them in remaining within their budgetary constraints
   d. all of the above

3. Which question may management find pertinent in generating pricing information?
   a. what are the type and location of the facility?
   b. what are the prices of competitors?
   c. what are the costs of preparing and providing the products or services?
   d. all of the above

4. Management would like to keep all of the following types of information from the public and competitors except:
   a. three cases of food-borne illness have occurred since yesterday's lunch
   b. a new product is being tested in the test kitchen
   c. sales figures have been down for the last month
   d. a faster process to produce certain items was developed

5. The dollar amount remaining after variable costs have been subtracted from the sales amount is:
   a. profit
   b. contribution margin
   c. break-even
   d. controllable cost

6. If a menu item is not popular, management may try:
   a. to change the face of the item to make it more acceptable
   b. to advertise the item more if the item has a low contribution margin
   c. to remove the item from the menu if the item has a large labor cost
   d. a and c

7. Management should consider the following option when advertising:
   a. radio for special events
   b. addressing advertising to the target market
   c. cost-effective advertising
   d. a shotgun approach

8. Placing too many food products on a menu can cause an operation to:
   a. lose focus of origins or goals
   b. lose sales
   c. increase spoilage, waste, and quality
   d. reduce the requirement for storage space

9. Food cost percentage can be obtained by:
   a. dividing sales by food cost
   b. dividing food cost by food sales
   c. dividing food cost by total sales
   d. multiplying food cost by cost of food sold

10. By analyzing the number and type of items sold, management can evaluate the following:
    a. which items should be removed from the menu
    b. which items are the most attractive to customers
    c. how much suggestive selling is being used
    d. all of the above

11. Name and give examples of three reasons why it is important to monitor the per person average of guest checks.

12. Explain four ways in which guest counts can signal the effectiveness or in-effectiveness of a hospitality operation.

13. Calculate the food and beverage cost percentages given the following data: Beverage sales for the month were $50,000 and total sales were $275,000. Food costs were $100,000 and beverage costs were $15,000.

14. Calculate the contribution margin of the daily special given the following data:

> Food cost = 30%
> Total food sales = $50,000
> Food cost for each serving = $7.00
> Menu price for daily special = $15.00

Examination Type Problems

1. Evaluate the importance of ongoing training for the waitstaff.

2. List and evaluate three reasons why it is important to analyze sales.

3. Calculate food and beverage percentages given the following income statement:

> | | |
> |---|---|
> | Food sales | $200,000 |
> | Beverage sales | $100,000 |
> | Total sales | $300,000 |
> | Food cost | $ 75,000 |
> | Beverage cost | $ 20,000 |
> | Total cost | $ 95,000 |

4. What contribution margin is reflected in question #3?

Case Study

You have been restaurant manager at Model for six months and have noticed in your profit and loss statements for the past few accounting periods that even though sales have remained the same your profit level is declining. You have checked prices of food and supplies and have also checked inventory and everything appears to be in order. According to your evaluations the problem is not occurring within the purchasing, receiving, issuing, or production areas. You know something is wrong and you cannot find the problem. Finally, you determine that perhaps sales analysis tools or reports may give you some information on this declining profit level. Name five reports or measurements for which you would collect data and explain what information each report and measurement will contain and why they were selected.

Appendix: Sample List of Web Sites

Company Information

Airline companies listed from Yahoo search
http://www.yahoo.com/Business_and_Economy/Companies/Travel/Airlines/
American Airlines Corporation
http://www.amrcorp.com/
Business-to-Business Magazine; special events in various cities
http://www.agendaonline.com
Company Financial Information Edgar Database
http://www.sec.gov/edgarhp.htm
Hilton Hotels Corporation
http://www.hilton.com
Hilton International
http://www.travelweb.com/TravelWeb/hl/common/hiltnint.html
Marriott Corporate Information
http://www.marriott.com/corporateinfo/
Marriott International: Company Information
http://www.199.170.0.159/ or http://marriott.com/
Other financial sources from Wall Street Net–Markets
http://www.netresource.com/wsn/intres.html
Switchboard Business and People Database
http://www.switchboard.com
Westin Resorts and Hotels
http://www.westin.com
Yahoo–Business: Corporations: Travel: Hotels
http://www.yahoo.com/Business/Corporations/Travel/Hotels/

Hospitality and Tourism Addresses

All the hotels on the Web
http://www.all-hotels.com
American Gaming Association
http://www.americangaming.org/
American Hotel and Motel Association
http://www.ahma.com/
Association for Corporate Travel Executives
http://www.acte.org
Atlanta Convention and Visitors Bureau
http://www.acvb.com
Center for Industry and Exposition Research
http://www.ceir.org
Culinary Professionals' Resource Center
http://www.thomson.com/rcenters/cul/cul.html
Eventsource Uniting the Events Industry
http://www.eventsource.com

ExpoGuide Trade Show and Conference Resources
   http://www.expoguide.com
Food Show Online
   http://www.foodshow.com
Hospitality Industry Resources
   http://www.hospitality.net
Hotel Discounts
   http://www.hoteldiscount.com
Hotels & Hospitality: Newspage
   http://www.newspage.com/NEWSPAGE/cgi-bin/walk.cgi/NEWSPAGE/
   info/d19/d2/d1
Hotel Online (daily news updates and reports)
   http://www.hotel-online.com/Neo/News/
Hotels and travel on the Net
   http://www.webscope.com:80/travel/
INNroads Homepage
   http://www.inns.com/home.htm
International Association of Conference Centers
   http:www.iacconline.com
International Exposition Management
   http://www.iame.org
Las Vegas Leisure Guide and Resource Directory
   http://www.pcap.com
Mapquest Interactive Mapping Service
   http://www.mapquest.com
National Indian Gaming Association
   http://www.indiangaming.org/
National Restaurant Association
   http://www.restaurant.org
New Jersey Gaming Commission
   http://www.state.nj.us/casinos/
Primenet (Internet provider)
   http://www.primenet.com
Professional Association of Innkeepers International
   http://www.paii.org/paii
Rooms with a View: Hotels and Electronic Commerce
   http://www.bart.nl/~moret/hotels.html
San Francisco Hotel and Reservations Available
   http://www.hotelres.com
Techweb: The Technology Super Site
   http://www.techweb.com/info/publications/publications.html
The Meetings Industry Mall
   http://www.mim.com
Tourism Research Links (for researchers, *not* travelers)
   http://www.tourism-montreal.org/tourism.htm
Trade Show in Asia
   http://www.tdb.gov.sg/trshow/tr_menu.html

Trade Shows
  http://www.tradegroup.com
Travel Industry Association of America
  http://www.tia.org/default.asp
Travel Web
  http://www.travelweb.com
Travelocity
  http://www.travelocity.com
Virtual Tourist (geographical tour of Web servers)
  http://www.vtourist.com
Welcome to Hospitality Net
  http://www.xxlink.nl/hospitalitynet
World Hotel Resources
  http://www.worldhotel.com/
World Tourism Organization
  http://www.world-tourism.org/
World Travel News
  http://www.world-travel-net.co.uk/events/country/ind_eve1.htm

Journals and Magazines

Adams Trade Press–Convention Sites
  http://www.aip.com
Casino Publications
  http://www.intersphere.com/casinoplayer/
Fodor's Travel
  http://www.fodors.com
Food and Travel Magazine
  http://www.epicurious.com/
Hotel & Motel Management
  email: suite@en.com
Internet Travel Newsletter
  http://www.travelet.com
Lodging Magazine
  http://lodgingmagazine.com/
Meeting News Magazine
  http://www.MeetingNews.com
Nations Restaurant News
  http://www.nrn.com
Successful Meetings Magazine
  http://www.successmtgs.com
Travel Weekly Homepage
  http://www.novalink.com/travel
Wall Street Journal
  http://www.adnet.wsj.com

Hospitality Education URLS

CHRIE
   http://www.access.digex.net/~alliance/about.html

Wine References

California Wine Club
   http://www.cawineclub.com/cwc3.html
Grapevine Wine Information Center
   http://www.winery.com/winery/
Spanish Wine Page
   http://www.eunet.es/
Wine French Regions
   http://www.nerdworld.com/nw269.

13
Labor Planning and Factors That Affect Labor Cost

Key Terms

absenteeism
fringe benefits
hiring
incentives
labor legislation

labor sources
orientation
selection
termination

time- and labor-saving
    devices
training
unionism

Learning Objectives

After completing this chapter, you should be able to:

- discuss and evaluate the importance of the five functions of human resources as they relate to cost control.
- identify the various sources of labor.
- identify the various factors that influence labor costs.

- design time- and labor-saving devices for various job positions.
- set labor standards for a hospitality organization.

Outline

Human Resources Management
    Selection, Hiring, and Orientation
    Training
    Termination
Sources of Labor
    Part-Time Staffing
    On-Call and Agency Staffing
    Cooperative Services
    Cross-Training

Factors That Influence Labor Costs
    Physical Facilities
    Equipment
    Hours of Operation
    Menu and Product
    External Factors
    Training, Benefits, and Accidents
    Employee Theft

The topics of labor turnover and burnout have been discussed over and over in trade journals and magazines. Some hospitality organizations have found ways to handle these issues, but most are still in the dark. Some sources blame the low wages employees receive, citing that it is difficult to motivate when money is not there. Long working hours are also named as a culprit. However, it is time for the industry and its management to stop blaming and to start acting. Psychological studies have proven that although some people think money motivates, an unhappy employee who earns a large paycheck will eventually leave the job. So, what actions can hospitality managers take to have a great crew and also avoid turnover and burnout? This chapter and the next will address this question, beginning with the employee selection process and looking at the various issues that affect labor costs.

Human Resources Management

The five categories under human resources management that can greatly impact labor quality and costs are selection, hiring, orientation, training, and termination. When management looks at labor cost from a cost-control point of view, they concentrate on the total payroll figure, that is, the number of hours worked multiplied by the different hourly rates. However, the actions of management in the selection, hiring, orientation, and training processes heavily influence the amount of money that is spent every accounting period on payroll and benefits.

Selection, Hiring, and Orientation

Because the hospitality industry is labor intensive, the need for personnel is of the utmost importance. When a restaurant does not have enough staff to wait on tables or a hotel does not have enough attendants to make up rooms, this affects level of service and operations may lose potential income. The hospitality industry is notoriously afflicted with "warm body syndrome" in that facilities are often in such desperate need to fill positions that lack of employee qualifications are sometimes overlooked. In doing so, most managers think they have solved the problem of short-staffing; and for a moment, everything looks good. However, a "warm body" that was just hired may not have worked in the industry before, and as there was no real selection process, there was also no orientation with regard to the philosophy of the workplace, the importance of customer service, the general concept of making guests feel welcome, and the like. In most of these instances, there is little or no training. Although most establishments have manuals for staff to follow, these manuals are often given to new employees without any real hands-on training. Many establishments use shadowing as a training technique, pairing employees so that rookies can learn the ropes from veterans. However, this often results in the blind leading the blind, as lack of proper training is the established pattern. The outcome of this type of ad hoc training is that an establishment may not be any better off than before, but it now has extra, albeit inexperienced, staff who may have the potential to become effective and efficient employees.

Training

Training is another important piece of the human resources puzzle. Training should not be done only when a crew is hired but should be an ongoing process to remind employees of the correct methods of performing their jobs and to update them with new techniques and information. Since training takes time, and time is money, this function is not the top priority on most lists. In fact, it is one of the functions that usually is eliminated when the phrase "controlling costs" appears. Unfortunately, this sacrifices long-term benefits in exchange for short-term increases to the bottom line. The more astute companies in the industry do realize the importance of selection, hiring, orientation, and training. These companies would rather commit time and resources to develop good employees who attend to guests' needs and wants than to let them work with guests in a substandard manner.

Termination

Termination is traumatic to both the organization and the people involved. Nobody enjoys firing people and nobody enjoys being fired. It is one of the more difficult tasks in the job description of a manager. However, this can easily be avoided if the other functions of human resources are carried out properly. In addition, termination is not simply telling an employee that he or she does not have a job anymore. It also puts a strain on the remaining crew because there is one less person to get the work done. This means that a new person needs to be hired as a replacement and thus the whole human resources cycle has to start all over. Worse still, guests can feel the effects of short-staffing. Scheduling can probably eliminate some of these effects in the short run; yet, the profits of an operation may suffer in the long run.

The monetary cost of selection, hiring, orientation, training, and termination is a topic of its own. When looking at labor cost control, the cost of each function must be considered—cost of advertising for the position, cost of printing all the forms, time for management to interview, time for orientation and training, time for administrative staff to process a new hire, and many others.

Treat human resources wisely and start well from the beginning so that the problem of constant turnover will not pose a problem to the operation.

Sources of Labor

There are many sources of labor where management can find quality and dedicated employees. Most of the time, management thinks of labor as full-time personnel; however, other categories such as part-time, on-call, and agency staffing and cooperative services should be considered.

Management often equates employees with positions and thus look for full-time candidates. A full-time staff garners obvious advantages. A full-time staff makes scheduling an easier task for management. Also, because employees work full-time, their job is probably a major source of their income; therefore, they view their job as a priority and take pride in the things they do. Also, because they work more hours than part-time staff, they are more skillful and knowledgeable in work procedures and practices. They are also often more dependable; however, when one or a few of them do not show up to work during the same time, it may not be easy for management to call in temporary replacement. Thus, the services provided to the guests may suffer.

Part-Time Staffing

Most establishments have a mix of full- and part-time staff. Part-time staffing offers flexibility in scheduling. Part-timers do not expect 30 to 40 hours of work per week and thus their hours can be cut back during slower periods. During peak check-in times at a hotel or during special foodservice functions, management can have enough staff on hand to handle the demand. Benefits and perks available to full-time staff may not be available to part-timers; in this respect, hospitality operations can save monetary resources. Part-time positions work well for a company and for members of the workforce who prefer more flexible schedules to spend time with their families, to work a second job to save money, or to go to school.

Although it appears that part-time labor is a win-win proposal, a few disadvantages need to be kept in mind. A part-time job is often not an employee's top priority, which may lead to substandard performance in rendering services to guests. Again, because of their major commitments, part-time staff sometimes may not be available when an establishment needs extra help. Management's goal should be to select the most dependable employees and to keep a good balance of part-time and full-time staff.

On-Call and Agency Staffing

Besides full-time and part-time staff, a few other labor sources are helpful to management. Wise and experienced managers keep a list of on-call staff for emergency purposes. This list may include ex-employees who might have sought a career change but still enjoy working with their previous co-workers once in a while, and may also include college students who might have worked with the establishment and know the ins and outs of the workplace. Hospitality establishments that are in proximity to hospitality programs at universities often set up on-call programs so that they can tap into the pool of college candidates.

Staffing agencies can provide staff with little notice. These companies generally charge a slightly higher rate than what would be paid for regular staff as staffing companies have to perform all of the human resources functions for the hospitality operations and help in their scheduling. However, these companies are quite handy and dependable. Hospitality establishments have no obligation to re-employ temporary personnel and staffing agencies can help establishments streamline their labor sources issues, and after some time, establishments may form their own pool of on-call personnel.

Cooperative Services

Hotels or restaurants that are chain affiliated or clubs that are managed by the same company can set up cooperative services whereby Hotel A can request two room attendants from Hotel B for a busy day and will return the favor when Hotel B needs extra help. The advantage of cooperative labor is that the operating procedures and standards of the same company should be uniform, so an employee from Hotel A can easily assume the responsibilities required by Hotel B.

Cross-Training

In large operations such as hotels and megaresorts, or even in smaller operations such as independent restaurants or clubs, labor sources can be borrowed not only from the same establishment but also from different departments. Cross-training takes cooperative services one step further. Front office employees who have also learned the skills needed for hosting in a fine-dining restaurant are more valuable to an establishment. Cross-trained employees understand the difficulties that their counterparts have in other departments so the entire staff tends to be more compassionate and appreciative and is able to work together better as a team.

Factors That Influence Labor Costs

Although payroll derived by multiplying the hourly wage and the number of hours worked, a fairly long list of factors can directly and indirectly affect payroll. These factors are all controllable and management must make adjustments as needed.

To begin with, management can directly control physical facilities, equipment, hours of operation, menu type, service type, and product, which can increase the efficiency and productivity of the staff so that a lesser amount of payroll can be achieved.

Physical Facilities

Physical facilities include the design of the building itself and the placement of all furniture and equipment. A well-built hotel and conference center has storage rooms for banquet tables of various sizes and banquet chairs right next to the conference rooms and banquet ballrooms. This saves employees the time needed to move the tables and chairs from one end of the establishment to another when setting up the rooms for different events. A well-designed clubhouse will not have the locker rooms next to the main entrance. Rather, there should be an exit from the locker rooms to the golf course, and another exit to the clubhouse. In addition, there should be plenty of storage space in the locker room area, so that linens will not have to be transported from one end of the clubhouse, through the lobby and offices, to the locker room. Even details as small as the placement of water pitchers and silverware stations in a dining room can help save steps for waitstaff. Time-and-motion studies have been performed on assembly lines and in cafeteria lines and catering outlets in which the assembly of packaged food products is monitored to ensure that there are no bottlenecks and to determine whether procedures can be modified to better the process. Analyze employees performing their various job functions so that procedures can be modified to increase productivity.

Equipment

Furniture, fixtures and equipment, (FF&E) are long-term assets on the balance sheets of all hospitality establishments. Yet, not all equipment is the equipment an establishment needs; in fact, some equipment may hinder productivity and thus increase labor cost. For example, standards are set whereby a pair of tongs is recommended to plate spaghetti for banquets. All the food has been prepared and placed in the right size pans in the steam table. The plates have been heated to the right temperature. The waitstaff just finished picking up the salads and are lining up to receive the entrees. However, a pair of tongs cannot be found and the next best piece of equipment is a scoop. It is not easy to serve spaghetti with a scoop, but these incidents happen quite often. It takes more time to plate spaghetti with a scoop than the entire plating process. Even employees who are efficient, come to work on time, and have the most dedicated and positive attitude cannot scoop spaghetti onto plates in an effective manner. Another example involves a front office in which the reservation process has always been performed manually. An employee takes down the reservation by hand and checks for availability in the reservation book. This reservation book might be handy or it might be in another part of the office. Because reservations sometimes are made months in advance, the reservations area has different books for different times of the year. Once the reservation is confirmed, the employee returns to his or her workstation and informs the guest. Then, when the guest arrives this information is transferred manually to a portfolio. If equipment such as a property management system is used, this process can be done as quickly as one minute and any future references to this reservation can be queried easily as well. The right equipment saves time and labor cost and increases guest satisfaction.

Hours of Operation

Hours of operation directly affect labor costs. The longer an establishment is open, the more labor costs will be incurred. Make sure that operation hours coincide with the needs and wants of the majority of customers. Survey the customers and observe their patterns. Obviously, it would not be cost-effective for a golf course to be open 24 hours a day, seven days a week because the grounds need to be maintained; moreover, no one wants to play golf at 3:00 a.m. By controlling the hours of operations, employees can be scheduled to ensure that costs are contained.

Menu and Product

In the foodservice area, the menu dictates the product and specifies an establishment's service style. Menu items that are made from scratch require more labor in the preparation process. Convenience foods may at times increase food cost but will invariably lower the labor needed in preparation, and thus will help control labor costs. In addition to preparation, labor costs are also incurred in the service of the product. The manner in which the food item needs to be served, whether a la carte or buffet, determines the style of service, and thus the required personnel and labor costs.

The effect product has on labor cost can also be seen in the hotel segment. Product differences, whether in a limited-service hotel or in a luxury establishment, can affect staffing in all areas, and thus labor costs. In a luxury hotel, due to guest room amenities and services, the time needed to clean a room is often more than that needed to clean a room in a limited-service hotel. Thus, labor costs are generally higher in luxury hotels.

External Factors

Labor costs are related to the economy in general, which includes labor legislation, union contracts, labor supply, and so on. Labor legislation, including laws pertaining to the level of minimum wage and paid holidays, can influence the amount of money that hospitality operations need to spend on labor. In areas where unionism is active, businesses have to abide by contracts and, again, labor dollars are affected. However, unionism may not be needed in companies that are positive and proactive and in which employees can trust management to treat the workforce fairly.

The supply and demand of labor dictate the price hospitality operations need to pay to hire and retain employees. In certain areas where labor shortage is a real problem, hospitality companies have imported labor from other countries for certain periods of the year in order to operate effectively. Obviously, when the economy is on the rise such as in the early 1980s and mid-1990s, the demand for skilled labor is much higher than during recessions.

Training, Benefits, and Accidents

This next set of factors that can influence labor costs needs the attention and work of management and great cooperation from employees. The first factor is training. Management must design the best possible training methods and motivate employees to improve themselves. Employees must be willing to be trained and to improve themselves before any real success can be achieved. Oftentimes, management half-heartedly puts together a training session and pays for the hours that the employees need to be present, and the employees show up but are not really interested. No positive results are accomplished, and productivity, though it may increase, may not reach the desired level.

Other factors in this area are incentives and fringe benefits. The more incentives and benefits that are given to employees, the more competitive a company will be, which in turn will create goodwill and loyalty among employees. Incentives and benefits appear on the surface to cost money; however, they need not simply be an increase in wages. They may be in the form of contests, recognition, or gifts. To address the problems of absenteeism and tardiness one restaurant pooled the names of employees with perfect attendance and bought lottery tickets. All of the employees in the pool were eligible to share the lottery winnings. Although the restaurant spent a minimal amount, employees started coming to work on time and did not call in sick as often. It is human nature to not want to be left out and just in case a lucky star shines that one day employees become encouraged to be part of the winning team.

The occurrence of accidents is a viable factor and can compound the monetary and time resources that have to be spent on labor costs. Employers should provide a safe workplace and appropriate training so that accidents and injuries will not happen. Accidents are costly, as employers have to pay for time off, workers' compensation, and medical bills. In addition, operations have to hire replacements because no matter how good employees may be, they cannot perform their duties if they are injured.

Employee Theft

Employee theft was discussed in detail in previous chapters, but one may wonder how theft relates to labor cost. Employees not only steal products and equipment, but they can also steal time if they are not managed correctly. Employees who punch in before the scheduled time or punch out after the scheduled time can cause overtime pay, and thus increase labor costs. Employees who take unscheduled breaks put a strain on the rest of the crew and reduce overall labor effectiveness. Incidents in which personnel create dummy employees in payroll and pocket the paychecks clearly poses a labor cost challenge.

To counteract employees who incorrectly punch in and out, employers need to institute time and attendance systems. Some point-of-sale systems can be programmed so that employees cannot clock in before the set time. A few minutes a day stolen by a small number of dishonest employees can add up to a substantial amount by the end of an accounting period. As labor cost is a major expense—the biggest one for the lodging segment of the hospitality business—time and attendance systems need to be closely monitored.

To counteract the dummy employee issue, operations with a large number of employees should require personnel of certain departments, at random, to pick up and sign for their paychecks at the accounting office rather than have the accounting office deliver the checks to all departments for distribution.

Time- and Labor-Saving Measures

Although this topic was included as part of the discussion on physical facilities, it is worth mentioning in a separate section because there are many measures that management can take to better the productivity of employees so that labor costs can be well spent and not wasted.

With regard to lodging operations, it is important to equip the front office with computer terminals and printers, keys that are issued to guests, and necessary supplies. It is annoying to guests to have to wait for a front desk agent to retrieve a key from a locked back office. Guests understand and appreciate the importance of security, but if an agent has to walk to the back every time a guest checks in, then the agent is not using his or her time wisely.

Strategic location also applies to waitstaff stations and cashier stations in foodservice operations. Computers and point-of-sale systems can process guest checks accurately and efficiently. For certain establishments such as cafeterias, it is wise to have the cash register at the end of the line. This gives patrons time to decide what they want; otherwise, they may stand at the cash register, thinking about their order and holding up the rest of the line. Other patrons certainly will not appreciate this, and the cashier will have to wait for the one guest to make up his or her mind without being able to help another patron in the meantime.

Uniforms can also play a part in employee effectiveness. Nicely designed pockets to hold guest checks and pens help waitstaff to be more organized and professional looking. If they can get a check and pen ready to take the order, the entire process can be sped up.

As for the back of the house, the placement of all equipment and utensils is important in helping employees to accomplish their tasks. Trays, racks, carts, spoons, ladles, and other supplies are included in this category. Imagine plating a banquet for 1000 guests. The plate warmers are stationed next to the conveyor belt, which is placed in front of the hot food line, and the plate covers, tray stands, and trays are all situated at the end of the conveyor belt. This is a great layout for plating a banquet; however, if the equipment is situated at the wrong places, the entire plating process will take more time and delays and possible mistakes may occur, which translates to increased labor costs. Access to food items needs to be regulated but once the items are requisitioned for use, they should be stored and placed in a manner that is convenient to employees.

The goal is to provide employees with the proper tools and processes so they can perform at a higher level. One way to get ideas about labor- and time-saving measures is to listen to employees. Solicit their input, as they are the people who do these tasks on a daily basis. If there is a better way, they will use it. In considering the opinions of the employees, management also establishes trust and respect for and from the employees, which fosters teamwork and motivates all. In the end, the operation comes up with better processes and the employees work more effectively.

Setting Labor Standards

Once a good crew has been recruited, the operation has to give them a welcome orientation to the team and train them by presenting them with the expected standards of their job performance. Good sources for such standards can often be obtained from trade or professional associations and industry averages or guidelines are also available. As a part of training, these standards of performance can be role-played or demonstrated so that there will not be any questions or misunderstandings.

Performance standards allow management to plan and set internal labor standards, that is, determine how many employees should be scheduled with a certain forecasted amount of sales. For instance, the standard for a room attendant in a limited-service hotel is to service 14 to 16 rooms per day; however, depending on the type of hotel, it may be as low as ten if the rooms are suites in a luxury hotel (see Figure 13–1). Therefore, because each operation is unique, management needs to assess its own operation and set standards to help in scheduling and thus in managing labor dollars. Various methods can be used to establish internal standards. One method is to videotape a random selection of employees to observe their workflow. This can help establish the steps required to complete the work and the time needed to accomplish each task. Another method is to present employees with detailed checklists that must be completed as employees perform their assigned tasks (see Figure 13–2).

Figure 13–1 *Sample Standards for Room Attendants*

	Rooms Cleaned Per Day
Luxury hotel	10–12
Full-service hotel	12–14
Limited-service hotel	14–16

Figure 13–2 *Checklist for Room Attendants in a Full-Service Hotel*

ROOM: _____

DATE: _____   INSPECTION: _____   ROOM ATTENDANT: _____

CLEAN - C	DIRTY - D	NEEDS REPAIR - R	MISSING - M

ENTRY
  Outside/inside door   _____
  Locks   _____
  Chain   _____
  Doorstop   _____
  "Do Not Disturb" sign   _____
  Emergency/evacuation flow chart   _____
  Fire pamphlets   _____
  Smoke detectors   _____
  Thermostat   _____

BEDROOM
  Carpet   _____
  Under the beds   _____
  Walls/ceiling   _____
  Drapes/curtains   _____
  Windows   _____
  Windowsills/frames   _____
  TV/travel host   _____
  Remote control   _____
  Bed frames   _____
  Headboards (straight)   _____
  Pictures (straight)   _____

LIGHTING
  Bulbs   _____
  Fixtures   _____
  Lamps/shades   _____

ON NIGHT STAND
  Telephone   _____
  Memo pad/pen   _____
  Guest services directory   _____
  Alarm clock/radio   _____
  Room service menu   _____

IN NIGHT STAND
  Bible   _____
  Guest book   _____

Figure 13–2 *continued*

ON DESK/DRESSER
  Folder:
    Stationery (5)   ———————
    Envelopes (3)   ———————
    Directory   ———————
    Pen   ———————
    Postcards   ———————
    Brochure   ———————
  Ice bucket   ———————
  Tray   ———————
  Glasses w/ caps (2)   ———————

IN CLOSET
  Shelves/rods   ———————
  Hangers—men's (6)   ———————
  Hangers—women's (6) ———————
  Laundry/dry cleaning price lists (2) ———————
  Luggage racks (2)   ———————
  Telephone books:
    White Pages (2)   ———————
    Yellow Pages (2)   ———————

ASHTRAYS
  Desk table   ———————
  Night stand   ———————
  End table   ———————
  Round table   ———————
  Bathroom   ———————

PARLOR
  Sleep sofa   ———————
  Love seat   ———————
  Desk   ———————
  Desk chair   ———————
  End table   ———————
  Floor lamp   ———————
  Dresser   ———————
  Remote control TV   ———————
  Brass coffee table   ———————
  Artificial plant   ———————
  Wastebaskets   ———————

LAVATORY/BATHROOM
  Amenities tray:
    Shampoo/conditioner ———————
    Shower cap   ———————
    Hand/body lotion   ———————

Figure 13–2 *continued*

LAVATORY/BATHROOM (continued)
   Amenities tray: (continued)
      Face soap   _____
      Bar soap   _____
      Mouthwash   _____
      Shoe polish   _____
      Shoe horn   _____
      Shoe mitt   _____
      Sewing kit   _____
   Soap dish   _____
   Liquid soap/dispenser   _____
   Glass tumblers w/ glass caps _____
   Facial tissue w/ cover   _____
   Toilet tissue/holder   _____
   Wastebaskets   _____
   Shower curtain   _____
   Clothesline   _____

TOWELS
   Bath towels (3)   _____
   Hand towels (3)   _____
   Washcloths—no logo (3)   _____
   Bath mat   _____
   Bath rug   _____
   Towel rack/bar   _____

MIRRORS
   Over lavatory   _____
   Bath door   _____

FURNITURE
   Dining room table   _____
   Dining table chairs (4)   _____
   Armoire   _____
   Chair/ottoman   _____
   Credenza/TV   _____

COMMENTS:

_____

_____

_____

_____

_____

_____

Summary

In hospitality businesses labor is a prime cost that impacts all areas; thus, control of labor is vital. Control begins with employee selection, hiring, orientation, and training. Management must provide a workplace that is conducive to efficiency, and employees' input should be sought to improve work processes. Management should use incentives to motivate employees. Once everything is in place, standards should be set, communicated, and maintained so that each person knows his or her performance expectations and can work toward a goal.

Review Exercises

1. Which of the following is not one of the categories included in human resources management?
   a. selection
   b. orientation
   c. labor cost calculation
   d. training

2. Sources of labor for the hospitality industry include:
   a. part-time employees
   b. on-call lists
   c. agency staffing
   d. all of the above

3. Which of the following is a disadvantage of using part-time staff?
   a. working at the establishment is their top priority
   b. they are trained according to the procedures and policies of the establishment
   c. they may not be available at the time needed by the establishment
   d. they are committed to the establishment

4. What might be a potential problem when using staffing agencies?
   a. they may conflict with union regulations
   b. they may incur higher labor rates
   c. their staff is already trained
   d. there is an obligation to re-employ their staff

5. Which of the following is not a factor that affects labor cost?
   a. hours of operation
   b. equipment
   c. menu
   d. cost of food

6. Which of the following external factors affect labor cost?
   a. labor legislation
   b. union contracts
   c. labor supply
   d. all of the above

7. Accidents can increase labor cost through:
   a. workers' compensation claims
   b. paper-work
   c. paid time off for an injured employee
   d. a and c

8. Which of the following is an example of a labor-saving measure?
   a. placing guest keys in the front office
   b. designing employee uniforms with pockets
   c. providing waitstaff with proper equipment
   d. all of the above

9. Setting labor standards can be useful in:
   a. determining food cost
   b. determining labor schedules
   c. determining type of service
   d. determining guest mix

10. Which of the following is an example of employee theft that directly affects labor cost?
    a. stealing food products
    b. punching in before the scheduled time without authorization
    c. giving food to friends
    d. short-changing guests

11. Describe the importance of the five functions of human resources as they relate to cost control.

12. Identify and explain five sources of labor.

13. Identify and explain five factors that influence labor costs.

14. Describe how an operation develops time- and labor-saving work procedures for room attendants.

Examination Type Problems

1. Describe the advantages and disadvantages of employing part-time and full-time staff from a cost-control point of view.

2. Describe the benefits of using staffing agencies.

3. List and explain three fringe benefits or incentives that you would use to motivate your employees and explain why you chose these particular benefits.

4. Describe how labor standards can be set for a bus person in a 100-seat restaurant.

Case Study _____

Your best friend has just accepted a job offer at Lawrencetown University (LU). LU is a new private college. It has a dining facility that can serve the 3000-plus student population and the 500-plus full-time and part-time faculty and staff. The facility will be open for breakfast weekdays from 6 a.m. to 10 a.m., for lunch weekdays from 11 a.m. to 3 p.m., and for dinner from Monday through Thursday from 5 p.m. to 8 p.m. Service is cafeteria style. Average estimated guest count is 500 for breakfast, 1000 for lunch, and 500 for dinner. The majority of guests will be students with board plans. The facility also has a boardroom that can hold up to 25 people. Catered events are usually held there and the facility can expect to cater fairly large parties on and off campus, mainly for university administration. Annual food and beverage sales are estimated to be about $3 million.

In three weeks, the university will start its fall semester. Your friend has been hired as the assistant food and beverage director and needs to hire and train a large group of employees to handle the business. Because Lawrencetown is a college town, he is wondering what he needs to do in order to hire the best people. Another challenge is the layout and design of the dining facilities. The boardroom is located down the hallway on the other side of the kitchen. A back hallway links the back door of the boardroom and the kitchen but servicing directly out of the kitchen would be quite challenging. The hallway is approximately 300 feet long, thus, if the waitstaff forget something from the kitchen, it will take a while to rectify the issue.

After assessing the situation, your friend calls you for some advice. He knows that you have been working with the Case Study Hotel and have extensive foodservice experience. He would like your help with the following tasks.

- Identify the various sources of labor available and determine how to reach them.
- Develop a list of at least 10 questions that you would ask when interviewing prospective employees in order to find the best crew for your dining facility.
- Develop a table-setting checklist for a three-course banquet service for 25 people. This list is to include all tableware, stemware, glassware, condiments, and the like so that a banquet crew can pull the necessary equipment to set up the room correctly.
- Develop a checklist of service items for a three-course banquet service for 25 people. This list is to include beverages, condiments, all food items, rolls, butter, serving utensils, refills, and the like so that a banquet crew can service the room appropriately.

14
Staffing and Scheduling

Learning Objectives

After completing this chapter, you should be able to:

- discuss the four steps in analyzing labor needs.
- perform a business demand analysis.
- complete a productivity schedule.
- compile a payroll budget.

- assign tasks and develop a schedule.
- measure and evaluate staff efficiency.
- discuss and evaluate the different means of increasing morale.

Chapter 13 featured a discussion on setting standards for an operation by conducting time-and-motion studies, gathering information from employees, seeking sources from trade and professional organizations, and, of course, drawing from past experiences. This chapter takes a look at the standards themselves and illustrates the need for management to measure standards to optimize the staffing and scheduling process.

Because payroll involves a human element, the latter part of this chapter features discussions on training techniques, morale, turnover, and the different types of benefits to ensure that managers can maximize the labor dollar. Cost control is not just cutting the dollar amount. If the utility of the labor dollars spent can be increased, an operation can also experience increases in sales and/or decreases in other costs, which can contribute to profit.

Production Standards

Products and Services

The hospitality business offers products and services. Products include rooms, food, beverage, and even rounds of golf. Productivity then, is measured by sales, number of guests served, rounds of golf played, and in the end, the net profit. However, the underlying factor in the hospitality industry is the service through which products are delivered to guests; thus, service and the labor used to deliver services within standards are the issues.

Measuring Production Standards

Standards in the hospitality industry are generally expressed in terms of rooms sold, sales dollars generated, guests served, net profit level, and labor cost percentage. Each department within an operation sets its own standards. For example, in a hotel, the rooms department sets a standard for the number of rooms serviced per attendant, while the food and beverage department sets a standard for average guest count. However, it is difficult to measure the productivity of the marketing department or administrative personnel. Thus, one way to measure efficiency is to calculate sales per labor dollar. Oftentimes, hospitality establishments also calculate sales per man-hour or sales per employee and use those standards for comparison. Similarly, net income per guest, net income per man-hour, and net income per employee are also calculated. These figures can be easily derived with the help of computers and spreadsheets. In this manner, managers can compare the efficiency of labor from one period to another or between establishments. Like grades on a report card, these measurements inform managers of the areas where an operation is performing well and where improvement may be needed.

In addition to their usefulness in determining labor efficiency, these standards are great assets in labor planning and scheduling. If the standard is five minutes per check-in or check-out for a front desk agent, then, on the average, a front desk agent can perform 12 check-ins or check-outs in an hour. Thus, when a certain number of check-ins or check-outs are expected, the proper number of front desk agents can be scheduled so that the hotel lobby will not be filled with lines of irate guests. Similarly, these standards can be used to schedule golf caddies, waitstaff, room attendants, cooks, utility personnel, and even security officers.

To maximize labor costs and to take full advantage of measuring productivity and planning labor, standards need to be set for each shift, each meal period, and each work category. Summer months may have higher sales and income levels than fall months when sales from vacation and pleasure travelers are measured. Breakfast normally brings in lower dollar amounts per customer than lunch or dinner due to menu prices. Third shift, or the graveyard shift (11:00 p.m. to 7:00 a.m.) services fewer guests than first shift (7:00 a.m. to 3:00 p.m.) or second shift (3:00 p.m. to 11:00 p.m.).

Analysis of Labor Needs

To accomplish an analysis of an operation's labor needs, management first has to perform business demand analysis, then productivity scheduling, payroll budgeting, and finally, task assignment.

Business Demand Analysis

Business demand analysis determines the needs of a business. Some important questions must be considered before an operation can determine what is needed in terms of labor. What is the estimated sales level for each meal period, day, place, or outlet? Will the competition take away some of the sales? Are there any local events or special promotions that may affect normal demand? Is the forecasted day a weekday, a weekend day, or a holiday?

Forecasting   Nothing is worse than an operation that is understaffed because a low level of sales was erroneously forecasted. The next worst scenario is that management has forecasted a high level of sales, but because something unexpected happened, the sales figure did not materialize and a full crew is left with nothing to do. Therefore, an accurate sales forecast is necessary. Per period and daily recap of sales and customer counts, check averages, historical data, special events, and seasonal and weather changes can all lend a hand in determining sales levels. The lunch business at a poolside restaurant will be better on a sunny and warm summer afternoon than on a cold and rainy day. Pizza places that offer carry-out and delivery services often experience higher sales volumes on rainy nights or when there are sports events on television.

Figure 14–1   *Sample Daily Recap Sheet of a Hotel with Two Dining Outlets*

Date:					
	Grill	Remarks	Fine Dining		Remarks
Breakfast	Sales: Cash Credit Over\<short> Customer count Average check # of hours worked Sales/labor hours		Breakfast	Sales: Cash Credit Over\<short> Customer count Average check # of hours worked Sales/labor hours	
Lunch	Sales: Cash Credit Over\<short> Customer count Average check # of hours worked Sales/labor hours		Lunch	Sales: Cash Credit Over\<short> Customer count Average check # of hours worked Sales/labor hours	
Dinner	Sales: Cash Credit Over\<short> Customer count Average check # of hours worked Sales/labor hours		Dinner	Sales: Cash Credit Over\<short> Customer count Average check # of hours worked Sales/labor hours	

Some daily recap sheets contain a column for remarks in which a manager can input data such as weather, special events, holidays, major advertising and promotion dollars spent, and the like to determine if a correlation exists between those factors and sales (see Figure 14–1). The more information an operation has and understands, the better it is able to prepare for guests by staffing accordingly. This information is also often used in production sheets in the kitchen to allow the chef and his or her crew to plan for special functions.

Competition   Competition can affect labor needs, as increased competition and new concepts present guests with more choices, which may affect the volume of business in a particular operation and thus the labor needs.

Marketing strategies, especially an analysis that addresses an operation's strengths, weaknesses, opportunities, and threats, is useful in this situation. If competition threatens a hospitality operation, then management must utilize the identified strengths and set strategies to increase, maintain, or recapture their market share.

Local Events and Holidays   A parade is scheduled to end right before the lunch period on New Year's Day. An establishment that serves lunch is located on the parade route. These two facts will most likely garner that particular establishment a high volume of sales for lunch that day. Most hotels do not maintain a full staff at Christmastime because occupancy usually is down during that period. Country clubs need extra staff on Memorial Day and Labor Day since most clubs organize special parties and functions for their members on those holidays. Therefore, operations must plan their labor needs accordingly. Chambers of Commerce and Convention and Visitors Bureaus can provide listings of local events and holiday promotions.

Advertising and Promotion   A resort may spend $200,000 for a three-week ad campaign on various media such as radio, television, newspapers, and billboards. If the scope of the campaign is national rather than regional or local, the advertising and promotion budget can be many times that amount. The effect of advertising and promotion can never be guaranteed. Thus, it is important to track the usefulness of each advertising and promotional medium. Special codes or 800 numbers may be used for different advertisement sources so that when a guest makes a reservation, the reservation agent can identify the medium that prompted the guest to make the call. Similarly, coupons indicate whether a particular promotional technique is working. Tracking systems allow management to accurately assess the effects of each advertising and promotion campaign, which can help determine future labor needs.

Productivity Scheduling

Productivity scheduling is like putting a puzzle together in that the estimated sales from the business demand analysis and set standards are used in conjunction to schedule and estimate labor needs. For example, if 300 check-outs are scheduled for a certain day and check-out time is before noon, the front office has to determine whether the 300 check-outs are all from the same conference. If so, and the final meeting of the conference is from 8:00 a.m. to 10:00 a.m., the hotel can expect heavy check-out periods before 8:00 a.m. and between 10:00 a.m. and noon. The room attendant staff has to be informed of the peak check-out periods so that the rooms can be turned around for sale by the check-in time for the next guest. If a breakfast break is not scheduled during the last meeting of the conference, the hotel's restaurant, coffee shop, snack bar, and coffee cart should prepare for extra business during the peak check-out periods.

In productivity scheduling, management needs to review each job category and determine how estimated sales will affect each job category and during what hours. Then, managers must plan the payroll by scheduling the personnel accordingly. In certain facilities, specific operating hours are busy while others are slow. Productivity scheduling allows management to stagger the schedule of waitstaff and kitchen personnel.

A manager must use the standards of his or her facility to determine the number of staff needed. Consider Figure 14–2, which is a sample productivity schedule for a banquet department in a hotel. A seated function in Room A for thirty guests will require five tables with six guests seated at each table. However, managers should always overset by a small percentage to allow for last-minute increases in counts. In this case, one table is the least amount that should be overset; therefore, six tables of six guests will be set for the function in Room A. The standard calls for two servers and one captain for a function with six tables of six.

Figure 14–2   *Productivity Schedule for a Banquet Department*

Standards for seated banquets
1 server for 3 tables of 6 or 2 tables of 8
1 server for the head table (if applicable)
1 captain for every 50 guests
Banquet manager needs to be present at all functions to check on progress

Standards for buffets
1 server for every 4 tables of 6 or 3 tables of 8
1 server for the head table (if applicable)
1 captain for every 60 guests
Banquet manager needs to be present at all functions to check on progress

Functions for Friday, May 30, 1997

Room	Style	# of Guests/Tables	# of Servers	# of Captains
A	Seated (6)	30/6	2 *	1
B	Seated (8)	100/13	7 **	2
C	Buffet (8)	500/63	21 ***	9

* 6 tables of 6, seated, standard 3 tables of 6 per server
    therefore, 6 tables ÷ 3 tables = 2
** 13 tables of 8, seated, standard 2 tables of 8 per server
    therefore, 13 tables ÷ 2 tables = 7 (approx.)
*** 63 tables of 8, buffet, standard 3 tables of 8 per server
    therefore, 63 tables ÷ 3 tables = 21

Payroll Budgeting

Once the staff positions are scheduled, an estimated payroll amount can be generated. Payroll budgeting is a blueprint that lets management know the monetary resources that will be needed in order to achieve the estimated sales level with appropriate service standards. Figure 14–3 is a payroll budget for a pizza buffet restaurant.

Budget versus Actual Cost If all things go as planned, an operation will hit the budget and will not be over or under targeted costs. However, any variance will require management to review the budget, the scheduling, and perhaps even the demand analysis and standards to determine what may have caused the deviation and make the necessary modification for the next period. Payroll analysis, comparing budgeted and actual amounts, is critical in cost management. Sometimes it may not be necessarily bad news if actual payroll costs are over the budgeted amount. In fact, although the dollar amount has exceeded the budget, there may not be an issue at all if an increase in labor cost is due to an increase in unexpected sales and the labor cost percentage stays in line with the normal amount. However, there should be some concern if actual payroll costs exceed that of the budgeted amount and sales have not increased. A manager

Figure 14–3 *Payroll Budget for a Pizza Buffet Restaurant*
(business hours: 10:00 a.m. to 10:00 p.m.)

Staff	Shift	# of Hours	Name	Rate	Extension (# of hours × rate)
Cook-lead	7–3	8	Jill	$8.25	$66.00
Cook 1	7–3	8	Jacqui	7.00	56.00
Cook 2	11–3	4	Hank	6.75	27.00
Utility 1	9–3	6	Norman	5.00	30.00
Utility 2	11–3	4	Thomas	5.00	20.00
Cashier 1	9–3	6	Christina	6.50	39.00
Cashier 2	9–3	6	Alex	6.50	39.00
Waitstaff 1	7–3	8	Judy	2.35	18.80
Waitstaff 2	7–3	8	Winnie	2.35	18.80
Waitstaff 3	9–3	6	Amy	2.35	14.10
Waitstaff 4	10–3	5	Dan	2.35	11.75
Waitstaff 5	11–3	4	Everett	2.35	9.40
Total payroll					$349.85

may need to review the steps for labor staffing and scheduling or use training, motivation, or incentives to ensure that standards are met. If employees are not efficient and effective, standards will not be met and managers may need to work with employees at an overtime rate or schedule extra personnel to complete the job, and thus ruin the labor budget.

Tolerable Variance Is it true that a budget has to be met to the cent? Are there tolerable variances? Answers to these questions depend on the philosophy of an operation. Because so many factors affect labor costs, some of which are beyond reasonable control, actual numbers often may not meet a budget to the cent. Thus, variances on either side may occur, and management needs to decide what variance percentage is acceptable. Normally, a variance of plus or minus 1% is deemed acceptable. However, if the amounts fluctuate in specific meal periods or on certain days, management should observe the action on the floor and monitor the back of the house during those meal periods or days of the week and make appropriate adjustments.

Assignment of Tasks

Once management knows how many employees are needed for each meal period, function or event, and day, the next step is to schedule specific employees and assign tasks. The productivity schedule and the payroll budget now serve as guides to a manager.

Employee Performance It may seem that all a manager needs to staff a function is to calculate the correct number of employees. To continue with the sample data in Figure 14–2, three employees—two servers and a captain—are scheduled for the function in Room A. The next managerial task is to determine which two servers and which captain should be assigned for the function in Room A. On the surface it may not appear to matter. The standard calls for three employees and three will be scheduled. However, it may matter which three staff members are scheduled for the same function due to differences in employee performance. It would be great if all employees were topnotch personnel. However, even topnotch personnel have to start from the bottom. Thus, an operation is made up of stronger, more experienced employees and those who might have just started or those who are good but not "strong." Therefore, measuring the efficiency of your employees and classifying their performance levels can help in scheduling and also in employee development. If an employee is performing well in most but not all areas, management can point out weak areas to the employee and assist him or her in doing better.

Measuring Employee Efficiency It is pertinent to measure efficiency, both for the good of the employees and for the operation. The best way to measure efficiency is to present employees with performance-based objectives. Then managers rate employees according to how these objectives are accomplished. This process may take some time but it is worth it.

Figure 14–4 *Efficiency Rating Scale*

	Time of Day									
Name	7 a.m.–8 a.m.	8 a.m.–9 a.m.	9 a.m.–10 a.m.	10 a.m.–11 a.m.	11 a.m.–12 p.m.	12 p.m.–1 p.m.	1 p.m.–2 p.m.	2 p.m.–3 p.m.	Total	%
Waitstaff A	2	2	2	2	0	3	3	3	17	121
Waitstaff B	1	1	2	2	0	3	2	2	13	93
Waitstaff C	3	3	3	0	3	3	3	3	21	150
Waitstaff D	2	2	1	0	1	1	1	2	10	71

Employee efficiency can also be measured through observation. Managers observe employees during their work periods and assign each a rating on an hourly basis. These ratings may be on a scale of 1 to 5, with 1 as the lowest score and 5 the highest. Ratings can be on a scale of 0 to 3 in which 0 indicates idle periods, such as employees' lunch hours and breaks; 1 is underexpectation, not performing to par; 2 is average, performing at par; and 3 is overexpectation, performing over par. Thus, for an 8-hour shift of 7:00 a.m. to 3:00 p.m., an employee will receive a total rating between 0 and 24. Because an hour is subtracted from each shift for lunch and breaks, the scale can be modified to rate only 7 hours and an employee will then receive a total rating between 0 and 21. Figure 14–4, is a sample efficiency ratings scale that features a ratings spectrum of 0 to 21, with 14 as the average. Waitstaff A has a total rating of 17, which translates into an above average percentage of 121% (17 ÷ 14 = 121%).

Efficiency ratings help managers identify their best performers and reward good work; they also motivate managers to have discussions with poor performers and decide what steps to take. Most importantly, employee ratings provide managers with a master plan for assigning tasks. With regard to the illustration of the three banquet staff members in Figure 14–2, a good manager most assuredly would not assign three weak employees for that function.

After the assignment of tasks, a manager must monitor actual labor productivity, compare actual cost of labor to the payroll budget, and make adjustments. Rating is a dynamic process and human resources grow with training and experience; thus, employee ratings may change for the better, which may improve the overall efficiency of an operation.

Morale and Turnover

Morale and turnover are two elements that appear to have an inverse relationship—the higher the morale, the lower the turnover rate, and vice versa. If this is true, it appears that management can solve many problems by simply raising morale. However, morale issues are not so cut-and-dried. They often are fairly difficult to deal with, and the relationship of morale and turnover is not as simple as it may seem.

Increasing Morale and Productivity

The hospitality industry provides many career opportunities; however, not all positions at all levels have great monetary remuneration. Many employees earn minimum wage or just a bit above that level. Many also have to rely on tips given by guests. This "low pay" image compounds the morale issue and it is management's responsibility to make the difference, as increased morale translates to increased productivity. Most people are motivated by extrinsic incentives such as money. A recent study by Robert Klara, published in *Restaurant Business*, cited that the challenge facing the restaurant industry is not the shortage of labor, but the shortage of qualified people. In addition, the money issue was reported as the number one reason why employees leave the industry. Although management may like to think that money does not motivate, this is not entirely true; however research shows that extrinsic incentives do not have a long-lasting effect. Money may motivate unhappy employees in the short run, but their performances most likely will return to substandard levels. Conversely, intrinsic incentives are touted to be more lasting. These incentives may include awards, praise, employee picnics, and the simple respect and care shown for employees by management.

The hospitality industry is a people-oriented industry, therefore, managers must select and train employees accordingly. An employee needs a positive attitude to deal with guests. Attitude can be learned, but it takes more time to learn an attitude that manifests itself through behavior than it does to memorize a fact. A human resources director of a hotel once said that a firm handshake and a great smile are good indicators that a candidate has the positive personality needed for the hospitality industry. Attitude is contagious. A positive attitude that stems from the top will be carried throughout the ranks. This does not mean that management should only hire candidates with exuberant personalities. Some soft-spoken employees may be great team members who help an operation in other ways. Managers simply need to operate human resources accordingly. One resort hotel that has employees who speak another language does not have "problems," just "challenges."

Management must treat employees with respect. If employees trust their workplace and feel that they are part of a team and not just a dispensable resource, they begin to take pride in their work, thus increasing morale and productivity. Some companies even do away with the terms "employee" and "employer" and use words such as "associate" or "team member" to convey a sense of equality. Some staff members say that they work "with" each other rather than "for" their bosses.

Credit must be given where credit is due. Oftentimes, employees would like a simple pat on the back for a job well done. In today's hectic society we have trained ourselves to measure the outcome without acknowledging the process and, more importantly, the people who make the process work. Monetary bonuses or increases should be awarded when appropriate. This can be done on either a regular or an irregular basis but with identifiable standards so all staff members will know how they are measured and there will not be any misunderstandings.

Benefits

Another way to motivate and reward employees is to give them a good benefits package. This can include health insurance and dental plans, paid vacation, tax breaks, retirement accounts, and discounts on food, hotel stays, and merchandise. Employee benefits may also include daily items such as discounted or free meals and parking. Certain management levels may receive significant privileges, car or gas allowances, and laundry and dry cleaning services. In recognition of the needs of the ever-increasing workforce, some companies offer childcare and family counseling programs as part of their benefits packages. If on-site childcare is not possible, many operations may offer pretax deductions to compensate for daycare expenses. Pretax deductions are quite popular because they are not considered taxable income and thus can lower the amount of taxes that an employee has to pay. Every perk aside from the base salary can be included as a benefit, thus, management can utilize a good benefits package to increase the value of any position and to increase morale and reduce turnover, which leads to satisfied employees who perform better and project a positive attitude to guests.

Management must also realize that the industry boasts many different types of employees. As Maslow explained in his hierarchy of needs, different people at different stages in life need different things. A woman with small children would like childcare benefits, but a teenager may want an extra 25 cents per hour to increase his or her earning power. Therefore, when designing a benefits package, management needs to be aware of all the needs of its employees.

Management should try to be consistently inconsistent, be creative, and come up with the unexpected from time to time. To increase productivity and attendance, one hotel company awards a million-dollar stock option to the property that has the highest guest comment card score for the year. The stocks are divided amongst all full-time staff, hourly employees and management alike. Guest satisfaction is important to the company's mission and employees are rewarded for a job well done.

Cost of Turnover

The cost of turnovers does not simply involve the loss of employee. It also involves completing the paperwork pertaining to the termination or resignation of an employee, placing an advertisement for the vacant position, interviewing potential candidates, and selecting and training a candidate. In addition, when an operation is short a person the extra burden is shared by those employees who are still at the establishment. This burden may be handled without compromising guest services; however, if standards are compromised, guests may become dissatisfied and sales may decrease, which compounds the cost of turnover.

If a restaurant has a healthy profit margin of 10% and an average cost of $500 is spent to replace one employee, the establishment will have to make an extra $5000 in sales in order to recoup the $500 employee replacement cost. This is by no measure a small amount. An additional $5000 in sales translates to an additional 500 guests if the average check is $10. For some restaurants, 500 guests may be the total number of guests for a few days.

Summary

Because the hospitality industry is a "people" business, labor cost is a prime cost in an operation, and in the lodging segment of the industry, labor is often the highest cost. Therefore, good control of the labor dollar is of the utmost importance. This all begins with careful business demand analysis through forecasting; studying the competition; consideration of local events, holidays, and special functions; and advertising and promotion campaigns that link an operation to its neighborhood and its locale.

Determining the efficiency of the staff is important in scheduling the right amount of resources to service the business forecasted. Standards of performance must be established and the strengths and weaknesses of each staff member should be matched to the demand. Once schedules are set, a payroll budget can be determined for control and measurement purposes.

Hospitality managers deal with human elements in staffing and scheduling. All employees want to be treated equitably and with respect. Management needs to employ creative methods to raise and keep employee morale high especially with regard to employees who earn minimum wage. Happy employees pass their feelings and attitudes to the customers. In the service business, attitude is one of the key factors of success.

Review Exercises

1. Which of the following is not generally regarded as a productivity measurement?
   a. number of managers
   b. guests served
   c. sales per meal period
   d. rounds of golf played

2. To take full advantage of measuring productivity and planning labor, productivity standards need to be set for:
   a. each shift
   b. each meal period
   c. each work category
   d. a and c

3. The following are all factors that affect the sales level except:
   a. competition
   b. weather
   c. local events
   d. labor needs

4. Which of the following is an effective method to track the success of a particular advertising and promotion program for a hotel?
   a. asking the advertising agency
   b. using a code or 800 number to track reservations
   c. looking at past history
   d. analyzing the weather

5. Which of the following is not one of the steps in the analysis of labor needs?
   a. business demand analysis
   b. morale assessment
   c. productivity scheduling
   d. payroll budgeting

6. An increase in food cost may not signal a problem in a restaurant if:
   a. it is accompanied by an increase in sales
   b. food has consistently been thrown away due to spoilage
   c. the food cost percentage also increases dramatically
   d. employees are allowed to take leftovers home

7. A scale of 1 through 5 is used to measure employee efficiency. If an employee works 7 hours and the average score is 3 per hour, an employee who receives a score of 28 is at a _____ % level.
   a. 100
   b. 125
   c. 133
   d. 148

8. Which of the following is regarded as a motivator to employees?
   a. increase in pay
   b. better work schedule
   c. benefits
   d. all of the above

9. If the scheduling standard calls for 1 server for every 25 seats in a restaurant, how many waitstaff does a manager need to schedule to ensure that an 180-seat restaurant will have sufficient personnel for a busy night?
   a. 5
   b. 7
   c. 8
   d. 9

10. Which of the following should a manager consider when assigning tasks?
    a. scheduling employees of different competency levels on the same shift to complement each other
    b. scheduling two weak employees for the same function to assist each other
    c. scheduling a captain to assist a new employee in learning the ropes
    d. scheduling according to the level of business

11. Explain the four steps in analyzing labor needs.

12. How can local events affect the volume of business in a hotel? How would that differ in a restaurant?

13. Calculate the total score and efficiency percentage rating for the housekeeping staff in Table 14–1. Scale: 0 = idle, 1 = lowest, 5 = highest. Use 21 (3 × 7) as the average score, with 3 as the average rating and 7 as the number of hours worked.

Table 14–1

Name				Time of Day					Total	%
	7 a.m.– 8 a.m.	8 a.m.– 9 a.m.	9 a.m.– 10 a.m.	10 a.m.– 11 a.m.	11 a.m.– 12 p.m.	12 p.m.– 1 p.m.	1 p.m.– 2 p.m.	2 p.m.– 3 p.m.		
Anne	2	1	2	3	3	4	0	2		
Betty	3	3	4	4	0	2	4	4		
Carol	3	3	3	3	3	3	0	2		
Diane	4	4	4	0	4	4	4	4		

Examination Type Problems

1. Calculate the total score and efficiency percentage rating for the kitchen staff in Table 14–2. Scale: 0 = idle, 1 = lowest, 2 = average, 3 = highest. Use 14 (2 × 7) as the average score, with 2 as the average and 7 as the number of hours worked.

Table 14–2

Name				Time of Day					Total	%
	3 p.m.– 4 p.m.	4 p.m.– 5 p.m.	5 p.m.– 6 p.m.	6 p.m.– 7 p.m.	7 p.m.– 8 p.m.	8 p.m.– 9 p.m.	9 p.m.– 10 p.m.	10 p.m.– 11 p.m.		
Joy	2	1	2	3	0	1	3	2		
Kim	3	3	2	2	0	2	3	2		
Lucy	3	3	3	0	3	3	3	2		
Mary	2	2	2	0	3	3	1	1		

2. Referring to question # 1, which employees are above average? Which are below average?

3. List five strategies that you can use to improve the efficiency of employees who rate below average.

Case Study

Your friend has recently inherited a restaurant from a distant relative. Knowing that you are successfully managing the Model Restaurant, she is seeking some advice from you in the area of labor staffing and scheduling. Her restaurant is a 100-seat midscale casual dining establishment situated in the downtown business district; therefore, most of the clients are employees office and bank buildings. Operating hours for lunch are 11 a.m. to 2 p.m., with the majority of business between 12 p.m. and 1 p.m. Most people only have one hour for lunch, therefore, quick and efficient service is of the utmost importance. Using the four steps of labor needs analysis:

- List ten factors that can affect your friend's business demand.
- If 200 guests are expected, how many front of the house personnel would you recommend to your friend? Please specify the number in each category such as host/hostess, waitstaff, buspersons, and so on. Explain the rationale of your recommendation.
- Using a spreadsheet program, formulate a spreadsheet file for a payroll budget for the front of the house. Use Figure 14–3 as an example for the format.
- Explain to your friend methods to measure labor efficiency. Use Figure 14–4 as an example.
- Recommend to your friend five strategies to combat poor morale.

References

Klara, R. (May 1997). Labor: Love 'em or lose them. *Restaurant Business, 96*(9), 42–44, 48, 50.

Maslow, A.H. (1954). Motivation and personality. New York: Harper & Row.

15
Controllable and Noncontrollable Expenses

Learning Objectives

After completing this chapter, you should be able to:

- identify the differences between controllable and noncontrollable expenses.
- identify the various subitems in each major expense category.
- evaluate the effectiveness of a department or expense category by examining its expense schedule.

- identify the different types of depreciation and evaluate their effects on taxes and profits.
- recommend actions to improve the effectiveness of a department or expense category.

In hospitality accounting, whether it is for hotels, restaurants, clubs, or casinos, certain expenses are controllable within a department or center while others are shared amongst the entire operation and are deemed noncontrollable. As discussed, food, beverage, and labor costs are known as the prime costs of a restaurant or a food and beverage department of a hotel or club. For departments in which food and beverage costs do not apply, labor expense is usually the largest portion of the entire departmental budget. In addition to food, beverage, and labor costs, a department has other expenses, some of which do not appear in departmental schedules or statements but are included in an operation's consolidated statement. This chapter will discuss these types of controllable and noncontrollable expenses.

Direct Operating Expenses

Direct operating expenses are similar to other operating expenses. In a restaurant or in a food and beverage department of a hotel or club, direct operating expenses can include items such as uniforms, laundry and dry cleaning, linen, china, glassware, silverware, kitchen fuel, cleaning supplies, paper supplies, bar supplies, menus, and so on. Figure 15–1 provides a more comprehensive list of direct operating expenses. These items may seem to be of little expense; however, when added together, they constitute a substantial percentage of a department's budget. These expenses can definitely be controlled to yield a better profit for an operation. For example, most managers view licenses as a fixed expense that cannot be avoided. Although there is truth in this statement, maintaining the right licenses and renewing them in a timely manner can save unnecessary expenses. If an operation only serves beer and wine, management only needs to obtain a beer and wine license rather than a full liquor license, which is more expensive.

If cooks improperly use aprons and towels to clean equipment, they may ruin them and the linen company may charge the operation more. This is also true when buspersons use napkins to clean tables rather than kitchen towels. When receiving linen, do not count only the bundles but also count the individual napkins in each bundle. If a bundle of 25 only has 24 an operation will still be charged for 25; and when the linen company picks up the dirty linen, one napkin will be missing and the company will then charge the operation a replacement cost for a napkin they never delivered.

China, glassware, and silverware are costly to an operation, especially if high-grade stainless steel, silver-plated, or real silver utensils are used. Care needs to be taken when handling such items. The amount spent on replacing these items should be well documented and monitored. If an uncharacteristically high amount is recorded, management needs to investigate the situation.

Figure 15–1   *Direct Operating Expenses*

Rooms Department:
  Cable/satellite television
  Commissions
  Complimentary guest services
  Contract services
  Guest relocation
  Guest transportation
  Laundry and dry cleaning
  Linen
  Operating supplies
  Reservations
  Telecommunications
  Training
  Uniforms
  Other

Food and Beverage:
  China, glassware, silver, linen
  Contract services
  Gratis food
  Laundry and dry cleaning
  Licenses
  Music and entertainment
  Operating supplies
  Telecommunications
  Training
  Uniforms
  Other

Others:
  Contract services
  Court maintenance
  Fertilizers, insecticides, and topsoil
  Gasoline and lubricants
  Licenses
  Management fee
  Nets and tapes
  Operating supplies
  Professional services
  Refuse removal
  Sand and top dressing
  Seeds, flowers, and shrubs
  Telecommunication
  Tournament expenses
  Uniforms

It is also good practice to take inventory of china, glassware, and silverware on a regular basis. This may deter employees from taking these items home if they know that management keeps track of them.

All cleaning supplies for an operation and fertilizers for golf courses or landscaping can be purchased through a bid process to ensure that the best prices and quality are obtained. All contract services, management fees, and professional services for golf or tennis professionals need to be carefully negotiated as well.

Monitoring telephone expenses and access and keeping a record of long-distance calls can be useful. Even if an operation implements a strict system of access codes to prevent employee theft of long-distance calls, customers or outside parties can still defraud an operation. Criminals posing as telephone company employees may dial into a hotel and ask for an outside line under the guise of checking the integrity of the hotel's telephone system. Trustworthy hotel employees do not realize that in doing this they start a hefty long-distance telephone bill by providing a line for anybody to call anywhere in the world. This form of theft, referred to as "slamming," is quite prevalent, and management needs to be on guard.

Music and Entertainment Expenses

Music and entertainment are classified as controllable expenses and according to the uniform system of accounts for the lodging industry, they are charged to an operation's food and beverage department. Figure 15–2 lists items that are included this category.

These expenses can vary, depending on the caliber of the entertainer and the type of entertainment an establishment would like to provide. In addition to performers' expenses, management cannot overlook the royalties that need to be paid to use certain background music in an establishment.

Figure 15–2   *Music and Entertainment Expenses*

This category includes all expenses associated with providing entertainment within a hotel or within a property's food and beverage facilities.

Booking agent's fees
Instrument rentals
Meals
Miscellaneous
Orchestra and musicians
Professional entertainers
Royalties

Marketing Expenses

Most large hotels have their own marketing departments. The marketing efforts of smaller hotels that belong to chains or franchises may be taken care of by their corporate offices. Independent hotels and restaurants most likely plan their own marketing activities, either through a marketing agency or their own staff. Figure 15–3 lists expenses that are included under marketing.

Marketing is a controllable expense; however, it is also true that one has to spend money in order to make money. Tracking the success rate and earning power of each marketing program allows management to wisely allocate financial resources. For instance, a hotel or a restaurant runs an advertisement on three radio stations, and if guests mention where they heard the advertisement they will receive a discounted room rate or a free appetizer or dessert. To track the effectiveness of each radio station, management may wish to assign a different 800 number to each radio station's advertisement so that when the reservations come into the hotel or restaurant, the reservations agent can track the source of the calls. Using special promotion coupons in direct mail can also achieve the same purpose. When the results are tabulated, management can easily ascertain which marketing program yielded the best return on the investment. It is also a good idea to train employees to ask guests whether they have visited the operation before, and if not, how they learned about the property. Employees can then make a notation on the voucher, coupon, or reservation to track the amount of new business each advertising program generates.

Figure 15–3 *Marketing Expenses*

Agency fees
Brochures
Civic and community projects
Circulars/point-of-sale materials
Complimentary guest passes
Direct mail
Donations
Dues and subscriptions
Frequent stay programs
Internet homepage
Magazines and trade journals
Miscellaneous
Newspaper
Postage for mailings
Program directories and guides/souvenirs
Signage
Special promotional vouchers
Telephone for advertising
Travel expenses

The recordkeeping of the effectiveness of marketing programs can be simple or high-tech, depending on the time and resources that are available to management. One franchise operator simply keeps a copy of each printed coupon that the restaurant issued in a three-ring binder. He notes the effective date of the coupon, the target market to which the coupon was sent, and the number of coupons redeemed. In this manner, he can build a substantial advertising history.

Utilities Expenses

Utilities include electricity, water, gas, oil, and other fuel. This category can be a substantial cost area if not managed properly. "Greening" has become not just a fad but a responsibility, and hospitality managers and owners have become more active in this pursuit. Greening an industry of this magnitude represents potentially huge savings of energy and natural resources. Energy must be consumed for hotels, restaurants, and clubs to operate in the right manner and provide quality service to guests; yet, energy used improperly can create an enormous amount of waste and decrease profit margins. Therefore, energy conservation is not only the right thing to do to help preserve the earth, but it is also the right thing to do for a more profitable business.

In the area of electricity, retrofits to replace incandescent bulbs with compact fluorescent bulbs has been one of the most widely used energy-saving techniques; but a myriad of initiatives has also proven to be profitable. One resort hotel in Scottsdale, Arizona, reduced its utility costs by $46,000 over a ten-month period by installing energy-efficient lighting, installing window shades in the accounting offices, reducing water heater temperature and pool temperature, and using seasonal thermostat settings. Another hotel in Boston, Massachusetts, installed energy-efficient thermopane windows in its 977 rooms, which saved 29,000 gallons of fuel oil and $126,450. Energy-efficient lighting in the corridors and service areas saved 25,000 watts per hour as compared to the old lighting system in yet another property.

Water usage may not seem to be a big issue in a single independent restaurant or club; however, hotels are major consumers of water in all areas of daily operation, from foodservice facilities to laundries and guestrooms. A 1989 study by Redlin and DeRoos surveyed 408 properties to determine average water consumption and water use trends in the lodging industry. They determined that the U.S. lodging industry used 154 billion gallons of water in 1988. This equated to average hotel guestroom use of 144 gallons of water per day. Using the national average of $2.25 per 1000 gallons, the total annual bill was approximately $346 million, or $118 per room (Shaw, 1990).

Hospitality operations can save water and financial resources through measures such as the simple installation of water flow restrictors to the more complex installation of rinse water reuse laundry systems. Two lodging properties in Seattle, Washington, and Long Beach, California, were retrofitted with laundry water reuse systems that treat the final rinse water of the preceding wash for use in the next wash cycle. The estimated savings amount to $39,000 per year. In another instance, ten properties of a well-known national chain in northern New Jersey send their laundry to a consolidated laundry facility, which uses congeneration and heat reclamation techniques that save more than $125,000 per year in water and energy costs. A hotel in Vancouver, British Columbia, installed low-consumption showerheads and toilets in its 75 designated "green rooms" and reduced water use by 40%.

Simple changes in operating procedures such as watering the lawn at dusk to reduce evaporation, sweeping the sidewalk rather than hosing it down, or implementing optional towel and bed linen reuse programs have also proven to be profitable. In initiating such programs, establishments need to consider services to guests. Most hotels put signs in the vanity and bath areas notifying guests of their towel and bed linen reuse program, which state that should guests choose not to subscribe to the reuse service, towels and bed linen will be changed on a daily basis. Responsible usage that does not compromise guest satisfaction can turn into profits.

Administrative and General Expenses

Administrative and general expenses are numerous. Even general insurance of a property may be included in administrative and general expenses, which is the case for restaurants and clubs. In hotels, it is recommended that general insurance be classified as an occupation expense, along with rent and property tax. Figure 15–4 lists items that are included in administrative and general expenses.

Administrative and general expenses are controllable. Credit and collection expenses, for instance, can be minimized with good credit policy and billing procedures. Credit card commissions can also be reduced as the average check, or per transaction revenue, and total revenue increase. It is advisable to update credit card commission quotes at least every two years, as the revenue level of an operation may change. In addition, electronic settlement processes speed up an operation's cash deposits in comparison to the manual process in which the credit card company sends checks, which then must be taken to a bank for deposit.

Management information system services, point-of-sales systems, and property management systems are classified under administrative and general expenses. Most managers are well versed in operational issues, however, some may not be as knowledgeable in the computer field. Thus, issues regarding contract services for maintenance and other services related to information systems can prove daunting. Management needs to gather all available information and may even wish to consult with other hotels, restaurants, and clubs that subscribe to the services to determine whether such systems or agreements meet their expectations. Thus, it is important to maintain industry contacts through associations and trade shows.

Items in this expense area that can easily be overlooked are operating supplies and equipment, which includes general office supplies, everything from photocopies to pencil sharpeners. Office items, especially smaller ones, tend to be consumed quickly. Office theft is often difficult to detect but needs

Figure 15–4 *Administration and General Expenses*

Bank charges
Cash overages and shortages
Communication systems
Contract services
Credit and collection
Credit card commissions
Donations
Dues and subscriptions
Head office
Human resources
Information systems
Internal audit
Internal communications
Loss and damage
Meals and entertainment
Operating supplies and equipment
Postage
Printing and stationery
Professional fees
Provision for doubtful accounts
Security
Telecommunications
Training
Transportation
Travel
Other

to be monitored. Such items should not be left in the open or easily accessible with an open-door policy. Although a requisition may be too much work, the simple use of a sheet that records the person's name and items drawn from the supply room may deter employees from taking excessive amounts or pocketing items for private use.

Repairs and Maintenance Expenses

This expense category falls in a gray area with regard to whether it is controllable, although when managed properly, repairs and maintenance should enhance an operation rather than burden it.

The items under repair and maintenance generally include painting and decorating, furniture and fixtures, building alternatives and improvements, upholstering, and maintenance contracts. A cost analysis might be beneficial to determine whether an operation should set up its own maintenance program, hire a service company, or combine the two options. Maintenance service companies are generally more technologically advanced than the staff of an independent operation. Maintenance contracts for equipment are recommended to off-set the cost of parts and labor. However, when it comes to furniture and fix-tures, it is the responsibility of the owner or manager to set up a maintenance schedule to clean the items regularly, to calibrate and adjust levels and temper-atures on a timely basis, and to inspect for symptoms and problems. These ac-tivities have to be accomplished to prevent breakdown. If properly cared for, furniture and fixtures should last at least five to eight years or more. Most cook-ing equipment can be maintained effectively if it is cleaned properly after every shift and is not abused by employees.

Occupation Expenses

Occupation expenses refer to rent and property taxes that your hotel, restau-rant, or club has to pay. If an operation owns a property, rental payment is a nonissue and property taxes play an important role.

Rent

Renting a property offers a number of advantages. Owners and managers do not have to worry about property taxes rising as a result of increases in prop-erty value. Depending on the economy, supply, and demand, owners and man-agers may also be able to negotiate a lease more in their favor.

The form of a lease can be fixed, variable, or mixed. Mixed lease agree-ments are also known as base minimum level agreements in which a tenant agrees to pay a "base minimum" rent regardless of sales and then an additional variable percentage of sales once a certain sales level is reached. Depending on an operation's level of sales and the stipulations of a lease, one type of agree-ment may favor a landlord and another may favor a tenant (see Figure 15–5).

Although most lease agreements only charge rent, some leases may re-quire a tenant to pay for part of the property insurance, maintenance, or real estate taxes. With regard to foodservice establishments in malls, leases on rent become more complex as additional items are usually apply. The common area maintenance charge is generally a percentage of the square footage occupied. Insurance expense is calculated in the same manner. Some malls also charge a merchant association fee, promotions fee, marketing fee, or trash removal fee.

Regardless of the terms, additional charges, and base rental amount, lease negotiation is vital because a lease can obligate a business for a period of a few years to 10 years or more. Thus, an astute decision can save financial resources and avert possible problems in the future.

Property Taxes

Property taxes are a noncontrollable expense that apply to operations that own property. The amount of property taxes depends on the value of the property; as the value of the property increases, so does the amount of taxes that needs to be paid. Property tax rates are based on a number of factors such as the location

Figure 15–5   *Leasing Scenarios*

Fixed lease $50,000 per year
Variable lease 4% of sales per year
Mixed lease $20,000 per year with 3% of sales over $500,000

1. Sales = $1,400,000
    Rental payment:
        Under fixed lease $50,000
        Under variable lease $56,000 $1,400,000 × 0.04
        Under mixed lease $35,000 $20,000 + ($1,400,000 − $500,000) × 0.03
        Best option: Mixed lease

2. Sales = $1,000,000
    Rental payment:
        Under fixed lease $50,000
        Under variable lease $40,000 $1,000,000 × 0.04
        Under mixed lease $35,000 $20,000 + ($1,000,000 − $500,000) × 0.03
        Best option: Variable lease

3. Sales = $2,000,000
    Rental payment:
        Under fixed lease $50,000
        Under variable lease $80,000 $2,000,000 × 0.04
        Under mixed lease $65,000 $20,000 + ($2,000,000 − $500,000) × 0.03
        Best option: Fixed lease

of the property and the type of business the property houses. If an owner or manager believes that a property has not been assessed correctly, he or she may submit an appeal. Oftentimes, such appeals lead to an adjustment, which may incur a lower amount of taxes.

Depreciation

Depreciation is known as a noncash expense; therefore, because it does not "cost" the business any cash, this cost is not closely monitored. Although depreciation is not paid in cash terms, it is still an expense, which enables an operation to reduce its taxable income and thus enjoy a better tax write-off.

The concept of depreciation is not to pay less tax, rather, if managed properly, depreciation expense should be a means for managers and owners to put away a certain amount of money to replace the depreciated asset when the time comes, to increase other assets for growth, to decrease liabilities, or for other purposes.

A number of depreciation methods are used in the hospitality industry. The two main methods are the straight-line method and accelerated types of methods. The straight-line method is perhaps preferred due to its simplicity. To obtain the annual depreciated amount the salvage value is deducted from the cost and the depreciable base is divided by the estimated number of years of its useful life. For instance:

Cost $10,000
Salvage $1000
Life   5 years

$$\text{Depreciation expense} = \frac{10,000 - 1000}{5}$$

$$= \frac{9000}{5}$$

$$= \$1800 \text{ per year}$$

The $1800 will then be recorded as an expense on an annual basis or divided into smaller amounts for every accounting period to offset the revenues earned, thus decreasing the amount of taxable income and the taxes paid.

Accelerated depreciation is also used widely in the industry due to the fact that more depreciation expenses can be taken during the first few years of depreciation. This enables owners and managers to write off a larger sum of money as the depreciation expense and thus pay less taxes in the early years. Many start-up businesses opt for this method because cash flow usually is tightest in the first few years of a business. Thus, any extra funds can be retained in the business for other purposes.

The most commonly used accelerated depreciation methods are double-declining balance and the modified accelerated cost recovery system. The double-declining balance (DDB), as its name suggests, doubles the amount of the straight-line rate. For instance, a 200% double-declining effectively depreciates twice the amount of the straight-line rate:

$$\text{Double-declining rate} = \frac{100\%}{\text{Useful life}} \times 2$$

Using the same data from the straight-line depreciation example:

$$\text{Double-declining rate} = \frac{100\%}{5} \times 2 = 40\%$$

The depreciation expense of the double-declining rate is calculated by multiplying the rate by the cost of the asset. Salvage is not used until the depreciated value approaches the salvage in later years. Table 15–1 illustrates the full depreciation of the $10,000 amount using the DDB method with a $1000 salvage. The depreciation amounts in years 1 and 2 are more than the $1800 as calculated using the straight-line method. The depreciation in year 3 is less than the $1800 level. The asset can only depreciate $296 in year 5 because any more than that amount will not yield the given $1000 salvage.

Table 15–1

Year	Calculation	Expense	Accumulated Depreciation	Salvage	Book Value
	Acquisition	0	0	1000	10,000
1	10,000 × 40%	4000	4000	1000	6000
2	6000 × 40%	2400	6400	1000	3600
3	3600 × 40%	1440	7840	1000	2160
4	2160 × 40%	864	8704	1000	1296
5	9000 − 8704	296	9000	1000	1000

The modified accelerated cost recovery system (MACRS) is similar to the DDB method and uses the 200% declining balance method but switches to straight-line depreciation at some point in the asset's life. To obtain the depreciation amount one determines the class life of the asset in question and applies the appropriate percentages to the cost of the asset. Figure 15–6 lists major class and asset lives for MACRS, and Figure 15–7 lists recovery allowance percentages for an asset.

Depending on the business strategy of an operation, owners and management may choose straight-line over accelerated or vice versa. For tax purposes, however, one must use either the straight-line method or the MACRS.

Interest

Interest is the dollar amount that is charged to a borrower for the use of money from a financial institution. This is usually for a loan or a mortgage. Interest is an expense that is controllable at the ownership level but not at the management level; however, this does not bar management from the need to understand how interest can affect the net income of an establishment.

Figure 15–6   *Major Class and Asset Lives for MACRS*

Class	Type of Property
3-year	Certain special manufacturing tools
5-year	Automobiles, light-duty trucks, computers, and certain special manufacturing equipment, restaurant equipment
7-year	Most industrial equipment, office furniture, and fixtures
10-year	Certain longer-lived types of equipment
27.5-year	Residential rental real property such as apartment buildings
39-year	All nonresidential real property, including commercial and industrial buildings

Figure 15–7   *Recovery Allowance Percentages for an Asset*

Ownership year	Class of Investment			
	3-year	5-year	7-year	10-year
1	33%	20%	14%	10%
2	45	32	25	18
3	15	19	17	14
4	7	12	13	12
5		11	9	9
6		6	9	7
7			9	7
8			4	7
9				7
10				6
11				3
	100%	100%	100%	100%

Loans and mortgages are obtained for many reasons. Most investors do not have enough cash to start a business and thus need liabilities to make up the entire investment budget. Even though some investors do have all the necessary cash, they still may want to obtain a loan or mortgage, using their business as collateral, to reduce their personal financial risk. This is especially true when interest rates are low. With low rates and tax deductions, most businesses prefer to maintain a certain balance of liability and equity rather than to structure a company with 100% equity.

Figure 15–8   *Levels of Interest Rates*

Loan amount $1,000,000

	Interest at 20%	Interest at 10%
Revenues	$1,000,000	$1,000,000
Cost of goods sold	400,000	400,000
Gross profit	600,000	600,000
All expenses	300,000	300,000
Earnings before interest and taxes	300,000	300,000
Interest expense	200,000	200,000
Gross earnings	100,000	200,000
Taxes (30%)	30,000	60,000
Net income	70,000	140,000

Interest and mortgage rates have been decreasing since the early 1980s, and many businesses refinanced their loans and mortgages in the early 1990s, because of the fall of interest rates in new loans. Although interest is tax deductible, it is still a cash expense that needs to be paid. Therefore, if a loan or a mortgage can be refinanced to obtain a lower interest rate, expenses can be reduced, thus increasing net income.

Figure 15–8 shows how low interest rates can increase net income. As seen in this figure, all revenues and costs are identical until they reach the entry pertaining to interest. At 20% interest, the interest expense comes to $200,000, leasing only $100,000 as the taxable income to net $70,000 after taxes. In reducing the original interest rate by half, income before taxes doubled to $200,000, netting the restaurant $140,000. It is true that higher gross earnings garner more taxes, but more is retained as net income.

Summary

The hospitality industry boasts myriad controllable and noncontrollable expenses. Some of these expenses are noncontrollable at management level, but are controllable at ownership level. Property tax is the only cost item that is considered to be completely noncontrollable.

Reducing expenses through acute decision-making, recordkeeping, and research can lower taxes and/or increase net income. Therefore, it is up to both management and ownership to make that profit.

Review Exercises

1. For departments in which food and beverage costs do not apply, which cost is the largest portion of the budget?
   a. advertising
   b. utilities
   c. labor
   d. property tax

2. Which of the following is not considered controllable?
   a. labor
   b. food
   c. beverage
   d. interest

3. Marketing expenses usually include:
   a. postage for mailing
   b. signage
   c. direct mail
   d. all of the above

4. Which of the following is true with regard to marketing?
   a. it is necessary to track the success of each marketing program
   b. time should not be wasted on calculations and analysis
   c. the more money spent, the more sales will be generated
   d. recordkeeping is not needed

5. Which of the following is not an initiative to conserve utilities?
   a. maintenance of water heater temperature at a constant level
   b. linen reuse program
   c. providing air-conditioning all year around
   d. compact fluorescent bulbs

6. One aspect that management should not lose sight of while saving energy is:
   a. guest satisfaction
   b. employee satisfaction
   c. dollars spent
   d. dollars saved

7. Credit card commission fees are dependent upon one of the following factors:
   a. number of employees
   b. total revenues
   c. total costs
   d. tax paid

8. Occupation expenses include:
   a. rent
   b. utilities
   c. repairs and maintenance
   d. all of the above

9. Property taxes:
   a. are a controllable expense
   b. can be appealed
   c. are in opposite relation to a property's value
   d. are always paid by a tenant

10. Which of the following is a depreciation method that is used in the hospitality industry:
    a. straight-line
    b. quadruple-declining balance
    c. modified accelerated cost recovery system
    d. a and c

11. Name two controllable and two noncontrollable expenses, and explain why they are categorized as such.

12. List three pieces of equipment in a fast-food restaurant and explain why a schedule is required for their maintenance.

13. Discuss ways to evaluate the effectiveness of an advertising or promotion campaign.

14. Discuss the differences between the straight-line depreciation method and the modified accelerated cost recovery system.

15. You have found a perfect spot for your fast-food operation in a new mall, and the rental agent offers you a choice of three leases: variable, fixed, or mixed. The variable lease stipulates that the rental charge will be 5% of sales, the fixed lease requires a rate of $55,000 per year, and the mixed lease charges a base minimum rent of $25,000 plus 3% of sales over $350,000. Determine the best option if your sales level is:
    a. $500,000
    b. $200,000
    c. $1,000,000

Examination Type Problems

1. You have recently purchased some new equipment for the office and it falls under the 3-year class life in the modified accelerated cost recovery system. Given that the equipment cost $100,000, has four years of useful economic life, and a salvage value of $25,000, calculate the:
    a. Depreciation expenses of the four years using the straight-line depreciation method
    b. Depreciation expenses of the four years using the double-declining balance method
    c. Depreciation expenses of the four years using the modified accelerated cost recovery system

2. Name three items under the direct operating expenses category and discuss how costs can be controlled and evaluated on these items.

3. The Internet features new ways to market hotels, restaurants, and foodservice operations. Discuss three marketing methods to explore should you have your own homepage or website.

4. You have a choice of three leases (variable, fixed, or mixed) for your fast-food operation. The variable lease stipulates that the rental charge will be 7% of sales, the fixed lease requires a rate of $60,000 per year, and the mixed lease charges a base minimum rent of $30,000 plus 4% of sales over $400,000. Determine the best option if your sales level is:
    a. $250,000
    b. $600,000
    c. $900,000

Case Study

You have managed the Model Restaurant so well that your hotel corporation has asked you to consult on a restaurant of a sister hotel. The general manager of the sister hotel explains to you that even though sales have remained the same for the last few months, there has been a constant decline in profit. Several advertising and promotion efforts were used to increase sales. You are not the owner and you have no control over noncontrollable costs, so your only alternative is to try to reduce controllable costs. List five specific controllable expenses and evaluate how each can be improved.

References

Club Managers Association of America. (1996). Uniform system of financial reporting for clubs. Dubuque, Iowa: Kendall/Hunt Publishing Company.

Deloitte & Touche LLP. (1996). Uniform system of accounts for restaurants. (1996). Seventh edition. Washington, DC: National Restaurant Association.

Hotel Association of New York City, Inc. (1996). Uniform system of accounts for the lodging industry. Ninth edition. East Lansing, Michigan: Educational Institute of the American Hotel & Motel Association.

Shaw, R. (1990). AH&MA gives stats on surveyed hotels' water consumption. *Hotel & Motel Management, 205*(19), B-2, B-28.

16
Forecasting and Budgeting

Key Terms

budgeting	market research	simple time series
contingency plan	moving averages	smoothing
decomposition	operations budget	static budget
Delphi method	ratio analysis	stockout
flexible budget	regression analysis	variance analysis
forecasting	sales force estimates	yield management
juries of executive opinion		

Learning Objectives

After completing this chapter, you should be able to:

- discuss the importance of forecasting and budgeting.
- explain all methods of forecasting.
- conduct forecasting using simple time series and moving averages.
- conduct static and flexible budgets.
- understand the five major categories of ratios.

- understand and perform variance analysis.
- take action and follow up significant variances.
- avoid the problem of stockout.
- design contingency plans for unforeseen circumstances.

Outline

Forecasting the Volume of Business
The Particulars of Forecasting
Preparing a Budget
The Particulars of Budgeting
Measuring Success and Budgetary
    Control
     Ratio Analysis
     Variance Analysis

Stockouts and Contingency Plans
Computerization
Summary
Review Exercises
Examination Type Problems
Case Study

The accuracy of forecasting and the precision of budgeting are major determinants of profitability in the hospitality industry. On the surface, forecasting and budgeting appear to be very similar in that they both involve prediction of the future; however, there are distinct differences. Forecasting predicts the outcomes of future events such as sales levels or guest counts. A budget is a formal plan of the revenues and expenses of an operation over a period of time and is usually expressed in terms of dollars. True budgeting is strategic planning and may contain forecasts for a number of years to provide estimates for the future, a coordinated management policy, a method of control to compare actual results to the estimates, and time to take corrective actions to improve situations. There are many types of budgets. This chapter concentrates on operations budgets and Chapter 17 discusses capital budgets.

After speaking with any controller, department head, or team of employees who has been involved with forecasting and/or budgeting, one will conclude that these are not easy tasks. Although owners and managers are generally satisfied with their forecasting and budgeting accuracy, they still desire improvement. Lasky (1988), who has helped rescue 130 hotels and motels from bankruptcy, cited that budgeting is one of the factors hoteliers ignore when opening an establishment. An accurate budget is essential to the profitability of an operation. Effective preparation of forecasts and budgets can lead to better knowledge of probable income on a departmental or unit level, and thus may expedite efficient control of operating expenses.

Forecasting the Volume of Business

In the hospitality business, forecasting gives restaurateurs, hoteliers, and club managers a plan for their actions. Forecasting is the estimation of potential sales levels given a set of circumstances. For the most part, forecasting relies heavily on historical data. The closer the forecasted period is to the present time line and the more accurate the historical data, the more useful the forecast will be to the business. In the lodging segment of the industry, forecasting is done in various departments and then a consolidated forecast of sales is compiled. These forecasts may consist of 7-, 10-, or 14-day forecasts for each department and sophisticated demand statistics analysis for yield management. Figure 16–1 is a 10-day forecast for a rooms department of a small hotel.

A survey of 140 controllers was conducted to assess the usefulness of departmental forecasting in the lodging industry. Respondents were given a list of uses of forecasting and were asked to rate the importance of such uses on a scale of 0 to 7, with 0 as "not applicable," 1 as "strongly disagree," and 7 as "strongly agree." Of the 13 uses, the controllers rated "staff properly" as the main benefit (5.82) and "motivate personnel" received the lowest rating (4.58).

Figure 16–1   Ten-Day Forecast

DAY	WED	THUR	FRI	SAT	SUN	MON	TUE	WED	THUR	FRI
DATE										
ROOMS	FC/ACT	FC/ACT	FC/ACT	FC/ACT	FC/ACT	FC/ACT	FC/ACT	FC/ACT	FC/ACT	FC/ACT
ARRIVALS										
DEPARTURES										
STAYOVERS										
TOTAL ROOMS OCCUPIED										
ROOMS ON THE BOOKS										
HOUSE COUNT										
FOOD AND BEVERAGE										
CATERING										
BREAKFAST										
LUNCH										
DINNER										
BREAK										
RECEPTION										
TOTAL CATERING COVERS										
IN HOUSE BANQUET										
BREAKFAST										
LUNCH										
DINNER										
BREAK										
RECEPTION										
TOTAL IN HOUSE BANQUET COVERS										
TOTAL BANQUET COVERS										
RESTAURANT										
BREAKFAST										
LUNCH/BRUNCH										
DINNER										
LATE NIGHT										
TOTAL RESTAURANT COVERS										

Figure 16–2   *Usefulness of Forecasting in Rank Order*

Uses	Mean Score	Standard Deviation
Staff properly	5.82	1.38
Control costs	5.74	1.50
Make decisions	5.68	1.34
Plan strategically	5.66	1.43
Maximize profits	5.56	1.46
Have a standard of comparison	5.51	1.51
Set prices accordingly	5.42	1.52
Examine alternative	5.24	1.37
Enhance communications	5.20	1.30
Order inventory effectively	5.07	1.45
Enhance commitment	5.01	1.45
Handle an unforeseen event	4.71	1.72
Motivate personnel	4.58	1.53

Figure 16–2 lists, in order of usefulness, the benefits of preparing a forecast. Such usefulness can also be realized in foodservice operations, clubs, and casinos.

The Particulars of Forecasting

The frequency of forecasting differs from one establishment to another. Moreover, because forecasts are not actual numbers and usually are not 100% accurate, management may be required to reforecast and update the numbers to match changing circumstances. In hotels, forecasting is performed on a departmental level by one to three persons. Monthly forecasting is the norm for most hotel departments except for rooms. Due to the sensitivity of yield management in capturing the highest rates possible, rooms departments generally prepare forecasts weekly, then monthly, and then annually. Yield management is a process by which rooms departments monitor the demand of rooms and sell them at different rates to maximize potential revenues. In other words, all rate categories are available for low demand days in order to sell the available rooms, however, when the forecast predicts that rooms are in high demand, then the lower rates are closed and discounts are restricted so the available rooms can be sold at higher rates.

Although monthly forecasting is the norm for food and beverage departments, weekly forecasting is also prevalent. In a freestanding food-service unit, management bears the main responsibility of establishing a forecast. This also holds true with multiunit food-service operations. The only difference is that headquarters may aid in the process by supplying the units with statistics.

A number of methods are used in preparing forecasts. The method used depends on the type of operation, the type of customers, the level of demand, the efforts spent on sales and marketing, seasonality, specific events, and availability and accuracy of historical data. The most common method in the lodging industry is sales force estimates. It is a bottom-up approach to aggregate unit managers' forecasts. This is done on a unit or departmental level by gathering data from first-line employees.

Another method is moving averages. Moving averages are compiled based on average past values of a time series. This method is popular due to its simple and quick calculation. Figure 16–3 shows the calculation for the number of meals served for Week 11 using a 3-week moving average.

When there are some events that may skew a regular moving average calculation, smoothing will be used. Smoothing gives more weight to the more recent past values of a time series, thereby discounting older data that may not have as much impact on the forecast. Simple time series are based on simple rules such as forecast equals last period's actual activity or add/subtract a certain percentage, and are especially useful for smaller scale food-service operations in which time, technology, or expertise is lacking. For example, assume that the golf revenues for a country club in January 1997 were $120,000. If a simple time series is used and the club expects a 10% increase in golf revenues in January 1998, then the calculation is:

Base $(1 + 10\%)$ = Forecast for January 1998
$120,000 (1.1) = $132,000

Simple time series may not yield the most accurate forecast; however, they provide trends to help operators make future decisions.

To obtain a more detailed analysis, decomposition is employed. Decomposition is a time series that is broken down into trends, cycles, seasons, and randomness. Another popular method is juries of executive opinion in which top executives jointly prepare forecasts.

For new products or services, market research is often performed to gather information from potential customers to estimate the rate of demand. This method is also used in existing hotels, foodservice operations, and clubs to ascertain their fair share of the market as compared to their competitors. The Delphi method, a formal process conducted by a group of experts to achieve consensus, is often used when performing a forecast for the entire industry. If data are available, regression analyses can also be performed to relate independent variables to dependent variables using the least squares method. This is perhaps the least used method in the industry due to the time needed for data collection, input, analysis, and interpretation. The R^2 statistic, having a value of 0 to 1, is derived from a regression analysis. It indicates the percentage of how much the independent variable can explain the changes that occurred in the dependent variable. Thus, a higher R^2 value indicates that the independent variable is a better predictor of the dependent variable. For example, the number of rooms sold can be a predictor of labor costs in the rooms department.

Figure 16–3   *Three-Week Moving Average*

Week	Actual Meals Served Per Day
1	850
2	1025
3	975
4	890
5	1115
6	968
7	1201
8	1106
9	1008
10	994

Moving average = Activity in previous N periods ÷ N
where N is the number of periods in the calculation of the moving average

Week 11 = Week 8 + Week 9 + Week 10 ÷ 3
        = 1106 + 1008 + 994 ÷ 3
        = 1036

While simple time series are used most in small food-service operations and hotels, combinations of forecasting methods are also used in the industry. For instance, a hotel front office manager may take into consideration actual reservations made and a variation of the moving average and simple time series methods to complete the 7-day forecast.

Although a wide variety of methods are used, there are certain reasons why one method is preferred over another. The 140 controllers from the aforementioned study stated the top reasons for using certain forecasting methods: the purpose for which the forecast is prepared, the period of time in which the forecast is prepared, the frequency of forecast updates, and the frequency of the forecast. If one method adequately serves the needs of an operation, management should continue to use that particular method; however, they may opt to use other methods to determine whether they yield better results.

Preparing a Budget

Budgeting and forecasting are both essential. However, the reasons why budgeting is important differ slightly from those for forecasting. Again recalling the survey that was discussed earlier, the same 140 hotel controllers rated the same 13 attributes for budgeting as were used in forecasting, using a scale of 0 to 7, with 0 as "not applicable," 1 as "strongly disagree," and 7 as "strongly agree." Of the 13 uses, the controllers rated "plan strategically" as the main benefit (5.93)

Figure 16–4   *Usefulness of Budgeting in Rank Order*

Uses	Mean Score	Standard Deviation
Plan strategically	5.93	1.26
Have a standard of comparison	5.92	1.31
Control costs	5.81	1.44
Make decisions	5.68	1.30
Maximize profits	5.58	1.39
Set prices accordingly	5.57	1.39
Staff properly	5.51	1.50
Enhance commitment	5.49	1.47
Examine alternatives	5.32	1.43
Enhance communications	5.28	1.45
Motivate personnel	4.80	1.57
Order inventory effectively	4.66	1.60
Handle an unforeseen event	4.00	1.83

and "handle an unforeseen event" received the lowest rating (4.00). Figure 16–4, lists, in order of usefulness, the benefits of preparing a budget.

The Particulars of Budgeting

Because budget periods normally cover a longer time span than that of forecasts, the frequency of the preparation of budgets is fairly uniform in that annual budgeting is the norm. In hotels, some departments may also prepare budgets monthly, quarterly, or semiannually, but they are somewhat insignificant. Although budgets are prepared annually, the ever-changing nature of the industry and the increased use of technology dictate that consolidated budgets be revised quite often. This is especially true in hotel settings when group functions are added or canceled.

Budgeting is done by unit managers in most food-service operations, by the various departments in hotels, and by the executive committee in clubs. In hotels, budgeting is performed by one to four persons at the departmental level, consolidated by the controller, and reviewed the by executive committee and the general manager. Food and beverage departments usually involve more people in the process because they have more outlets and personnel than other departments.

Figure 16–5 is a sample budget for a small-scale restaurant. An average number of covers and an average check amount are estimated for budgeting purposes. The costs of food and other controllable items are expressed as a percentage of revenues while fixed costs such as depreciation, property taxes, and rent are calculated separately.

Figure 16–5   *Sample Budget of a Small-Scale Restaurant*

Budget for the Month of May 20XX

Average check $10.00
Customer count per day = 285

Sales revenues	($10 × 285 × 31)	88,350.00
Food cost	(31.5%)	27,830.25
Salaries and wages	(29.9%)	26,416.65
Employee benefits	(3.8%)	3,357.30
Direct operating expenses	(6.6%)	5,831.10
Music and entertainment	(0.2%)	176.70
Marketing	(3.5%)	3,092.25
Utilities	(4.0%)	3,534.00
Repairs and maintenance	(1.7%)	1,501.95
General and administrative	(3.0%)	2,650.00
Interest	(6.0%)	5,301.00
Occupancy cost	3,350.00	
Depreciation	1,760.00	
Gross income	3,548.80	

The operations budget is also known as the revenues and expense budget. It mirrors the income statement by providing the operator an estimate of the income or loss potential before the actual accounting period. It serves as a benchmark for the company to compare past efforts and also serves as a realistic, attainable goal.

Operations budgets are mainly classified into two categories: static (fixed) and flexible (scenario analysis). A static budget reflects one level of forecasted sales, and a flexible budget reflects two or more levels. A static budget is the base of a flexible budget, and a flexible budget is just a matter of a few formulas with spreadsheet technology. Figure 16–6 is a sample flexible budget.

Most small operations may not see the need to develop flexible budgets. However, flexible budgets do provide management with revenues, expenses, and profit information at different levels of activities. Therefore, flexible budgets are usually performed in large hotels or foodservice organizations because of the many departments and variables that make up the entire budget.

Measuring Success and Budgetary Control _____

Budgets and forecasts are important documents; however, they are only as important as their use. If management does not analyze and take action from these figures, an operation will not benefit from the budgeting process. The two types of analyses that are used involve ratios and variance.

Figure 16–6   *Sample Flexible Budget*

Flexible Operations Budget for 20XX

Given:

Average room rate	$65.00
Days per year	365
Number of rooms	86
Telephone revenue	2.4% of rooms revenue
Room expenses	26% of rooms revenue
Telephone expenses	80% of telephone revenue
Administrative expenses	29% of total revenue
Repairs and maintenance	2% of total revenue
Energy	4% of total revenue
Depreciation	$14,500.00
Interest	$112,050.00
Insurance	$5,500.00
Property tax	$6,000.00
Tax rate	30%

	Activity Levels—Occupancy %		
	65.00	70.00	75.00
Revenue:			
Rooms	$1,326,227.50	$1,428,245.00	$1,530,262.50
Telephone	31,829.46	34,277.88	36,726.30
Total	1,358,056.96	1,426,522.88	1,566,988.80
Departmental expenses:			
Rooms	344,819.15	371,343.70	397,868.25
Telephone	25,463.57	27,422.30	29,381.04
Total	370,282.72	398,766.00	427,249.29
Departmental income:			
Rooms	981,408.35	1,056,901.30	1,132,394.25
Telephone	6,365.89	6,855.58	7,345.26
Total	987,774.24	1,063,756.88	1,139,739.51
Undistributed operating expenses:			
Administrative expenses	393,836.52	424,131.64	454,426.75
Repairs and maintenance	27,161.14	29,250.46	31,339.78
Energy	54,322.28	58,500.92	62,679.55
Total	475,319.94	511,883.01	548,446.08
Total interest before fixed charges:	512,454.31	551,873.87	591,293.43
Depreciation	14,500.00	14,500.00	14,500.00
Interest	112,050.00	112,050.00	112,050.00
Insurance	5,500.00	5,500.00	5,500.00
Property tax	6,000.00	6,000.00	6,000.00
Gross income	374,404.31	413,823.87	453,243.43
Income taxes	112,321.29	124,147.16	135,973.03
Net income	262,083.02	289,676.71	317,270.40

Ratio Analysis

Financial ratio is a tool often used to interpret information presented in financial statements. Ratio analysis is essentially a mathematical calculation of one value divided by another, expressed in the form of times or percentages. It is in the presentation of such relationships that ratios generate new information, making the numbers and values more meaningful, informative, and useful. Financial ratios are primarily used to assess the performance of businesses. Financial ratios transform absolute numbers into meaningful relative terms from which owners and managers can extract valuable information.

The four categories of ratios that are used most are liquidity, debt (solvency), turnover (activity), and profitability. Schmidgall (1989) also includes operating ratios, which examine the efficiency of daily operations in the hospitality industry, especially in hotels. Liquidity ratios measure an operation's ability to meet its short-term debts. Debt, or solvency, ratios measure the degree of debt financing and indicate an operation's ability to meet its long-term debts. Turnover, or activity, ratios reflect company's use of available assets, prompt payment of trade payables, and expenses. Profitability ratios are most often discussed because they show the amount of money earned, such as return on assets and return on sales. Operating ratios such as sales mix, average daily rate (ADR), and revenue per available room (REVPAR) help determine the managerial efficiency of hotels (Schmidgall, 1995; Volk, 1995).

As early as 1963 the National Restaurant Association (NRA) started analyzing ratios for the restaurant industry. In one of its publications, *A Financial Analysis of the Restaurant Industry,* the association recommended six basic ratios as most appropriate to the needs of most foodservice operators: 1) current ratio, 2) net sales to net working capital, 3) return on equity, 4) return on asset, 5) fixed asset turnover, and 6) profit margin. The association also used these ratios to project trends for restaurants. Figure 16–7 provides a list of ratios and their calculations.

Variance Analysis

The difference between budgeted and actual figures is known as the variance. Depending on whether it is a revenue variance or cost variance, a positive or negative difference may be favorable or unfavorable. When the actual amount exceeds the budgeted amount, the variance is positive and thus favorable; when the actual amount is less than budgeted, the variance is negative and thus unfavorable. Therefore, when actual expenses are less than budgeted, the variance is favorable; when actual expenses are more than budgeted, the variance is unfavorable (see Figure 16–8).

Obviously, the aim of forecasting and budgeting is to be on target; however, variances do occur because it is unlikely that budgeted figures will exactly match actual figures. Variances should never be ignored. Significant variances need to be investigated and action must be taken. Even if the variance is favorable, better planning may enable an operation to capture a bigger profit margin. Every operation should set up its own guidelines with regard to what are deemed significant variances, and dollar amounts and percentages should be

Figure 16–7 *Ratios Most Used in the Hospitality Industry*

Ratio	Formula
Liquidity ratios:	
Current ratio	Current assets ÷ Current liabilities
Acid-test ratio	Cash, marketable securities, notes, and accounts receivable ÷ Current liabilities
Operating cash flows to current liabilities ratio	Operating cash flows ÷ Average current liabilities
Working capital turnover	Revenue ÷ Average working capital
Solvency ratios:	
Solvency ratio	Total assets ÷ Total liabilities
Debt-equity ratio	Total liabilities ÷ Total owners' equity
Long-term debt to total capitalization ratio	Long-term debt ÷ Long-term debt and owners' equity
Number of times interest earned ratio	EBIT ÷ Interest expense
Fixed charge coverage ratio	EBIT + Lease expense ÷ Interest expense and lease expense
Operating cash flows to total liabilities ratio	Operating cash flows ÷ Average total liabilities
Activity ratios:	
Accounts receivable turnover	Revenue ÷ Average accounts receivable
Average collection period	365 ÷ Accounts receivable turnover
Inventory turnover:	
Food inventory turnover	Cost of food used ÷ Average food inventory
Beverage turnover	Cost of beverages used ÷ Average beverage inventory
Property and equipment turnover	Total revenues ÷ Average property and equipment
Asset turnover	Total revenues ÷ Average total assets
Profitability ratios:	
Profit margin	Net income ÷ Total revenue
Return on assets	Net income ÷ Average total assets
Gross return on sales	EBIT ÷ Average total assets
Return on owners' equity	Net income ÷ Average owners' equity
Return on common stockholders' equity	Net income − Preferred dividend ÷ Average common stockholders' equity
Earnings per share	Net income ÷ Average common shares outstanding
Price earnings ratio	Market price per share ÷ Earnings per share
Efficiency ratios:	
Paid occupancy percentage	Paid rooms occupied ÷ Rooms available
Complimentary occupancy	Complimentary rooms ÷ Rooms available
Average occupancy per room	Number of room guests ÷ Number of rooms occupied
Multiple occupancy percentage	Rooms occupied by two or more people ÷ Rooms occupied by guests
Operating efficiency ratio	Income before fixed charges ÷ Total revenue
Mix of sales	Departmental revenues are totaled: Percentages of total revenue ÷ Number of rooms sold
ADR	Room revenue ÷ Number of rooms sold
Revpar	Paid occupancy percentage ÷ ADR
Average food service check	Total food revenue ÷ Number of rooms sold
Food cost percentage	Cost of food sold ÷ Food sales
Beverage cost percentage	Cost of beverages sold ÷ Beverage sales
Labor cost percentage	Labor cost by department ÷ Department revenues

Figure 16–8   *Budget Report with Variances*

Summary Budget Report for May 20XX

	Budget	Actual	Variance ($)	Variance (%)
Revenue:				
Rooms	$14,998.00	$15,640.00	$642.00	4%
Telephone	460.00	501.00	41.00	9%
Total	15,458.00	16,141.00	683.00	4%
Departmental expenses:				
Rooms				
Payroll	2,546.00	2,236.00	310.00	12%
Laundry	130.00	147.00	(17.00)	−13%
Linen	329.00	335.00	(6.00)	−2%
Commissions	159.00	156.00	3.00	2%
All other expenses	222.00	198.00	24.00	11%
Total	3,386.00	3,072.00	314.00	9%
Telephone	451.00	438.00	13.00	3%
Total	3,837.00	3,510.00	327.00	9%
Departmental income:				
Rooms	11,612.00	12,568.00	956.00	8%
Telephone	9.00	63.00	54.00	600%
Total	11,621.00	12,631.00	1,010.00	9%
Undistributed operating expenses:				
Administration	3,109.00	2,879.00	230.00	7%
Maintenance and energy costs	1,890.00	2,301.00	(411.00)	−22%
Total	4,999.00	5,180.00	(181.00)	−4%
Total gross income	6,622.00	7,451.00	829.00	13%
Depreciation	1,250.00	1,250.00	–	–
Property taxes	550.00	550.00	–	–
Insurance	500.00	500.00	–	–
Interest expense	1,456.00	1,456.00	–	–
Gross income	2,866.00	3,695.00	829.00	29%
Income taxes (30%)	859.80	1,108.50	(248.70)	−29%
Net income	$2,006.20	$2,586.50	$248.70	12%

evaluated. The best method of evaluation is to common-size the budgeted and actual figures and then compare the dollar amounts and percentages. For instance, some chefs at country clubs worry if food cost is half a percentage point over budget, regardless of the dollar amount. This is because food service in country club restaurants is fairly steady and banquets are prebooked so revenues are well planned. Due to these factors, the amount of food used should also be well controlled; thus, a half-percent variance may be significant for clubs but not for a restaurant with a varied clientele.

There is usually more tolerance in labor cost percentages than in food and beverage cost percentages. If an operation is short-staffed and only certain individuals are available to fill in, these individuals may be on overtime, which increases the labor cost tremendously. Again, management has to determine which variances are reasonable and which are significant. Also, variance reports on performances need to be timely and concise so that management can take appropriate action.

When comparing the budget to actual costs, most hospitality operations are concerned with prime cost items as these items account for such a large percentage of operational cost. If these costs are in line with the standards established in the budget, then management may seek to raise the standards unless it is understood that the operation is functioning at maximum efficiency and effectiveness. However, if there is a variance in the standard, then the cause of the variance must be evaluated. The cause of variance is most effectively examined through the following actions:

- Retaking inventory
- Examining prices of products in inventory
- Comparing production sheets to sales or guest checks
- Comparing sales to inventory
- Comparing voids, waste, and spillage sheets to inventory
- Comparing time cards to schedules
- Comparing schedules to sales
- Comparing sales to forecasted sales
- Ensuring that all operational activities are in accordance with standards

In many cases in which costs are out of line, it is due to a mistake in taking inventory. Because of the amount of space available in most facilities and the time of day in which inventory is taken, it is difficult to obtain an accurate inventory. The end of the week, in most hospitality facilities, occurs on Sunday or Monday night and inventory is usually taken in the late hours of the night after the facility has closed. Therefore, if costs are out of line, management may want to go back and verify that inventory has been taken correctly. Also, in foodservice operations, procedure must be established as to how production tables and behind the bar beverages are to be counted. If items on the production table or beverages behind the bar are to be counted in the inventory, they must always be added to the inventory. If a decision is made not to count these items, then they should always be omitted, otherwise this could cause a fluctuation in inventory.

Prices used to calculate inventory should also be examined. If the price was increased on an item that is purchased in large quantities, this could cause a major difference in overall cost. Receiving personnel may think that management is aware of a change in price when in fact the change may not have been noted. This is also why a consistent method must be used for establishing the price of items in inventory.

Comparing production sheets to sales or guest checks assists management in determining if the variance is due to overproduction, theft, or waste. Management must routinely compare production sheets to sales to ascertain whether the amount to be prepared was actually prepared. If the items are not accounted for they may have been stolen or discarded as waste. Production personnel may also waste products through improper production procedures. Therefore, all of these areas should be routinely evaluated.

In the same way that production is compared to sales, the amount sold should be compared to inventory to ensure that all products are accounted for and that all numbers balance. The amount on hand during the ending inventory, plus the amount purchased, minus the amount sold indicates the amount that should be on hand at the beginning of the inventory cycle. This process should never be taken for granted. Management must ensure that the amount sold was actually given to customers. Just because the numbers balance does not mean that guests received the products. This step in the control process is often neglected.

Managers should also compare voids, waste, and spillage sheets to inventory. Quite often a mistake can be an honest mistake. An unaccounted for void can cause sales to appear out of balance and can take several hours to detect. This is why it is important to have a trail tape in the cash register or some other means of reviewing sales. Waste, spillage, complimentary food or drinks, and food or drinks that have been sent back for remake must be accounted for if the cause for variance is to be detected.

The number of hours that employees actually worked should be compared to the number of hours that were scheduled. Time cards should be checked against schedules and employees should be informed that clocking in early and clocking out late will not be tolerated. Management may want to initial time cards when employees clock in and out to prevent these occurrences.

Comparing schedules to sales informs managers whether they have scheduled more labor hours or less labor hours than needed. An operation may want to establish standards such as sales per man-hour—each hour of labor used should reflect a certain volume in sales. An estimation of the amount of labor that should be used reveals whether labor and sales are compatible. Scheduling is a difficult process, and because the volume of business fluctuates so much in the hospitality industry, scheduling and sales must be evaluated constantly.

Management must compare actual sales to forecasted sales to ensure that labor and production were estimated correctly. Overproduction and overscheduling employee hours can cause additional expenditures; underproduction and short-staffing can also cause problems. Items with a higher contribution margin may not be available or guests may go elsewhere because of slow and poor service.

Anytime there is a variance management must ensure that all operational activities are in accordance with established objectives and standards. Because the budget is the overall operating standard for an organization, it will be difficult for an operation to achieve success if budgetary standards are not met. All operational procedures and guidelines must support the budget. Corrective action must be taken if procedures are not designed to meet budgetary standards.

Stockouts and Contingency Plans

Many problems arise because of lack of planning. If a restaurant forecasts for 100 customers but 200 show up due to a concert at a theater down the road, then both sales and costs will go up. The increase in sales theoretically should cover the increase in costs, because certain costs such as rent and insurance stay the same; however, the forecasted profit margin may not be achieved. Labor may not be as efficient because extra help is not available when needed. This is not just a short-term issue of efficiency; miscalculated forecasts may also lead to poor service and bad experiences for the customers. Worse still, the restaurant may experience stockout, in which there is not enough food to fill the orders, especially if a situation such as this falls on the last day of the order cycle and the restaurant is expecting a shipment of goods the next morning.

Thus, every situation needs a contingency plan. A contingency plan is a backup plan for possible events or future emergencies. For example, a contingency plan is required if a restaurant staff member discovers a shortage of dinner rolls half an hour before the dinner shift is scheduled to begin. Management must make a decision. Should the restaurant not serve rolls with their meals and not inform the customers? Or should guests be informed before they order? Should the restaurant offer a substitution? If so, what might that substitution be? If the restaurant is a chain or multiunit operation, it may be able borrow stock from another unit, supposing there is one in the vicinity, and return it when their own order arrives. Otherwise, a manager may need to go to the neighborhood grocery store to buy enough to last the meal period. There is not a textbook answer to this situation or any other situation. Management should develop guidelines for certain situations and should consider the circumstances involved. Managers must think on their feet and react quickly, although accurate forecasting and budgeting and efficient ordering procedures can help avert these types of situations.

Computerization

Due to sweeping technology and the widespread use of computers, the importance, frequency, and preparation methods of forecasting and budgeting have changed dramatically. Today's technology is far more advanced that it was just a decade ago. Various software packages are available—either as stand-alone products or as modules in a system—for the different functions of hotels, restaurants, clubs, and casinos. According to a 1988 report compiled by the National

Figure 16–9 Sample Inventory Spreadsheet with Extensions and Order Amounts

Product Description	Pack Size	Units/Pack	Amount	Measure	Price/Pack	Price/Unit	On-hand Packs	On-hand Units	Extension Units
Butter, 90 CT/PAT	Case/6	6	5.00	Pound	49.49	8.25	15	90	742.35
	Case/6	6	5.00	Pound	50.63	8.44	25	150	1265.75
Butter, balls, .25 oz	Case/6	6	3.00	Pound	39.02	6.50	19	114	741.38
Butter, chip, 47 ct	Case/4	4	4.25	Pound	39.49	7.62	7	28	213.43
Butter, bakers	Case	36	1.00	Pound	81.00	2.25	11	396	891.00
Butter, rosettes	Case	600	1.00	Each	28.28	0.05	2	1200	56.56
Butter, solids, unsalted	Case/36	36	1.00	Pound	53.97	1.50	10	360	539.70
Butter, blue, crumbles	Case/4	4	5.00	Pound	41.50	10.38	19	76	788.50
Cheese, Havarti, Danish, oz	Pound	1	1.00	Pound	3.35	3.35	45	45	150.75
Cheese, American, 120 ct/oz	Case/4	4	5.00	Pound	35.00	8.75	24	96	840.00
Cheese, American, yellow, loaf, oz	Case/6	6	5.00	Pound	51.21	8.54	6	36	307.26
Cheese, Asiago	Pound	1	1.00	Pound	4.30	4.30	18	18	77.40
Cheese, Bel Paese, oz	Pound	1	1.00	Pound	4.68	4.68	2	2	9.36
Cheese, Boursin Baby, 5.5 oz	Each	1	1.00	Each	4.13	4.13	34	34	140.42
Cheese, Brie, wheel, domestic, oz	Case/2	2	1.00	Each	17.90	8.95	7	14	125.30
Cheese, Cambazola	Case/2	10	1.00	Pound	74.50	7.45	5	50	372.50
Cheese, Camembert, 4.5 oz	Each	1	1.00	Each	1.70	1.70	30	30	51.00
Cheese, cheddar, mild, mini	Case/100	100	1.00	Each	18.04	0.18	17	1700	306.68
Cheese, cheddar, sharp, NY, oz	Pound	1	1.00	Pound	2.90	2.90	14	14	40.60
Cheese, cheddar, sharp, oz	Case/100	10	1.00	Pound	21.06	2.11	3	30	63.18
Cheese, cheddar, white	Pound	1	1.00	Pound	2.80	2.80	5	5	14.00

Restaurant Association, computers were used in many functional areas, including accounting, bookkeeping, and inventory (see Figure 16–9). In the lodging segment, a 1989 survey reported that close to 70% of the respondents used computers to prepare forecasts (Schmidgall). This increased to 96.38% in a 1997 study (DeFranco). Lotus 1-2-3 was the software most widely used by the respondents with Microsoft Excel reported as the second most commonly used tool. Even more respondents (99.26%) used computers and spreadsheets for budgeting purposes.

Because computers have made the budgeting and forecasting processes more manageable, many operations develop more than one forecast and one budget on an annual basis. Reforecasting and rebudgeting are quite common, as computers and spreadsheet applications allow figures to be changed easily to reflect current situations or unforeseen circumstances.

Summary

Three major elements determine the effectiveness of forecasting and budgeting: accuracy, timeliness, and relevancy. Use all data and personnel available when developing forecasts and budgets. Historical data are important yet future events that have impact on your hospitality concern are also vital. Even if a first attempt has deficiencies, management and responsible parties should not simply abandon forecasts or budgets and "go by experience."

When forecasts and budgets are not on target or are not prepared in a timely manner, management needs to provide updated forecasts and budgets to reflect current situations. An incorrect or late forecast will not benefit an operation.

Managers may often complain about the stacks of paperwork on their desks; for this reason, all reports, including forecasts and budgets, must be concise. They should not contain pages of peripheral information, as information overload has an adverse effect on the efficiency of an operation.

Review Exercises

1. Which of the following is not an important factor to consider when estimating sales incomes?
   a. food costs
   b. sales histories
   c. inflation
   d. nearby street improvement

2. Over a 60-day period, 600 guests are served and 120 prime rib dinners are sold. What is the percentage of guests who ordered prime rib dinners?
   a. 12%
   b. 20%
   c. 40%
   d. 45%

3. Past records show that 40% of dinner guests order some type of chicken entree. In view of this, what percentage of the 160 guests forecasted for next Tuesday's dinner will order chicken entrees?
   a. 40%
   b. 46%
   c. 60%
   d. 64%

4. When budgeted sales are $17,000 and actual sales are $15,000, the variance is:
   a. +$2000 favorable
   b. +$2000 unfavorable
   c. −$2000 favorable
   d. −$2000 unfavorable

5. Which is not a method used in forecasting?
   a. guests' comments
   b. simple time series
   c. market research
   d. decomposition

6. Which is a good method to use if forecasting for the sales of new products or services?
   a. guests' comments
   b. Delphi method
   c. moving average
   d. market research

7. If Great Food Restaurant uses a 4-week moving average to predict customer counts, what count is predicted for Week 8?

Week	Count
3	1000
4	1020
5	1040
6	980
7	1008

   a. 1000
   b. 1012
   c. 1020
   d. 1028

8. A simple time series of add 5% will make the last guest count of 200 for lunch become:
   a. 201
   b. 205
   c. 210
   d. 220

9. What is the occupancy percentage of Sky Lodge if it has 300 rooms and housed 200 guests (all single occupancy) last night?
   a. 40%
   b. 60%
   c. 67%
   d. 70%

10. In reference to question #9, if 50 rooms were each occupied by two people, what is the double occupancy percentage?
   a. 20%
   b. 25%
   c. 30%
   d. 33%

11. The Red Fish Cafe uses a 3-week moving average method in forecasting. Given the following data, what will be its expected guest count for Week 20?

Week	Actual Guest Count
15	1840
16	1760
17	1882
18	1823
19	1799

12. The Golden Eagle, a 300-room hotel, uses simple time series to forecast its guest counts and occupancy percentages. The current month, April, records a guest count of 5400. As the summer months approach, the hotel expects an increase in guest count of 1% per month for the next five months. Assuming all single occupancy, what will the guest counts and occupancy percentages be for the months of May through September?

13. Given the following information, prepare a budget for Restaurant Max Profit for the month of April.

   Average check: $15.40
   Customer count per day: 302
   Days in April: 30
   Food cost: 33.4%
   Salaries and wages: 28.6%
   Employee benefits: 4.0%
   Direct operating expense: 6.9%
   Music and entertainment: 0.5%
   Marketing: 2.5%
   Utilities: 2.9%
   Repairs and maintenance: 1.1%
   Administrative and general expenses: 3.0%
   Interest: 5.5%
   Occupation expense: $3110
   Depreciation: $1337

14. The Evergreen Country Club has established a budget for its Grill with 2400 guests forecasted for the month of July. However, its Grill business depends heavily on the number of golfers that the club attracts. Knowing that the weather in July is unpredictable, the manager would like to see what would happen to profit levels if the guest count fluctuated to 2000 or 2800. Given the following level budget for 2400 guests, develop a flexible budget for the Grill at Evergreen for the month of July. Note: All controllable expenses are calculated as a percentage of sales and noncontrollable expenses are fixed. The tax rate for Evergreen is 35%.

	2400 guests
Revenues:	
Food Sales	$46,000
Controllable expense:	
Food cost	16,200
Labor cost	11,880
Administrative and general expense	1440
Utilities	1560
Marketing	900
Repairs and maintenance	870
Noncontrollable expense:	
Occupation expense	2000
Depreciation	1560
Insurance	2000
Property tax	2750
Gross income	4840
Income tax (35%)	1694
Net income	$ 3146

Examination Type Problems

1. The Blue Monkey Bar and Grill uses a 3-week moving average method in forecasting. Given the following data, what will be its expected guest count for Week 11?

Week	Actual Guest Count
6	340
7	260
8	382
9	323
10	299

2. The White Horse, a 150-room inn, uses simple time series to forecast its guest counts and occupancy percentages. The current month, September, records a guest count of 2300. As the winter months approach, the hotel expects a decrease in guest count of 1% per month for the next five months. Assuming all single occupancy and that it is not a leap year, what will the guest counts and occupancy percentages be for the months of October through February?

3. Given the following information, prepare a budget for Restaurant Atlanta for the month of September.

> Average check: $13.00
> Customer count per day: 258
> Days in September: 30
> Food cost: 31.4%
> Salaries and wages: 28.8%
> Employee benefits: 4.0%
> Direct operating expense: 6.5%
> Music and entertainment: 0.5%
> Marketing: 3.0%
> Utilities: 3.9%
> Repairs and maintenance: 1.5%
> Administrative and general expenses: 3.0%
> Interest: 7.5%
> Occupation expenses: $2110
> Depreciation: $1637

4. The Mountain Peak Ski Resort has established a budget for its Cafe with 1300 guests forecasted for the month of February. However, its Cafe business depends heavily on the number of skiers that the resort attracts. Knowing that the weather in February is unpredictable, the manager would like to see what would happen to profit levels if the guest count fluctuated to 1000 or 1800. Given the following level budget for 1300 guests, develop a flexible budget for the Cafe at Mountain Peak for the month of February. Note: All controllable expenses are calculated as a percentage of sales and noncontrollable expenses are fixed. The tax rate for Mountain Peak is 35%.

	1300 guests
Revenues:	
Food sales	$28,000
Controllable expense:	
Food cost	9200
Labor Cost	5880
Administrative and general expense	990
Utilities	1050
Marketing	500
Repairs and maintenance	660
Noncontrollable expense:	
Occupation expense	1000
Depreciation	1110
Insurance	900
Property tax	1130
Gross income	5580
Income tax (35%)	1953
Net income	$ 3627

Case Study _____

The Case Study Hotel is contemplating opening another food and beverage outlet to complement the services offered by Model Restaurant. The general manager would like you to develop a formal budget for the upcoming year. The
budget will serve as a control document for you and the hotel. The hotel is in
a 40% tax bracket, and as the new manager, you will receive a bonus of 5% of
income before occupation cost.

The first step in developing the budget is to research external factors that
may affect your business during the upcoming year.

- The local economy has improved steadily since early last year and
  predictions are that it will continue to strengthen in the next year.
- Because of adverse weather conditions, the Department of Agriculture
  and the Commerce Department predict that beef prices will increase by
  10%. Last year the average food cost of similar restaurants was 35% of
  sales. You predict, with the increase in the price of beef, that the food
  cost for this new venture will be 38%.
- A new 100-seat steak house will open in June of next year. The
  restaurant will be located two blocks from you. The local chamber of
  commerce predicts employment in the area to increase by 1500 jobs
  over the next year. There are 500 apartments, 200 single-family
  dwellings, and 100 condominiums under construction or planned for
  completion before the end of the year. Therefore, you expect a net
  increase in the number of guests and check averages.

Using all available information, you have drawn up the following budget
for the new restaurant.

- With 100 seats in a 2000 square-foot dining room turnover is 2 times for
  lunch and 1.5 times for dinner.
- The average check dinner is $21.00.
- The average check lunch is $12.00.
- The restaurant will be open 26 days per month.
- Payroll: Payroll is 35% of sales, including benefits. Employee meals (30
  meals per day) are $12,355.20. Insurance for 24 employees is $6.93 per
  week.
- Direct operating expenses: Uniforms are estimated to be a fixed cost of
  $600 per month. Laundry and linens are estimated to be $6200 per year.
  China and glassware are estimated to be a fixed cost of $7030 per year.
- Advertising expenses are estimated to be 2% of sales.
- Utility Expenses are estimated to be 4% of sales.
- Administrative and general expenses are estimated to be 4% of sales.
- Occupation costs are expected to be $2000 for the year while property
  taxes are $2780.
- Insurance is 3% of sales.

References

Borchgrevink, C. P., & Schmidgall, R. S. (1995). Budgeting practices of U.S. lodging firms. *The Bottomline, 10*(5), 13–17.

Chamberlain, D. (1991). Finance: Cost control: A written budget is a valuable tool for tracking your meeting dollars. *Successful Meeting, 40*(6), 89–90.

Coltman, M. M. (1994). *Hospitality management accounting.* 5th ed. New York: Van Nostrand Reinhold.

Dale, J. C., & Kluga, T. (1992). Energy conservation: More than a good idea. *The Cornell Hotel and Restaurant Administration Quarterly, 33*(6), 30–35.

DeFranco, A. L. (1997). The importance and use of financial forecasting and budgeting at the departmental level in the hotel industry as perceived by hotel controllers. *Hospitality and Research Journal, 20*(3), 99–110.

DeMyer, J. P., & Wang-Kline, D. (1990). What's on the books?: A practical guide to forecasting and budgeting. *Hotel & Resort Industry, 13*(1), 64.

Karch, R. (1992). Streamlining your hotel cost. *Hotel & Resort Industry, 15*(11), 88–90.

Lasky, M. (1988). An Rx for hotel health. *Lodging Hospitality, 44*(6), 75–77.

Malk, M., & Schmidgall, R. S. (1995). Analyzing food operations. *The Bottomline, 10*(3), 23–27.

Malk, M., & Schmidgall, R. S. (1993/1994). Financial analysis of the rooms division. *The Bottomline, 8*(6), 18–21.

McCarthy, T. (1992). Budgeting: A key to marketing success. *Hotel Resort Industry, 15*(1), 16–17.

National Restaurant Association. (1988). Tableservice operator survey. Washington, D.C.: Author.

Quain, W. J. (1992). Analyzing sales-mix profitability. *The Cornell Hotel and Restaurant Administration Quarterly, 33*(2), 57–62.

Schmidgall, R. S. (1989). While forecasts hit targets, GMs still seek better guns. *Lodging, 15*(3), 101–106.

Schmidgall, R. S., & Ninemeier, J. D. (1989). Budgeting practices in lodging and food service chains: An analysis and comparison. *International Journal of Hospitality Management, 8*(1), 35–41.

Schmidgall, R. S., & Ninemeier, J. D. (1987). Budgeting in hotel chains: Coordination and control. *The Cornell Hotel and Restaurant Administration Quarterly, 28*(1), 79-84.

Tilzer, J. S., & Julian, J. P. (1988). Budgeting: Management's game plan. *Lodging Hospitality, 44*(11), 114–117.

17
Capital Budgeting

Learning Objectives

After completing this chapter, you should be able to:

- discuss the importance of capital budgeting.
- explain the differences between the various types of capital budgets.
- determine the relevancy of the different forms of cash flow in capital budgets.
- evaluate the worth of potential investment projects through the use of capital budget criteria.

- understand the significance of capital rationing as it pertains to capital budgets.
- discuss the significance of the three stages of control in capital budgeting.

Outline

Classifications of Capital Budgets
    Replacement to Improve Revenues
    Replacement to Reduce Costs
    Replacement for Maintenance
    Expansion of Existing Concepts
    Expansion into New Concepts
    Safety and Environmental Projects
Elements in a Capital Budget
    Relevant and Incremental Cash Flows
    Initial Cash Flow

    Operating Cash Flow
    Terminal Cash Flow
    Total Project Cash Flow
Time Value of Money and Investment
    Opportunities
    Present and Future Values of a Lump
      Sum
    Present and Future Values of an Annuity
    Perpetuities

The topics of forecasting and budgeting were discussed in Chapter 16. It is important to understand the significance of these two functions because sales forecasting is a key element in capital budgeting decisions. An error in forecasting may cause an operation to invest too much in assets and thus incur unnecessary expenses and high depreciation. In the lodging industry, overcapacity may force a hotel to reduce its targeted average daily rate in order to attract the needed occupancy to break even. Conversely, if a forecast is extremely below the actual level, an operation will not have ample assets to produce the services and goods needed to meet the demand. Worse still, an operation may lose its portion of the growing market demand to a competitor and may have to spend a huge amount on advertising and promotion to woo customers back. Thus, an operating requires an accurate forecast to plan accordingly and set forth its capital budget.

Capital budgeting, also known as capital expenditure analysis or capital request, is the entire process of analyzing potential projects and deciding whether they should be included in an operation's investment plan. This process should not be taken lightly.

Expenditures are usually classified into operating expenses and capital expenses. If a restaurant buys a small piece of equipment and expenses it as a regular replacement expense, then it is classified as an operating expense and will be written off during that particular accounting period. However, expenses that continue to benefit an operation in years to come are classified as capital expenses. Capital expenses may include major new kitchen equipment, renovations, and expansions. Capital expenses are costly, and if a poor decision is made, it not only affects the operation negatively during that one accounting period but it continues to hurt the business until the project is discarded.

The timing of capital expenditure is also pertinent. Because business operates on the economics of supply and demand, a hospitality operation must maximize its return by purchasing capital assets at the right time. If the hospitality industry is on an upward trend and many hotels and restaurants plan to expand at the same time, the demand for new equipment and products may cause back-orders.

Please note that graduates of a two-year or four-year hospitality program most likely will not be making major capital investment decisions upon graduation; however, even management-level purchases of a few thousand dollars should be given the same analysis and attention. In some instances, owners may want managers to know the theories involved in capital budgeting.

Classifications of Capital Budgets

Why would an operation spend so much money on a project? What items and situations should be considered as potential investments? In the hospitality industry the reasons why large amounts of money need to be spent and capitalized as assets can be classified into six main categories.

Replacement to Improve Revenues

This category includes investments in assets that bring about more revenues through better efficiency. If an operation reaches maximum capacity a new investment can reduce production time and thus can increase guest count and revenues.

Replacement to Reduce Costs

This goes hand in hand with the previous category. An old piece of equipment, such as a deep-fat fryer or an air conditioner, may still work but may use too much energy because of its old design. In such a case, it is more efficient for an operation to invest in a newer model to reduce energy costs.

Replacement for Maintenance

Equipment, furniture, fixtures, china, glassware, silverware, and linen are "must haves" in the hospitality industry. For many reasons, from carelessness of employees to theft by guests, items such as silverware and linen have to be replaced constantly. This category differs from the first two in that if replacement is not made, business cannot continue. A hotel can still sell rooms while running a high energy cost, but a hotel cannot sell rooms if there are no towels and sheets, nor could its restaurant serve guests without adequate tableware.

Expansion of Existing Concepts

There are times when a corporation finds a niche in the market and business is superb. An increase in efficiency will not solely satisfy the demand of a growing market. Thus, a company may wish to open another unit on the other side of town to satisfy the demand and also to bring in new guests from the area. Expenses involved in opening new units or expanding an old unit by adding more seats, a new wing of rooms, or an additional nine holes of golf fall into this category. Decisions in this category are more complex than the first three in that these types of investments are usually more costly and involve a major commitment.

Expansion into New Concepts

This is similar to the previous category except that the concept under consideration is brand new. Instead of an additional nine holes of golf, a country club may want to introduce a program in which moms can leave their kids in a supervised play area while they play golf or have lunch with their friends. A hotel may want to add a yogurt and gourmet coffee stand to the lobby or patio area. This category is sometimes risky because it calls for an operation to sail into new waters. A new concept can do very well; however, if a forecast and feasibility study are overly optimistic, an investment can hurt an operation tremendously.

Safety and Environmental Projects

Investments in this category can be minimal or substantial and may include projects implemented to comply with mandatory governmental regulations or insurance policies. The hospitality industry works in conjunction with the Occupational Safety and Health Administration (OSHA) to ensure a safe environment for employees and guests alike.

All purchases require a sum of money as an initial investment. Some may also need additional sums in the following years for upgrades and maintenance. Capital budgeting, therefore, analyses the costs and benefits of such investments. Of course, conditions are right for investment if the benefits outweigh the costs; however, due to government and insurance regulations, an operation may have to invest in projects that do not yield a profitable return.

Elements in a Capital Budget _____

Relevant and Incremental Cash Flows

When cash flows are calculated for capital budgeting purposes, it is not the same as accounting income. Cash flow is the actual cash generated by a particular project or investment. Therefore, noncash expenses such as depreciation and amortization need to be added to the accounting income to determine the net cash flow. Similarly, interest expenses and dividends are not included in the analysis because the return required by the investors or the company furnishing the capital is accounted for in the cost of capital percentage rate, hence interest and dividends would be double-counted if included in the financing cash flows.

A project's incremental cash flow is the difference between the operation's cash flow with the project and without the project. Thus, costs such as rehabilitation and brokerage fees that were incurred in the past and have been expensed are counted as sunk costs and should not be included. Along the same lines, if an operation buys new equipment and decides that it would be a good time to paint the kitchen for maintenance purposes before the new equipment is installed, those painting costs are deemed irrelevant to the project or investment, and although they can be expensed as maintenance costs for the period, they should not be included in the capital budgeting analysis. However, if an operation decides to use the same space for a project that it had previously been leasing to another company, consequently foregoing the rent it could have collected, then the rent income becomes an opportunity cost and is relevant to the project and needs to be included in the analysis.

Initial Cash Flow

Once the relevant costs are identified, the initial cash outlay has to be determined. The initial outlay is the initial investment or the total dollar amount needed to start a project. The cash flows included in this category are the price of the project, freight, installation, and any changes in net working capital, which is the difference between current assets and current liabilities. A new project, be it replacement or expansion, may increase the sales level, which in turn may increase the amount of cash, inventory, accounts receivable, and other current assets. More sales may require more cash to make change or to pay for additional inventory, which is needed because of the anticipated increase in sales. By buying more inventory, and with good credit, an operation will owe more to its purveyors in accounts payable. The operation may also need to increase its staff, thus increasing salary and wages payable, taxes payable, and the like. These costs have to stabilize before extra sales can be generated as a result of a replacement, renovation, or expansion.

Operating Cash Flow

Once a project is in operation, the operating cash flow (OCF) for each year of the life of the project can be calculated. The viability of a project can be estimated by obtaining the OCF for each year of the project. This can be done the long way by preparing an income statement that ignores interest expenses and adding back the noncash expenses after taxes or it can be done quickly by using a formula in which

R = revenues
E = expenses
T = tax
D = depreciation

First, calculate net income (NI):

$$(R - E - D)(1 - T) = NI$$
$$(R - E)(1 - T) - D + DT = NI$$

OCF = NI + D, therefore, the variables should be rearranged so that NI + D is on the right side of the equation.

$$(R - E)(1 - T) + DT = NI + D$$
$$(R - E)(1 - T) + DT = OCF, \text{ or, rearranged,}$$
$$OCF = (R - E)(1 - T) + DT$$

The advantage of using the formula is not only because it is quicker, it also accounts for tax credits if an operation losses money, as the carry-back/carry-forward tax function is built into the calculation.

Terminal Cash Flow

The end of the life of a project may present one of three situations: 1) if a project is sold at its book value, which is the monetary amount by which an asset is valued in business records, there is neither gain nor loss, and thus no tax considerations; 2) if a project's sale value is higher than its book value, there is a gain, and thus the operation will have to pay tax; 3) if a project's sale value is lower than its book value, there is a loss, and thus the operation can claim a tax credit. Besides calculating gains and losses, there is also the recovery of the net working capital amount that was spent at the beginning of the project. The rationale is that now that the project is over, extra money and cash flows should not be necessary, and the money will flow back into the business as incoming cash.

Total Project Cash Flow

After terminal cash flow has been determined, the numbers should be entered on a time line to calculate the feasibility of the project. The total project cash flow is not the simple addition of all these numbers. The value of money changes as time passes. Any dollar amount today is not going to have the same value five years from now. Therefore, money needs to be assigned a proper place in a time continuum so that its value can be objectively assessed.

Time Value of Money and Investment Opportunities

Because the value of money decreases as time passes, the only way to protect the value of your money is through investment.

Present and Future Values of a Lump Sum

Present value is the value of a lump sum at this very moment and future value is what the value will become with interest after a period of time. For instance, if one puts $100 (present value) in the bank for 5 years, and the bank promises a 6% return on investment, one can compute the future value of this $100. There are many ways to derive future value (FV). A formula approach may be used.

$$FV = PV(1 + i)^n$$
$100 = PV (present value)
5 = n (number of compounding periods)
6 = i (interest rate)

Substitute the numbers for the values:

$$100 \times 1.06^5 = 133.82$$

A future value table such as that in Figure 17–1 can also be used. Look for 6% and 5 periods to locate the interest factor, and then multiply the interest factor by the present value of $100. If the table does not provide the exact value for the required percentage or number of periods, one may have to interpolate to get to an approximate value. However, the easiest and most direct way to compute future value is to use a business financial calculator. Enter $100 as PV (present value), 5 as n (number of compounding periods), 6 as i (interest rate). The calculator method has advantages. It provides you a more accurate answer because the computation can be taken out a few more decimal points, and it provides an answer quickly.

Some computer spreadsheets even have function wizards to facilitate an analysis. Such function wizards merely require an operator to click the mouse and enter variable, and the answer, in this case the future value, is instantly computed.

Of course, calculation of future value is key; however, capital budgeting is often more concerned with present value because an operation may need to estimate a future sum of money to determine whether that sum of money is more than, less than, or equal to must be invested today (present value). The formula is as follows:

$$PV = \frac{FV}{(1+i)^n}$$

$133.82 = FV (future value)
5 = n (number of compounding periods)
6 = i (interest rate)

Substitute the numbers for the values:

$$PV = \frac{133.82}{(1 + .06)^5} = 100$$

Figure 17–2 is present value table that provides the interest factor that is to be multiplied by the future value. However, a financial calculator or computer spreadsheet will provide the most accurate figure.

Present and Future Values of an Annuity

Instead of just one sum of money, an operation may invest a certain amount of money regularly every compounding period. The payment received from such an investment is referred to as an annuity. The present and future values of an annuity can be calculated in the same fashion as a lump sum. If an investment promises an annuity of $500 per year over the next 10 years, and the interest rate is 6%, then the amount that an operation has to pay today (present value)

$$FV_{n,k} = (1 + K)^n$$

Number of Periods	1%	2%	3%	4%	5%	6%	7%	8%	9%	10%	12%	14%	15%	16%
1	1.0100	1.0200	1.0300	1.0400	1.0500	1.0600	1.0700	1.0800	1.0900	1.1000	1.1200	1.1400	1.1500	1.1600
2	1.0201	1.0404	1.0609	1.0816	1.1026	1.1236	1.1449	1.1664	1.1881	1.2100	1.2544	1.2996	1.3225	1.3456
3	1.0303	1.0612	1.0927	1.1249	1.1576	1.1910	1.2250	1.2597	1.2950	1.3310	1.4049	1.4815	1.5209	1.5609
4	1.0406	1.0824	1.1255	1.1699	1.2155	1.2625	1.3108	1.3605	1.4116	1.4541	1.5735	1.6890	1.7490	1.8106
5	1.0510	1.1041	1.1593	1.2167	1.2763	1.3382	1.4026	1.4693	1.5386	1.6105	1.7623	1.9254	2.0114	2.1003
6	1.0615	1.1262	1.1941	1.2653	1.3401	1.4185	1.5007	1.5869	1.6771	1.7716	1.9738	2.1950	2.3131	2.4364
7	1.0721	1.1487	1.2299	1.3159	1.4071	1.5036	1.6058	1.7138	1.8280	1.9487	2.2107	2.5023	2.6600	2.8262
8	1.0829	1.1717	1.2668	1.3686	1.4775	1.5938	1.7182	1.8509	1.9926	2.1436	2.4760	2.8526	3.0590	3.2784
9	1.0937	1.1951	1.3048	1.4233	1.5513	1.6895	1.8385	1.9990	2.1719	2.3579	2.7731	3.2519	3.5179	3.8030
10	1.1046	1.2190	1.3439	1.4802	1.6289	1.7908	1.9672	2.1589	2.3674	2.5937	3.18058	3.7072	4.0456	4.4114
11	1.1157	1.2434	1.3842	1.5395	1.7103	1.8983	2.1049	2.3316	2.5804	2.8531	3.4785	4.2262	4.6524	5.1173
12	1.1268	1.2682	1.4258	1.6010	1.7959	2.0122	2.2522	2.5182	2.8127	3.1384	3.8960	4.8179	5.3503	5.9360
13	1.1381	1.2936	1.4685	1.6651	1.8856	2.1329	2.4098	2.7196	3.0658	3.4523	4.3635	5.4924	6.1528	6.8858
14	1.1495	1.3195	1.5126	1.7317	1.9799	2.2609	2.5785	2.9372	3.3417	3.7975	4.8871	6.2613	7.0757	7.9875
15	1.1610	1.3495	1.5580	1.8009	2.0789	2.3966	2.7590	3.1722	3.6425	4.1772	5.4736	7.1379	8.1371	9.2655
16	1.1726	1.3728	1.6047	1.8730	2.1829	2.5404	2.9522	3.4259	3.9703	4.5950	6.1304	8.1372	9.3576	10.748
17	1.1843	1.4002	1.6528	1.9479	2.2920	2.6928	3.1588	3.7000	4.3276	5.0545	6.8660	9.2765	10.761	12.468
18	1.1961	1.4282	1.7024	2.0258	2.4066	2.8543	3.3799	3.9960	4.7171	5.5599	7.6900	10.575	12.375	14.463
19	1.2081	1.4568	1.7535	2.1068	2.5270	3.0256	3.6165	4.3157	5.1417	6.1159	8.6128	12.056	14.232	16.777
20	1.2202	1.4859	1.8061	2.1911	2.6533	3.2071	3.8697	4.6610	5.6044	6.7275	9.6463	13.743	16.367	19.461
21	1.2324	1.5157	1.8603	2.2783	2.7860	3.3996	4.1406	5.0338	6.1088	7.4002	10.804	15.668	18.822	22.574
22	1.2447	1.5460	1.9161	2.3699	2.9253	3.6035	4.4304	5.4365	6.6586	8.1403	12.100	17.861	21.645	26.186
23	1.2572	1.5769	1.9736	2.4647	3.0715	3.8197	4.7405	5.8715	7.2579	8.9543	13.552	20.362	24.891	30.376
24	1.2697	1.6084	2.0328	2.5633	3.2251	4.0489	5.0724	6.3412	7.9111	9.8497	15.179	23.212	28.625	35.236
25	1.2824	1.6406	2.0938	2.6658	3.3864	4.2919	5.4274	6.8485	8.6231	10.835	17.000	26.462	32.919	40.874
26	1.2953	1.6734	2.1566	2.7725	3.5557	4.5494	5.8074	7.3964	9.3992	11.918	19.040	30.167	37.857	47.414
27	1.3082	1.7069	2.2213	2.8834	3.7335	4.8223	6.2139	7.9881	10.245	13.110	21.325	34.390	43.535	55.000
28	1.3213	1.7410	2.2879	2.9987	3.9201	5.1117	6.6488	8.6271	11.167	14.421	23.884	39.204	50.066	63.800
29	1.3345	1.7758	2.3566	3.1187	4.1161	5.4184	7.1143	9.3173	12.172	15.863	26.750	44.693	57.575	74.009
30	1.3478	1.8114	2.4273	3.2434	4.3219	5.7435	7.6123	10.063	13.268	17.449	29.960	50.590	66.212	85.850
40	1.4889	2.2080	3.2620	4.8010	7.0400	10.286	14.974	21.725	31.409	45.259	93.051	188.88	267.86	378.72
50	1.6446	2.6916	4.3839	7.1067	11.467	18.420	29.457	46.902	74.358	117.39	289.00	700.23	1083.7	1670.7
60	1.8167	3.2810	5.8916	10.520	18.679	32.988	57.946	101.26	176.03	304.48	897.60	2595.9	4384.0	7370.2

Figure 17–1   Interest Factor Table of the Future Value of a Lump Sum

Figure 17–2   Interest Factor Table of the Present Value of a Lump Sum

$PV_{n,k} = 1/(1 + K)^n$

Number of Periods	1%	2%	3%	4%	5%	6%	7%	8%	9%	10%	12%	14%
1	.9901	.9804	.9709	.9615	.9524	.9434	.9346	.9259	.9174	.9091	.8929	.8772
2	.9803	.9612	.9426	.9246	.9070	.8900	.8734	.8573	.8417	.8264	.7972	.7695
3	.9706	.9423	.9151	.8890	.8638	.8396	.8163	.7938	.7722	.7513	.7188	.6750
4	.9610	.9238	.8885	.8548	.8227	.7921	.7629	.7350	.7084	.6830	.6355	.5921
5	.9515	.9057	.8626	.8219	.7835	.7473	.7130	.6806	.6499	.6209	.5674	.5194
6	.9420	.8880	.8375	.7903	.7462	.7050	.6663	.6302	.5963	.5645	.5066	.4556
7	.9327	.8706	.8131	.7599	.7107	.6651	.6227	.5835	.5470	.5132	.4523	.3996
8	.9235	.8535	.7894	.7307	.6768	.6274	.5820	.5403	.5019	.4665	.4039	.3506
9	.9143	.8368	.7664	.7026	.6446	.5919	.5439	.5002	.4604	.4241	.3606	.3075
10	.9053	.8203	.7441	.6756	.6139	.5584	.5083	.4632	.4224	.3855	.3220	.2697
11	.8963	.8043	.7224	.6496	.5847	.5268	.4751	.4289	.3875	.3505	.2875	.2366
12	.8874	.7885	.7014	.6246	.5568	.4970	.4440	.3971	.3555	.3186	.2567	.2076
13	.8787	.7730	.6810	.6006	.5303	.4688	.4150	.3677	.3262	.2897	.2292	.1821
14	.8700	.7579	.6611	.5775	.5051	.4423	.3878	.3405	.2992	.2633	.2046	.1597
15	.8613	.7430	.6419	.5553	.4810	.4173	.3624	.3152	.2745	.2394	.1827	.1401
16	.8528	.7284	.6232	.5339	.4581	.3936	.3387	.2919	.2519	.2176	.1631	.1229
17	.8444	.7142	.6050	.5134	.4363	.3714	.3166	.2703	.2311	.1978	.1456	.1078
18	.8360	.7002	.5874	.4936	.4155	.3503	.2959	.2502	.2120	.1799	.1300	.0946
19	.8277	.6864	.5703	.4746	.3957	.3305	.2765	.2317	.1945	.1635	.1161	.0829
20	.8195	.6730	.5537	.4564	.3769	.3118	.2584	.2145	.1784	.1486	.1037	.0728
21	.8114	.6598	.5375	.4388	.3589	.2942	.2415	.1987	.1637	.1351	.0926	.0638
22	.8034	.6468	.5219	.4220	.3418	.2775	.2257	.1839	.1502	.1228	.0826	.0560
23	.7954	.6342	.5067	.4057	.3256	.2618	.2109	.1703	.1378	.1117	.0738	.0491
24	.7876	.6217	.4919	.3901	.3101	.2470	.1971	.1577	.1264	.1015	.0659	.0431
25	.7798	.6095	.4776	.3751	.2953	.2330	.1842	.1460	.1160	.0923	.0588	.0378
26	.7720	.5976	.4637	.3607	.2812	.2198	.1722	.1352	.1064	.0839	.0525	.0331
27	.7644	.5859	.4502	.3468	.2678	.2074	.1609	.1252	.0976	.0763	.0469	.0291
28	.7568	.5744	.4371	.3335	.2551	.1956	.1504	.1159	.0895	.0693	.0419	.0255
29	.7493	.5631	.4243	.3207	.2429	.1846	.1406	.1073	.0822	.0630	.0374	.0224
30	.7419	.5521	.4120	.3083	.2314	.1741	.1314	.0994	.0754	.0573	.0334	.0196
35	.7059	.5000	.3554	.2534	.1813	.1301	.0937	.0676	.0490	.0356	.0189	.0102
40	.6717	.4529	.3066	.2083	.1420	.0972	.0668	.0460	.0318	.0221	.0107	.0053
45	.6391	.4102	.2644	.1712	.1113	.0727	.0476	.0313	.0207	.0137	.0061	.0027
50	.6080	.3715	.2281	.1407	.0872	.0543	.0339	.0213	.0134	.0085	.0035	.0014
55	.5785	.3365	.1968	.1157	.0683	.0406	.0242	.0145	.0087	.0053	.0020	.0007
60	.5504	.3048	.1697	.0951	.0535	.0303	.0173	.0099	.0057	.0033	.0011	.0004

for this incoming cash flow over the next 10 years can be calculated. The formula is as follows:

$$PV = A \times \left[\frac{1}{i} - \frac{1}{i(1 + i)^n} \right]$$

$500 = A$ (annuity)
$10 = n$(number of compounding periods)
$6 = i$ (interest rate)

Substitute the numbers for the values:

$$PV = 500 \times \left[\frac{1}{.06} - \frac{1}{.06(1 + .06)^{10}} \right] = \$3680$$

Figure 17–3 is a present value table that provides the interest factor that is to be multiplied by the annuity. However, a financial calculator or computer spreadsheet can compute the present value a lot faster.

The future value of an annuity can also be calculated using the same three methods. The formula is as follows:

$$FV = A \times \left[\frac{(1 + i)^n - 1}{i} \right]$$

$500 = A$ (annuity)
$10 = n$ (number of compounding periods)
$6 = i$ (interest rate)

Substitute the numbers for the values:

$$FV = 500 - \left[\frac{(1 + .06)^{10} - 1}{.06} \right] = \$6590.40$$

Figure 17–4 is a future value table that provides the interest factor that is to be multiplied by the annuity. Again, a financial calculator or computer spreadsheet can also be used.

Perpetuities

Some investments pay a set amount indefinitely. This payment is known as a perpetuity. One should not be overly optimistic about this type of investment. Remember that money today does not have the same purchasing power it had a decade ago. Therefore, the worth of the money has to be considered. Also, not many investment vehicles like this exist nowadays; and the stock of those that still do exist was most likely issued years ago. However, the application of a perpetuity is useful in capital budgeting and stock valuation.

A generally accepted accounting principle indicates that a corporation is a "going concern," which implies that it will exist indefinitely. If a corporation issues

Figure 17–3   Interest Factor Table of the Present Value of an Annuity

$$PVA_{n,k} = \frac{1 - \dfrac{1}{(1 + K)^n}}{k}$$

Number of Periods	1%	2%	3%	4%	5%	6%	7%	8%	9%	10%	12%	14%	15%	16%
1	0.9901	0.9804	0.9709	0.9615	0.9524	0.9434	0.9346	0.9259	0.9174	0.9091	0.8929	0.8772	0.8696	0.8621
2	1.9704	1.9416	1.9135	1.8861	1.8594	1.8334	1.8080	1.7833	1.7591	1.7355	1.6901	1.6467	1.6257	1.6052
3	2.9410	2.8839	2.8286	2.7751	2.7232	2.6730	2.6243	2.5771	2.5313	2.4869	2.4018	2.3216	2.2832	2.2459
4	3.9020	3.8077	3.7171	3.6299	3.5460	3.4651	3.3872	3.3121	3.2397	3.1699	3.0373	2.9137	2.8550	2.7982
5	4.8534	4.7135	4.5797	4.4518	4.3295	4.2124	4.1002	3.9927	3.8897	3.7908	3.6048	3.4331	3.3522	3.2743
6	5.7955	5.6014	5.4172	5.2421	5.0757	4.9173	4.7665	4.6229	4.4859	4.3553	4.1114	3.8887	3.7845	3.6847
7	6.7282	6.4720	6.2303	6.0021	5.7864	5.5824	5.3893	5.2064	5.0330	4.8684	4.5638	4.2883	4.1604	4.0386
8	7.6517	7.3255	7.0197	6.7327	6.4632	6.2098	5.9713	5.7466	5.5348	5.3349	4.9676	4.6389	4.4873	4.3436
9	8.5660	8.1622	7.7861	7.4353	7.1078	6.8017	6.5152	6.2469	5.9952	5.7590	5.3282	4.9464	4.7716	4.6065
10	9.4713	8.9826	8.5302	8.1109	7.7217	7.3601	7.0236	6.7101	6.4177	6.1446	5.6502	5.2161	5.0188	4.8332
11	10.3676	9.7868	9.2526	8.7605	8.3064	7.8869	7.4987	7.1390	6.8052	6.4951	5.9377	5.4527	5.2337	5.0286
12	11.2551	10.5753	9.9540	9.3851	8.8633	8.3838	7.9427	7.5361	7.1607	6.8137	6.1944	5.6603	5.4206	5.1971
13	12.1337	11.3484	10.6350	9.9856	9.3936	8.8527	8.3577	7.9038	7.4869	7.1034	6.4235	5.8424	5.5831	5.3423
14	13.0037	12.1062	11.2961	10.5631	9.8986	9.2950	8.7455	8.2442	7.7862	7.3667	6.6282	6.0021	5.7245	5.4675
15	13.8651	12.8493	11.9379	11.1184	10.3797	9.7122	9.1079	8.5595	8.0607	7.6061	6.8109	6.1422	5.8474	5.5755
16	14.7179	13.5777	12.5611	11.6523	10.8378	10.1059	9.4466	8.8514	8.3126	7.8237	6.9740	6.2651	5.9542	5.6685
17	15.5623	14.2919	13.1661	12.1657	11.2741	10.4773	9.7632	9.1216	8.5436	8.0216	7.1196	6.3729	6.0472	5.7487
18	16.3983	14.9920	13.7535	12.6593	11.6896	10.8276	10.0591	9.3719	8.7556	8.2014	7.2497	6.4674	6.1280	5.8178
19	17.2260	15.6785	14.3238	13.1339	12.0853	11.1581	10.3356	9.6036	8.9501	8.3649	7.3658	6.5504	6.1982	5.8775
20	18.0456	16.3514	14.8775	13.5903	12.4622	11.4699	10.5940	9.8181	9.1285	8.5136	7.4694	6.6231	6.2593	5.9288
21	18.8570	17.0112	15.4150	14.0292	12.8212	11.7641	10.8355	10.0168	9.2922	8.6487	7.5620	6.6870	6.3125	5.9731
22	19.6604	17.6580	15.9369	14.4511	13.1630	12.0461	11.0612	10.2007	9.4424	8.7715	7.6446	6.7429	6.3587	6.0113
23	20.4558	18.2922	16.4436	14.8568	13.4886	12.3034	11.2722	10.3711	9.5802	8.8832	7.7184	6.7921	6.3988	6.0442
24	21.2434	18.9139	16.9355	15.2470	13.7986	12.5504	11.4693	10.5288	9.7066	8.9847	7.7843	6.8351	6.4338	6.0726
25	22.0232	19.5235	17.4131	15.6221	14.0939	12.7834	11.6536	10.6748	9.8226	9.0770	7.8431	6.8729	6.4641	6.0971
26	22.7952	20.1210	17.8768	15.9828	14.3752	13.0032	11.8258	10.8100	9.9290	9.1609	7.8957	6.9061	6.4906	6.1182
27	23.5596	20.7069	18.3270	16.3296	14.6430	13.2105	11.9867	10.9352	10.0266	9.2372	7.9426	6.9352	6.5135	6.1364
28	24.3164	21.2813	18.7641	16.6631	14.8981	13.4062	12.1371	11.0511	10.1161	9.3066	7.9844	6.9607	6.5335	6.1520
29	25.0658	21.8444	19.1885	16.9837	15.1411	13.5907	12.2777	11.1584	10.1983	9.3696	8.0218	6.9830	6.5509	6.1656
30	25.8077	22.3965	19.6004	17.2920	15.3725	13.7648	12.4090	11.2578	10.2737	9.4269	8.0552	7.0027	6.5660	6.1772
35	29.4086	24.9986	21.4872	18.6646	16.3742	14.4982	12.9477	11.6546	10.5668	9.6442	8.1755	7.0700	6.6166	6.2153
40	32.8347	27.3555	23.1148	19.7928	17.1591	15.0463	13.3317	11.9246	10.7574	9.7791	8.2438	7.1050	6.6418	6.2335
45	36.0945	29.4902	24.5187	20.7200	17.7741	15.4558	13.6055	12.1084	10.8812	9.8628	8.2825	7.1232	6.6543	6.2421
50	39.1961	31.4236	25.7298	21.4822	18.2559	15.7619	13.8007	12.2335	10.9617	9.9148	8.3045	7.1327	6.6605	6.2463
55	42.1472	33.1748	26.7744	22.1086	18.6335	15.9905	13.9399	12.3186	11.0140	9.9471	8.3170	7.1376	6.6636	6.2482
60	44.9550	34.7609	27.6756	22.6235	18.9293	16.1614	14.0392	12.3766	11.0480	9.9672	8.3240	7.1401	6.6651	6.2492

Figure 17–4   Interest Factor Table of the Future Value of an Annuity

$$FVA_{n,k} = \frac{(1+K)^n - 1}{k}$$

Number of Periods	1%	2%	3%	4%	5%	6%	7%	8%	9%	10%	12%	14%	15%	16%
1	1.0000	1.0000	1.0000	1.0000	1.0000	1.0000	1.0000	1.0000	1.0000	1.0000	1.0000	1.0000	1.0000	1.0000
2	2.0100	2.0200	2.0300	2.0400	2.0500	2.0600	2.0700	2.0800	2.0900	2.1000	2.1200	2.1400	2.1500	2.1600
3	3.0301	3.0604	3.0909	3.2160	3.1525	3.1836	3.2149	3.2464	3.2781	3.3100	3.3744	3.3396	3.4725	3.5056
4	4.0604	4.1216	4.1836	4.2465	4.3101	4.3746	4.4399	4.5061	4.5731	4.6410	4.7793	4.9211	4.9934	5.0665
5	5.1010	5.2040	5.3091	5.4163	5.5256	5.6371	5.7507	5.8666	5.9847	6.1051	6.3528	6.6101	6.7424	6.8771
6	6.1520	6.3081	6.4684	6.6330	6.8019	6.9753	7.1533	7.3359	7.5233	7.7156	8.1152	8.5355	8.7537	8.9775
7	7.2135	7.4343	7.7625	7.8983	8.1420	8.3938	8.6540	8.9228	9.2004	9.4872	10.089	10.730	11.067	11.414
8	8.2857	8.5830	8.8923	9.2142	9.5491	9.8975	10.260	10.637	11.028	11.436	12.300	13.233	13.727	14.240
9	9.3685	9.7546	10.159	10.583	11.027	11.491	11.978	12.488	13.021	13.579	14.776	16.085	16.786	17.519
10	10.462	10.950	11.464	12.006	12.578	13.181	13.816	14.487	15.193	15.937	17.549	19.337	20.304	21.321
11	11.567	12.169	12.808	13.486	14.207	14.972	15.784	16.645	17.560	18.531	20.655	23.045	24.349	25.733
12	12.683	13.412	14.192	15.026	15.917	16.870	17.888	18.977	20.141	21.384	24.133	27.271	29.002	30.850
13	13.809	14.680	15.618	16.627	17.713	18.882	20.141	21.495	22.953	24.523	28.029	32.089	34.352	36.786
14	14.947	15.974	17.086	18.292	19.599	21.015	22.550	24.215	26.019	27.975	32.393	37.581	40.505	43.672
15	16.097	17.293	18.599	20.024	21.579	23.276	25.129	27.152	29.361	31.772	37.280	43.842	47.580	51.660
16	17.258	18.639	20.157	21.825	23.657	25.673	27.888	30.324	33.003	35.950	42.753	50.980	55.727	60.925
17	18.430	20.012	21.762	23.698	25.840	28.213	30.840	33.750	36.974	40.545	48.884	59.118	65.075	71.673
18	19.615	21.412	23.414	25.645	28.132	30.906	33.999	37.450	41.301	45.599	55.750	68.394	75.836	84.141
19	20.811	22.841	25.117	27.671	30.539	33.760	37.379	41.446	46.018	51.159	63.440	78.969	88.212	98.603
20	22.019	24.297	26.870	29.778	33.066	36.786	40.995	45.762	51.160	57.275	72.052	91.025	102.44	115.38
21	23.239	25.783	28.676	31.969	35.719	39.993	44.865	50.423	56.765	64.002	81.699	104.77	118.81	134.84
22	24.472	27.299	30.537	34.248	38.505	43.392	49.006	55.457	62.873	71.403	92.503	120.44	137.63	157.41
23	25.716	28.845	32.453	36.618	41.430	46.996	53.436	60.893	69.532	79.543	104.60	138.30	159.28	183.60
24	26.973	30.422	34.426	39.083	44.502	50.816	58.177	66.765	76.790	88.497	118.16	158.66	184.17	213.98
25	28.243	32.030	36.459	41.646	47.727	54.865	63.249	73.106	84.701	98.347	133.33	181.87	212.79	249.21
26	29.526	33.671	38.553	44.312	51.113	59.156	68.676	79.954	93.324	109.18	150.33	208.33	245.71	290.09
27	30.821	35.344	40.710	47.084	54.669	63.706	74.484	87.351	102.72	121.10	169.37	238.50	283.57	337.50
28	32.129	37.051	42.931	49.968	58.403	68.528	80.698	95.339	112.97	134.21	190.70	272.89	327.10	392.50
29	33.450	38.792	45.219	52.966	62.323	73.640	87.347	109.97	124.14	148.63	214.58	312.09	377.17	456.30
30	34.785	40.568	47.575	56.085	66.439	79.058	94.461	113.28	136.31	164.49	241.33	356.79	434.75	530.31
40	48.886	60.402	75.401	95.026	120.80	154.76	199.64	259.06	337.88	442.59	767.09	1342.0	1779.1	2360.8
50	64.463	84.579	112.80	152.67	209.35	290.34	406.53	573.77	815.08	1163.9	2400.0	4994.5	7217.7	10436.
60	81.670	114.05	163.05	237.99	353.58	533.13	813.52	1253.2	1944.8	3034.8	7471.6	18535.	29220.	46058.

preferred stock that promises 3% per year, then this, in essence, is a perpetuity. An investor's financial responsibility for a perpetuity is calculated as follows:

$$\text{Present value} = \frac{\text{Perpetuity}}{\text{Interest}}$$

Perpetuity calculations are useful in estimating a selling price. For example, if Company A would like to sell a hotel, which is estimated to net $100 in cash flow per year, then the value that Company B is willing to pay for the hotel is $100 divided by Company B's cost of capital. If it costs Company B 10% to obtain funds for the investment, then the value that Company B is willing to pay is $1000 (100 ÷ 0.10). If it costs Company B 20% to raise the money, which is a riskier proposition, then the most that Company B is willing to pay for the hotel is $500 ($100 ÷ 0.20). Anything more than $500 will cause Company B to lose money on the investment.

Uneven Cash Flows

Life is not neat and tidy and an operation hardly ever deals with only one sum of money at only one period of time. In most situations, an operation's analysis consists of uneven cash flow. Unfortunately, there is not a simple formula for uneven cash flow nor is there an interest table. So an investor has to consider each cash flow by itself or combine consecutive like ones to calculate present or future values. Financial calculators and computers, however, make such calculations a lot easier. Calculating uneven cash flows is similar to calculating net present value; therefore, these two aspects will be jointly explained in the next section.

Now that the theories have been discussed, an example and corresponding calculations (Figure 17–5) can further illustrate how cash flows work and how an operation can make an educated decision as to whether it should invest in a project. Skyline Hotels has been in business since the early 1930s. It has a strong management team and is renowned for purchasing distressed properties, turning them into profitable ventures, and selling them in 5 to 10 years to maximize returns. Skyline uses brokerage firms nationwide to locate these properties.

Independent Hotel was spotted by one of Skyline's brokerage firms last year at a fee of $75,000. Skyline's plan is to remodel Independent and operate it at a professional level for 5 years. It is estimated that the end of the fifth year will be the best time to sell, as operating cash flows of Independent will have stabilized.

After final negotiations, Independent can be bought at a price of $3,000,000 with an estimated book value, using straight-line depreciation, of $1,250,000 in 5 years. In order for Independent to become competitive, Skyline has to invest another $200,000 and increase Independent's net working capital by $175,000 at the beginning of this venture.

Using historical data and scenario analysis, Skyline has determined that Independent will be able to reach revenues of $1,500,000 at the end of the first year. It also has estimated a growth in sales of 12% per year for the next 4 years

Figure 17–5 Cash Flow Estimation

Skyline Hotels—Feasibility for the Purchase of Independent Hotel

Cost	3,000,000
Depreciation (# of years)	5
Salvage	1,250,000
Other initial costs	200,000
Change in net working capital	175,000
Sales in year 1	1,500,000
Growth in sales	12%
Expenses in year 1	1,000,000
Growth in expenses	6%
Tax rate	34%
Cost of capital	10%

Depreciable base			
Cost	3,000,000	Depreciation	390,000
Other initial costs	200,000		
	3,200,000		

Sale price 8,571,494
Cash flow of year 5 ÷ Cost of capital

Tax on sale			
Cost	3,200,000	Gain	7,321,494
Accumulated depreciation	1,950,000	Tax	2,489,308
Book value	1,250,000		

Item	Year 0	Year 1	Year 2	Year 3	Year 4	Year 5
Cost	3,000,000					
Other initial costs	200,000					
Change in net working capital	175,000					
Operating cash flow						
Revenues		1,500,000	1,680,000	1,881,600	2,107,392	2,360,279
Expenses		1,000,000	1,060,000	1,123,600	1,191,016	1,262,477
Depreciation		390,000	390,000	390,000	390,000	390,000
Expenses before taxes		110,000	230,000	368,000	526,376	707,802
Tax		37,400	78,200	125,120	178,968	240,653
Net income		72,600	151,800	242,880	347,408	467,149
Net income + Depreciation		462,600	541,800	632,880	737,408	857,149
Sale price						8,571,494
Recovery of net working capital						175,000
Tax on recaptured depreciation and gain						(2,489,308)
TOTAL CASH FLOWS	(3,375,000)	462,600	541,800	632,880	737,408	7,114,335
NET PRESENT VALUE	2,889,908					
INTERNAL RATE OF RETURN	0.276593174, or 27.66%					

of this investment. At the same time, expenses for Independent are estimated to be $1,000,000 at the end of the first year with a growth rate of 6%. The cost of purchasing Independent will be 10% and the average tax rate for Skyline is 34%.

The total initial outlay of $3,375,000 was obtained by adding the price of the hotel, other initial costs, and the change in net working capital. It may be advisable to calculate depreciation expenses before obtaining the yearly operating cash flow. Using a 5-year straight-line depreciation, the salvage of $1,250,000 is subtracted from the depreciable base of $3,200,000, which is divided by 5 years to obtain an annual depreciation of $390,000. To calculate its operating cash flows for the 5 years, Skyline can follow the income statement format or the formula method.

At the very end, the sale price is calculated by the knowledge of a perpetuity, dividing the year 5 operating cash flow by the cost of capital to arrive at $8,571,494. Comparing that to the book value of $1,250,000, there is a gain of $7,321,494. Therefore, $2,489,308 in taxes (34% of the gain) will have to be paid. Thus, total cash flow, both operating and terminal, for year 5 is $7,114,335.

This may seem to be quite a complex process; however, it can be simplified by using a computer spreadsheet program such as Lotus or Excel. In this way, if any variable has to be changed, a new calculation can easily be done. Figure 17–6 shows the formulas Excel uses for this calculation.

Capital Budget Feasibility Criteria

After the cash flows are obtained, an operation can employ one of four methods to determine the feasibility of a proposal: accounting rate of return, payback, net present value, or internal rate of return.

Accounting Rate of Return

The accounting rate of return (ARR) is one of the simpler methods to determine whether an operation should invest in an opportunity. ARR is a ratio of the average annual project income, or cash flow, and the total investment. This ratio is known as return on investment (ROI). If assets are outlaid rather than investment, it is called return on assets (ROA); if equity is used, it is called return on equity (ROE).

$$\text{ROI} = \frac{\text{Average annual project income}}{\text{Total investment}}$$

$$\text{ROA} = \frac{\text{Average annual project income}}{\text{Total assets}}$$

$$\text{ROE} = \frac{\text{Average annual project income}}{\text{Total equity}}$$

If a project has a life of 3 years, then the numerator is the total income, or cash flows, of those 3 years divided by 3. If it is a 10-year project, the same

Figure 17–6 Cash Flow Estimation with Excel Formulas

Skyline Hotels—Feasibility for the Purchase of Independent Hotel

Cost	3000000
Depreciation (# of years)	5
Salvage	1250000
Other initial costs	200000
Change in net working capital	175000
Sales in year 1	1500000
Growth in sales	0.12
Expenses in year 1	1000000
Growth in expenses	0.06
Tax rate	0.34
Cost of capital	0.1

Depreciable base
Cost	=C4
Other initial costs	=C8
	=SUM(C19:C20)

Depreciation =(C22-C7)/C6

Sale price =H49/C15
Cash flow of year 5 ÷ Cost of capital

Tax on sale
Cost	=C22	Gain	=D25-C31
Accumulated depreciation	=E19*C6	Tax	=E28*C14
Book value	=C28-C29		

Item	Year 0	Year 1	Year 2	Year 3	Year 4	Year 5
Cost	=C4					
Other initial costs	=C8					
Change in net working capital	=C9					
Operating cash flow						
Revenues		=C10	=D41*(1+$C$11)	=E41*(1+$C$11)	=F41*(1+$C$11)	=G41*(1+$C$11)
Expenses		=C12	=D42*(1+$C$13)	=E42*(1+$C$13)	=F42*(1+$C$13)	=G42*(1+$C$13)
Depreciation		=$E$19	=$E$19	=$E$19	=$E$19	=$E$19
Expenses before taxes		=D41-D42-D43	=E41-E42-E43	=F41-F42-F43	=G41-G42-G43	=H41-H42-H43
Tax		D45*0.34	E45*0.34	F45*0.34	G45*0.34	H45*0.34
Net income		=D45-D46	=E45-D46	=F45-D46	=G45-D46	=H45-D46
Net income + Depreciation		=D48+D43	=E48+D43	=F48+F43	=G48+G43	=H48+H43
Sale price						=D45
Recovery of net working capital						=C9
Tax on recaptured depreciation and gain						=-E31
TOTAL CASH FLOWS	=-SUM(C37:C39)	=D49	=E49	=F49	=G49	=SUM(H49:H54)

NET PRESENT VALUE =C57+NPV(C15,D57:H57)

INTERNAL RATE OF RETURN =IRR(C57:H57,0.15), or =C61

rule applies for adding the income of the 10 years and dividing that by 10. Average investment is the total cost of the project and its salvage value divided by 2. If the salvage value happens to be 0, then the cost of the project is divided by 2. Average total assets are the average of beginning and ending total assets on the balance sheet; and average equity is the average of beginning and ending common equities on the balance sheet.

A company sets its own criterion for ARR. If a company has a minimum ARR of 35%, then anything 35% and above is acceptable to the company. Otherwise, the project is rejected.

Using the data in Figure 17–5, the ARR of Independent Hotel can be calculated as follows:

$$\text{Average annual project income} = \frac{1,282,838}{5}$$
$$= 256,368$$

$$\text{Average investment} = \frac{3,200,000 + 1,250,000}{2}$$
$$= 2,225,000$$

$$\text{ARR} = \frac{256,368}{2,225,000}$$
$$= 11.52\%$$

The total cash flows of the 5 years amounts to $9,489,023, which averages to $1,897,805 per year. The cost of $3,200,000 and the salvage value of $1,250,000 average to $2,225,000. Therefore, the ARR is 11.52%. If Skyline sets its ARR hurdle at 35%, then this project is way under the requirement and should be rejected.

There are two major reasons why a project can look so good, as in Figure 17–5, and can be sold for millions of dollars and yet is not a good investment according to the ARR method. First, this method concentrates on income and not cash flows; therefore, the end sale price is not included in the calculation. Investments that are calculated using cash flows give a more accurate picture. Also, because money from different time periods is simply added together, the time value of money is ignored. This method does have good points, such as the ease of calculation and perhaps the ease of understanding, as most people care about income as a measurement of return. However, for hotels, restaurants, casinos and clubs, where the sale prices of property can generate huge sums of money, this may not be the preferred method.

Payback

Payback, like ARR, is simple to calculate, as it is also a ratio. Its set criterion is number of years, so if a company's maximum payback is 2 years, any project that takes 2 years or more to recuperate its costs will be rejected. However, payback differs from ARR because it uses cash flows rather than net income, which gives a more realistic picture of the investment return. Unlike ARR, results in a percentage, the calculation of payback yields a number. Payback is defined as project cost divided by annual cash flow. If a project yields uneven cash flows in its lifetime, then the annual cash flow is subtracted until the year in which costs are totally recovered is reached.

Consider the following example. It costs a restaurant $5000 to buy a new pizza oven. Assume that in 5 years, the oven will be deemed worthless and the restaurant will not be able to sell it for anything. There is no change in net working capital, so the restaurant does not need to worry about the recovery of net working capital or any tax considerations in gains or losses. The annual cash flow from this new pizza oven is estimated to be $3000 a year. Following is the calculation for even cash flows using the payback method.

$$\text{Payback} = \frac{5,000}{3,000}$$
$$= 1.67 \text{ years}$$

If the restaurant's payback is set at 2 years, then this project falls within its criterion and the restaurant can take on the project of purchasing the oven.

Calculation of uneven cash flows is not difficult; it just requires a few more steps. Again consider the data in Figure 17–5. The cash flows for that project are listed below:

Year	Cash Flows
0	$(3,375,000)
1	462,600
2	541,800
3	632,880
4	737,408
5	7,114,335

The calculation goes step by step and year by year until the $3,375,000 is recovered.

$$
\begin{array}{rr}
\text{Project cost} = & \$3,375,000 \\
- \text{ Cash flow 1} & \underline{462,600} \\
& 2,912,400 \\
- \text{ Cash flow 2} & \underline{541,800} \\
& 2,370,600 \\
- \text{ Cash flow 3} & \underline{632,880} \\
& 1,737,720 \\
- \text{ cash flow 4} & \underline{737,408} \\
& 1,000,312 \\
\end{array}
$$

Cash flow 5 is $7,114,335, which is more than enough to cover $1,000,312, therefore, a portion of cash flow 5, will be needed to cover the remaining cost.

$$\frac{1,000,312}{7,114,335} = 0.14$$

It will take 4.14 years for the project to pay for its own costs, so the payback period is 4.14 years. If the payback criterion for this particular project is anything less than 4.14, the company should accept this project.

Again, the point may arise that perhaps the project in Figure 17–5 is a bad investment because it does not meet ARR and payback criteria. As discussed, the ARR method has shortcomings, and payback is not without its faults as well.

Payback is better than ARR because it uses cash flows rather than income; however, it falls into the same trap as ARR in that time value of money is not considered. For instance, money in year 4 is compared to the value of money today at cost. In addition, payback does not consider cash flow beyond the calculated payback period. Once the payback period is calculated, in this case 4.14 years, the financial impact of the cash flows that follows is ignored. Usually, the first few years of a business are extremely difficult because it is just getting off the ground and still has to build a client base and provide good products and services to clientele. Profits do not come until later. But if an operation solely uses smaller cash flows at the beginning and obtains a higher number than the set payback criterion, then the operation is throwing away a good investment that can earn a lot more in the long run. Moreover, the example in Figure 17–5 only pertains to one end of the spectrum in that Skyline is in the business of turning around hotels and selling them to achieve profit; the other end of spectrum involves running a business on a day-to-day basis to obtain profit.

If ARR and payback have so many disadvantages, why are they used? They are still good indicators and are quick and easy to calculate. However, neither method should be used as the sole criterion for any capital budget. Net present value and internal rate of return are much better indicators.

Net Present Value

As the name suggests, net present value (NPV) has to do with netting present values with a certain number. If an operation spends $10 and makes $40, it nets $30, a positive gain; if an operation spends $10 and makes $10, it breaks even; if an operation spends $40 and makes $10, the net value is negative and there is a loss of $30.

Net present value follows this train of thought. The only difference is that the time value of money has to be considered; therefore, an operation performing an NPV analysis first has to discount all future values by changing the cost of capital of the project to the present. When they are all at year 0, the present, an operation adds all the future cash flows that have been discounted to present values, and nets them with the cost of the project. If the number is positive, the investment should be accepted; if the number is 0, it is at break-even; and if the number is negative, a loss has been incurred and the investment should be rejected. In Figure 17–7 a financial table was used to obtain the calculations of the viability of the purchase of Independent Hotel (recall Figure 17–5). Because the net present value is a positive figure, the project should be accepted.

Figure 17–7 *Calculations of NPV and IRR*

TOTAL CASH FLOWS	(3,357,000)	462,000	541,800	632,880	737,408	7,114,225
NET PRESENT VALUE	2,889,908					
INTERNAL RATE OF RETURN	0.276593174, or 27.66%					

Some types of financial calculators feature a function key for NPV. Once the cost, all cash flows, and the cost of capital are entered, NPV can be computed in a matter of one or two seconds. NPV considers all cash flows and the time value of money and is an accurate way to make capital budgeting decisions.

Internal Rate of Return

Investments are evaluated with regard to dollar amounts as well as percentages. Internal rate of return (IRR) falls into the latter category. Like NPV, IRR considers all cash flows and the time value of money; however, unlike NPV, it gives the rate of return of the investment, that is, what the project earns in terms of percentages. The interest rate that equates cash flows and the cost of the project is the IRR. In other words, if an operation invests $X as the cost and obtains $Y in return, the interest rate that equates $X and $Y is the rate of return of the project.

Again using the data in Figure 17–5, the internal rate of return, as calculated by a spreadsheet program, is 27.66%. The cost to raise capital is only 10%, which means that the gain is 17.66% after paying investors and creditors. The cost of capital is also known as the capitalization rate or hurdle rate. One has to pass the hurdle before one can win, so the IRR has to be larger than the cost of capital before an operation should accept a project. If the IRR is the same as the cost of capital, it is at break-even; and if the IRR is less than the cost of capital, the project will not earn enough to pay off the investors and creditors so it is not a good investment.

Computers are taking over a number of accounting functions. Spreadsheet applications are extremely useful in calculating NPV and IRR, as values are calculated through simple commands. Figure 17–8 shows the spreadsheet commands for NPV and IRR, which determine the viability of the acquisition of Independent Hotel (recall Figure 17–5).

Comparison of Net Present Value and Internal Rate of Return

It has been established that NPV and IRR are the preferred methods to determine a project's feasibility. But is one method better than the other? In using formulas and financial tables, the NPV method is invariably easier to calculate

Figure 17–8   *Excel Spreadsheet Commands for NPV and IRR*

TOTAL CASH FLOWS	=SUM(C38:C40) =D50 =E50 =F50 =G50 =SUM(H50:H55)
NET PRESENT VALUE	=C58+NPV(C16,C58:H58)
INTERNAL RATE OF RETURN	=IRR(C58:H58,0.15), or =C62

and is more accurate. The IRR may require guess work and interpolation and thus may take more time; however, with today's technology in calculators and computers, time is not the deciding factor here; rather, it is whether one prefers to evaluate numbers or percentages. Some people always go by the numbers with the theory that one can take dollars to the bank but not percentages. Others believe that percentages are easier to interpret than big dollar amounts.

One must understand the underlying assumptions of these two methods. Refer back to the data in Figure 17–5 in which the NPV of almost three million dollars is calculated with the 10% cost of capital. This assumes that the cash flow that the hotel receives each year can be reinvested at 10%. The IRR, however, assumes that the cash flows earned every year can be reinvested at the rate of the IRR, which is 27.66%; a huge difference. Realistically, the chance of reinvesting the cash flow at 10% is more likely than reinvesting at 27.66%. Therefore, if there is a conflict between the results of NPV and IRR, it may prove wise to rely on NPV with regard to whether a project is accepted. The topics of NPV and IRR are more financially oriented than those related to control, thus, readers may wish to consult a hospitality finance book to gain more insight into the two methods.

Other Considerations

Other factors must be considered with regard to capital budgeting. This chapter provided a sample project and worked through the numbers and followed the criteria to determine whether it is a good investment. In the real world, if an operation wants to buy just one pizza oven, it may have to evaluate a few different brands of pizza ovens. These different proposals are known as mutually exclusive projects. Mutually exclusive projects dictate that an operation must try to pick the best of the lot, and by accepting one project, it must reject all others.

Other projects are known as independent projects in which the acceptance or rejection of one project does not influence the decision to accept or reject another. If a restaurant needs a new oven and new furniture for the dining room, both projects can be accepted, if they both look good and pass the set criteria.

In the case of capital rationing an operation has to prioritize investment analysis results because of limited capital. In this manner, an operation has to pick the project that yields the highest NPV and then go down the list until the budget cannot accommodate any more investments. Again, in the real world, the last penny of a budget most likely will not be spent on one or two priority investments. If an operation has already picked two projects and has $20,000 left in its budget but the next highest yield project costs $40,000, what should the operation do? The operation may have to reassess all the options to reach the combination that can use up the most funds and yield the highest combined NPV.

Uneven life spans in mutually exclusive projects must also be considered. As previously discussed, mutually exclusive projects dictate that an operation must pick the best investment; however, this precludes the possibility that different projects may span different periods. For instance, a country club needs to buy a grill for its restaurant. The two bids have different cash flows because one grill has a life of 7 years and the other has a life of 10 years. The club could ignore the 3-year difference and simply calculate the ARR, payback, NPV, and IRR and make a decision. But common sense suggests that if the 7-year grill is selected, the club will need to replace it sooner than it would have had to replace the 10-year grill.

The option of lease versus purchase should be explored when analyzing investments. Leasing has definite advantages. For a high technology product that may need to be upgraded often, leasing may be the smart way to go so that an operation is not stuck with obsolete equipment or materials. Leases can also be treated as expenses that can be written off every accounting period to reduce taxes. In addition, when interest rates are high, leasing may be a more viable option, as it allows an operation to circumvent the high cost of capital. Obviously, when an operation has neither a budget to spend nor a lump sum of money to invest in upgrading, leasing becomes a means to obtain the assets that a facility needs to carry it through day-to-day operations. All investment decisions should be made on a case-by-case basis, as one option is not always better than another.

Capital Budgeting and the Control Function

All upgrades and purchases cost money. Even regular maintenance sometimes costs so much that it has to be capitalized. Thus, capital budgeting is important to the control function of every operation.

Once a capital budget is set, the control function takes over in three distinct stages. First, a manager needs to oversee any extensive installation, renovation, or construction so that a project has no serious delays or cost overruns. Delays and other problems can significantly increase costs.

Second, once installation, renovation, or construction is finished, a manager must perform a postaudit, which is much like the debriefing that takes place after a laboratory session to discuss what went well and what went wrong. These investigations help a manager identify the accuracy of the original forecast and any problems that might have occurred during construction. With this information a manager will be able to control similar projects better.

Third, management must compare the actual figures that a project yields to the figures shown in the forecast and capital budget analysis. Also, management must execute continuing control through performance measurement of the operation.

Summary

Capital expenditure decisions are important to an operation because the effects such decisions have on the operation may last a number of years. Although capital expenditure decisions generally involve large sums of money, decisions that involve a few thousand dollars should be given the same analysis procedures and attention. Therefore, knowledge of capital budgeting is essential.

The capital budgeting process starts with identifying the relevant cash flows and classifying them into a project time line with initial cash flow, operating cash flow, and terminal cash flow. Then management employs a capital budgeting technique to make an informed decision. The technique known as accounting rates of return features ratios that pertain to return on investment, return on assets, and return on equity. Other techniques include payback period, net present value, and internal rate of return. Of these techniques, the last two are preferred because they take into consideration time value of money. Time value of money calculations include present and future values of lump sums, present and future values of annuities, perpetuities, and uneven cash flow. Uneven cash flow resembles the cash flow time line in a capital budget analysis.

Once a capital budgeting decision is made, the control function starts. Management needs to monitor all expenses and revenues to ensure that the figures projected for the capital budget analysis are in line.

Review Exercises

1. The present value of $500 after 3 years in an account that pays 6% annual interest will become:
   a. $565.60
   b. $570.50
   c. $595.51
   d. $599.51

2. If you need to save $200,000 to open a restaurant in 10 years, how much do you have to save per month if your investment will yield 14%?
   a. $771.99
   b. $799.71
   c. $817.63
   d. $871.67

3. Which of the following is not a feasibility criterion for capital budgeting?
   a. ARR
   b. NPV
   c. IRR
   d. NRR

4. Why is payback not the best feasibility criterion?
   a. it is easy to compute
   b. a computer is not required for the computation
   c. it does not consider the time value of money
   d. it considers all cash flows

5. The formula for calculating the present value of a perpetuity is:
   a. present value ÷ interest
   b. future value ÷ interest
   c. interest ÷ payment
   d. payment ÷ interest

6. To accept a project using NPV criterion, the NPV has to be:
   a. 0
   b. more than 0
   c. less than 0
   d. the NPV is irrelevant

7. To accept a project using IRR criterion, the IRR has to be:
   a. equal to the cost of capital
   b. less than the cost of capital
   c. more than the cost of capital
   d. more than 10%

8. Given the following cash flows, the payback of this project is:

Year	Cash Flows
0	(100)
1	70
2	50
3	20

   a. 1.6 years
   b. 2.0 years
   c. 2.4 years
   d. 3.0 years

9. Using the cash flows in question #8 and a 10% cost of capital, the NPV of this project is:
   a. $18.86
   b. $18.95
   c. $19.99
   d. $21.25

10. Using the cash flows in question #8, the IRR of this project is:
    a. 20%
    b. 21.54%
    c. 22.46%
    d. 23.56%

11. What is the PV of $550 after 6 years if the interest rate is 10%?

12. What is the FV of $500 after 5 years if it is in an account that pays 11% annual interest?

13. What is the FV of a 4-year annuity of $300 if the interest rate is 10%? What is the PV of the annuity?

14. An investor is considering the purchase of 1000 acres of land. His analysis is that if the land is used for cattle grazing, it will produce a cash flow of $5000 per year indefinitely. If the investor requires a return of 10% on investment, what is the most he is willing to pay for the land?

15. The Roasting Company is evaluating the purchase of a new coffee cart for its outdoor patio. The cost of capital for the cart is 8%, and the expected costs and cash flows are listed below. Should the company take on this investment using the payback criterion if the set limit is 1.5 years?

Year	Expected Cash Flows
0	($5000)
1	1000
2	4000
3	3000
4	2000
5	4000

16. Restaurant Rosebud is considering buying a new stove that costs $4900. The stove will be deemed worthless in 6 years and the restaurant will not be able to sell it for anything. There is no change in net working capital. If the estimated annual cash flows from this new stove are as follows, what is the estimated payback period for the stove?

Year	Cash Flows
0	($4900)
1	120
2	239
3	401
4	1488
5	1170
6	2001

17. Hotel Wave is deciding whether it should open a tea room. The cost of capital is 12%. If the expected net cash inflows are as follows, what is the project's NPV?

Year	Expected Net Cash Flows
0	($560,000)
1	230,000
2	290,000
3	180,000
4	150,000

18. Using the data from question #17, what is the IRR of the tea room project?

Examination Type Problems _____

1. What is the PV of $1250 after 6 years if the interest rate is 8%?

2. What is the FV of $900 after 5 years if it is in an account that pays 12% annual interest?

3. What is the FV of a 5-year annuity of $220 if the interest rate is 6%? What is the PV of the annuity?

4. A farmer is considering the purchase of 5000 acres of land. His analysis is that if the land is used for growing avocados, it will produce a cash flow of $25,000 per year indefinitely. If the investor requires a return of 10% on investment, what is the most he is willing to pay for the land?

5. A diner is evaluating the purchase of an ice-cream machine. The cost of capital for the machine is 11%, and the expected costs and cash flows are listed below. What is the NPV of this investment and should the diner invest in this ice-cream machine?

Year	Expected Cash Flows
0	($7700)
1	1200
2	4000
3	3900
4	2000
5	4000

6. JJ's Pub is considering buying a new ice machine that costs $5500. The ice machine will be deemed worthless in 4 years and the pub will not be able to sell it for anything. There is no change in net working capital. If the estimated annual cash flows from this new ice machine are as follows, how long would it take until the investment starts paying off?

Year	Cash Flows
0	($5500)
1	3100
2	2000
3	950
4	130

7. Hotel Star is deciding whether it should open an American grill. The cost of capital is 12%. If the expected net cash flows are as follows, what is the project's NPV?

Year	Expected Net Cash Flows
0	($960,000)
1	330,000
2	590,000
3	400,000
4	150,000

8. Using the data from question #7, what is the IRR of the American grill project?

Case Study

Brick-oven pizza is a new trend and the customers at Model Restaurant are asking for such an item. The general manager asks you to decide whether Model should buy a pizza oven or sign a contract with a local pizza restaurant for them to deliver the pizzas.

Discounting all the expenses, you have calculated the net cash flows to be $5580 per year for the next 5 years. By the end of this 5-year period, you have the option to sell the pizza oven for $500. The cost of a new oven is $17,000.

If a contract is signed with a local pizza restaurant, there will be no initial investment. However, the cash flow that your restaurant will receive as part of the contract agreement will only be $2260 per year.

If the cost of capital is 8% and the minimum time commitment to the contract is 5 years, would you suggest that Model buy the oven or sign the contract?

18
Casinos: The Wild Card in Hospitality Cost Control

Learning Objectives

After completing this chapter, you should be able to:

- discuss the role of a gaming control board.
- identify issues addressed by the minimum internal control standards.
- calculate hold percentages.
- compare and contrast the organization of an accounting department in a hotel and that of a casino hotel.
- describe the flow of a casino revenue audit.

- evaluate the main cashiering activities at the cage and recommend at least five control procedures.
- evaluate the revenue flows in the various table games and slots and recommend at least three control procedures for each game.

Outline

For the past decade in the United States, casinos have been the fastest growing segment of the hospitality industry. There are solid reasons to propose that the casino segment is an industry of its own. The acquisition of Caesar's World by ITT Sheraton; the spin-off of Harrah's from Promus; the merger of Hilton, Bally's, and Grand Casinos; the continuing expansion of Mirage Resorts and Circus Circus from the Excalibur; and new properties like the Luxor, Beau Rivage, and Bellagio attest that hotel companies realize that a substantial profit margin can be achieved in casinos. Because of this and the fact that a large amount of cash changes hands, internal controls in casinos are of the utmost importance. The objective of this chapter is to provide a broad overview of an internal control system in a casino operation.

Regulations Set by Gaming Control Boards

Legalized casino gaming was limited to the state of Nevada until 1976 when New Jersey entered the scene. Since then, the industry has exploded. In the 1990s, many other states passed referendums that made casino gaming legal. In states with a more established casino industry, such as Nevada and New Jersey, gaming control boards regulate daily operations. Professional associations have also come together in the last couple of years to help set standards for accounting so that more uniform reporting of financial data can be achieved.

Minimum Internal Control Standards

According to regulations set by gaming control boards, casinos must establish and present a system of internal controls that comply with generally accepted accounting principles. This system of controls includes organizational structure, accounting procedures, authorization processes, recordkeeping, safeguarding of assets, and the accuracy and reliability of financial records. Most jurisdictions require these controls, known as minimum internal control standards (MICS), as part of the application for a casino license. The respective regulatory agencies review the MICS to ensure that they conform to jurisdiction requirements. After approval, gaming operations can start. Any subsequent changes in the MICS require approval as well. Regulatory agencies also audit casinos to determine the degree of compliance with the MICS. If the MICS are not followed, a casino's license can be revoked.

Figure 18–1   *Signature Authority and Sensitive Access*

Position Title	Signature Authority					Sensitive Access						
	A	B	C	D	E	F	G	H	I	J	K	L
Board of Directors						Only with key person						
President	X	X	X	X	X	X	X	X	X	X	X	X
VP of Casino Operations	X	X	X	X	X		X	X			X	
VP of Finance	X	X	X			X	X			X	X	
VP of Marketing		X										
VP of Food and Beverage												
VP of Human Resources												
VP of Security						X	X	X		X		
Surveillance Director							X		X			
EGD Director	X	X	X	X			X				X	X
EGD Shift Manager	X			X								X
EGD Lead Technician												X
EGD Changeperson Pit Boss	X			X				X			X	
Casino Supervisor				X				X			X	
Dealer				X								
Credit Collection Clerk											X	
Accounting Manager							X		X			
Cage Shift Manager							X				X	
Director of Player Development	X	X	X					X			X	
Casino Executive Host	X	X	X					X			X	
Security Supervisor						X	X	X			X	

Signature Authority
A = Complimentary privileges
B = Approval of credit
C = Check cashing approval
D = Fills and credits
E = Jackpots of $10

Sensitive Access
F = Drop Boxes
G = Cage
H = Pit podium
I = Surveillance
J = Hard or soft count
K = Credit information
L = Slot machines and other electronic gaming device (EGD) components

Source: Gaming Education and Research Institute, University of Houston, Houston, Texas.

In adhering to MICS, a licensee must clearly identify the positions and functions within an operation and determine how they are segregated. This can be achieved through an organizational chart, which includes detailed descriptions of the duties and responsibilities for each position. A licensee also has to identify sensitive areas and the positions or individuals that have access to such areas. Sensitive areas include drop boxes, the cage, pit podiums, surveillance, hard and soft count, credit information, and slot machines and other electronic gaming devices. In addition, the positions or individuals that can grant signature authority on various matters need to be identified. Signature authority is similar to the dispensation of complimentary privileges in a hotel. Such matters more unique to casino operations include approval of customer credit, check cashing approval, fills and credits, and jackpots over certain amounts. Figure 18–1 is part of an organizational chart that indicates signature authority and sensitive access.

A licensee must also identify the administrative and accounting procedures that it will follow. As seen in Figure 18–2, MICS spell out everything to

Figure 18–2   *Minimum Internal Control Standards*

Organizational chart
  Identifies positions and functions within operation
  Determines segregation of positions and functions
  Describes duties and responsibilities of each position
  Identifies positions with sensitive access and signature authority

Administrative and accounting procedures
  Opening and closing tables
  Table inventories
  Transporting chips and tokens to and from gaming tables
  Shift changes at gaming tables
  Physical characteristics of drop boxes
  Transportation of drop boxes to and from gaming tables
  Drop buckets to and from electronic gaming devices
  Chip and token purchases
  Hopper fills
  Transportation of electronic gaming devices
  Hand-paid jackpots
  Layout and physical characteristics of cashier's cage
  Accounting controls
  Exchange of checks submitted by gaming patrons
  Credit card and debit card transactions
  Accounting and redemption of patron cash deposits
  Control of coupon redemption and other complimentary distribution programs
  Federal cash transaction reporting
  Control maximum loss per customer (riverboat gaming jurisdictions have typically established such guidelines)
  Accounting for the total number and amount of money received from admissions (riverboat gaming jurisdictions have such guidelines)

Source: Gaming Education and Research Institute, University of Houston, Houston, Texas.

---

reduce, if not eliminate, theft, collusion, and other illegal activities by employees and guests.

Accounting Control

Terminology

To understand the accounting control function of a casino, it is a good idea to first discuss the terminology involved.

The word "win" does not need much explanation. If one succeeds in a game, for instance, and the reward or prize is $10, then one wins $10. However, in casino accounting and controls, win pertains to the winnings of the casino and not the players. It is the net intake of the casino. The wagers that players make are called drop. Drop is the measurement of the wagering activity in a casino. Payout refers to the winning wages of the players. These terms apply to all table games.

Win = Drop − Payouts

Drop in slot machine terminology is the amount of coins in the collection or overflow bucket at the bottom of the machine. The total wager, or number of coins deposited, in a slot machine is known as the handle. In machines in which wagers are made with a card rather than coins, an electronic meter device measures the handle.

Win = Handle − Payouts

In some casinos, drop refers to the amount of money, foreign chips, and other denominations placed in the table drop box. This is especially true when the amount is used for game win calculation which will be discussed presently. It is imperative that all casino employees know the correct interpretations of the terms to avoid mistakes.

Hold is the same as win, the net amount retained by a casino. Hold percentage is the amount of win as related to the amount of wager and is widely used to measure the performance of the various games. If the total wager is $10 and the casino pays out $8 and retains $2, then 20% is the hold percentage.

Hold percentage = Win ÷ Drop

As a result of drops and payouts, the table inventory of chips may be reduced or may have excessive amounts. A table inventory must operate like a regular cash till, which has different denominations to make change. Thus, if there is too much or not enough of some chip denominations, a dealer can issue a fill or a credit to the main cashiering station, known as the cage. A fill, as the word suggests, adds to the table inventory and a credit takes away from the inventory. In this instance, the word "credit" does not refer to the extension

Figure 18–3 *Fill and Credit Slip*

DATE		GAME	PIT/TABLE	SHIFT		
				D	**S**	**G**
CHIP DENOMINATION		AMOUNT				
	5000.					.00
	1000.					.00
	500.					.00
	100.					.00
	25.					.00
	5.					.00
	2.50					
	1.00					.00
	.50					
	.25					
	TOTAL					

CASINO SUPERVISOR   LIC. NO.

of credit from a casino to customers; instead, it refers to the transfer of excess chips or currencies from a table to the cage to avoid possible confusion of operation and temptation of stealing and cheating. Figure 18–3 is an example of a fill and credit slip.

The following formula is used to calculate game win, which is the increase in money after inventories, fills, credits, and drop have been tabulated. Note that drop here is the amount in the drop box, not the amount wagered by the players.

> Ending table inventory
> − Beginning table inventory
> − Fills
> + Credits
> + Drop (drop box amount)
> Game win

In the sample game win calculations in Figure 18–4, Example A features just ending and beginning inventory amounts and drop; Example B, however, also considers fills and credits. The drop of $100 in Example A does not necessarily indicate a win, as that $100 may have been dropped in the box because a player changed his or her currency into chips and only played one game. In addition to the drop, inventory amounts must also be considered to determine the win. The same procedures apply when fills and credits are involved. Because fills add to a table and make the original inventory bigger, they need to be subtracted from the win to get back to the original table inventory

Figure 18–4   *Sample Game Win Calculations*

Game Win	Example A	Example B
Ending table inventory	2000	2000
− Beginning table inventory	300	300
− Fills	0	500
+ Credit	0	400
+ Drop	100	600
Game win	1800	2200

amount; otherwise, the win will be inflated. Similarly, because credits represent money removed from a table, they need to be added back when calculating the win.

Organization

A typical accounting department of a casino operation is similar to that of a standard hotel. The chief financial officer, also known as the controller or comptroller, presides over all activities. Under this position are the food and beverage controller or auditor, the hotel revenue controller, payroll, and general accounting, which consists of payables, receivables, and cashiering. The one major difference is the presence of the casino revenue controller or auditor, who is in charge of the slot count, or hard count (coins and tokens) and the pit-game count, or soft count (bills). This person also supervises the cage cashiers, and thus the fills and credits.

General Accounting

As mentioned, the general accounting function includes the duties of payables, receivables, and cashiering; however, in casinos, the cashiering function also includes cashiers in the cage and on the floor. The cashiering function must be controlled yet it cannot be so bureaucratic and time-consuming that it hinders the time that players are able to spend on the games. Another important point about cashiering is that the amount of strict cash exchange should not be counted as the revenue of the casino; otherwise, the operating results will be distorted. Due to the complexities of this function the cashiering processes of each game will be explained in subsequent sections of this chapter.

Accounts receivable in a casino approves credit as would a standard hotel; however, the credit requested by some casino guests may be a significant amount. These credits, also known as markers or IOUs, are simple documents that guests sign, denoting the amount that they receive from the casino. The availability of credit to guests is an important element in the operation and marketing strategy of a casino hotel. Most players are not local residents and many are visitors from other countries. Therefore, credit granting is crucial. The procedures of credit granting will be explored in more detail later in the chapter.

Casinos want to issue credit because the more credit one has, the more one will spend. This is why credit exists. To make money and not incur debt, however, it is vital that casinos grant credit to the right players. Players who have exceeded their credit limit should be denied further credit, as a casino may have a difficult time collecting.

It is advisable that only one person control credit at any given time. That person is responsible for the accounting, supervision, evaluation, approval, and collection of credits. He or she can delegate duties, in particular, those related to the processing of payments received during collections.

Casino Revenues Accounting

The main concern in the organizational structure of casino accounting is to divide the responsibilities of the department to the extent that it will minimize collusion and other types of fraud. From the time the money comes into the casino through the front doors to when it ends up in the back office vault, casino revenues accounting can be divided into three major areas: casino operations, cage operations, and count rooms. In casino operations, the people who collect the coins, tokens, and money from the players are the dealers at the various games, the pit clerks who record the game transactions, and the drop teams that collect the drop boxes. In cage operations, the main personnel are the cage cashiers who change out chips and tokens for cash and the credit cashiers who give the players their chips and tokens once credit is approved. In the count room, the hard and soft count personnel count, verify, and record the values of all coins, chips, tokens, and bills according to the procedures set out in the MICS.

Principal Revenue Flows and Cashiering

Money flows into a casino through the cashier cage and the play of games. The main cashier cage exchanges the players' money for chips and cashes in the players' chips or winnings. The cage also takes care of fills and credits. As for games, there are primarily six categories: table games, poker, keno, bingo, sports and race bookings, and slots and other electronic gaming devices. The money that comes from the cage goes directly back to the vault for deposits or replenishment and the accounting records are sent to the accounting office. The money from games goes through drop and count procedures in the count room and then is sent to the vault and the accounting records are sent to the accounting office.

Main Cashiering and the Cage

The cage is where the main cashiering functions take place, especially in smaller casino operations. It is the focal point of all cash activities in that it exchanges players' currency for chips or vice versa and carries out fills and credits for table games and slots. It also serves as a midstation between the floor and the vault. If money is running out at a game or if there is an excess accumulation of chips at a table, the cage can provide or store money and/or chips, and this way, the vault need not be opened and locked as many times during the day. In addition to preparing fills and credits for the games on the floor, the cage takes care of the credits that are extended to the customers by receiving their approved markers or IOUs and giving them the chips to play.

MICS in the cage encompass cashiers banks, the daily deposit, credits, cash deposits and withdrawals, and cashing in. The cage may have several individual banks for fills, change, and other purposes. At the beginning of each day, the opening cage cashier performs a blind count to verify the amounts. If the banks are not at impress, the cage cashier informs the cage supervisor who will investigate and reconcile the differences. During changes of shift, the incoming and outgoing cashiers agree on the inventory amounts and sign a two-part window count.

In addition, a bank settlement sheet is prepared for each bank. This not only counts the inventory amounts but also balances the items that are included in the beginning and ending inventories. The shift manager then consolidates all the bank settlement sheets and reconciles all opening and ending inventories. The original documents are sent to accounting where they will be audited and copies are kept in the cage. Once a day, the vault supervisor also prepares a bank deposit. According to casino procedures, the amount to be deposited is usually determined by a senior ranking casino officer such as the vice president of administration.

Applications for credit can be obtained at the cage. An application must include information such as customer's name, address, date of birth, verification of identification, signature, bank account number, and social security number. Credit bureaus, banks, and other financial institutions are contacted to evaluate the worth of the application. Central Credit is a casino credit bureau that can provide information on a player's past credit history with other casinos. Once the credit is approved, the cage issues a player a marker.

The marker is a four-part form that a player must sign and return to the cage to obtain the cash, tokens, or chips for gaming. A player also signs a payment agreement, which stipulates when payment is expected (usually within 30 days). All information is then forwarded to accounting for processing and monitoring of payments.

Another duty of the cage is to provide safekeeping services for players. A customer may exchange cash or cash equivalents at the cage for a deposit slip on which the customer's name, date of birth, social security number, and valid identification are recorded. Also included are the numeric and written amounts of the deposit, data, type of deposit, and the signatures of the customer and the cashier. The same slip is filled out for a withdrawal. If only a partial withdrawal is made, the net balance in the account is verified between the cashier and the player. If a player losses the original deposit slip, a new one is made out with all the necessary information.

The main cage also controls cashing-in procedures. Most cashing in can be done with no formalities; however, if a total exceeds $10,000 from multiple transactions or a single transaction within a 24-hour period, according to the law, the casino has to prepare a currency transaction report. This is usually done at the cage, but the pit follows the same procedures. The cage cashier first obtains and verifies a player's name, address, and social security number. Then a photo of the player is taken, notated with his or her name, signed by the cashier, and attached to the report. The report has to be signed by the cashier and filed within 15 days after the date of transaction.

Table Games

Cashiering for table games involves players giving the dealer money, markers, other chips, or documents in exchange for gaming chips. The money, markers, chips, and documents are placed in the drop box and the chips for which those items were exchanged are usually added to the table inventory of chips to be counted.

Poker

Poker and other card games usually take place in a separate room off the floor. Because of this, the cashiering function is significant. Chips can be bought and sold at the table just like in blackjack or craps. For the convenience of the players and to increase their gaming time, some casinos may also have a cashier cage outside the card room because most card rooms are not located near the main cage. Also, because card rooms typically operate on a commission basis, it is wise from a control standpoint to have cashier activities taken care of by a cashier rather than by a dealer at the table.

Keno, Bingo, and Sports and Race Bookings

Keno does not involve a lot of cashiering activities because when a player buys a keno ticket that is the end of the transaction. The only cashiering involved is when a player pays with a larger bill and change is needed. In this respect, keno cashiering resembles regular sales transactions.

Bingo cashiering is much the same as keno. Players buy bingo cards and collect from the casino if they win. Sports and race bookings involve a similar process in which players purchase bet tickets wait for the results, and collect any payouts.

Slots and Other Electronic Gaming Devices

Cashiering activities are more with regard to slot machines and other electronic gaming devices. In table games, a dealer is on hand to provide cashiering services. In slots, players usually exchange currency at the cage for a small container or bucket of coins or tokens to play. It does not take long to play a round of slots, therefore, a continuous flow of coins or tokens is required.

In addition to the main cashier cage, a slot booth is usually located strategically in or near the slot area for the ease of change—the easier it is for players to get money to play, the more they tend to play. Larger slot operations may even have change personnel, known as carousel barkers, runway personnel, or carnival barkers, who provide players easy access to change. They may use microphones to encourage people to play and to announce the winners of jackpots to add to the atmosphere.

Many casinos offer video poker and other video slot machines. The one-arm bandit sometimes is replaced by electronic devices that require a player to push a button rather than to pull a handle. Also, if a player does not want to be bothered by exchanging money or getting his or her hands dirty from coins and tokens, a card with a magnetic strip can be used. This card operates much like a debit card, recording the amount of plays made and thus the amount of cash used. However, most people who play slots want to pull the handle and hear the reels roll and the sound of coins coming down the hopper and hitting the payout tray.

Table Game Operations

The flow of revenue does not automatically mean revenue income for the casino. As previously discussed, the win and the hold percentage need to be calculated. Reviewing the operations of games can determine how control systems can be set up. The internal control on table games focuses on the procedures that begin with the gaming chip itself, the opening of a game, fills and credits during operation, the contents and amounts in the drop box, the closing of a game, and finally the count. The MICS, therefore, outline the procedures and auditors ensure that these procedures are followed.

Gaming Chips

Chips come in various sizes, shapes, colors, denominations, and uses such as primary, secondary, and reserve. An inventory must be maintained so that it can be reconciled within the operation or with other operations (in case of outside chips). Procedures for destroying chips are required as well.

A typical chip is round and has a diameter of 1⁹⁄₁₆ inches. Denominations vary from $1 to $5000 with a different primary color for each denomination. A contrasting secondary color is used for the edge spots on each denomination of the value chip. Some chips do not carry a value and are usually used for roulette. The name of the casino and the specific value have to be permanently impressed upon each chip.

MICS require a secondary set of chips that has a different color scheme than that of the primary set. In situations in which a casino suspects the use of counterfeit chips by its players, it will replace the primary set with the secondary set. Although a casino may accept wagers made with chips from a casino down the road, most casinos do not redeem foreign chips.

When new chips are shipped to a casino, personnel from the accounting department and personnel from security perform the receiving function. The chips are checked against the invoice, entered in the casino's chip inventory log, and stored in the vault until usage is required. During operations, the chips are counted daily; during off hours, all chips are secured either in the cage, the count room, the vault, or a locked transparent compartment on the gaming tables.

When chips are worn out or have to be destroyed due to security reasons, the casino administrator records the date, location, number and value of chips to be destroyed, and the method of destruction. A representative from the respective casino regulatory agency and from the accounting department have to be present during destruction.

Opening a Table

To open a game, a table inventory slip and a two-part duplicate form that records the beginning and ending inventory are needed. At the close of the previous game, the dealer fills out this form. The top original copy, the closer, is given to the casino supervisor and the duplicate copy, the opener, is deposited in the chip rack and locked under a clear lid. This is also known as the table float.

At the beginning of the next game, the casino supervisor unlocks the table float and the dealer counts the table inventory and compares the count to that on the duplicate slip in the table float. The table number, and sometimes shift number, is clearly marked on the table float so that if the inventory is not correct there will be a trail to follow in the investigation. When the inventory is in order, the game can begin.

Drop Boxes

Because chips are used for all table games, players have to exchange currency for chips at the main cage, present a credit marker to the dealer, or exchange currency at the table to start playing. MICS strictly prohibit cash wagering, as it is confusing to commingle cash and chips and it is definitely not a good control to have cash lying all over the table. When the dealer receives a marker or currency, he or she places it in the drop box and gives the player the corresponding amount in chips. MICS also require the casino to specify the procedures of this exchange. Thus, a dealer will put the cash or marker on the table in clear view of the players, call out the amount of cash or marker loud enough to be heard by the players, distribute the chips, and then deposit the cash or marker in the box.

The drop box is similar to the table float in that it is labeled with the table number, and perhaps shift number. It is locked but has an opening for deposit of items and is removed at the end of the shift to be replaced by an empty one for the next shift. The removed drop box is transported to the count room and the contents are included in the calculation of the win. Per MICS, transportation of a drop box from a table to the count room should follow the most direct route possible to alleviate any security issues.

Fills and Credits

While the game is going on, there are times when a dealer may be low in his of her table inventory or times when there is an excess amount of chips because a dealer is winning most bets. A fill or credit will be issued in such cases. The casino supervisor and pit shift manager are generally in charge of initiating such actions. They oversee the games at all times to ensure a good flow of activities and compliance with MICS.

A fill is initiated with the completion of a two-part form of which the original is kept at the table and the copy is sent to the pit clerk, who enters the request into the computer system. A printout then appears at the cage where the request is transferred to a fill slip. The fill slip usually consists of four-parts of which the original, first, and second copies are removed from the printer and the third copy stays in the machine. The cashier signs the fill slip and gives the requested chips to security or accounting personnel. This person verifies the amount, signs the form, returns the second copy of the form to the cashier, and transports the chips and original and first copy of the fill slip to the pit.

When the money arrives at the pit, the pit shift manager verifies the amount of chips and directs the security or accounting personnel to the appropriate table. The dealer at the table verifies the chips in front of the players, signs the original and first copy of the fill slip, places the original fill slip and the original request in the drop box, and gives the security or accounting personnel the first copy. The first copy of the fill slip, which now has the signatures of the pit boss and the dealer, is then returned to the cage to be attached to the second copy. All these fill slips and requests are to be turned into accounting for audits.

A credit is done in the same manner. The request is initiated from the pit, except that instead of chips and the slip coming from the cage, the slip comes back from the cage for signatures and chips are removed from the table inventory with the first copy of the credit slip to be attached to the second copy in the cage after verification of the chips.

Electronic surveillance of fills and credits can further ensure that all procedures are followed and that theft does not occur. Some casinos may limit surveillance to fills and credits over certain amounts. Generally, $10,000 is the minimum amount for which surveillance would be employed.

Closing a Game

When a game or a shift is finished, the dealer counts the chips on the table, fills out a two-part inventory slip, and has the amount verified by the casino supervisor. They both sign the slip, deposit the original copy (closer) in the drop box, and place the copy (opener) in the table float. The table is now equipped for the next shift with chips and an inventory slip, which may require the signatures of incoming personnel (see Figure 18–5).

Soft Count

The MICS that pertain to this area are specific and well defined. All the keys to the count room are recorded in a security log and the room is monitored 24 hours a day. After all necessary personnel enter the room, the door is locked

Figure 18–5   *Table Inventory Slip*

DATE		GAME	PIT/TABLE	CLOSER FOR		
				D	D(A)	G
CHIP DENOMINATION		AMOUNT				
	5000.					.00
	1000.					.00
	500.					.00
	100.					.00
	25.					.00
	5.					.00
	2.50					
	1.00					.00
	.50					
	.25					
TOTAL						

SIGNATURES

OUTGOING CASINO SUPERVISOR _____ LICENSE NO. _____

INCOMING CASINO SUPERVISOR _____ LICENSE NO. _____

OUTGOING DEALER/BOX PERSON _____ LICENSE NO. _____

INCOMING DEALER/BOX PERSON _____ LICENSE NO. _____

before the drop boxes are opened for counting. The soft-count team and the security personnel who transported the drop boxes to the room are the only personnel allowed inside the room during the count. The team consists of three people for three distinct job functions: recorder, counter, and verifier. Team members are rotated on a periodic basis and do not work with the same team members more than four days per week. Once the counting starts, no one is allowed to enter or exit the room until the count is completed. In case of an emergency, all employees have to show their hands to the surveillance camera and to other personnel to prove that nothing is being taken out of the room before they can leave the room.

The count table is made of transparent material and team members are required to wear an outer garment with no pockets so that contents in the count room cannot be hidden or taken outside. If members need to reach inside the garment for any reason, they first have to show their hands to the camera and to other personnel as mentioned. All of these precautions are implemented to lessen the temptation and ease of theft.

The soft-count team members are the only people who have access to the drop boxes. The boxes are opened one at a time and the contents are emptied out. Per MICS, a member must verbalize the number of the box, which will be recorded on the surveillance tape. He or she also has to show the camera and the other members that the box is completely empty. The empty box is then re-locked for use during the next shift.

The contents of the box are counted and placed on a drop cash card. One member initiates the count of all contents by a machine, records the count, and passes the contents to another member to verify. The machine tape is then at-tached to the drop cash card. The second member does his or her own count and calls out the results to the member who did the original count. If the two counts do not match, the difference must be reconciled before they can proceed to open and count the next drop box. The third member then prepares a table game summary, in ink, for each box, calculating the game win as discussed pre-viously in this chapter. The amount of the opener, fills, credits, and closer are added to the drop box amount on the drop cash card. Because the table sum-mary is prepared in ink, any errors are to be crossed out and initialed by at least two count team members. The members sign the table game summary sheet after the entire count is completed.

A vault supervisor then enters the room, counts the contents, and resolves any differences. All personnel now exit the room, transport the cash to the vault, and forward the documents to accounting where an income auditor will check their accuracy.

Slot Operations

MICS for slot machines and other electronic gaming devices include registration, minimum standards, integrity, fills, jackpot, counts, computer monitoring, and currency acceptors.

Machine Features

Years ago a $100 jackpot may have been considered a great payout; however, progressive slots now offer jackpots in denominations of millions. In the early 1980s video poker also increased players' attention to the slots. Through the use of microcomputer chips, slots can now generate gaming statistics and account-ing data, incorporate security and diagnostics functions, and offer various graph-ics and audio effects. Computerized slots are generally more reliable than the electromechanical type, however, certain characteristics are still the same.

Whether computerized or driven by electromechanical devices, slots have coin-in and coin-out functions. Although computerized slots offer these func-tions in the form of a magnetic card, the sound of coins dropping into the machine or filling up the payout tray is still available. Slots either have a handle or a button to activate play. A hopper holds the coins and a bucket collects extra coins when the hopper is full.

Profile

Just like people, slots have personalities or profiles. This not only pertains to the type of game the machine plays but to a lot of other information that is useful to the control function, including the date the machine is purchased, price, manufacturer, model and serial numbers, hold percentage, stand number, denomination, when it was put on or taken off the floor, program identification, and whether it is an asset or a leased unit. With this information, management can monitor the performance of each machine to ensure that the casino is receiving the proper amount of profits.

Cashiering

As discussed earlier, cashiering activities can make or break a slots operation. Change has to be constantly available and easily accessible to maximize the playtime on each slot. Again, the easier it is for players to get money to play, the more they tend to play.

Hard Count

The slot drop count, or hard count, is usually scheduled a few times per week or more depending on the frequency of plays and these counts are most often performed during off hours for business and security reasons. A casino has to advise the gaming control board of such schedules. All of the drop buckets inside each machine are permanently labeled and a second set of buckets of a different color is used for rotation.

The count team consists of at least three people, including a security guard. The membership of the count team is controlled by the MICS and must be independent of the slot management. Team members are rotated so that the same people will not work together more than so many days a week. The security guard ensures that the process is not interrupted, thus minimizing opportunities for theft.

The hard count starts when the supervisor obtains the key to the count room. He or she must sign the key out, indicating the time. The team then obtains the drop buckets. Numbered bags are also used in some casinos. The team also needs the keys to the slots. When on the floor, each slot is opened individually to verify the drop bucket number and the machine number. The bucket is then removed from the locked slot machine compartment. If some of the coins or tokens fall out, the team member must call out "loose tokens" to alert security before placing the tokens in the bucket. All of these precautions help ensure the integrity of the count procedures. Once all of the buckets are replaced, the team retires to the count room where coin machines are used to count the amount. As in the soft-count room, the hard-count room is equipped with surveillance cameras. When the individual buckets are emptied into the count machines, the team member holds the empty bucket to the camera to show that all the contents are removed from the bucket and that no coins or tokens have been taken. A different member of the team records the meter readings and completes all reports in ink. When all counts are recorded, the coins and tokens are wrapped. A vault supervisor verifies the drop by performing a random count of approximately 10% of the total. He or she then fills out a settlement sheet to be sent to the accounting office. When all is done, the count team supervisor returns the count room key.

Computerization

Computerization has brought about many changes in slots, with regard to players and casino management alike. For players, it has added more game choices, more options of playing, and most importantly, larger jackpots. For casino management, computerized slots provide much better control with updated information. In the area of marketing, these slots can track wagers and frequency of play. They also can record player information and identify high rollers, the types of games players like, complimentary items, current and previous trips' activities, and wins and losses. From a control standpoint, these machines can tell management the number of coins or tokens taken in, the metal count, the weight and size of the coins, where a coin ends up (out, hopper, or bucket), speed of the mechanism, who opens the slot machine door, time and date opened, purpose of opening the door, number of free plays given, and whether there were any payout alterations and exception and incident reports. While these available functions are all good, they must be used wisely instead of simply to generate more reports to be piled on managers' desks.

Summary

The control function is more significant in casinos than it is in other hospitality facilities because of the increased number of cash transactions. Although technology aids the recreational and operational aspects of casinos, ultimately, it is still management's responsibility to maintain an enjoyable yet structured and temptation-free environment for employees and guests.

Review Exercises

1. MICS stands for:
   a. minimum international casino status
   b. maximum international casino standards
   c. maximum internal control standards
   d. minimum internal control standards

2. MICS dictate that:
   a. licensees must identify the functions and responsibilities within the organization
   b. licensees must identify sensitive areas
   c. licensees must identify positions and individuals who have access to the sensitive areas
   d. all of the above

3. Win in casino terminology means:
   a. win of the players
   b. win of the casino
   c. win of the rooms department
   d. win of the food and beverage department

4. Win can be defined as:
   a. wager (drop) minus payouts
   b. payouts minus wager (drop)
   c. wager (drop) plus payouts
   d. wager (drop) plus fills

5. A win for slots can be defined as:
   a. handle minus payouts
   b. payouts plus handle
   c. payouts minus handle
   d. handle plus credits

6. The hold percentage, given a $100 drop and a $20 win, is:
   a. 5 times
   b. 500%
   c. 20%
   d. 5%

7. Which of the following is not a major area in casino revenue accounting?
   a. food and beverage operations
   b. casino operations
   c. cage operations
   d. count room

8. Money flows into a casino through:
   a. the cashier cage and the count room
   b. the cashier cage and the play of games
   c. the count room and the play of games
   d. the count room and the players themselves

9. MICS are set up for:
   a. table games
   b. slot games
   c. a and b
   d. a, b, and main cashiering

10. Computerized slot machines have not:
    a. added more game choices
    b. provided better control with updated information
    c. caught all illegal activities in slot operations
    d. recorded player information

11. Calculate the game win using the following data:

Ending table inventory	5560
Beginning table inventory	250
Fills	1100
Drop	900

12. Ann is a new dealer at Luxury Casino. In order to do her job correctly, she needs to learn how to calculate table win. If $5000 is her game win and she has the following information, what is her ending table inventory?

Fills	1000
Credit	800
Drop	2000
Beginning table inventory	1000
Game win	5000

13. Describe the issues that are addressed in the MICS.

14. What is the hold percentage for Magic Casino if the total wager is $150 and the casino pays out $105?

Examination Type Problems

1. Calculate the game win using the following data:

Ending table inventory	9000
Beginning table inventory	300
Fills	5060
Credit	100
Drop	500

2. Casino Windmill has a new dealer who needs to learn how to calculate table win. If $7000 is game win and the following information is given, what is the ending table inventory?

Fills	2200
Credit	700
Drop	2000
Beginning table inventory	450
Game win	7000

3. List at least five control procedures for the main cashiering activities in the cage.

4. What is the hold percentage for Casino Thunderbird if the total wager is $1150 and the casino pays out $700?

Case Study

What is unique to a casino operation is that there is a built-in method of rewarding customers for their play. This method of reward is the issuing of complimentary items, or "comps." There are two types of comps that a casino is able to offer a player. "Soft" comps require only a paper-transfer from one department budget to another department revenue budget line. Examples of soft comps are meals, lodging, and transportation. Generally speaking, any in-house service may be issued to a player as a soft comp. The other type of comp is known as a "hard" comp. This comp involves the actual transfer of moneys to a vendor. Examples of hard comps are airline tickets, specialty restaurants, and off-site shows or boxing matches. A casino operator is more likely to require greater justification for issuance of a hard comp. Justification for all comps is generally found in the casino operation's player rating computer files.

When a comp is requested, the issuer, usually the casino marketing department or the pit boss, looks up the requester's account in the computer files. This account is a lot like a bank account. Frequent, lengthy play helps to build up the theoretical win, and the granting of comp requests lowers the theoretical win. The issuer will grant a comp of up to 30% of theoretical win for soft comps and 15% for hard comps.

In a casino operation, one of the most common but least publicized forms of theft is comp theft, and one of the increasingly more common types of comp theft is the barter system. Smith is a floor person at the local casino. His neighbor, Jones, is a salesman at the local car dealership. They strike a deal. In return for Jones' assistance in getting Smith the lowest price on his new car and preferred repair service time, Smith agrees to submit false player ratings in Jones' name. Jones agrees not to go to the casino for a number of months, so that his casino "savings account" can build. A few months later, on some special occasion (birthday, anniversary) Jones will call the casino marketing department and request dinner and a show for two. The marketing department will review the account. If there is an adequate amount available, it will make the reservations and issue the comp. The casino is then down a few hundred dollars in stolen services.

This type of theft is difficult to detect. The primary reason for the difficulty is that there are multiple departments involved. Without the complete cooperation of internal audits, casino games, casino marketing, food and beverage, surveillance, comp accounting, and security, this form of theft will go undetected and unpunished. What measures can you recommend to deter such thefts?

Index